Preface

Foreword to the First Edition (1962)

The phonetic detail of the pronunciation of British English has already been described in several excellent works, notably those of Daniel Jones. This present book, written after a number of years of teaching the spoken language both to English students and to foreign learners, sets out to place the phonetics of British English in a larger framework than has been customary. For this reason, emphasis is given to the function of the spoken medium as a form of communication. Some treatment of the historical background and the linguistic implications of the present sound system is included, as well as information concerning the acoustic nature of English sounds. Those sections in Part II, in which detailed descriptions of the realizations of phonemes are given, deal with spelling forms, articulatory and acoustic features, variants and chief historical sources. In addition, throughout Parts II and III, general advice to the foreign learner is included.

The book is intended to serve as a general introduction to the subject which will encourage the reader to consult more specialized works on particular aspects. Though my own views and observations intrude both in the material and in its presentation, much of the information given is derived from the numerous sources quoted in the Bibliography. In particular, new evaluations, which seem to me to reflect more nearly the current trend of RP forms, are made of the phonetic characteristics of certain phonemes. In the acoustic field, where so much remains to be investigated and where research proceeds so rapidly, an attempt has been made to sum up the results of work done in the post-war period, though many of the conclusions must as yet be regarded as tentative. It was tempting to apply to British English a logical, elegant, and economical phonemic analysis such as is now commonplace in the United States, involving a very much simplified phonemic notation. If this has not been done, it is mainly because a type of analysis was required which was explicit on the phonetic level as well as reasonably tidy on the phonemic level; it seemed easier, for instance, to deal with phonetic developments and variants in terms of the largely traditional (for British English) transcription which has been used.

Throughout the book, the influence of my teachers, Professor Daniel Jones and Dr H. N. Coustenoble, will be obvious. To them my sincere thanks are due, not only for their teaching over the past twenty-five years but also for the example of dedication which they gave me. My gratitude is also due to Professor D. B. Fry and all my colleagues of the Department of Phonetics, University

College, London, whose brains I have constantly picked during the writing of this book. In particular, I have valued the help of Mr J. D. O'Connor and Dr A. J. Fourcin, who have read sections of the book, made corrections, and suggested improvements. I am also much indebted to Professor Randolph Quirk for his helpful comments on several points of Old English phonology. I am most grateful, too, to Mr J. C. Wells, who has generously allowed me to use unpublished figures resulting from his work on the formants of RP vowels.

A. C. Gimson

University College
London
December 1961

Foreword to the Fifth Edition (1994)

Gimson's *Pronunciation of English* has retained its pre-eminence as the standard reference book on the pronunciation of English over a period of thirty-two years. It has therefore seemed appropriate to undertake a major revision. The substantial additions made by Gimson himself in later editions (in particular a new chapter on the teaching of English to foreign learners) and by Susan Ramsaran (in particular sections on current changes in RP and stylistics) have been kept albeit with minor corrections.

I have rewritten large parts of the book and altered details on almost every page, to include new facts and new approaches. The parts which have been least altered are those concerned with the history of phonetics and the history of the language (the whole of the new Chapter 6, the subsections entitled '*Chief Sources*' under each phoneme and the section headed '*Elision*' in Chapter 10). Discussion of the present situation in RP, of other standards, and of regional accents now forms a separate chapter from that on the historical background. Theoretically the book remains almost entirely within a phonemic framework in its description of vowels and consonants (although very limited reference is made to other approaches in Part I). To present a similar amount of detailed information in any other way would have necessitated a different book, besides lessening its accessibility.

Major revisions and additions concern the discussion of the terms syllable, vowel, and consonant (§§5.5, 5.6), prosodic, paralinguistic, and extralinguistic features (§§5.7, 5.8), standard and regional accents, including brief but systematic treatments of General American, Scottish English, Cockney, Northern English and Australian English (Chapter 7), the acoustics of vowels (§8.6), word accent (§10.1), phonotactics (§10.10), and intonation (§11.6). I have added at appropriate points brief discussions of aspects of the acquisition of English by native learners, since the book is regularly used by speech therapists. Information on spelling frequencies has been included in the sections on each phoneme. This information was kindly supplied by Edward Carney, and more detail on this topic can be found in Carney (1994).

Newly published figures are presented for the formant frequencies of RP vowels. The figures for the (relatively) pure vowels are taken from Deterding (1990) with the kind permission of the author. The figures for the diphthongs were compiled in the Phonetics Laboratory in Manchester. They were obtained from two renderings of each diphthong by three speakers of each sex (from four samples of each component of each diphthong). This work was supported by a small grant from the Research Support Fund of the Faculty of Arts, University of Manchester.

The diagrams of variants of vowels have been redrawn to take account of various changes in pronunciation and symbolization (partly stemming from the latest revision of the International Phonetic Alphabet (1989)). The sagittal sections for the consonants have been supplemented by new palatograms produced by electropalatography. The source of the sagittal sections in the original edition was not made explicit; I have checked them against available X-ray sources (in particular Perkell, 1969) and against the palatograms, and made some slight emendments. But no systematically collected data is available for all the consonants (radiation hazards have inhibited such research) and thus the sections can only be regarded as informed estimates. With the advent of the technique of Magnetic Resonance Imaging it may be possible to include more objectively compiled diagrams in a future edition. The palatograms were made recently in Manchester and represent the relevant consonants before /ɑː/, apart from /ŋ/ in *long* and [ɫ] in *doll*. Figure 27, showing formant transitions and bursts for plosives, is reproduced from Lieberman and Blumstein (1988) with the permission of Cambridge University Press.

The bibliography has been thoroughly revised. References in previous editions which are still relevant have been kept and new references which I have used and in some cases referred to in footnotes have been included.

Many people have helped me with this revision. In particular I have to thank David Deterding for supplying the formant frequencies of the (relatively) pure vowels from his Ph.D. thesis, Kathleen Newton for spending a summer producing similar data for the diphthongs, Ted Carney for the spelling information previously mentioned, Martin Barry for supplying the palatograms together with regular computational advice and general phonetic discussion, Mike MacMahon for advice on some historical points, Peter Ladefoged for supplying a computer version of the IPA chart which served as the basis for Table 1 and Ken James and Gerry Abbott for advice on the teaching aspect of the final chapter. Various people have assisted with the typing and computerization including Carolyn Cook, Irene Pickford, Pat Lowe, and Gavin Probyn. Most importantly of all I have to thank my wife Margaret for drawing all the diagrams on computer (50 figures and 82 text diagrams); the time she has spent on the book has been nearly as great as my own. Lastly I must mention the encouragement given to me by Nigel Vincent and the indulgence of colleagues in my Department which has allowed me to have extended periods during which I could devote myself almost entirely to this new edition.

Alan Cruttenden

Department of Linguistics
University of Manchester
July 1993

Foreword to the Sixth Edition (2000)

The sixth edition has involved updating throughout the book, including an updating of all the references. I have rewritten large parts of the sections on the syllable, on phonotactics, and on word accent in Chapters 5 and 10. The sections on the current state of RP and its variants (including Estuary English) have also been rewritten. Other sections extensively revised include those dealing with advice to foreign learners (for whom a new subsection on pronouncing dictionaries has been added), and with acoustic information (for which new spectrograms have been produced). Many people have helped with the sixth edition but those to whom thanks are necessary are people already mentioned in the fifth edition, in particular David Deterding for allowing me to use the new formant information in Chapter 8, Ted Carney, whose statistics on spelling frequencies I have plundered even more widely than in the fifth edition, and Martin Barry, who helped with the acoustic sections. My thanks also go to Hector Ortiz-Lira and Rastislav Šuštaršič for pointing out mistakes in the fifth edition which have now been corrected.

Alan Cruttenden

Department of Linguistics
University of Manchester
July 2000

Contents

Part III Words and Connected Speech

List of Phonetic Symbols and Signs, and Abbreviations

AN	Anglo-Norman
ANE	Australian English
a	Cardinal Vowel no. 4 (approximately as in French *patte*); also used for first element of RP diphthong /aɪ/
æ	front vowel between open and open-mid (RP vowel in *cat*)
ɑ	Cardinal Vowel no. 5 (approximately as in French *pas*); also used for RP /ɑ:/ in *car*
ɒ	Cardinal Vowel no. 13 (RP vowel in *dog*)
b	voiced bilabial plosive (Eng. *b* in *labour*)
ɓ	voiced bilabial implosive (see §4.3.10)
β	voiced bilabial fricative (sometimes heard for *f* in a sequence like *of blue*)
C	Cardinal Vowel
c	voiceless palatal plosive (sometimes for *qu* in French *quai*)
ç	voiceless palatal fricative (as in German *ich*)
ɔ	Cardinal Vowel no. 6 (approximately as in German *Sonne*); also used for RP /ɔ:/ in *saw* and first element of diphthong /ɔɪ/
d	voiced alveolar plosive (Eng. *d* in *lady*)
ɗ	voiced alveolar implosive (see §4.3.10)
ɖ	voiced retroflex plosive
ð	voiced dental fricative (Eng. *th* in *other*)
e	Cardinal Vowel no. 2 (approximately as in French *thé*; also used for RP /e/ in *bed*, and for the first element of the diphthong /eɪ/
eModE	Early Modern English
ə	unrounded central vowel (Eng. initial and final vowels in *another*)
ɚ	unrounded retroflexed central vowel (General American *er* in water)
ɛ	Cardinal Vowel no. 3 (approximately as in French *père*)
ɜ	unrounded central vowel (RP *ir* in *bird*)
ɝ	unrounded retroflexed central vowel (General American *ir* in *bird*)
f	voiceless labiodental fricative (Eng. *f* in *four*)
ɟ	voiced palatal plosive (sometimes in French *guide*)
GA	General American
g	voiced velar plosive (Eng. *g* in *eager*)
ɠ	voiced velar implosive (see §4.3.10)
h	voiceless glottal fricative (Eng. *h* in *house*)

ɦ	voiced glottal fricative (sometimes Eng. *h* in *behind*)
i	Cardinal Vowel no. 1 (approximately as in French *si*); also used for Eng. /iː/ in see
ɨ	unrounded close central vowel (a realization of English /iː/ in some dialects)
ɪ	centralized unrounded close-mid vowel (Eng. vowel in *sit*)
j	voiced palatal approximant (Eng. *y* in *you*)
ʝ	voiced palatal fricative (sometimes *j* in Eng. *yeast*)
ɾ	voiced alveolar tap (sometimes *r* in Eng. *very*)
k	voiceless velar plosive (Eng. *c* in *car*)
l	voiced alveolar lateral approximant (Eng. *l* in *lazy*)
ɫ	voiced alveolar lateral approximant with velarization (RP *ll* in *ill*)
ɬ	voiceless alveolar lateral fricative (Welsh *ll*)
ME	Middle English
m	voiced bilabial nasal (Eng. *m* in *me*)
ɱ	voiced labiodental nasal (Eng. *m* in *comfort*)
ɯ	Cardinal Vowel no. 16 (like Eng. /uː/ with spread lips)
NE	Northern (England) English
n	voiced alveolar nasal (Eng. *n* in *no*)
ŋ	voiced velar nasal (RP *ng* in *sing*)
ɲ	voiced palatal nasal (French *gn* in *vigne*)
OE	Old English
OF	Old French
o	Cardinal Vowel no. 7 (approximately as in French *eau*)
ø	Cardinal Vowel no. 10 (approximately as in French *peu*)
œ	Cardinal Vowel no. 11 (approximately as in French *peur*)
θ	voiceless dental fricative (Eng. *th* in *thing*)
p	voiceless bilabial plosive (Eng. *p* in *pea*)
PresE	Present-day English
RP	Received Pronunciation
r	voiced alveolar trill (an emphatic pronunciation of *r* in Scottish English)
ɹ	voiced post-alveolar approximant (RP *r* in *red*)
ɻ	voiced retroflex approximant (sometimes for General American *r* in *red*)
ʀ	voiced uvular trill (an emphatic pronunciation of French *r* in *rouge*)
ʁ	voiced uvular fricative or approximant (French *r* in *peur*)
SSE	Standard Scottish English
s	voiceless alveolar fricative (Eng. *s* in *see*)
ʃ	voiceless palato-alveolar fricative (Eng. *sh* in *she*)
t	voiceless alveolar plosive (Eng. *t* in *tea*)
ʈ	voiceless retroflex plosive
u	Cardinal Vowel no. 8 (approximately as in French *doux*); also used for Eng. /uː/ in *do*
ʉ	rounded close central vowel (a realization for Eng. /uː/ in some dialects)
ʊ	centralized rounded close-mid vowel (RP. *u* in *put*)
v	voiced labiodental fricative (Eng. *v* in *ever*)
ʌ	Cardinal Vowel no. 14; also used for Eng. /ʌ/ in *cup*
ʋ	voiced labiodental approximant (a speech defective pronunciation of Eng. *r* in *red*)

w	voiced labial-velar approximant (Eng. *w* in *we*)
ʍ	voiceless labial-velar fricative (sometimes Eng. *wh* in *why*)
x	voiceless velar fricative (Scottish English *ch* in *loch*)
y	Cardinal Vowel no. 9 (approximately as in French *but*)
ʎ	voiced palatal lateral approximant (Italian *gl* in *egli*)
ɤ	Cardinal Vowel no. 15 (a realization of Eng. /ʊ/ in some dialects)
ɣ	voiced velar fricative (Spanish *g* in *luego*)
z	voiced alveolar fricative (Eng. *z* in *lazy*)
ʒ	voiced palato-alveolar fricative (Eng. *s* in *measure*)
ɸ	voiceless bilabial fricative (sometimes *f* in the sequence *of peace*)
‖	alveolar lateral click (the sound to make horses 'gee-up')
ǀ	dental click (as in the Eng. vocalization written 'tut-tut')
ʔ	glottal plosive (as in an emphatic pronunciation of Eng. *accent*)
.	indicates a syllable boundary
–	indicates a morpheme boundary
+	indicates a word boundary
ː	indicates full length of preceding vowel
ˑ	indicates half length of preceding vowel
˘	indicates short, non-prominent, vowel
ˋ	high falling nuclear tone (and used to indicate primary accent in citation forms)
ˎ	low falling nuclear tone
ˊ	high rising nuclear tone
ˏ	low rising nuclear tone
ˇ	falling-rising nuclear tone
ˆ	rising-falling nuclear tone
>	mid-level nuclear tone
=	stylized tone (high level followed by mid level)
ˈ	syllable carrying (high) secondary accent
ˌ	syllable carrying (low) secondary accent
~	nasalization, e.g. [õ]
¨	centralization, e.g. [ö]
⊤	more open quality, e.g. [ǫ]
⊥	closer quality, e.g. [ɔ̣]
˳	devoiced lenis consonant, e.g. [z̥] (above in the case of [ŋ̊,ʒ̊,g̊])
ˌ	syllabic consonant, e.g. [n̩] (above in the case of [ŋ̍])
ˌ	dental articulation, e.g. [t̪]
ˍ	post-alveolar articulation, e.g. [t̠]
[ ]	phonetic (allophonic) transcription
/ /	phonemic transcription
>	changed to
<	developed from
→	is realized as
*	common in RP (Figs 12–30 and in Chapter 10)
†	considered substandard in RP
< >	orthographic form

PART I

Speech and Language

1

Communication

1.1 *Speech*

One of the chief characteristics of human beings is their ability to communicate to their fellows complicated messages concerning every aspect of their activity. A man possessing the normal human faculties achieves this exchange of information mainly by means of two types of sensory stimulation, auditory and visual. Children learn from a very early age to respond to the sounds and tunes which their elders habitually use in talking to them; and, in due course, from a need to communicate, they begin to produce themselves the recurrent sound patterns with which they have become familiar. In other words, they begin to make use of speech; and their constant exposure to the spoken form of their own language, together with their need to convey increasingly subtle types of information, leads to a rapid acquisition of the framework of spoken language. Nevertheless, with all the conditions in favour, a number of years pass before they master the sound system used in their community. It is no wonder, therefore, that the learning of another language later in life, acquired artificially in brief and sporadic spells of activity and often without the stimulus arising from an immediate need for communication, will tend to be tedious and rarely more than partially successful. In addition, the more firmly consolidated the basis of a first language becomes and the later in life that a second language is begun, the more learners will be subject to resistances and prejudices deriving from the framework of their original language. As we grow older, the acquisition of a new language will normally entail a great deal of conscious, analytical effort, instead of children's ready and facile imitation.

1.2 *Writing*

Later in childhood children will be taught the conventional visual representation of speech—they will learn to use writing. Today, in considering those languages which have long possessed a written form, we are apt to forget that the writing was originally an attempt at reflecting the spoken language and that the latter precedes the former for both the individual and the community. Indeed, in many languages, so parallel are the two forms felt to be that the written form may be responsible for changes in pronunciation or may at least tend to impose restraints upon its development. In the case of English, this sense of parallelism, rather than of derivation, may be encouraged by the obvious lack of consistent relationship between sound and spelling. A written form of English, based on the Latin alphabet, has existed for more than 1,000 years and, though the pronunciation of English has been constantly changing during this time, few basic changes of spelling have been made since the fifteenth century. The result is that written English is often an inadequate and misleading representation of the spoken language of today. Clearly it would be unwise, to say the least, to base our judgements concerning the spoken language on prejudices derived from the orthography. Moreover, if we are to examine the essence of the English language, we must make our approach through the spoken rather than the written form. The primary concern of this book will be the production, transmission, and reception of the sounds of English—in other words, the phonetics of English.

1.3   *Language*

From the moment that we abandon orthography as our starting point, it is clear that the analysis of the spoken form of English is by no means simple. Each of us uses an infinite number of different speech sounds when we speak English. Indeed, it is true to say that it is difficult to produce two sounds which are precisely identical from the point of view of instrumental measurement: two utterances by the same person of the word *cat* may well show quite marked differences when measured instrumentally. Yet we are likely to say that the same sound sequence has been repeated. Additionally we may hear clear and considerable differences of quality in the vowel of *cat* as, for instance, in the London and Manchester pronunciations of the word; yet, though we recognize differences of vowel quality, we are likely to feel that we are dealing with a 'variant' of the 'same' vowel. It seems, then, that we are concerned with two kinds of reality: the concrete, measurable reality of the sounds uttered, and another kind of reality, an abstraction made in our minds, which appears to reduce this infinite number of different sounds to a 'manageable' number of categories. In the first, concrete, approach, we are dealing with sounds in relation to SPEECH; at the second, abstract, level, our concern is the behaviour of sounds in a particular LANGUAGE. A language is a system of conventional signals used for communication by a whole community. This pattern of conventions covers a system of significant sound units (the PHONEMES), the inflexion and arrangement of 'words', and the association of meaning with words. An utterance, an act of speech, is a single concrete manifestation of the system at work. As we have seen, several utterances which are plainly different on the concrete, phonetic level may fulfil the same function, i.e. are the 'same', on the systematic language level. It is important in any analysis of spoken language to keep this distinction in mind and we shall later be considering in some detail how this dual approach to the utterance is to be made. It is not, however, always possible or desirable to keep the two levels of analysis entirely separate: thus, as we shall see, we will draw upon our knowledge of the linguistically significant units to help us in determining how the speech continuum shall be divided up on the concrete, phonetic level; and again, our classification of linguistic units will be helped by our knowledge of their phonetic features.

1.4   *Redundancy*

Finally, it is well to remember that, although the sound system of our spoken languages serves us primarily as a medium of communication, its efficiency as such an instrument of communication does not depend upon the perfect production and reception of every single element of speech. A speaker will, in almost any utterance, provide the listener with far more cues than he needs for easy comprehension. In the first place, the situation, or context, will itself delimit very largely the purport of an utterance. Thus, in any discussion about a zoo, involving a statement such as 'We saw the lions and tigers', we are predisposed by the context to understand *lions*, even if the *n* is omitted and the word actually said is *liars*. Or again, we are conditioned by grammatical probabilities, so that a particular sound may lose much of its significance, e.g. in the phrase 'These men are working', the quality of the vowel in *men* is not as vitally important for deciding whether it is a question of *men* or *man* as it would be if the word were said in isolation, since here the plurality is determined in addition by the demonstrative adjective preceding *men* and the verb form following. Then again, there are particular probabilities in every language as to the different combinations of sounds which will occur. Thus in English, if we hear an initial *th* sound [ð], we expect a vowel to follow, and of the vowels some are much more likely than the others. We distinguish sequences such as -*gl* and -*dl* in final positions, e.g. in *beagle* and *beadle*, but this distinction is not relevant initially, so that even if *dloves* is said, we understand *gloves*. Or again, the total rhythmic shape of a word may provide an important cue to its recognition: thus, in a word such as *become*, the general rhythmic pattern may be said to contribute as much to the recognition of the word as the precise quality of the vowel in the first, weakly accented, syllable. Indeed, we may come to doubt the relative importance of vowels as a help to intelligibility, since we can replace our twenty English vowels by the single vowel [ə] in any utterance and still, if the rhythmic pattern is kept, retain a high degree of intelligibility. An utterance, therefore, will provide a large complex of cues for the listener to interpret, but a great deal of this information will be REDUNDANT as far as the listener's needs are concerned. On the other hand, such an over-proliferation of cues will serve to offset any disturbance such as noise or to counteract the sound-quality divergences which may exist between speakers of two dialects of the same language. But to insist, for instance, upon exaggerated articulation in order to achieve clarity may well be to go beyond the requirements of speech as a means of communication; indeed, certain obscurations of quality are, and have been for many centuries, characteristic of English. Aesthetic judgements on speech, such as those which deplore the use of the 'intrusive *r*', take into account social considerations of a somewhat different order from those involved in a study of speech as communication.

1.5   *Phonetics and Linguistics*

This book describes the sound system of English, but it should be remembered that such a description forms only part of the total description of a language. A complete description of the current state of a language provides information on a number of interrelated components.

The PHONETICS of a language concerns the concrete characteristics (articulatory, acoustics, auditory) of the sounds used in languages, whereas PHONOLOGY concerns how sounds function in a systemic way in a particular language. The traditional approach to phonology is through PHONEMICS, which analyses the stream of speech into a sequence of contrastive segments, 'contrastive' here meaning 'contrasting with other segments which might change the meaning' (see further in §5.3 below). The phonemic approach to phonology is not the only type of phonological theory but it is the most accessible to those with no training in linguistic theory, besides being more relatable to the writing system. Hence the major part of this book is set within phonemic analysis. Besides being concerned with the sounds of a language, both phonetics and phonology must also describe the combinatory possibilities of the sounds (the PHONOTACTICS or SYLLABLE STRUCTURE) and the PROSODY of the language, that is, how features of pitch, loudness, and length work to produce accent, rhythm, and intonation. Additionally, a study can be made of the relationship between the sounds of a language and the letters used in its writing system (GRAPHOLOGY or GRAPHEMICS).

Although this book presents a detailed description of the phonetics and phonemics of English, reference will need to be made from time to time to other components of the language:

(1) The LEXICON—the words of the language, the sequence of phonemes of which they are composed, together with their meanings.

(2) The MORPHOLOGY—the structure of words, in particular their inflexion (e.g. *start/started*—here the past-tense morpheme is added to the stem morpheme). Statements can be made of the phonemic structure of morphemes—the MORPHOPHONEMICS. So the morphophonemics of the English plural morpheme involve the MORPHOPHONEMIC ALTERATIONS illustrated by the /s/ in *cats*, the /z/ in *dogs* and the /ɪz/ in *losses*.

(3) The SYNTAX—the description of categories like noun and verb, and the system of rules governing the structure of phrases, clauses, and sentences in terms of order and constituency.

(4) The SEMANTICS—the meaning of words and the relationship between word meanings, and the way such meanings are combined to give the meanings of sentences.

(5) The PRAGMATICS—the influence of situation on the interpretation of utterances.

Moreover various other aspects of linguistics will involve phonetics and phonology. STYLISTICS concerns the variations involved in different situations and in different styles of speech. SOCIOLINGUISTICS concerns the interaction between language and society (e.g. the variation involved across classes and between the sexes). DIALECTOLOGY (often considered a branch of sociolinguistics) concerns the variation in the same language in different regions. PSYCHOLINGUISTICS concerns the behaviour of human beings in their production and perception of language (e.g. how far do we plan ahead and how much of an utterance do we decode at a time?). LANGUAGE ACQUISITION concerns children's learning of their first language, whereas APPLIED LINGUISTICS principally concerns the acquisition of a second language.

Finally, it is clear that the various components of a language are always undergoing change in time. The state of a language at any (SYNCHRONIC) moment must be seen against a background of its historical (DIACHRONIC) evolution. It is for this reason that this book includes information on earlier states of the sound system of English, with some speculation on possible developments in the future.

2

The Production of Speech: The Physiological Aspect

2.1 *The Speech Chain*

Any manifestation of language by means of speech is the result of a highly compli-cated series of events. The communication in sound of such a simple concept as 'It's raining' involves a number of activities on the part of the speaker. In the first place, the formulation of the concept will take place at a linguistic level, i.e. in the brain; the first stage may, therefore, be said to be psychological. The nervous system transmits this message to the so-called 'organs of speech' and these in turn behave in a conventional manner, which, as we have learned by experience, will have the effect of producing a particular pattern of sound; the second important stage for our purposes may thus be said to be articulatory or physiological. The movement of our organs of speech will create disturbances in the air, or whatever the medium may be, through which we are talking; these varying air pressures may be investigated and they constitute the third stage in our chain, the physical, or acoustic. Since communication generally requires a listener as well as a speaker, these stages will be reversed at the listening end: the reception of the sound waves by the hearing apparatus (physiological) and the transmission of the information along the nervous system to the brain, where the linguistic interpretation of the message takes place (psychological). Phonetic analysis has often ignored the role of the listener. But any investigation of speech as communication must ultimately be concerned with both the production and the reception ends.

Our immediate concern, however, is with the speaker's behaviour and more especially, on the concrete speech level, with the activity involved in the produc-tion of sounds. For this reason, we must now examine the articulatory stage (the speech mechanism) to discover how the various organs behave in order to produce the sounds of speech.

2.2 *The Speech Mechanism*

Man possesses, in common with many other animals, the ability to produce sounds by using certain of his body's mechanisms. The human being differs from other animals in that he has been able to organize the range of sounds which he can emit into a highly efficient system of communication. Non-human animals rarely progress beyond the stage of using the sounds they produce as a reflex of certain basic stimuli to signal fear, hunger, sexual excitement, and the like. Nevertheless, like other animals, man when he speaks makes use of organs whose primary physiological function is unconnected with vocal communication; in particular, those situated in the respiratory tract.

2.2.1 Sources of Energy: The Lungs

The most usual source of energy for our vocal activity is provided by an airstream expelled from the lungs. There are languages which possess sounds not requiring lung (pulmonic) air for their articulation, and, indeed, in English we have one or two extralinguistic sounds, such as the one that we write as *tut-tut* and the noise of encouragement made to horses, which are produced without the aid of the lungs; but all the essential sounds of English use lung air for their production. Our utterances are, therefore, largely shaped by the physiological limitations imposed by the capacity of our lungs and by the muscles which control their action. We are obliged to pause in articulation in order to refill our lungs with air and the number of energetic peaks of exhalation which we make will to some extent condition the division of speech into sense-groups. In those cases where the airstream is not available for the upper organs of speech, as when, after the removal of the larynx, lung air does not reach the mouth but escapes from an artificial aperture in the neck, a new source of energy, such as stomach air, has to be employed; a new source of this kind imposes restrictions of quite a different nature from those exerted by the lungs, so that the organization of the utterance into groups is changed and variation of energy is less efficiently controlled.

A number of techniques are available for the investigation of the activity in speech of the lungs and their controlling muscles. At one time air pressure within the lungs was observed by the reaction of an air-filled balloon in the stomach. On the basis of such evidence from a gastric balloon, it was at one time claimed that syllables were formed by chest pulses.[1] Such a primitive procedure was replaced by the technique of electromyography, which demonstrated the electrical activity of those respiratory muscles most concerned in speech, notably the internal intercostals; this technique disproved the relationship between chest pulses and syllables.[2] X-ray photography can reveal the gross movements of the ribs and hence by inference the surrounding muscles, although the technique of Magnetic Resonance Imaging (MRI) is now preferred on medical grounds.

2.2.2 The Larynx and Vocal Folds

The airstream provided by the lungs undergoes important modifications in the upper parts of the respiratory tract before it acquires the quality of a speech

---

[1] Stetson (1951)
[2] Ladefoged (1967)

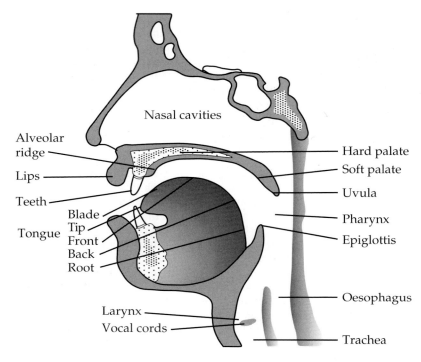

Fig. 1. Organs of speech.

sound. First of all, in the TRACHEA or windpipe, it passes through the LARYNX, containing the so-called VOCAL FOLDS, often, less correctly, called the vocal cords, or even vocal chords (see Fig. 1).

   The larynx is a casing, formed of cartilage and muscle, situated in the upper part of the trachea. Its forward portion is prominent in the neck below the chin and is commonly called the 'Adam's apple'. Housed within this structure from back to front are the vocal folds, two folds of ligament and elastic tissue which may be brought together or parted by the rotation of the arytenoid cartilages (attached at the posterior end of the folds) through muscular action. The inner edge of these folds is typically approximately 17–22 mm long in males and approximately 11–16 mm in females.[3] The opening between the folds is known as the GLOTTIS. Biologically, the vocal folds act as a valve which is able to prevent the entry into the trachea and lungs of any foreign body, or which may have the effect of enclosing the air within the lungs to assist in muscular effort on the part of the arms or the abdomen. In using the vocal folds for speech, the human being has adapted and elaborated upon this original open-or-shut function in the following ways (see Fig. 2):

---

[3] Clark and Yallop (1995: 181)

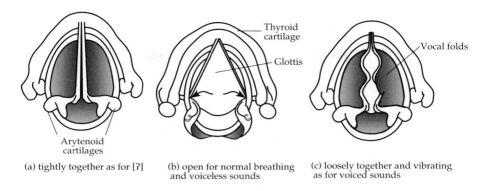

(a) tightly together as for [ʔ]

(b) open for normal breathing and voiceless sounds

(c) loosely together and vibrating as for voiced sounds

Fig. 2. The vocal cords as seen from above.

(1) The glottis may be held tightly closed, with the lung air pent up below it. This 'glottal stop' [ʔ] frequently occurs in English, e.g. when it precedes the energetic articulation of a vowel as in *apple* [ʔæpl] or when it reinforces /p,t,k/ as in *clock* [klɒʔk] or even replaces them, as in *cotton* [kɒʔn]. It may also be heard in defective speech, such as that arising from cleft palate, when [ʔ] may be substituted for the stop consonants, which, because of the nasal air escape, cannot be articulated with proper compression in the mouth cavity.

(2) The glottis may be held open as for normal breathing and for voiceless sounds like [s] in *sip* and [p] in *peak*.

(3) The action of the vocal folds which is most characteristically a function of speech consists in their role as a vibrator set in motion by lung air—the production of voice, or phonation; this vocal fold vibration is a normal feature of all vowels or of a consonant such as [z] compared with voiceless [s]. In order to achieve the effect of voice the vocal folds are brought sufficiently close together that they vibrate when subjected to air pressure from the lungs. This vibration, of a somewhat undulatory character, is caused by compressed air forcing the opening of the glottis and the resultant reduced air pressure permitting the elastic folds to come together once more; the vibratory effect may easily be felt by touching the neck in the region of the larynx or by putting a finger over each ear flap when pronouncing a vowel or [z] for instance. In the typical speaking voice of a man, this opening and closing action is likely to be repeated between 100 and 150 times in a second, i.e. there are that number of cycles of vibration (called Hertz, which is abbreviated to Hz); in the case of a woman's voice, this frequency of vibration might well be between 200 Hz and 325 Hz. We are able, within limits, to vary the speed of vibration of our vocal folds or, in other words, are able consciously to change the pitch of the voice produced in the larynx; the more rapid the rate of vibration, the higher is the pitch (an extremely low rate of vibration being partly responsible for what is usually called creaky voice). Normally the vocal folds come together rapidly and part more slowly, the opening phase of each cycle thus being longer than the closing phase. This gives rise to 'modal' (or 'normal') voice which is used for most of English speech. Other modes of vibration result in other voice

qualities, most notably breathy and creaky voice which are used contrastively in a number of languages. (See also §5.8.) Moreover, we are able, by means of variations in pressure from the lungs, to modify the size of the puff of air which escapes at each vibration of the vocal folds; in other words, we can alter the amplitude of the vibration, with a corresponding change of loudness of the sound heard by a listener. The normal human being soon learns to manipulate his glottal mechanism so that most delicate changes of pitch and loudness are achieved. Control of this mechanism is, however, very largely exercised by the ear, so that such variations are exceedingly difficult to teach to those who are born deaf, and a derangement of pitch and loudness control is liable to occur among those who become totally deaf later in life.

(4) One other action of the larynx should be mentioned. A very quiet whisper may result merely from holding the glottis in the voiceless position. But the more normal whisper, by means of which we are able to communicate with some ease, can be felt to involve energetic articulation and considerable stricture in the glottal region. Such a whisper may in fact be uttered with an almost total closure of the glottis and an escape of air in the region of the arytenoids.

The simplest way of observing the behaviour of the vocal folds is by the use of a laryngoscope, which gives a stationary mirrored image of the glottis. By use of stroboscopic techniques, it is possible to obtain a moving record and high-speed films have been made of the vocal folds, showing their action in ordinary breathing, producing voice and whisper, and closed as for a glottal stop. The modern technique of observation is to use fibre-optic endoscopy coupled, if required, with a videocamera.

2.2.3   The Resonating Cavities

The airstream, having passed through the larynx, is now subject to further modification according to the shape assumed by the upper cavities of the pharynx and mouth, and according to whether the nasal cavities are brought into use or not. These cavities function as the principal resonators of the voice produced in the larynx.

2.2.3.1 The Pharynx   The pharyngeal cavity (see Fig. 1) extends from the top of the trachea and oesophagus, past the epiglottis and the root of the tongue, to the region at the rear of the soft palate. It is convenient to identify these sections of the pharynx by naming them: laryngopharynx, oropharynx, nasopharynx. The shape and volume of this long chamber may be considerably modified by the constrictive action of the muscles enclosing the pharynx, by the movement of the back of the tongue, by the position of the soft palate which may, when raised, exclude the nasopharynx, and by the raising of the larynx itself. The position of the tongue in the mouth, whether it is advanced or retracted, will affect the size of the oropharyngeal cavity; the modifications in shape of this cavity should, therefore, be included in the description of any vowel. It is a characteristic of some kinds of English pronunciation that certain vowels e.g. the [æ] vowel in *sad* are articulated with a strong pharyngeal contraction; in addition, a constriction may be made between the lower rear part of the tongue and the wall of the pharynx so that friction, with or without voice, is produced, such fricative sounds being a feature of a number of languages.

The pharynx may be observed by means of a laryngoscope or fibre-optic nasendoscopy and its constrictive actions are revealed by lateral X-ray photography or, nowadays, preferably by MRI.

The escape of air from the pharynx may be effected in one of three ways:

(1) The soft palate may be lowered, as in normal breathing, in which case the air may escape through the nose and the mouth. This is the position taken up by the soft palate in articulation of the French nasalized vowels in a phrase such as *un bon vin blanc* [œ̃ bõ vẽ blɑ̃], the particular quality of such vowels being achieved through the function of the nasopharyngeal cavities. Indeed, there is no absolute necessity for nasal airflow out of the nose, the most important factor in the production of nasality being the sizes of the posterior oral and nasal openings (some speakers may even make the nasal cavities vibrate through nasopharyngeal mucus or through the soft palate itself).[4]

(2) The soft palate may be lowered so that a nasal outlet is afforded to the airstream, but a complete obstruction is made at some point in the mouth, with the result that, although air enters all or part of the mouth cavity, no oral escape is possible. A purely nasal escape of this sort occurs in nasal consonants such as [m,n,ŋ] in the English words *ram, ran, rang*. In a snore and some kinds of defective speech, this nasal escape may be accompanied by friction between the rear side of the soft palate and the pharyngeal wall.

(3) The soft palate may be held in its raised position, eliminating the action of the nasopharynx, so that the air escape is solely through the mouth. All normal English sounds, with the exception of the nasal consonants mentioned, have this oral escape. Moreover, if for any reason the lowering of the soft palate cannot be effected, or if there is an enlargement of the organs enclosing the nasopharynx or a blockage brought about by mucus, it is often difficult to articulate either nasalized vowels or nasal consonants. In such speech, typical of adenoidal enlargement or the obstruction caused by a cold, the French phrase mentioned above would have its nasalized vowels turned into their oral equivalents and the English word *morning* would have its nasal consonants replaced by [b,d,g]. On the other hand, an inability to make an effective closure by means of the raising of the soft palate—either because the soft palate itself is defective or because an abnormal opening in the roof of the mouth gives access to the nasal cavities—will result in the general nasalization of vowels and the failure to articulate oral stop consonants such as [b,d,g]. This excessive nasalization (or hypernasality) is typical of a condition such as cleft palate.

It is evident that the action of the soft palate is accessible to observation by direct means, as well as by lateral X-ray photography and MRI; the pressure of the air passing through the nasal cavities may be measured at the nostrils or within the cavities themselves.

---

[4] Laver (1980: 77ff)

2.2.3.2 *The Mouth*   Although all the cavities so far mentioned play an essential part in the production of speech sounds, most attention has traditionally been paid to the behaviour of the cavity formed by the mouth. Indeed, in many languages the word *tongue* is used to refer to our speech and language activity. Such a preoccupation with the oral cavity is doubtless due to the fact that it is the most readily accessible and easily observed section of the vocal tract; but there is in such an attitude a danger of gross oversimplification. Nevertheless, it is true that the shape of the mouth determines finally the quality of the majority of our speech sounds. Far more finely controlled variations of shape are possible in the mouth than in any other part of the speech mechanism.

The only boundaries of this oral chamber which may be regarded as relatively fixed are, in the front, the teeth; in the upper part, the hard palate; and, in the rear, the pharyngeal wall. The remaining organs are movable: the lips, the various parts of the tongue, and the soft palate with its pendant uvula (see Fig. 1). The lower jaw, too, is capable of very considerable movement; its movement will control the gap between the upper and lower teeth and also to a large extent the disposition of the lips. The space between the upper and lower teeth will often enter into our description of the articulation of sounds; in all such cases, it is clear that the movement of the lower jaw is ultimately responsible for the variation described. Movement of the lower jaw is also one way of altering the distance between the tongue and the roof of the mouth.

It is convenient for our descriptive purposes to divide the roof of the mouth into three parts: moving backwards from the upper teeth, first, the teeth ridge (adjective: ALVEOLAR) which can be clearly felt behind the teeth; secondly, the bony arch which forms the hard palate (adjective: PALATAL), which varies in size and arching from one individual to another; and finally, the soft palate (adjective: VELAR), which, as we have seen, is capable of being raised or lowered, and at the extremity of which is the uvula (adjective: UVULAR). All these parts can be readily observed by means of a mirror.

(1) Of the movable parts, the lips (adjective: LABIAL), constitute the final orifice of the mouth cavity whenever the nasal passage is shut off. The shape which they assume will, therefore, affect very considerably the shape of the total cavity. They may be shut or held apart in various ways. When they are held tightly shut, they form a complete obstruction or occlusion to the airstream, which may either be momentarily prevented from escaping at all, as in the initial sounds of *pat* and *bat*, or may be directed through the nose by the lowering of the soft palate, as in the initial sound of *mat*. If the lips are held apart, the positions they assume may be summarized under five headings:

(a) held sufficiently close together over all their length that friction occurs between them. Fricative sounds of this sort, with or without voice, occur in many languages and the voiced variety [β] is sometimes wrongly used by foreign speakers of English for the first sound in the words *vet* or *wet*;

(b) held sufficiently far apart for no friction to be heard, yet remaining fairly close together and energetically spread. This shape is taken up for vowels like that in *see* and is known as the SPREAD lip position;

(c) held in a relaxed position with a lowering of the lower jaw. This is the position taken up for the vowel of *sat* and is known as the NEUTRAL position;

(d) tightly pursed, so that the aperture is small and rounded, as in the vowel of *do*, or more markedly so in the French vowel of *doux*. This is the CLOSE ROUNDED position;

(e) held wide apart, but with slight projection and rounding, as in the vowel of *got*. This is the OPEN ROUNDED position.

Variations of these five positions may be encountered, e.g. in the vowel of *saw*, for which a type of lip-rounding between open-rounded and close-rounded is commonly used. It will be seen from the examples given that lip position is particularly significant in the formation of vowel quality. English consonants, on the other hand, even including [p,b,m,w] whose primary articulation involves lip action, will tend to share the lip position of the adjacent vowel. In addition, the lower lip is an active articulator in the pronunciation of [f,v], a light contact being made between the lower lip and the upper teeth.

(2) Of all the movable organs within the mouth, the tongue is by far the most flexible and is capable of assuming a great variety of positions in the articulation of both vowels and consonants. The tongue is a complex muscular structure which does not show obvious sections; yet, since its position must often be described in considerable detail, certain arbitrary divisions are made. When the tongue is at rest, with its tip lying behind the lower teeth, that part which lies opposite the hard palate is called the FRONT and that which faces the soft palate is called the BACK, with the region where the front and back meet known as the CENTRE (adjective: CENTRAL). These areas, together with the root, are sometimes collectively referred to as the body of the tongue. The tapering section facing the teeth ridge is called the blade (adjective: LAMINAL) and its extremity the tip (adjective: APICAL). The edges of the tongue are known as the rims.

Generally, in the articulation of vowels, the tongue tip remains low behind the lower teeth. The body of the tongue may, however, be 'bunched up' in different ways, e.g. the front may be the highest part as when we say the vowel of *he*; or the back may be most prominent as in the case of the vowel in *who*; or the whole surface may be relatively low and flat as in the case of the vowel in *ah*. Such changes of shape can be felt if the above words are said in succession. These changes moreover, together with the variations in lip position, have the effect of modifying very considerably the size of the mouth cavity and of dividing this chamber into two parts: that cavity which is in the forward part of the mouth behind the lips and that which is in the rear in the region of the pharynx.

The various parts of the tongue may also come into contact with the roof of the mouth. Thus, the tip, blade, and rims may articulate with the teeth as for the *th* sounds in English, or with the upper alveolar ridge as in the case of /t,d,s,z,n/ or the apical contact may be only partial as in the case of /l/ (where the tip makes firm contact whilst the rims make none) or intermittent in a trilled /r/ as in some forms of Scottish English. In some languages, notably those of India, Pakistan, and Sri Lanka, the tip contact may be retracted to the very back of the teeth ridge or even slightly behind it; the same kind of retroflexion, without the tip contact, is typical of some kinds of English /r/, e.g. those used in south-west England and in the USA.

The front of the tongue may articulate against or near to the hard palate. Such a raising of the front of the tongue towards the palate (palatalization) is an essential part of the [ʃ,ʒ] sounds in English words such as *she* and *measure*, being additional to an articulation made between the blade and the alveolar ridge; or again, it is the main feature of the [j] sound initially in *yield*.

The back of the tongue can form a total obstruction by its contact with the soft palate, raised in the case of [k,g] and lowered for [ŋ] as in *sing*; or again, there may merely be a narrowing between the soft palate and the back of the tongue, so that friction of the type occurring finally in the Scottish pronunciation of *loch* is heard. And finally, the uvula may vibrate against the back of the tongue, or there may be a narrowing in this region which causes uvular friction, as at the beginning of the French word *rouge*.

It will be seen from these few examples that, whereas for vowels the tongue is generally held in a position which is convex in relation to the roof of the mouth, some consonant articulations, such as the Southern British English /r/ in *red* and the /l/ in *table*, will involve the 'hollowing' of the body of the tongue so that it has, at least partially, a concave relationship with the roof of the mouth.

Moreover, the surface of the tongue, viewed from the front, may take on various forms: there may be a narrow groove running from back to front down the mid-line as for the /s/ in *see*, or the grooving may be very much more diffuse as in the case of the /ʃ/ in *ship*; or again, the whole tongue may be laterally contracted, with or without a depression in the centre (sulcalization), as is the case with various kinds of *r* sounds.

(3) The oral speech mechanism is readily accessible to direct observation as far as the lip movements are concerned as are many of the tongue movements which take place in the forward part of the mouth. A lateral view of the shape of the tongue over all its length and its relationship with the palate and the velum may be obtained by means of still and moving X-ray photography and by MRI. It is not, however, to be expected that pictures of the articulation of, say, the vowel in *cat* will show an identical tongue position for the pronunciation of a number of individuals. Not only is the sound itself likely to be different from one individual to another, but, even if the sound is for all practical purposes the 'same', the tongue positions may be different, since the boundaries of the mouth cavity are not identical for two speakers; and, in any case, two sounds judged to be the same may be produced by the same individual with different articulations. When, therefore, we describe an articulation in detail, it should be understood that such an articulation is typical for the sound in question, but that variations are to be expected.

Palatography, showing the extent of the area of contact between the tongue and the roof of the mouth, has long been a more practical and informative way of recording tongue movements. At one time the palate was coated with a powdery substance, the articulation was made, and the 'wipe-off' subsequently photographed. But the modern method uses electropalatography, whereby electrodes on a false palate respond to any tongue contact, the contact points being simultaneously registered on a visual display. This has the advantage of showing a series of representations of the changing contacts between the tongue and the top of the mouth during speech. Electropalatograms of this sort are used to illustrate the articulations of consonants in Chapter 9.

2.3   *Articulatory Description*

We have now reviewed briefly the complex modifications which are made to the original airstream by a mechanism which extends from the lungs to the mouth and nose. The description of any sound necessitates the provision of certain basic information:

(1) The nature of the airstream; usually, but not always, this will be expelled by direct action of the lungs.

(2) The action of the vocal folds; in particular, whether they are closed, wide apart, or vibrating.

(3) The position of the soft palate, which will decide whether or not the sound has nasal resonances.

(4) The disposition of the various movable organs of the mouth, i.e. the shape of the lips and tongue, in order to determine the nature of the related oral and oropharyngeal cavities.

In addition, it may be necessary to provide other information concerning, for instance, a particular secondary narrowing, or tenseness which may accompany the primary articulation; or again, when it is a question of a sound with no steady state to describe, an indication of the kind of movement which is taking place. A systematic classification of possible speech sounds is given in Chapter 4.

3

The Sounds of Speech: Acoustic and Auditory Aspects

3.1 *Sound Quality*

To complete an act of communication, it is not normally sufficient that our speech mechanism should simply function in such a way as to produce sounds; these in turn must be received by a hearing mechanism and interpreted, after having been transmitted through a medium, such as the air, which is capable of conveying sounds. We must now, therefore, examine briefly the nature of the sounds which we hear, the characteristics of the transmission phase of these sounds, and the way in which these sounds are perceived by a listener.

When we listen to a continuous utterance, we perceive an ever-changing pattern of sound. As we have seen, when it is a question of our own language, we are not conscious of all the complexities of pattern which reach our ears: we tend consciously to perceive and interpret only those sound features which are relevant to the intelligibility of our language. Nevertheless, despite this linguistic selection which we ultimately make, we are aware that this changing pattern consists of variations of different kinds: of SOUND QUALITY—we hear a variety of vowels and consonants; of PITCH—we appreciate the melody, or intonation, of the utterance; of LOUDNESS—we will agree that some sounds or syllables sound 'louder' than others; and of LENGTH—some sounds will be appreciably longer to our ears than others. These are judgements made by a listener in respect of a sound continuum emitted by a speaker and, if the sound stimulus from the speaker and response from the listener are made in terms of the same linguistic system then the utterance will be meaningful for speaker and listener alike. It is reasonable to assume, therefore, that there is some constant relationship between the speaker's articulation and the listener's reception of sound variations. In other words, it should be possible to link through the transmission phase the listener's impressions of changes of quality, pitch, loudness, and length to some articulatory activity on the part of the speaker. It will in fact be seen that an exact parallelism or correlation between the production, transmission, and reception phases of speech is not always easy to establish, the investigation of such relationships being one of the tasks of present-day phonetic studies.

The formation of any sound requires that a vibrating medium should be set in motion by some kind of energy. We have seen that in the case of the human speech mechanism the function of vibrator is often fulfilled by the vocal folds, and that these are activated by air pressure from the lungs. In addition, any such sound produced in the larynx is modified by the resonating chambers of the pharynx, mouth and, in certain cases, the nasal cavities. The listener's impression of sound quality will be determined by the way in which the speaker's vibrator and resonators function together.

Speech sounds, like other sounds, are conveyed to our ears by means of waves of compression and rarefaction of the air particles (the most common medium of communication). These variations in pressure, initiated by the action of the vibrator, are propagated in all directions from the source, the air particles themselves vibrating at the same rate (or frequency) as the original vibrator. In speech, these vibrations may be of a complex but regular pattern, producing 'tone' such as may be heard in a vowel sound; or they may be of an irregular kind, producing 'noise', such as we have in the consonant /s/; or there may be both regular and irregular vibrations present, i.e. a combination of tone and noise, as in /z/. In the production of normal vowels, the vibrator is normally provided by the vocal folds; in the case of many consonant articulations, however, a source of air disturbance is provided by constriction at a point above the larynx, with or without accompanying vocal fold vibrations.

Despite the fact that the basis of all normal vowels is the glottal tone, we are all capable of distinguishing a large number of vowel qualities. Yet the glottal vibrations in the case of [ɑː] are not very different from those for [iː], when both vowels are said with the same pitch. The modifications in quality which we perceive are due to the action of the supraglottal resonators which we have previously described. To understand this action, it is necessary to consider a little more closely the nature of the glottal vibrations.

It has already been mentioned that the glottal tone is the result of a complex, but mainly regular, vibratory motion. In fact, the vocal folds vibrate in such a way as to produce, in addition to a basic vibration over their whole length (the FUNDAMENTAL FREQUENCY), a number of overtones or HARMONICS having frequencies which are simple multiples of the fundamental or first harmonic. Thus, if there is a fundamental frequency of vibration of 100 Hz, the upper harmonics will be of the order of 200, 300, 400 etc. Hz. Indeed, there may be no energy at the fundamental frequency, but merely the harmonics of higher frequency such as 200, 300, 400 Hz. Nevertheless, we still perceive a pitch which is appropriate to a fundamental frequency of 100 Hz, i.e. the fundamental frequency is the highest common factor of all the frequencies present, whether or not it is present itself.

The number and strength of the component frequencies of this complex glottal tone will differ from one individual to another and this accounts at least in part for the differences of voice quality by which we are able to recognize speakers. But we can all modify the glottal tone so as to produce at will vowels as different as [iː] and [ɑː], so that despite our divergences of voice quality we can convey the distinction between two words such as *key* and *car*. This variation of quality, or timbre, of the glottal tone is achieved by the shapes which we give the resonators above the larynx—the pharynx, mouth, and nasal cavities. These chambers are capable of assuming an infinite number of shapes, each of which will have a characteristic vibrating resonance of its own. Those harmonics of the glottal tone which coincide with the chamber's own resonance are very considerably amplified. Thus, certain bands of strongly reinforced harmonics are characteristic of a particular arrangement of the resonating chambers which produces, for instance, a certain vowel sound. Moreover, these bands of frequencies will be reinforced whatever the fundamental frequency. In other words, whatever the pitch on which we say, for instance, the vowel [ɑː], the shaping of the resonators and their resonances will be very much the same, so that it is still possible, except on extremely high or low pitches, to recognize the quality intended. It is found that, for male speakers, the vowel [iː] has one such characteristic band of strong components in the region of 300 Hz and another at about 2,200 Hz, whereas for female speakers these bands of energy are at about 275 Hz and 2,700 Hz.

3.2   *The Acoustic Spectrum*

This complex range of frequencies of varying intensity which go to make up the quality of a sound is known as the ACOUSTIC SPECTRUM, and those bands of energy which are characteristic of a particular sound are known as the sound's FORMANTS. Thus, formants of [ɑː] are said to occur, for male speakers, in the regions around 700 Hz and 1,100 Hz.

Such complex waveforms can be analysed and displayed as a SPECTROGRAM (see Fig. 3). Originally this display required a special instrument, a spectrograph, but nowadays it is generally done by computer. The spectrogram consists of a three-dimensional display: frequency is shown on the vertical axis, time on the horizontal axis, and the energy at any frequency level either by the density of blackness in a black and white display, or by colours in a colour display. Thus the concentrations of energy at particular frequency bands (the formants) stand out very clearly. Fig. 3 shows, in the spectrogram of *Manchester music shops*, the

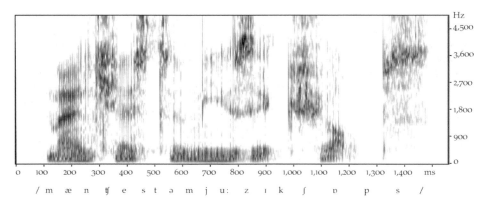

Fig. 3. Spectrogram of the phrase *Manchester music shops* as said by a male speaker of RP.

extent to which utterances are not neatly segmented into a succession of sounds but, on the contrary, there is considerable overlap. Such spectrographic analysis provides a great deal of acoustic information in a convenient form. Nevertheless, much of the information given is, in fact, irrelevant to our understanding of speech and the phonetician is obliged to establish by other methods the elements of the spectrum which are essential to speech communication.

For instance, two, or at most three, formants appear to be sufficient for the correct identification of vowels. As far as the English vowels are concerned, the first three formants are all included in the frequency range 0–4,000 Hz, so that the spectrum above 4,000 Hz would appear to be largely irrelevant to the recognition of our vowels. In both older (analogue) telephone systems with a frequency range of approximately 300–3,000 Hz and in newer (digital) systems with a range up to around 4,000 Hz, we have little difficulty in identifying the sound patterns of speakers and even in recognizing individual voice qualities. Indeed, when we are dealing with a complete utterance in a given context, where there is a multiplicity of cues to help our understanding, a high degree of intelligibility may be retained even when there are no frequencies above 1,500 Hz.

As one would suspect, there appear to be certain relationships between the formants of vowels and the cavities of the vocal tract (i.e. the shapes taken on by the resonators, notably the relation of the oral and pharyngeal cavities). Thus, the first formant appears to be low when the tongue is high in the mouth: e.g. [iː] and [uː] having high tongue positions, and have first formants around 280–320 Hz, whereas [ɑː] and [ɒ] have their first formants in the region 600–800 Hz, their tongue positions being relatively low. On the other hand, the second formant seems to be inversely related to the length of the front cavity: thus [iː], where the tongue is raised high in the front of the mouth, has a second formant around 2,200–2,700 Hz, whereas [uː], where the tongue is raised at the back of the mouth and lips are rounded, has a relatively low second formant around 1,100–1,400 Hz. (For averages for the first and second formants of all RP vowels for male and female speakers see Table 3 and Figs 10 and 11 in Chapter 8.)

It is also confirmed from spectrographic analysis that a diphthong, such as that in *my*, is indeed a glide between two vowel elements (reflecting a perceptible articulatory movement), since the formants bend from those positions typical of one vowel to those characteristic of another (see Table 4 and Fig. 9 in Chapter 8).

For many consonant articulations (e.g. the initial sounds in *pin, tin, kin, thin, fin, sin, shin*, in which the glottal vibrations play no part) there is an essential noise component, deriving from an obstruction or constriction within the mouth, approximately within the range 2,000–8,000 Hz (see Fig. 32 in Chapter 9). This noise component is also present in analogous articulations in which vocal fold excitation is present, as in the final sounds of *ruse* and *rouge* where we are dealing with sounds which consist of a combination of glottal tone and noise. Relevant acoustic data concerning vowel and consonant articulations in RP is given in Chapters 8 and 9.

Spectrographic analysis also reveals the way in which there tends, on the acoustic level, to be a merging of features of units which, linguistically, we treat separately. Thus, our discrimination of [f] and [θ] sounds would appear to depend not only on the frequency and duration of the noise component but also upon a characteristic bending of the formants of the adjacent vowel. Indeed, in the case of consonants such as [p,t,k], which involve a complete obstruction of the airstream and whose release is characterized acoustically by a relatively brief burst of noise, the vowel TRANSITION between the noise and the steady state of the vowel appears to be of prime importance for our recognition of the consonant.

3.2.1   Fundamental Frequency: Pitch

Our perception of the pitch of a speech sound depends directly upon the frequency of vibration of the vocal folds. Thus we are normally conscious of the pitch caused by the 'voiced' sounds, especially vowels; pitch judgements made on voiceless or whispered sounds, without the glottal tone, are limited in comparison with those made on voiced sounds, and are induced mainly by variations of intensity or by the dominance of certain harmonics brought about by the dispositions of the resonating cavities.

The higher the glottal fundamental frequency, the higher our impression of pitch. A male voice may have an average pitch level of approximately 120 Hz and a female voice a level in the region of 220 Hz.[1] The pitch level of voices, however, will vary a great deal between individuals and also within the speech of one speaker, the total range of one speaking voice being liable to have a range as extensive as 80–350 Hz. Following adolescence men's voices become lower until the fourth decade after which they rise continuously into old age; women's voices generally become lower up to the time of the menopause, remain much the same for 20 years or so and then possibly rise slightly.[2] Yet our perception of frequency extends further than the limits of glottal fundamental frequency, since our recognition of quality depends upon frequencies of a much higher order. In fact, the human ear perceives frequencies from as low as 16 Hz to about 20,000 Hz and in some cases even higher. As one becomes older, this upper limit may fall considerably, so that at the age of 50 it may extend no higher than approximately 10,000 Hz. As we have seen, such a reduced range is no impediment to perfect understanding of speech, since a high percentage of acoustic cues for speech recognition fall within the range 0–4,000 Hz.

Our perception of pitch is not, however, solely dependent upon fundamental frequency. Variations of intensity on the same frequency may induce impressions of a change of pitch; and conversely, tones of very high or very low frequency, if they are to be audible at all, require greater intensity than those in a middle range of frequencies.[3]

Instrumental measurement of fundamental frequency based on signals received through a microphone employs two general methods. The first is to count the number of times that a particular pattern is repeated within a selected segment of a waveform such as that provided on an oscillogram. The second is to track the progress of the fundamental frequency on a spectral display like that provided on a spectrogram, or, alternatively, to track the progress of a particular

---

[1] Fant (1956)
[2] Hollien and Shipp (1972); Russell, Penny and Pemberton (1995)
[3] Denes and Pinson (1993: 101ff)

harmonic and divide by the relevant number. Nowadays various computer programs are available which average the results from a range of measurements based on the two general methods noted above. But even with such sophisticated programs there are still likely to be the occasional mistakes like octave jumps (each doubling in Hz representing an octave).

A third method of fundamental frequency extraction involves direct measurement of the vibration of the vocal folds either by glottal illumination or by electroglottography. The best-known technique in the latter class involves use of a LARYNGOGRAPH.[4] In this technique electrodes are attached to the outside of the throat and the varying electrical impedance is monitored and projected onto a visual display. The signal generated by the variation in impedance can also be stored, enabling this technique to be used outside the laboratory.

Measures of fundamental frequency do not always correspond to our auditory perception of pitch. Besides the dependence on intensity mentioned above, different segments affect the fundamental frequency in different ways: for example, other things being equal, an [i] will have a higher fundamental frequency than an [a] and a [p] will produce a higher frequency on a following vowel than a [b]. Such (slight) changes in frequency will generally be undetectable by the ear. As in many other cases of instrumental measurement, we still have to use our auditory perception to interpret what instruments tell us.

3.2.2   Intensity: Loudness

Our sensation of the relative loudness of sounds may depend on several factors, e.g. a sound or syllable may appear to stand out from its neighbours—be 'louder'—because a marked pitch change is associated with it or because it is longer than its neighbours. It is better to use a term such as PROMINENCE to cover these general listener-impressions of variations in the perceptibility of sounds. More strictly, what is 'loudness' at the receiving end should be related to INTENSITY at the production stage, which in turn is related to the size or AMPLITUDE of the vibration. An increase in amplitude of vibration, with its resultant impression of greater loudness, is brought about by an increase in air pressure from the lungs. As we shall see (§10.2), this greater intensity is not in itself usually the most important factor in rendering a sound prominent in English. Moreover, all other things being equal, some sounds appear by their nature to be more prominent or sonorous than others, e.g. the vowel in *barn* has more carrying power than that in *bean*, and vowels generally are more powerful than consonants.

The judgements we make concerning loudness are not as fine as those made for either quality or pitch. We may judge which of two sounds is the louder, but we find it difficult to express the extent of the difference. Indeed, in terms of our linguistic system, we need to perceive and interpret only gross differences of loudness, despite the fact that when we judge quality we are, in recognizing the formant structure of a sound, reacting to characteristic regions of strong intensity in the spectrum.

---

[4] Abberton and Fourcin (1984)

3.2.3   Duration: Length

In addition to affording different auditory impressions of quality, pitch, and loudness, sounds may appear to a listener to be of different length. Clearly, whenever it is possible to establish the boundaries of sounds or syllables, it will be possible to measure their duration by means of such traces as are provided by oscillograms or spectrograms. Such delimitation of units, in both the articulatory and acoustic sense, may be difficult, as we shall see when we deal with the segmentation of the utterance. But, even when it can be done, variations of duration in acoustic terms may not correspond to our linguistic judgements of length. We shall, for instance, refer later to the 'long' vowels of English such as those of *bean* and *barn*, as compared with the 'short' vowel in *bin*. But, in making such statements, we shall not be referring to absolute duration values, since the duration of all vowels will vary considerably from utterance to utterance, according to factors such as whether the utterance is spoken fast or slowly, whether the syllable containing the vowel is accented or not, and whether the vowel is followed by a voiced or voiceless consonant. In the English system, however, we know that no more than two degrees of length are ever linguistically significant and all absolute durations will be interpreted in terms of this relationship. This distinction between measurable duration and linguistic length provides another example of the way in which our linguistic sense interprets from the acoustic material only that which is significant.

The sounds comprising any utterance will have varying durations and we will have the impression that some syllables are longer than others. Such variations of length within the utterance constitute one manifestation of the rhythmic delivery which is characteristic of English and so is fundamentally different from the flow of other languages, such as French, where syllables tend to be of much more even length.

As already mentioned, the absolute duration of sounds or syllables will depend, among other things, upon the speed of utterance. An average rate of delivery might contain anything from about six to 20 sounds per second, but lower and much higher speeds are frequently used without loss of intelligibility. The time required for the recognition of a sound will depend upon the nature of the sound and its pitch, vowels and consonants differing considerably in this respect, but it seems that a vowel lasting only about 4 msecs may have a good chance of being recognized.

3.2.4   'Stress'

We have purposely avoided the use of the word 'stress' in this chapter because this word has been used in different and ambiguous ways in phonetics and linguistics. It has sometimes been used as simply equivalent to loudness, sometimes as meaning 'made prominent by means other than pitch' (i.e. by loudness or length), and sometimes as referring just to syllables in words in the lexicon and meaning something like 'having the potential for accent on utterances'. Throughout this book we will avoid use of the term 'stress' altogether, using PROMINENCE as the general term referring to segments or syllables, SONORITY as the particular term referring to the carrying power of individual sounds, and ACCENT as referring to those syllables which stand out above others, either in individual words or in longer utterances.

3.3   *Hearing*

Our hearing mechanism must be thought of in two ways: the physiological mechanism which reacts to the acoustic stimuli—the varying pressures in the air which constitute sound; and the psychological activity—which, at the level of the brain, selects from the gross acoustic information that which is relevant in terms of the linguistic system involved. In this way, measurably different acoustic stimuli may be interpreted as being the 'same' sound unit. As we have seen, only part of the total acoustic information seems to be necessary for the perception of particular sound values. One of the tasks which confront the phonetician is the disentanglement of these relevant features from the mass of acoustic material that modern methods of sound analysis make available. The most fruitful technique of discovering the significant acoustic cues is that of SPEECH SYNTHE-SIS, controlled by listeners' judgements. After all, the sounds [ɑː] and [s] are [ɑː] and [s] only if listeners recognize them as such. Thus, it has been established that only two formants are necessary for the recognition of vowels, because machines which generate sound of the appropriate frequency bands and intensity produce vowels which are correctly identified by listeners.

Listeners, without any phonetic training, can, therefore, frequently give valuable guidance by their judgements of synthetic qualities. But it is important to be aware of the limitations of such listeners, so as to be able to make a proper evaluation of their judgements. A listener's reactions are normally conditioned by his experience of handling his own language. Thus, if there are only five significant vowel units in his language, he is liable to allow a great deal more latitude in his assessment of what is the 'same' vowel sound than if he has 20. An Englishman, for instance, having a complex vowel system and being accustomed to distinguishing subtle distinctions such as those in *sit, set, sat,* will be fairly precise in his judgement of vowel qualities. A Spaniard, however, whose vowel system is made up of fewer significant units, is likely for this reason to be more tolerant of variation of quality. Or again, if a listener is presented with a system of synthetic vowels which is numerically the same as his own, he is able to make allowance for considerable variations of quality between his and the synthetic system and still identify the vowels correctly—by their 'place' in a system rather than by their precise quality; this is what he does when he listens to and understands his language as used by a speaker of a different dialect.

Our hearing mechanism also plays an important part in monitoring our own speech; it places a control upon our speech production which is complementary to our motor, articulatory, habits. If this feedback control is disturbed, e.g. by the imposition of an artificial delay upon our reception of our own speech, disturbance in the production of our utterance is likely to result. Those who are born deaf or who become deaf before the acquisition of speech habits are rarely able to learn normal speech; similarly, a severe hearing loss later in life is likely to lead eventually to a deterioration of speech, although not down to the same level as that of those born deaf.

4

The Description and Classification of Speech Sounds

4.1 *Phonetic Description*

We have considered briefly both the mechanism which produces speech sounds and also some of the acoustic and auditory characteristics of the sounds themselves. It is now important to formulate a method of description and classification of the sound types which occur in speech and, more particularly, in English. We have seen that a speech sound has at least three stages available for investigations—the production, transmission, and reception stages. A complete description of a sound should, therefore, include information concerning all three stages. To describe the first sound in the word *ten* merely in terms of the movements of the organs of speech is to ignore the nature of the sound which is produced and the features perceived by a listener. Nevertheless, to provide all the information in respect of all phases entails a lengthy description, much of which may be irrelevant to a particular purpose. For example, since the description of the sounds of a language has in the past been most commonly used in the teaching of the language to foreigners, the emphasis has always been laid on the articulatory event. Moreover, it is only comparatively recently that there has existed any considerable body of acoustic information concerning speech. The most convenient and brief descriptive technique continues to rely either on articulatory criteria or on auditory judgements, or on a combination of both. Thus, those sounds which are commonly known as 'consonants' are most easily described mainly in terms of their articulation, whereas 'vowel' sounds require for their description a predominance of auditory impressions.

4.2 *Vowel and Consonant*

Two types of meaning are associated with the terms 'vowel' and 'consonant'. Traditionally consonants are those segments which, in a particular language, occur at the edges of syllables, while vowels are those which occur at the centre of syllables. So, in *red, wed, dead, lead, said,* the sounds represented by <r,w,d,l,s> are consonants, while in *beat, bit, bet, but, bought,* the sounds represented by <ea,i,e,u,ough> are vowels. This reference to the functioning of sounds in syllables in a particular language is a phonological definition. But once any attempt is made to define what sorts of sounds generally occur in these different syllable-positions, then we are moving to a phonetic definition. This type of definition might define vowels as median (air must escape over the middle of the tongue, thus excluding the lateral [l]), oral (air must escape through the mouth, thus excluding nasals like [n]), frictionless (thus excluding fricatives like [s]), and continuant (thus excluding plosives like [p]); all sounds excluded from this definition would be consonants. But difficulties arise in English with this definition (and with others of this sort) because English /j,w,r/, which are consonants phonologically (functioning at the edges of syllables) are vowels phonetically. Because of this these sounds are often called semi-vowels. The reverse type of difficulty is encountered in words like *sudden* and *little* where the final consonants /n/ and /l/ form syllables on their own and hence must be the centre of such syllables even though they are phonetically consonants, and even though /n/ and /l/ more frequently occur at the edges of syllables, as in *net* and *let.* When occurring in words like *sudden* and *little,* nasals and laterals are called syllabic consonants.

In this chapter we will be describing and classifying speech sounds phonetically (in the next chapter we return to the phonological definitions). We shall find that consonants can be voiced or voiceless, and are most easily described wholly in articulatory terms, since we can generally feel the contacts and movements involved. Vowels, on the other hand, are voiced, and, depending as they do on subtle adjustments of the body of the tongue, are more easily described in terms of auditory relationships.

4.3   *Consonants*

We have seen, in the preceding chapters, that the production of a speech sound may involve the action of a source of energy, a vibrator, and the movement of certain supraglottal organs. In the case of consonantal articulations, a description must provide answers to the following questions:

(1) Is the airstream set in motion by the lungs or by some other means? (pulmonic or non-pulmonic)
(2) Is the airstream forced outwards or sucked inwards? (egressive or ingressive)
(3) Do the vocal folds vibrate or not? (voiced or voiceless)
(4) Is the soft palate raised, directing the airstream wholly through the mouth, or lowered, allowing the passage of air through the nose? (oral, or nasal or nasalized)
(5) At what point or points and between what organs does closure or narrowing take place? (place of articulation)
(6) What is the type of closure or narrowing at the point of articulation? (manner of articulation)

In the case of the sound [z], occurring medially in the word *easy,* the following answers would be given:

(1) pulmonic
(2) egressive
(3) voiced
(4) oral
(5) tongue blade–alveolar ridge
(6) fricative

These answers provide a concise phonetic label for the sound; a more detailed description would include additional information concerning, for instance, the shape of the remainder of the tongue, the relative position of the jaws, and the lip position.

4.3.1   Egressive Pulmonic Consonants

Most speech sounds are made with egressive lung air. Virtually all English sounds are so made, the exception being [p,t,k], which in some dialects become ejectives (see §4.3.9 below).

4.3.2   Voicing

At any place of articulation, a consonantal articulation may involve the vibration of the vocal folds, i.e. may be voiceless or voiced.

4.3.3   Place of Articulation

The chief points of articulation are the following:

BILABIAL—the two lips are the primary articulators, e.g. [p,b,m].
LABIODENTAL—the lower lip articulates with the upper teeth, e.g. [f,v].
DENTAL—the tongue tip and rims articulate with the upper teeth, e.g. [θ,ð], as in *think* and *then*.
ALVEOLAR—the blade, or tip and blade, of the tongue articulates with the alveolar ridge, e.g. English [t,d,l,n,s,z].
POST-ALVEOLAR—the tip of the tongue articulates with the rear part of the alveolar ridge, e.g. [ɹ] as at the beginning of English *red*.
RETROFLEX—the tip of the tongue is curled back to articulate with the part of the hard palate immediately behind the alveolar ridge, e.g. [ɻ] such as is found in south-west British and some American English pronunciations of *red*.
PALATO-ALVEOLAR—the blade, or the tip and blade, of the tongue articulates with the alveolar ridge and there is at the same time a raising of the front of the tongue towards the hard palate, e.g. [ʃ,ʒ,tʃ,dʒ] as in English *ship, measure, beach, edge.*[1]

---

[1] These are called post-alveolar on the chart of the International Phonetic Alphabet (Table 1)

PALATAL—the front of the tongue articulates with the hard palate, e.g. [j] or [ç] as in *queue* [kju:] or [kçu:] or a very advanced type of [k,g] = [c,ɟ], as in French *quitter* or *guide*.

VELAR—the back of the tongue articulates with the soft palate, e.g. [k,g,ŋ], the last as in *sing*.

UVULAR—the back of the tongue articulates with the uvula, e.g. [ʁ] as in French *rouge*.

GLOTTAL—an obstruction, or a narrowing causing friction but not vibration, between the vocal folds, e.g. English [h].

In the case of some consonantal sounds, there may be a secondary place of articulation in addition to the primary. Thus, in the so-called 'dark' [ɫ], as at the end of *pull*, in addition to the partial alveolar contact, there is an essential raising of the back of the tongue towards the velum (velarization); or, again, some post-alveolar articulations of [ɹ] are accompanied by slight lip-rounding (labialization). The place of PRIMARY ARTICULATION is that of the greatest stricture, that which gives rise to the greatest obstruction to the airflow. The SECONDARY ARTICULATION exhibits a stricture of lesser rank. Where there are two co-extensive strictures of equal rank an example of DOUBLE ARTICULATION results.

4.3.4 Manner of Articulation

The obstruction made by the organs may be total, intermittent, partial, or may merely constitute a narrowing sufficient to cause friction. The chief types of articulation, in decreasing degrees of closure, are as follows:

(1) *Complete Closure*

PLOSIVE—a complete closure at some point in the vocal tract, behind which the air pressure builds up and can be released explosively, e.g. [p,b,t,d,k,g,ʔ].

AFFRICATE—a complete closure at some point in the mouth, behind which the air pressure builds up; the separation of the organs is slow compared with that of a plosive, so that more extended friction is a characteristic second element of the sound, e.g. [tʃ,dʒ].

NASAL—a complete closure at some point in the mouth but, the soft palate being lowered, the air escapes through the nose, e.g. [m,n,ŋ]. These sounds are continuants and, in their (most usual) voiced form, have no noise component; they are, to this extent, vowel-like.

(2) *Intermittent Closure*

TRILL (OR) ROLL—a series of rapid intermittent closures made by a flexible organ on a firmer surface, e.g. [r], where the tongue tip trills against the alveolar ridge as in Spanish *perro*, or [ʀ] where the uvula trills against the back of tongue, as in a stage pronunciation of French *rouge*.

TAP—a single tap made by a flexible organ on a firmer surface, e.g. [ɾ] where the tongue tip taps once against the teeth ridge, as in many Scottish pronunciations of English /r/.

(3) *Partial Closure*

LATERAL—a partial (but firm) closure is made at some point in the mouth, the airstream being allowed to escape on one or both sides of the contact. These sounds may be continuant and frictionless and therefore vowel-like, (i.e. approximants in (5) below), as in [l,ɫ], as pronounced in southern British *little* [lɪtɫ] or they may be accompanied by a little friction [l̥] as in *fling* or by considerable friction [ɬ] as in *please*.

(4) *Narrowing*

FRICATIVE—two organs approximate to such an extent that the airstream passes between them with friction, e.g. [ɸ,β,f,v,ʍ,θ,ð,s,z,ʃ,ʒ,ç,x,h]. In the bilabial region, a distinction is to be made between those purely bilabial such as [ɸ,β] where the friction occurs between spread lips, and a labial-velar sound like [ʍ] where the friction occurs between rounded lips and is accompanied by a characteristic modification of the mouth cavity brought about by the raising of the back of the tongue towards the velum. [ç] occurs at the beginning of *huge*, [x] and [ʍ] in Scottish pronunciations of *loch* and *which*, and [β] in Spanish *haber*.

(5) *Narrowing without Friction*

APPROXIMANT (OR FRICTIONLESS CONTINUANT)—a narrowing is made in the mouth but the narrowing is not quite sufficient to cause friction. In being frictionless and continuant, approximants are vowel-like; however, they function phonologically as consonants, i.e. they appear at the edges of syllables. They also differ phonetically from such sounds functioning as vowels in either of two ways. Firstly, the articulation may not involve the body of the tongue, e.g. post-alveolar [ɹ] and labiodental [ʋ], the former the usual pronunciation in RP at the beginning of *red*, the latter a speech-defective pronunciation of the same sound. Secondly, where they do involve the body of the tongue, the articulations represent only brief glides to a following vowel: thus [j] in *yet* is a glide starting from the [i] region and [w] in *wet* is a glide starting from the [u] region.

4.3.5   Obstruents and Sonorants

It is sometimes found useful to classify categories of sounds according to their noise component. Those in whose production the constriction impeding the airflow through the vocal tract is sufficient to cause noise are known as OBSTRUENTS. This category comprises plosives, fricatives and affricates. SONORANTS are those voiced sounds in which there is no noise component (i.e. voiced nasals, approximants and vowels).

4.3.6   Fortis and Lenis

A voiceless/voiced pair such as English /s,z/ are distinguished not only by the presence or absence of voice but also by the degree of breath and muscular effort involved in their articulation. Those English consonants which are usually voiced tend to be articulated with relatively weak energy, whereas those which are always voiceless are relatively strong. Indeed, we shall see that in certain situations, the so-called voiced consonants may have very little voicing. so that the energy of articulation becomes a significant factor in distinguishing the voiced and voiceless series.

Table 1. The International Phonetic Alphabet (revised to 1993; corrected 1996)

CONSONANTS (PULMONIC)

	Bilabial	Labiodental	Dental	Alveolar	Postalveolar	Retroflex	Palatal	Velar	Uvular	Pharyngeal	Glottal
Plosive	p b			t d		ʈ ɖ	c ɟ	k g	q ɢ		ʔ
Nasal	m	ɱ		n		ɳ	ɲ	ŋ	N		
Trill	B			r					R		
Tap or Flap				ɾ		ɽ					
Fricative	ɸ β	f v	θ ð	s z	ʃ ʒ	ʂ ʐ	ç ʝ	x ɣ	χ ʁ	ħ ʕ	h ɦ
Lateral fricative				ɬ ɮ							
Approximant		ʋ		ɹ		ɻ	j	ɰ			
Lateral approximant				l		ɭ	ʎ	L			

Where symbols appear in pairs, the one to the right represents a voiced consonant. Shaded areas denote articulations judged impossible.

CONSONANTS (NON-PULMONIC)

Clicks	Voiced implosives	Ejectives
ʘ Bilabial	ɓ Bilabial	' as in:
ǀ Dental	ɗ Dental/alveolar	p' Bilabial
ǃ (Post)alveolar	ʄ Palatal	t' Dental/alveolar
ǂ Palatoalveolar	ɠ Velar	k' Velar
ǁ Alveolar lateral	ʛ Uvular	s' Alveolar fricative

VOWELS

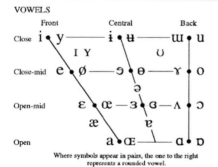

Where symbols appear in pairs, the one to the right represents a rounded vowel.

OTHER SYMBOLS

ʍ Voiceless labial-velar fricative
w Voiced labial-velar approximant
ɥ Voiced labial-palatal approximant
ʜ Voiceless epiglottal fricative
ʢ Voiced epiglottal fricative
ʡ Epiglottal plosive

ɕ ʑ Alveolo-palatal fricatives
ɺ Alveolar lateral flap
ɧ Simultaneous ʃ and x

Affricates and double articulations can be represented by two symbols joined by a tie bar if necessary.

k͡p t͡s

SUPRASEGMENTALS

ˈ	Primary stress
ˌ	Secondary stress

ˌfoʊnəˈtɪʃən

ː	Long	eː
ˑ	Half-long	eˑ
˘	Extra-short	ĕ
.	Syllable break	ɹi.ækt
ǀ	Minor (foot) group
‖	Major (intonation) group
‿	Linking (absence of a break)

TONES & WORD ACCENTS

LEVEL			CONTOUR		
e̋ or ˥	Extra high	ě or ˬ	Rising
é	˦	High	ê	˥	Falling
ē	˧	Mid	e᷄	˧	High rising
è	˨	Low	e᷅	˩	Low rising
ȅ	˩	Extra low	e᷈	˧	Rising-falling
↓ Downstep			↗ Global rise		etc.
↑ Upstep			↘ Global fall		

DIACRITICS

Diacritics may be placed above a symbol with a descender, e.g. ŋ̊

◌̥	Voiceless	n̥ d̥	◌̤	Breathy voiced	b̤ a̤	◌̪	Dental	t̪ d̪
◌̬	Voiced	s̬ t̬	◌̰	Creaky voiced	b̰ a̰	◌̺	Apical	t̺ d̺
ʰ	Aspirated	tʰ dʰ	◌̼	Linguolabial	t̼ d̼	◌̻	Laminal	t̻ d̻
◌̹	More rounded	ɔ̹	ʷ	Labialized	tʷ dʷ	◌̃	Nasalized	ẽ
◌̜	Less rounded	ɔ̜	ʲ	Palatalized	tʲ dʲ	ⁿ	Nasal release	dⁿ
◌̟	Advanced	u̟	ˠ	Velarized	tˠ dˠ	ˡ	Lateral release	dˡ
◌̠	Retracted	i̠	ˤ	Pharyngealized	tˤ dˤ	◌̚	No audible release	d̚
◌̈	Centralized	ë	~	Velarized or pharyngealized	ɫ		
◌̽	Mid-centralized	e̽	◌̝	Raised	e̝ (ɹ̝ = voiced alveolar fricative)		
◌̩	Syllabic	l̩	◌̞	Lowered	e̞ (β̞ = voiced bilabial approximant)		
◌̯	Non-syllabic	e̯	◌̘	Advanced Tongue Root	e̘		
˞	Rhoticity	ɚ	◌̙	Retracted Tongue Root	e̙		

4.3.7   Classification of Consonants

The chart of the International Phonetic Alphabet (IPA) (see Table 1) shows manner of articulation on the vertical axis, place of articulation on the horizontal axis, and a pairing within each box thus created shows voiceless consonants on the left and voiced consonants on the right.

4.3.8   Ingressive Pulmonic Consonants

Consonants of this type, made as we are breathing in, sometimes occur in languages as variants of their egressive pulmonic equivalents. So we may use such sounds when we are out of breath, but have not got time to pause, either because the need for communication is pressing, or because we do not wish someone else to have a chance to speak. The use of such an ingressive pulmonic airstream is, however, variable between languages, and is not especially common in English. Individual sounds made on an ingressive pulmonic airstream may occur as speech defects. Some sounds may also occur extralinguistically, so in English a common way of expressing surprise or pain involves the energetic inspiration of air accompanied by bilabial or labiodental friction.

4.3.9   Egressive Glottalic Consonants

In the production of these sounds, known as EJECTIVES, the glottis is closed, so that lung air is contained beneath it. A closure or narrowing is made at some point above the glottis (the soft palate being raised) and the air between this point and the glottis is compressed by a general muscular constriction of the chamber and a raising of the larynx. Thus, a bilabial ejective plosive sound [p'] may be made by compressing the air in this way behind the lips. However, it is not only plosives which may be ejective; affricates and fricatives commonly have this type of compression in a number of languages, e.g. [ts', tl', s', x' etc.]. If the glottis is tightly closed, it follows that this type of articulation can apply only to voiceless sounds. [p', t', k'] occur sometimes in final positions in some dialects of English (e.g. in south-east Lancashire). These are not to be confused with the more common variants of final [p,t,k] which are frequently (e.g. in London English) replaced or reinforced by a glottal stop; thus the final sound in the word *stop* may be replaced by a glottal stop or have a glottal closure accompanying the bilabial one, but there is no compression between the glottal and bilabial closures.

4.3.10   Ingressive Glottalic Consonants

For these sounds a complete closure is made in the mouth but, instead of air pressure from the lungs being compressed behind the closure, the almost completely closed larynx is lowered so that the air in the mouth and pharyngeal cavities is rarefied. The result is that outside air is sucked in once the mouth closure is released; at the same time, there is sufficient leakage of lung air through the glottis to produce voice. It will be seen that the resulting sound is made by means of a combined airstream mechanism, namely a pulmonic airstream in combination with ingressive glottalic air. Such ingressive stops (generally voiced) are known as IMPLOSIVES and occur with bilabial [ɓ], dental or alveolar [ɗ], or velar [ɠ] mouth closures. Though such sounds occur in a number of languages, sometimes in the speech of the deaf and in types of stammering, they are not found in normal English. In some languages voiceless implosives may occur, which of course means that in these cases the larynx must be completely closed.

4.3.11   Ingressive Velaric Consonants

Another set of sounds involving an ingressive airstream is produced entirely by means of closures within the mouth cavity; normal breathing through the nose may continue quite independently if the soft palate is lowered and may even produce accompanying nasalization. Thus, the sound made to indicate irritation or sympathy (often written as 'tut-tut') is articulated by means of a double closure, the back of the tongue against the velum and the tip, blade, and sides against the teeth, teeth ridge, and side teeth. The cavity contained within these closures is then enlarged mainly by tongue movement, so that the air is rarefied. The release of the forward closure causes the outer air to be sucked in; the release may be crisp in which case a sound of a plosive type is heard, or relatively slow, in which case an affricated sound is produced. These sounds are known as CLICKS, the one referred to above being a dental click [ǀ]. The sound made to encourage horses is a lateral click, i.e. the air is sucked in by releasing one side of the tongue [ǁ]. These clicks and several others occur as significant sounds in a small number of languages in Africa (e.g. Zulu) and paralinguistically in most languages (as in English).

4.4   *Vowels*

This category of sounds is normally made with a voiced egressive airstream, without any closure or narrowing such as would result in the noise component characteristic of many consonantal sounds; moreover, the escape of the air is characteristically accomplished in an unimpeded way over the middle line of the tongue. We are now concerned with a glottal tone modified by the action of the upper resonators of the mouth, pharyngeal and nasal cavities. As we have seen (chapters 2 and 3), the movable organs mainly responsible for shaping these resonators are the soft palate, lips, and tongue. A description of vowel-like sounds must, therefore, note:

(1) The position of the soft palate—raised for oral vowels, lowered for nasalized vowels.
(2) The kind of aperture formed by the lips—degrees of spreading or rounding.
(3) The part of tongue which is raised and the degree of raising.

Of these three factors, only the second—the lip position—can easily be described by visual or tactile means. Our judgement of the action of the soft palate depends less on our feeling for its position than on our perception of the presence or absence of nasality in the sound produced. Again, the movements of the tongue, which so largely determine the shape of the mouth and pharyngeal cavities, may be so minute that it is impossible to assess them by any simple means; moreover, there being normally no contact of the tongue with the roof of the mouth, no help is given by any tactile sensation. A vowel description will usually, therefore, be based mainly on auditory judgements of sound relationships, together with some articulatory information, especially as regards the position of the lips. In addition, an acoustic description can be given in terms of the disposition of the characteristic formants of the sound (see section §3.1 above).

4.4.1   Difficulties of Description

The description of vowel sounds, especially by means of the written word, has always presented considerable difficulty. Certain positions and gross movements of the tongue can be felt. We are, for instance, aware that when we pronounce most vowel sounds the tongue tip lies behind the lower teeth; moreover, in comparing two such vowels as /iː/ (*key*) and /ɑː/ (*car*) (Fig. 4), we can feel that, in the case of the former, the front of the tongue is the part which is mainly raised, whereas in the case of the latter, such raising as there is is accomplished by the back part of the tongue. Therefore, it can be stated in articulatory terms that some vowel sounds require the raising of the front of the tongue while others are articulated with a typical 'hump' at the back; and these statements can be confirmed by means of X-ray photography. But the actual point and degree of raising is more difficult to judge. It is not, for instance, helpful to say that a certain vowel is articulated with the front part of the tongue raised to within 5 mm of the hard palate. This may be a statement of fact for one person's pronunciation, but an identical sound may be produced by another speaker with

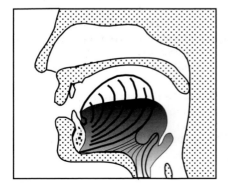

Fig. 4. *Tongue positions of* [iː], [ɑː].

a different relationship between the tongue and palate. Moreover, we would not find it easy to judge whether our tongue was at 4 or 5 mm from the palate. It is no more helpful to relate the vowel quality to a value used in a particular language, as is still so often done. A statement such as 'a vowel quality similar to that in the English word *cat*' is not precise, since the vowel in *cat* may have a wide range of values in English. The statement becomes more useful if the accent of English is specified, but even then a number of variant interpretations will always be possible.

4.4.2   Cardinal Vowels

It is clear that a finer and more independent system of description is needed, on both the auditory and articulatory levels. The most satisfactory scheme is that devised by Daniel Jones and known as the CARDINAL VOWEL system. The basis of the system is physiological, i.e. the two qualities upon which all the others were 'hinged' were produced with the tongue in certain easily felt positions: the front of the tongue raised as close as possible to the palate without friction being produced, for the Cardinal Vowel [i]; and the whole of the tongue as low as possible in the mouth, with very slight raising at the extreme back, for the Cardinal Vowel [ɑ]. Starting from the [i] position, the front of the tongue was lowered gradually, the lips remaining spread or neutrally open and the soft palate raised. The lowering of the tongue was halted at three points at which the vowel qualities seemed, from an auditory standpoint, to be equidistant. The tongue positions of these qualities were X-rayed and were found to be fairly equidistant from a spatial point of view. The symbols [e,ɛ,a] were assigned to these vowel values. The same procedure was applied to vowel qualities depending on the height of the back of the tongue, this raising the back of the tongue from the [ɑ] position; the lips were changed progressively from a wide open shape (for [ɑ]) to a closely rounded one and the soft palate remained raised. Again, three auditorily equidistant points were established from the lowest to the highest position; the corresponding tongue positions were photographed and the spatial relationships confirmed as for the front vowels. These values were given the symbols [ɔ,o,u]. Thus a scale of eight primary Cardinal Vowels was set up, denoted by the following numbers and symbols: 1, [i]; 2, [e]; 3, [ɛ]; 4, [a]; 5, [ɑ]; 6, [ɔ]; 7, [o]; 8, [u].

It is to be noticed that the front series [i,e,ɛ,a] and [ɑ] of the back series are pronounced with spread or open lips, whereas the remaining three members of the back series have varying degrees of lip-rounding. The combination of tongue and lip positions in the primary Cardinal Vowels are the most frequent in languages, i.e. front and open vowels are most commonly unrounded while back vowels other than in the open position are most commonly rounded. A secondary series can be obtained by reversing the lip positions, e.g. lip-rounding applied to the [i] tongue position, or lip-spreading applied to the [u] position. Such a secondary series is denoted by the following numbers and symbols: 9, [y]; 10, [ø]; 11, [œ]; 12, [ɶ]; 13, [ɒ]; 14, [ʌ]; 15, [ɣ]; 16, [ɯ].

This complete series of 16 Cardinal Vowel values may be divided into two lip shape categories, with corresponding tongue positions:

unrounded—[i,e,ɛ,a,ɑ,ʌ,ɤ,ɯ]
rounded—[y,ø,œ,ɶ,ɒ,ɔ,o,u]

Such a scale is useful because (a) the vowel qualities are unrelated to particular values in languages, though many may occur in various languages, and (b) the set is recorded, so that reference may always be made to a standard, invariable scale.[2] Thus a vowel quality can be described as being, for instance, similar to that of Cardinal 2 ([e]), or another as being a type half-way between Cardinal 6 ([ɔ]) and Cardinal 7 ([o]), but somewhat centralized. Diacritics are available in the IPA alphabet to show modifications of Cardinal values, e.g. a subscript ˕ to mean more open, a subscript ˔ meaning closer, and raised dots ¨ to mean centralized. The last example given above might in this way be symbolized as [ɔ̝̈] or [ö̞].

It is, moreover, possible to give a visual representation of these vowel relationships on a chart which is based on the Cardinal Vowel tongue positions. The simplified diagram shown in Fig. 5 is obtained by plotting the highest point of tongue raising for each of the primary Cardinal Vowels and joining the points together. The internal triangle, corresponding to the region of central or [ə]-type vowel sounds, is made by dividing the top line into three approximately equal sections and drawing lines parallel to the two sides, so that they meet near the base of the figure. On such a figure, the sound symbolized by [ɔ̝̈] or [ö̞] may have its relationship to the cardinal scale shown visually (see the open circle (O) on Fig. 5).

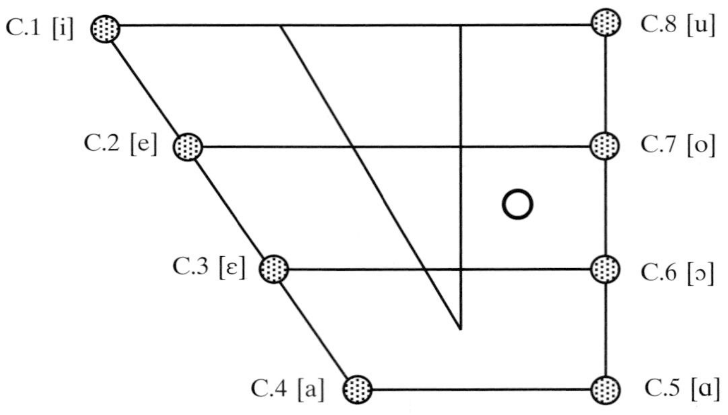

Fig. 5. *The primary Cardinal vowels; the area symbolised by* [ɔ̝̈] *or* [ö̞] *shown as a circle.*

It must be understood that this diagram is a highly conventionalized one which shows, above all, quality relationships. Some attempt is, however, made to relate the shape of the figure to actual tongue positions: thus, the range of movement

[2] Copies of the original recording of the Cardinal Vowels by Daniel Jones are available from the author at the Department of Linguistics, University of Manchester, Manchester M13 9PL

is greater at the top of the figure, and the tongue raising of front vowels becomes more retracted as the tongue position lowers. Nevertheless, it has been shown that it is possible to articulate vowel qualities without the tongue and lip positions which this diagram seems to postulate as necessary. It is, for instance, possible to produce a sound of the Cardinal 7 ([o]) type without the lip–tongue relationship suggested. But, on the whole, it may be assumed that a certain auditorily identified vowel quality will be produced by an articulation of the kind suggested by the Cardinal Vowel diagram. Moreover, it is a remarkable fact that the auditory judgements as to vowel relationships made by Daniel Jones have been largely supported by recent acoustic analysis; in fact, a chart based on an acoustic analysis of Cardinal Vowel qualities corresponds very well with the traditional Cardinal Vowel figure (see Figs 10 and 11 in Chapter 8).

4.4.3 Nasality

Besides the information concerning lip and tongue positions which the above chart and symbolization denote, a vowel description must also indicate whether the vowel is purely oral or whether it is nasalized. The 16 Cardinal Vowels mentioned may all be transformed into their nasalized counterparts if the soft palate is lowered. It is unusual, however, to find such an extensive series of nasalized vowels, since it is unusual (though not unknown) for languages to make such fine, significant distinctions of nasalized qualities as are common in the case of the purely oral values.

4.4.4 Relatively Pure Vowels vs Gliding Vowels

It is clearly not possible for the quality of a vowel to remain absolutely constant (or, in other words, for the organs of speech to function for any length of time in an unchanging way). Nevertheless, we may distinguish between those vowels

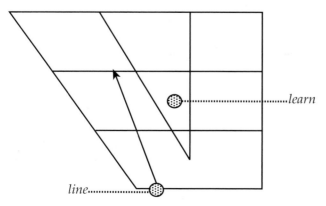

Fig. 6. *The vowels of* learn *and* line.

which are relatively pure (or unchanging), such as the vowel in *learn,* and those which have a considerable and voluntary glide, such as the gliding vowel in *line.* The so-called pure vowels will be marked on the diagram as a dot, showing the highest point of the tongue or, better, a ring, since it would be inadvisable to attempt to be over-precise in the matter of these auditory judgements; the gliding (or diphthongal) vowel sound will be shown as an arrow, which indicates the quality of the starting point and the direction in which the quality change is made (corresponding to a movement of the tongue). Fig. 6 shows the way in which the vowels of *learn* and *line* will be marked.

We are now in a position to give a practical and comprehensive description of a vowel sound, partly in articulatory terms, partly in auditory terms. The vowel which we have symbolized above as [ɜ] or [ö] might be described in this way: 'A vowel quality between Cardinal Vowels 6 and 7, but somewhat centralized'. Such a written description will have a meaning in terms of sound for anyone who is familiar with the Cardinal Vowel scale. The position of the lips and the soft palate is subsumed in this description. There may, of course, be other features of the sound which may be worth mentioning in a full phonetic description, e.g. a breathy or creaky voice quality.

4.4.5 Articulatory Classification of Vowels

Although precise descriptions of vowels are better done auditorily, nevertheless it is convenient to have available a rough scheme of articulatory classification. Such a scheme is represented by the vowel diagram on the chart of the International Phonetic Alphabet as shown in Table 1. It will be noticed that this is of similar shape to the Cardinal Vowel diagram, although a single line is used centrally rather than a triangle. Labels are provided to distinguish between front, central, and back, and between four degrees of opening: close, close-mid, open-mid, and open (see Fig. 7). At each intersection point on the periphery of the

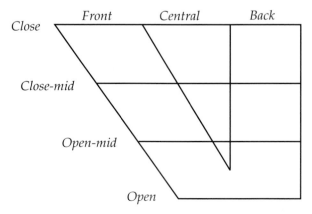

Fig. 7. *Articulatory labels combined with the Cardinal Vowel diagram.*

diagram on the IPA chart (Table 1) two symbols are supplied; these symbols are the same as those used for the Cardinal Vowels. However, on the IPA chart the unrounded vowel is always the first of the pair and the rounded the second; this means that we cannot say that the first corresponds to the primary Cardinal and the second to the secondary Cardinal. (It will be remembered that primary Cardinals involve the most frequent lip positions, back vowels being more usually rounded.) The IPA diagram also supplies us with a number of additional symbols for vowels in certain positions, [ɪ,æ,ɨ,ə,ɐ] being used for unrounded vowels and [ʉ,ʊ,ɵ] for rounded vowels.

5

Sounds in Language

5.1 *Speech Sounds and Linguistic Units*

We have now considered a method of describing and classifying the sounds capable of being produced by the speech organs. Speech is, however, a manifestation of language and spoken language is normally a continuum of sound. A speech sound, produced in isolation and without the meaningfulness imposed by a linguistic system, may be described in purely phonetic terms; but any purely phonetic approach to the sounds of language encounters considerable difficulties. Two initial problems concern, firstly, the identification and delimitation of the sound unit (or segment) to be described and, secondly, the way in which different sounds are treated, for the purpose of linguistic analysis, as if they were the same.

As we have seen, in any investigation of speech, it is on the physiological and acoustic levels that most information is available to us. Yet, especially on the articulatory level, as is revealed by moving X-ray photography, any utterance consists of apparently continuous movements by a very large number of organs; it is well-nigh impossible to say, simply from an X-ray film of the speech organs at work, how many speech sounds have been uttered. A display of acoustic information is easier to handle (see Fig. 3), but even here it is not always possible, because of the way in which many sounds merge into one another, to delimit exactly the beginning and end of sound segments. Moreover, even if it were possible to identify the main characteristics of certain sounds without being sure of their limits, it would not follow that the phonetic statement we might accordingly make concerning the sequence of sound segments would be a useful one in terms of the language which we were investigating. Thus, the word *tot* is frequently pronounced in the London region in such a way that it is possible to identify five sound segments: [t], [s], [h], [ɒ], [t]. Yet much of this phonetic reality may be discarded as irrelevant when it is a question of the structure of the word *tot* in terms of the sound system of English. Indeed, the speaker himself will probably feel that the utterance *tot* consists of only three 'sounds' (not only because of the influence of the spelling), such a judgement on his part being a highly sophisticated one which results from his experience in hearing and speaking English. In other words, the [s] and [h] segments are to be treated as part of the phonological, or linguistic, unit /t/.[1] The phonetic sequence [tsh] does not, in an initial position in this type of English, consist of three meaningful units; in other languages, on the other hand, such a sequence might well constitute three linguistic units as well as three phonetic segments.

This same example illustrates how different sounds may count, in respect of their function in a language, as the same linguistic unit. In such a pronunciation of *tot*, as is noted above, the first realization of /t/ might be described as consisting of:

(1) A voiceless stop made by the tongue tip and rims against the alveolar ridge and side teeth.

(2) A slow release of the compressed air, so that friction is heard—[s].

(3) The complete disengagement of the tongue from the roof of the mouth, so that no friction is caused in the mouth; but an interval before the beginning of the next sound, during which there is friction in the glottis (and voiceless resonance in the supraglottal cavities)—[h].

The second manifestation of /t/, on the other hand, might have an articulation which could be described phonetically as follows:

(1) An alveolar stop made as before, but with a simultaneous stop made in the glottis.

(2) The glottal closure is released, but the oral stop is retained slightly longer, during which time the air escapes through the nasal passage, the soft palate being lowered.

The first [t] might be briefly described as a voiceless alveolar plosive, released with affrication and aspiration; the second as an unexploded voiceless alveolar plosive made with a simultaneous glottal stop. These two different articulations, with the resultant difference of sound, function, nevertheless, as the same linguistic unit, the first sound occurring predictably under strong accent initially in a syllable and the second being a typical manifestation of the unit in a final position. Such an abstract linguistic unit, which will include sounds of different types, is called a PHONEME; the different phonetic realizations of a phoneme are known as its ALLOPHONES.

5.2 *The Linguistic Hierarchy*

It is clear, as we hinted in Chapter 1, that speech and language require in their analysis different types of unit. An utterance, on the concrete speech level, will consist of the continuous physiological activity which results in a continuum of sound; the largest unit will, therefore, be the span of sound occurring between

---

[1] It is customary to distinguish sound segments from linguistic sound units (phonemes) by using [ ] to enclose the former and / / to enclose the latter

two silences. Within this unit of varying extent it may be possible to find smaller segments. It is, however, from the abstract, linguistic level of analysis that we receive guidance as to how the utterance may be usefully segmented in the case of any particular language. We might find, for instance, that an utterance such as 'The boys ran quickly away and were soon out of sight' is spoken without a pause or interruption for breath; it might be said to constitute a single breath group on the articulatory level. But, on the linguistic level, we know that this utterance is capable of being analysed as a sentence consisting of two CLAUSES. Moreover, certain extensive sequences occurring within the utterance might be meaningfully replaced by other sound sequences, e.g. *boys* might be replaced by *dogs*, ran by *walked, quickly* by *slowly* etc. These replaceable sound sequences are able to stand by themselves and are called WORDS. In written forms of language, it usually happens that words are separated from each other by spaces, this being a sophisticated convention which is not reflected in speech. (We shall see, however, in Chapter 11, that words may retain at their boundaries certain characteristics in connected speech, so that their presence and span is signalled on a phonetic as well as an orthographic level.) Yet there are meaningful units smaller than the word. The word *boys* may be divided into *boy* and *s* ([z]), where the presence or absence of [z] indicates the plural or singular form; *quickly* may be said to consist of *quick* and the adverbial suffix *-ly*. These are smaller sound sequences which may be interchanged meaningfully, but which may or may not be capable of standing by themselves. These smaller units, known as MORPHEMES, may correspond with words, e.g. *boy*, in which case they may stand alone, or they may not normally occur other than in association with a word. There is, however, yet a lower level at which meaningful commutation is possible. The word *ran* is also a morpheme; but if, instead of saying [ræn], we say [rʌn], we have, by changing an element on a lower level than the morpheme, changed the meaning and function of the word. This basic linguistic element, beyond which it is not necessary to go for practical purposes, is what we have already referred to as a PHONEME. A phoneme may, therefore, be thought of as the smallest contrastive linguistic unit which may bring about a change of meaning.

5.3 *Phonemes*

It is possible to establish the phonemes of a language by means of a process of commutation or the discovery of MINIMAL PAIRS, i.e. pairs of words which are different in respect of only one sound segment. The series of words *pin, bin, tin, din, kin, chin, gin, fin, thin, sin, shin, win* supplies us with 12 words which are distinguished simply by a change in the first (consonantal) element of the sound sequence. These elements, or phonemes, are said to be in CONTRAST or OPPOSITION; we may symbolize them as /p,b,t,d,k,tʃ,dʒ,f,θ,s,ʃ,w/. But other sound sequences will show other consonantal oppositions, e.g.

(1) *tame, dame, game, lame, maim, name*, adding /g,l,m,n/ to our inventory;
(2) *pot, tot, cot, lot, yacht, hot, rot*, adding /j,h,r/;
(3) *pie, tie, buy, thigh, thy, vie*, adding /ð,v/;
(4) *two, do, who, woo, zoo*, adding /z/.

Such comparative procedures reveal 22 consonantal phonemes capable of contrastive function initially in a word.

It is not sufficient, however, to consider merely one position in the word. Possibilities of phonemic opposition have to be investigated in medial and final positions as well as in the initial. If this is done in English, we discover in medial positions another consonantal phoneme, /ʒ/, cf. the word oppositions *letter, leather, leisure* or *seater, seeker, Caesar, seizure*. This phoneme /ʒ/ is rare in initial and final positions (e.g. in *rouge*). Moreover, in final positions, we do not find /h/ or /r/, and it is questionable whether we should consider /w,j/ as separate, final, contrastive units (see §8.2). We do, however, find one more phoneme that is common in medial and final positions but unknown initially, viz. /ŋ/ cf. *simmer, sinner, singer* or *some, son, sung*.

Such an analysis of the consonantal phonemes of English will give us a total of 24 phonemes, of which four (/h,r,ʒ,ŋ/) are *of restricted occurrence*—or six, if /w,j/ are not admitted finally. Similar procedures may be used to establish the vowel phonemes of English (see Chapter 8).

The final inventories of vowel and consonant phonemes will constitute a statement of the total oppositions in all positions in the word or syllable; when any particular place in the word or syllable is taken into consideration (e.g. in consonantal clusters in initial position), the number of terms in the series of oppositions is likely to be more restricted.

5.3.1 Diversity of Phonemic Solutions

It is important to emphasize the fact that it is frequently possible to make several different statements of the phonemic structure of a language, all of which may be equally valid from a logical standpoint. The solution chosen will be the one which is most convenient as regards the use to which the phonemic analysis is to be put. Thus, one solution might be appropriate when it is a question of teaching a language to a particular group of foreigners, when similarities and differences between two languages may need to be underlined; another solution might be appropriate if it is a question of using the phonemic analysis as a basis for an orthography, when sociolinguistic considerations (for example, relations with other countries having particular orthographic conventions) have to be taken into account. Even without such considerations, discrepancies in analysis frequently arise in the case of such sound combinations as affricates (e.g. [tʃ,dʒ,tr,dr]) and diphthongs (e.g. [eɪ,əʊ,aɪ,aʊ]), which may be treated as single phonemes or combinations of two. Such problems concerning particular English sounds will be dealt with when vowels and consonants are considered in detail.

5.3.2 Distinctive Features

Up to now we have obtained an inventory of phonemes for English which is no more than a set of relationships or oppositions. The essence of the phoneme /p/, for instance, is that it is not /t/ or /k/ or /s/ etc. This is a negative definition, which it is desirable to amplify by means of positive information of a phonetic type. Thus, we may say that /p/ is, from a phonetic point of view, characteristically voiceless (compared with voiced /b/); labial (compared with the places of articulation of such sounds as /t/ or /k/); plosive (compared with /f/). The /p/ phoneme may, therefore, be defined positively by stating the combination of distinctive features which identify it within the English phonemic system: voiceless, labial, plosive.

As originally conceived, the distinctive features of a language were stated in articulatory terms using as a basis the phonetic classification of consonants described in the previous chapter. So the distinctive features of English /p/ were voiceless, labial, and plosive. Here there are three dimensions of variation: voicing, place, and manner. But it was conceded that the distinctive features of a language might involve more or less than three dimensions. For example, in some languages (e.g. in Tamil, a language of south India) voicing is not a distinctive feature (so changing from [p] to [b] does not bring about a change of meaning) and so only place and manner are distinctive. In other languages we may need to state four dimensions of variation. In Hindi not only is voicing (and place and manner) distinctive but aspiration is also separately distinctive from voice; compare, for example, /kaan/ 'ear', /kʰaan/ 'mine', /gaan/ 'anthem', /gʰaan/ 'quantity'. Such articulatory distinctive features sometimes involve two terms (voiceless vs voiced, aspirated vs unaspirated), sometimes three (e.g. labial /p,b/ vs alveolar /t,d/ vs velar /k,g/ in English), and sometimes more.

Later developments in the theory of distinctive features have involved explaining all the contrasts of a language in terms of BINARY distinctive features and suggesting that there is a set of binary features (involving around 12 or 13 distinctions) which will account for all languages. An apparent three-term distinction like labial vs. alveolar vs. velar is turned into two features with plus or minus values; using 'coronal' to mean 'made with the blade of the tongue raised above the neutral position,' and 'anterior' to mean 'made in front of the hard palate,' the English plosives /p,b,t,d,k,g/ are then defined as follows:

	p,b	t,d	k,g
coronal	–	+	–
anterior	+	+	–

In the most well-known set of binary distinctive features[2] many are still articulatory, although some are auditory or acoustic (e.g. 'strident').

In this book we use distinctive feature analysis (of the more traditional kind which allows non-binary dimensions) where such analysis is not in doubt and where it is obviously explanatory. This means that we frequently refer to feature analysis when describing the consonants of English, but use it very little when describing the vowels, since almost all distinctive feature analysis in this area is disputed and not always helpful.

5.3.3   Allophones

No two realizations of a phoneme are the same. This is true even when the same word is repeated; thus, when the word *cat* is said twice, there are likely to be

---

[2] Chomsky and Halle (1968)

slight phonetic variations in the two realizations of the phoneme sequence /k+æ+t/. Nevertheless, the phonetic similarities between the utterances will probably be more striking than the differences. But variants of the same phoneme will frequently show consistent phonetic differences; such consistent variants are referred to as ALLOPHONES. We have seen (§5.1) how different the initial and final allophones of /t/ in the word *tot* may be. Or again, the [k] sounds which occur initially in the words *key* and *car* are phonetically clearly different: the first can be felt to be a forward articulation, near the hard palate, whereas the second is made further back on the soft palate. This difference of articulation is brought about by the nature of the following vowel, [iː], having a more advanced articulation than [ɑː]; the allophonic variation is in this case conditioned by the context. In some varieties of English the two [l] sounds of *lull* [lʌɫ] show a variation of a different kind. The first [l], the so-called 'clear' [l] with a front vowel resonance, has a quality very different from that of the final 'dark' [ɫ] with a back vowel resonance. Here the difference of quality is related to the position of the phoneme in the word or syllable and depends on whether a vowel or a consonant or a pause follows. It is possible, therefore, to predict in a given language which allophones of a phoneme will occur in any particular context or situation: they are said to be in conditioned variation or COMPLEMENTARY DISTRIBUTION. Statements of complementary distribution can refer to preceding or following sounds (e.g. fronted k̟ before front vowels like /iː/ in *key* but retracted k̠ before back vowels like /ɑː/ in *car*); to positions in syllables (plosives are strongly aspirated when initial in accented syllables); or to positions in any grammatical unit, e.g. words (vowels may optionally be preceded by a glottal stop when word-initial) or morphemes (Cockney has a different allophone of /ɔː/ in morpheme-medial and morpheme-final positions (cf. *board* [bɔʊd] vs. *bored* [bɔwəd])).

Complementary distribution does not take into account those variant realizations of the same phoneme in the same situation which may constitute the difference between two utterances of the same word. When the same speaker produces noticeably different pronunciations of the word *cat* (e.g. by exploding or not exploding the final /t/), the different realizations of the phonemes are said to be in FREE VARIATION. Again, the word *very* may be pronounced [veɹɪ] (where the middle consonant is an approximant) or [veɾɪ] (where the middle consonant is a tap). The approximant and the tap are here in free variation. Variants in free variation are also allophones (since, like those in complementary distribution, they are not involved in changes of meaning).

It is usually the case that there is some phonetic similarity between the allophones of a phoneme: for example both the [l] sounds discussed above, as well as the voiceless fricative variety which follows /p/ or /k/ in words such as *please* and *clean*, are lateral articulations. It sometimes happens that two sounds occur in complementary distribution, but are not treated as allophones of the same phoneme because of their total phonetic dissimilarity. This is the case of [h] and [ŋ] in English; they are never significantly opposed, since [h] occurs typically in initial positions in the syllable or word, and [ŋ] in final positions. A purely logical arrangement might include these two sounds within the same phoneme, so that *hung* might be transcribed phonemically as either /hʌh/ or /ŋʌŋ/; but such a solution would ignore the total lack of phonetic similarity and also the feeling of native speakers. The ordinary native speaker is, in fact, often unaware of the allophonic variations of his phonemes and will, for instance, say that the various allophones of /l/ we have discussed are the 'same' sound; [h] and [ŋ], however, he will always consider to be 'different' sounds. When he makes a statement of this kind, he is usually referring to the function of the sounds in the language system and can thereby offer helpful, intuitive, information regarding the phonemic organization of his language. In the case of a language such as English prejudices induced by the existence of written forms have naturally to be taken into account in evaluating the native speaker's reaction.

5.3.4 Neutralization

It sometimes happens that a sound may be assigned to either of two phonemes with equal validity. In English, examples of this kind are to be found in the plosive series. The contrast between English /p,t,k/ and /b,d,g/ is shown in word-initial position by pairs like *pin/bin, team/deem, come/gum*. However, following /s/ there is no such contrast. Words beginning /sp-, st-, sk-/ are not contrasted with words beginning /sb-, sd-, sg-/, although a distinction sometimes occurs word-medially, as in *disperse/disburse*, and *discussed/disgust* (which suggests a syllable division between the /s/ and the following plosive). In such circumstances we say that the contrast between /p,t,k/ and /b,d,g/, the contrast between voiceless and voiced, is neutralized following /s/ in word-initial position. Words like *spin, steam*, and *scar* could equally well be transcribed with /b,d,g/ as with /p,t,k/. Indeed, even though the writing system itself suggests /p,t,k/ (/k/ may be written with <k> or <c>), the sounds which actually occur following /s/ can in some respects be considered closer to /b,d,g/ since the aspiration which generally accompanies /p,t,k/ in initial position is not present after /s/ (although vowels following /p,t,k/ generally start from a higher pitch and vowels following /sp,st,sk/ have this higher pitch, which argues for /p,t,k/).[3]

Another case of neutralization concerns the allophones of /m/ and /n/ before /f/ or /v/ in words like *symphony* and *infant*. The nasal consonant in each case is likely to be [ɱ] in rapid speech, i.e. a labiodental sound anticipating the labiodental [f]. Here again, /m/ and /n/ are not opposed, so that the sound could be allocated to either the /m/ or the /n/ phoneme. In practice, since in a slow pronunciation an [ɱ] would tend to be used in *symphony* and an [n] in *infant*, the [ɱ] is usually regarded as an allophone of /m/ in the one case and of /n/ in the other.

5.3.5 Phonemic Systems

Statements concerning phonemic categories and allophonic variants can be made in respect of only one variety of one language. It does not follow that, because [l] and [ɬ] are not contrastive in English and belong to the same phoneme, that this is so in other languages—in some kinds of Polish [l] and [ɬ] constitute separate phonemes. Or again, although /ŋ/ is a phoneme in English, in Italian the

---

[3] Wingate (1982)

velar nasal [ŋ] is an allophone of /n/ which occurs before /k/ and /g/. Indeed, in English, too, /ŋ/ has not always had phonemic status. Nowadays, [ŋ] might be considered an allophone of /n/ before /k/ and /g/, as in *sink* and *finger*, were it not for the fact that the /g/ in words such as *sing* was lost about 400 years ago; once this situation had arisen, a phonemic opposition existed between *sin* and *sing*. In some parts of north-west England, the situation is still the same as it was 400 years ago, e.g. not only is *sink* pronounced [sɪŋk] but *sing* is pronounced [sɪŋg], and in such dialects [ŋ] can be considered an allophone of /n/.

Thus the number of phonemes may differ as between various types of the same language. In present-day southern British English, the words *cat, half, cart* contain the phonemes /æ/, /ɑː/, and /ɑː/ respectively. But one type of Scottish English has only one vowel phoneme for all three words, the words being phonemically /kat, haf, kart/ (the pre-consonantal /r/ being pronounced). Such a dialect of English has one phoneme less than southern British English, since the opposition *Sam/psalm* is lost. On the other hand, this smaller number of phonemes is sometimes counterbalanced by the regular opposition of the first elements of a pair such as *witch/which*, which establishes a phonemic contrast between /w/ and /ʍ/.

It should not, however, be assumed that the phonemic systems of two dialects are different only because they have a lesser or greater number of phonemes in certain areas. The sound sequence [sɛt], i.e. with a vowel in the region of Cardinal 3, may be a realization of *sat* in one dialect and of *set* in another; the phonemic categories commonly represented as /ɪ,e,æ/ etc, may nevertheless be present in both dialects, the system of short front vowels in the first dialect being somewhat more 'closed' than that of the second. Or again, the diphthong [əʊ] is a realization of the phoneme of *boat* in educated southern British, but is frequently a realization of the vowel in *boot* in one type of Cockney; however, the same number of vowel phonemes occurs in both kinds of English.

Moreover, speakers of different dialects may distribute their phonemes differently in words, as when a speaker from the north of England pronounces *after, bath* and *pass* with /æ/ where a speaker from the south of England pronounces them with /ɑː/. Even speakers of the same dialect (as well as those of different dialects) may distribute the same number of phonemes differently among the words they use. In southern British English, some will say *elastic* with /æ/ in the second syllable, others /ɑː/ and some will say /ˈjuːnɪzn/ for *unison*, others /ˈjuːnɪsn/.

Lastly, even individuals are inconsistent; in certain situations, they may change the number of their phonemes, e.g. the occasional use of /ʍ/ in southern British in words like *which*, and they may not always use the same phoneme in a particular word or group of words, e.g. the erratic use, in the same person's speech, of /ɒ/ or /ɔː/ in words like *off*.

To sum up, we may conclude that a phonemic analysis of a number of varieties of one language is likely to reveal: different coexistent phonemic systems; considerable phonetic discrepancies in the realizations of comparable phonemes in different systems; variation in the distribution of phonemes in words and even within the speech of one individual according to the situation. It is important to remember this likelihood of complication in both the system and its realization, not only in the present situation but also when it is a question of investigating past states of the language. (For a more detailed analysis of variation between dialects, see §7.4.)

5.4   Transcription

The transcription of an utterance (analysed in terms of a linear sequence of sounds) will naturally differ according to whether the aim is to indicate detailed sound values—an ALLOPHONIC (or NARROW) transcription—or the sequence of significant functional elements—a PHONEMIC (or BROAD) transcription.

In the former, allophonic type of transcription, an attempt is made to include a considerable amount of information concerning our knowledge of articulatory activity or our auditory perception of allophonic features. The International Phonetic Alphabet (IPA) provides numerous diacritics for a purpose such as this; e.g. the word *titles* might be transcribed as [ˈtˢʰä·ët̸ɫz]. Such a notation would show the affrication and aspiration of the initial [t], the fact that the first element of the diphthong is centralized from Cardinal 4 and is long compared with the second element, which is a centralized Cardinal 2, that the [ɫ] has a back vowel resonance and is partly devoiced in its first stage, and that the final [z] is completely devoiced. Such a notation is relatively explicit and detailed, but gives no more than an impression of the complexity of the utterance as revealed by the various methods of physiological and acoustic investigation. This type of transcription is useful when the focus is on particular details of pronunciation.

In phonemic transcription a different principle operates—namely, that of one symbol per phoneme. Thus a phonemic transcription of the type of English described in this book uses 44 different symbols (24 consonants and 20 vowels). The basis on which an actual symbol is chosen depends on two further principles: (a) using the phonetic symbols of the most frequent allophones, and (b) replacing non-Roman symbols arising from (a) by Roman symbols where these are not already in use. Thus the phonetic symbol for the most common allophone of the phoneme at the beginning of *red* is /ɹ/ but the phonemic transcription replaces /ɹ/ by /r/ on the basis of (b). But in the transcription of vowels Romanization (i.e. the principle under (b)) is not completely carried through in this book, e.g. the transcription uses /ɒ/ and /ɔː/ for the vowels in *cot* and *caught* where it would be possible to use /o/ and /oː/. Transcription of these vowels as used here is called COMPARATIVE PHONE-MIC because it allows comparison with vowels in other languages to be made, even though a phonemic transcription is being used. It follows from the principles mentioned above that, even using the IPA, it is possible to construct different sets of symbols for the 44 symbols of English, although the one used in this book is the most common one in use for the type of English described.

It must be remembered that a phonemic transcription does not by itself indicate how a sequence is to be pronounced. Only if we know the conventions which tell us how a phoneme is to be realized in different positions do we know its correct pronunciation. Nevertheless a phonemic transcription is particularly useful as a corrective instrument in a language like English where the orthography does not consistently mirror present-day pronunciation.

By now it will have become clear that slant brackets are used for a phonemic transcription, e.g. /taɪtlz/ while square brackets indicate an allophonic transcription, e.g. [ˈtʰä·ëtɬz]. Sometimes we may wish to show just the phonetic detail of one segment in an otherwise phonemic transcription. In such cases square brackets must still be used, e.g. [taɪtɬz]. Slant brackets may only be used if the whole sequence is represented phonemically.

5.5   Syllables

The concept of a unit at a higher level than that of the phoneme or sound segment, yet distinct from that of the word or morpheme, has existed since ancient times. It is significant that most alphabets, such as our own, which have as their basis the representation of phonemes by letters (however approximately), have reached this state by way of a form of writing which symbolized a group of sounds—a SYLLABARY. Indeed, the basis of the writing of many languages, e.g. that of the Semitic group, remains syllabic in this sense. The notion that there exists at this higher level a unit known as the syllable has led to many attempts in recent times to define the term. The best-known approach is that which used to be called a theory of prominence[4] but is nowadays better known as the SONORITY HIERARCHY.

5.5.1   The Sonority Hierarchy

In any utterance some sounds stand as more prominent or sonorous than others, i.e. they are felt by listeners to stand out from their neighbours. Another way of judging the sonority of a sound is to imagine its 'carrying power'. A vowel like [a] clearly has more carrying power than a consonant like [z] which in turn has more carrying power than a [b]. Indeed the last sound, a plosive, has virtually no sonority at all unless followed by a vowel. A sonority scale or hierarchy can be set up which represents the relative sonority of various classes of sound; although there is some argument over some of the details of such a hierarchy, the main elements are not disputed. One version of the hierarchy is as follows (the most sonorous classes are at the top of the scale):

> open vowels
> close vowels
> laterals
> nasals
> approximants
> trills
> fricatives
> affricates
> plosives and flaps

Intermediate vowels are appropriately placed between open and close. Within the last three categories voiced sounds are more sonorous than voiceless sounds.

---

[4] Jones (1918 [1960: 55])

The class 'approximants' sits somewhat awkwardly in this hierarchy, since the approximants [j,w] are, as already remarked in §4.3.4(5), are merely short versions of close vowels in the [i,u] regions. However, the short gliding nature of [j,w] means that they are much less prominent than [i,u] and other approximants like [ɹ,ʋ] have a sonority somewhat less than of laterals and nasals.[5]

Using the sonority hierarchy we can then draw a contour representing the varying prominences of an utterance, e.g.

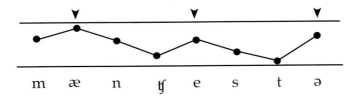

m   æ   n   ʧ   e   s   t   ə

The number of syllables in an utterance equates with the number of peaks of sonority, in this case three (marked with arrows). This accords with native speakers' intuition. However, there are some cases where contours plotted with the sonority hierarchy do not produce results which accord with our intuition. Many such cases in English involve /s/ in clusters, as, for example, in *stop*:

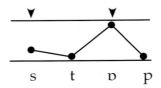

s   t   ɒ   p

The contour of *stop* implies two syllables while native speaker intuition is certain that there is only one syllable. This suggests that sounds below a certain level on the hierarchy cannot constitute peaks, i.e. that classes from fricatives downwards cannot constitute peaks in English (though the cut-off point may be drawn at different levels in different languages). Formal statements about the clustering possibilities of English consonants sometimes treat /s/ as an appendix to syllables which may consequently violate restrictions on their sonority (see §10.10.1(11)).[6]

5.5.2   Syllable Constituency

In the previous section reference was made to syllable peaks. In a word like *print* /prɪnt/ the vowel /ɪ/ constitutes the peak and the consonants around it are

---

[5] For a variation on the sonority scale, see Giegerich (1992: 133)
[6] Giegerich (1992: 147–50)

sometimes said to constitute the syllable margins, with those before the peak being called the onset and those after the peak being called the coda. The onset, peak and coda of a syllable form a hierarchy of constituents, in which the coda is more closely associated with the peak than with the onset. This can be represented diagrammatically as

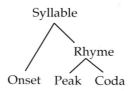

Evidence for the greater coherence of the peak and the coda compared with that between the onset and the peak comes from the use of rhyming in verse in which *pat, cat, sat* rhyme but *pat, pad, pack* do not rhyme (and hence the use of the term 'rhyme' itself), added to which there are very often restrictions between the peak and the coda in ways in which there are not between the onset and the peak, e.g. the consonant /ŋ/ as in *sing* can only follow short vowels. Moreover, onset consonants are involved in slips of the tongue but coda consonants are not, e.g. *pat the cake* may be produced with a slip to *cat the cake* or even *cat the pake* but slips do not produce *pak the cake* or *pak the cate*.

As implied by the sonority scale discussed above, and illustrated in a word like *prints*, onsets generally involve increasing sonority up to the peak (e.g. /r/ is more sonorous than /p/ while the peak /ɪ/ is more sonorous than /r/), whereas codas generally involve decreasing sonority (e.g. /t/ is less sonorous than /n/ which is less sonorous than the peak /ɪ/). In English the exceptions are constituted mainly by the occurrence of /s/ which does not constitute a syllable despite being of higher sonority than a sound which precedes or follows.

5.5.3 Syllable Boundaries

Although the onsets and codas of syllables are obviously clearly identifiable at the beginnings and ends of words, dividing word-medial sequences of consonants between coda and onset can be problematical. In many languages such dividing of words into syllables is a relatively straightforward process (e.g. in Bantu languages, in Japanese, and in French). In other languages, like English, it is not. The sonority hierarchy tells us how many syllables there are in an utterance by showing us a number of peaks of sonority. Such peaks represent the centres of syllables (usually vowels). Conversely it would seem reasonable for the troughs of sonority to represent the boundaries between syllables. Sounds following the trough would then be in ascending sonority up to the peak and sounds following the peak would be in descending sonority up to the trough. But problems arise because the hierarchy does not tell us whether to place the trough consonant itself with the preceding or the following syllable; an additional problem is caused by the downgraded /s/ mentioned in the previous sections. So, for example, syllable division is problematical in words like *funny, bitter, mattress, extra* /ˈekstrə/. Various principles can be applied to decide between alternatives: align syllable boundaries with morpheme boundaries where present (the morphemic principle); align syllable boundaries to parallel syllable codas and onsets at the ends and beginnings of words (the phonotactic principle); align syllable boundaries to best predict allophonic variation, e.g. the devoicing of /r/ following /t/. Unfortunately, such principles often conflict with one another. A further principle is often invoked in such cases, the maximal onset principle, which assigns consonants to onsets wherever possible and is said to be a universal in languages; but this itself often conflicts with one or more of the principles above. The syllabification of word-medial sequences in English is dealt with in detail in §10.10.2.

5.6 *Vowel and Consonant*

It was seen in the previous chapter that attempts to arrive at a universal phonetic definition of the two terms, from an articulatory or an auditory standpoint, encounter difficulties as regards certain borderline sounds such as [j,w,r] in English. If, however, the syllable is defined phonologically, i.e. from the point of view of distribution of phonemes, a solution can be given to most of these problems. It will be found that the phonemes of a language usually fall into two classes, those which are typically central in the syllable (occurring at the peak) and those which typically occur at the margins (or onsets and codas) of syllables. The term 'vowel' can then be applied to those phonemes having the former function and 'consonant' to those having the latter. The frictionless English sounds /j,w,r/, which, according to most phonetic descriptions are vowel-like, nevertheless function in the language as consonants, i.e. are marginal in the syllable. The English lateral and nasal sounds are commonly classed phonetically as of the consonantal type because of the complete or partial mouth closure with which they are articulated. From a functional viewpoint, too, they generally behave as consonants, since they are usually marginal in the syllable. Sometimes, however, they operate as a separate peak of sonority, e.g. in *middle* /mɪdl̩/ and *button* /bʌtn̩/, and thus function in the peaks of syllables. In such occurrences they are referred to as syllabic laterals and nasals.

A further illustration of the consonantal function of /j,w,r/ is provided by the behaviour of the English articles when they combine with words beginning with these phonemes. *The* is pronounced /ðiː/ or /ðɪ/ before a vowel and /ðə/ before a consonant; we also have the forms *a* or *an an* according to whether a consonant or vowel follows. Since it is normal to pronounce *the yacht, the watch, the rabbit* with /ðə/ and to prefix *a* to *yacht* and *watch* and *rabbit* rather than *an*, /j/ and /w/ may be said to behave as if they belong to the consonant class of phonemes, despite their vocalic quality.

It is clear that if the elements of the utterance are divided into two categories, some units which are assigned to one class according to phonetic criteria may fall into the other class when it is a question of phonological (functional) analysis.

5.7   *Prosodic Features*[7]

We have so far dealt with the description and organization of the qualitative features of utterances. As we have seen in Chapter 3, a sound not only has a quality, whose phonetic nature can be described and whose function in the language can be determined, but also features of length, pitch, and loudness. There may be phonemic oppositions in a language based solely or in part on length differences; alternatively, differences in the length of a phoneme may relate to different contexts, as when English vowels are generally shorter before voiceless consonants than before voiced consonants.

The features of pitch, length, and loudness may contribute to patterns which extend over larger chunks of utterance than the single segment and when used thus are called suprasegmental or PROSODIC. Pitch is used to make differences of TONE in tone languages, where a syllable or word consisting of the same segmental sequence has different lexical meanings according to the pitch used with it (e.g. in Chinese). Outside tone languages (and even within tone languages, although to a lesser extent) pitch also makes differences of INTONATION whereby different pitch contours produce differences of attitudinal or discoursal meaning (discoursal here refers to the way successive chunks of utterances are linked together). While tone is a feature of syllables or words, intonation is a feature of phrases or clauses. Some combination of the features of pitch, length, and loudness will also produce ACCENT, whereby particular syllables are made to stand out from those around them. There are a number of other prosodic features whose linguistic use is far less understood. These include RHYTHM, the extent to which there is a regular 'beat' in speech; TEMPO (the average conversational tempo of speakers of British English is around four syllables per second),[8] and VOICE QUALITY, which includes both supralaryngeal settings of the mouth and tongue, and laryngeal settings (or phonation types) involving either the vocal folds or the larynx as a whole. Sometimes a voice quality conveys meaning, as when a creaky voice indicates boredom; sometimes a quality is appropriate to a situation, e.g. breathy voice is known as 'bedroom voice' and whispery voice as 'library voice'.

5.8   *Paralinguistic and Extralinguistic Features*

In addition to prosodic features which spread over more than one segment, there are also PARALINGUISTIC features, which are essentially interruptive rather than co-occurrent. The most common interruptive effect is pause, which functions sometimes as part of the intonation system where it is one of the indicators of an intonational phrase boundary, but at other times functions as a hesitation marker. In the latter case a filled pause is often involved, by some combination of [ʔ] [m] and [ə] in southern British, but by other sounds in other dialects and

---

[7] For a detailed classification of prosodic and paralinguistic features, see Crystal and Quirk (1964)

[8] Byrd (1992a) finds men speaking 6.2% faster than women

languages (e.g. by an [n] in Russian). Many other paralinguistic effects are more commonly called VOCALIZATIONS: these include single phonemes or sequences of phonemes like [ʃː] for 'be quiet', [pst] as an attention-getter, and [ǁ] (a reduplicated dental click) for 'irritation' or 'naughty' (often written *tut-tut*), and various conventionalized types of cough and whistle. Since the foreign learner is likely to pause to think of the right word or grammar far more often than the native speaker, it is undoubtedly the hesitation markers which are the most important feature for him to master. With the acquisition of correct hesitations a foreign learner can dramatically increase his ability to sound like an Englishman.

While prosodic and paralinguistic features are used to convey meaning, (although this meaning is in various ways outside the central phonemic system) the term EXTRALINGUISTIC is used for those features over which the speaker has no immediate control. Some of these features may be physical, e.g. sex, age, and larynx size; others may simply be speaker habits, e.g. a particular speaker may always speak with a creaky voice; others may be specific to languages, e.g. speakers of one language may make much more use of an ingressive pulmonic airstream than other languages—this is reported to be so in Finnish—or to particular accents, e.g. Scouse, the dialect of Liverpool, is said to have an adenoidal quality, produced by retracting and raising the tongue, tightening the pharynx, raising the larynx and keeping the jaws close together, even for open vowels.[9] Many extralinguistic features are, of course, ones which may also function prosodically or paralinguistically, e.g. breathy voice may be understood prosodically as 'bedroom voice', yet a particular speaker may have this as a constant characteristic of his speech, and voice qualities involving a raised or lowered larynx, while being habitual, may also be interpreted as 'strained' or 'gloomy' respectively.[10] For further description of voice quality see under §11.8 below.

---

[9] Knowles (1978)
[10] Laver (1974, 1980)

PART II

The Sounds of English

6

The Historical Background

6.1 *Phonetic Studies in Britain*

Although linguistic science has made rapid and spectacular progress in the present century, it is not merely in modern times that speech and language have been the object of serious study. Extensive accounts of the pronunciation of Greek and Latin were written 2,000 years ago and, in India, at about the same time, there appeared detailed phonological analyses of Sanskrit, which reveal remarkable affinities with modern ways of thought—'These early phoneticians speak in fact to the twentieth century rather than to the Middle Ages or even to the mid-nineteenth century. . .'.[1] In this country, too, printed works containing information of a phonetic kind extend back for at least 400 years. It is true that the very earliest writers in England rarely had as their main interest a purely phonetic investigation; and the descriptive accounts which they provided are less rigorous and satisfactory, by modern standards, than those of the Indian grammarians. But, by the seventeenth century, we find a considerable body of published work, which is already entirely phonetic in character and which contains observations and theories still adhered to today.

6.1.1 Palsgrave and Salesbury

Some of the first writers whose work we possess were concerned with the relation between the sounds of English and those of another language. Thus, John Palsgrave's French grammar *Lesclarcissement de la Langue Francoyse* (1530) includes a section which deals with the pronunciation of French, much as any modern grammar would. In order to explain the values of the French sounds, Palsgrave compares them with the English. This is done in no objective fashion, and it is not easy for us now to know what precise sound is indicated in either language. But this difficulty of communicating sound values in print—especially those of vowels—was one which was shared by all writers until some system of objective evaluation, such as that of the Cardinal Vowels, was devised and this

---

[1] Allen (1953: 7)

of course depended on the development of recording techniques. At least John Palsgrave was sufficiently aware of divergent associations of letters and sound to provide some passages of French in a kind of phonetic transcription. Another early writer concerned with pronunciation is William Salesbury, a Welshman, whose *Dictionary in Englyshe and Welshe* (1547) contained comments on the sounds of English. Sound values are indicated by means of a method of transliteration in Welsh or English. Indeed, though grammars of foreign languages published during the next three centuries increasingly attempted more exact description and comparison of sounds, for the great majority of them the section devoted to pronunciation continued to rely mainly on transliteration for indicating approximate values. Even today, grammars of foreign languages frequently make use of this approximate method of 'simulated' pronunciation.

6.1.2   Spelling Reformers: Smith, Hart, Gil

A more important type of phonetic inquiry stemmed from the activities of those who, particularly in the sixteenth and seventeenth centuries, were concerned at the increasing inconsistency of the relationship of Latin letters and the sounds which they represented, especially in English. There had been during the previous five or six centuries great changes of pronunciation, particularly as far as the vowel sounds were concerned, so that letters no longer had their original Latin values. The same sound could be written in a number of ways, or the same spelling do service for several sounds; moreover, the same word might be spelt in different ways by different writers. Thus, 400 years before the activities of Bernard Shaw and the Simplified Spelling Society, men were aware of the need to bring some order into English spelling. During the four centuries that have elapsed since these early efforts, our pronunciation has continued to evolve without any radical changes of spelling having been made, with the result that today discrepancies between sound and spelling are greater than they have ever been. It can, however, be said that for more than 200 years our spelling forms, inconsistent though they may be as far as sound symbolization is concerned, have been standardized.

The early spelling reformers were obliged, if they were to propose a more logical relationship of sound and spelling, to investigate the sounds of English. A writer such as Thomas Smith, *De Recta et Emendata Linguae Anglicae Scriptione* (1568), makes many pertinent phonetic comments on matters such as the aspiration of English plosives and the syllabic nature of /n/ and /l/, as well as providing correct descriptions of the articulation of consonants. Yet, he, as a phonetician, is overshadowed in the sixteenth century by John Hart, whose most important work, the *Orthographie*, was published in 1569. Besides making out his case for spelling reform and proposing a revised system, Hart describes the organs of speech, defines vowels and consonants (distinguishing between front and back vowels and between voiced and voiceless consonants), and notes the aspiration of voiceless plosives. Of the numerous seventeenth-century orthoepists, only Alexander Gil, *Logonomia Anglica* (1619, 1621), can be compared with Hart on the phonetic level, though even his observations lack the objectivity of Hart's.

6.1.3 Phoneticians: Wallis, Wilkins, Cooper

If the writers mentioned above used phonetic methods of analysis and transcription as a means to their end of devising an improved spelling, there emerged in the seventeenth century a group of writers who were interested in speech and language for their own sake. Because of their preoccupation with detailed analysis of speech activity, the comparative study of the sounds of various languages, the classification of sound types, and the establishment of systematic relationships between the English sounds, they can be said to be the true precursors of modern scientific phoneticians. Two of the most celebrated, John Wallis and Bishop Wilkins, were among the founders of the Royal Society; and, indeed, Isaac Newton, the greatest of the early members of the Society, was interested in phonetic analysis and has left notes of his own linguistic observations. Language was considered a proper object of the attention of the writers of this new scientific age, their view of speech and pronunciation being set against a framework of the universal nature and characteristics of language.

The linguistic fame of John Wallis, primarily a mathematician, spread throughout Europe and lasted into the eighteenth century, his work being copied long after his death. His principal linguistic work, *Grammatica Linguae Anglicanae*, was first published in 1653 and the last authoritative edition appeared in 1699; but other, unauthorized, editions continued to appear in the eighteenth century, the last being dated 1765. Wallis intended his *Grammar* to help foreigners to learn English more easily and also to enable Englishmen to understand more thoroughly the true nature of their language. He admits in his preface that he is not the first to undertake such a task, but claims that he does not seek to fit English into a Latin mould, as most of his predecessors had done, but rather to examine the sounds of English as constituting a system in their own right. By his methods, he says, he has succeeded in teaching not only foreigners to pronounce English correctly but also the deaf and dumb to speak. The introductory part of the work (*Tractatus de Loquela*), besides giving a short history of English, describes in detail the organs of speech and attempts to establish a general system of sound classification which will do service for all languages (illustrations of qualities are taken from French, Welsh, German, Greek and Hebrew as well as English). Vowels are classified in *Guttural, Palatal*, and *Labial* categories, subdivided into *Wide, Medium*, and *Narrow* classes. The degrees of aperture are similar to those which are used even today, but the divisions Guttural, Palatal, and Labial, which take into account both the area of raising of the tongue and also lip action, show a confusion of dimensions not to be found in more modern analyses.

Consonants, like vowels, are divided into three classes: *Labial, Palatal*, and *Guttural*, being different from vowels in that the airstream from the lungs is obstructed or constricted at some point. Wallis remarks that the airstream may pass entirely through the mouth, almost completely through the nose, or almost equally divided between the mouth and the nose, the position of the uvula determining the difference of direction. Thus, nine basic consonantal articulations are postulated. In addition, the airstream may be completely shut off (*Closed* or *Primitive*) or merely constricted (*Open, Derivative*, or *Aspirate*), the latter being articulated with a narrow aperture or with a wider, rounder, opening. The 'closed' consonants (stops) consist of the *mutes* [p,t,k] the *semi-mutes* [b,d,g], and the *semi-vowels* [m,n,ŋ]. The corresponding 'open' or 'aspirated' consonants are: mute [f,s,x], semi-mutes [v,z,x] or [ɣ];[2] and those with a wider opening: mute [f] (again), [θ,h], semi-mutes [w,ð,j]; [l,r] are related to the [d] or [n] articulations; [ʃ,ʒ] are regarded as compound sounds. Wallis's detailed remarks on the pronunciation of English are made in terms of this general system stated in the *Loquela*. It will be seen that such a classification, despite errors and inadequacies which are apparent today, represents a serious attempt at the establishment of universal sound categories. Although the elements of Wallis's system have been quoted briefly here, it should be pointed out that his is merely the most celebrated of a number of similar analyses made at about the same time.

His fellow member of the Royal Society, Bishop John Wilkins, published in 1668 an *Essay towards a Real Character and a Philosophical Language*. Written in English, this work of 454 pages, with a dictionary appended, is of much wider scope than that of Wallis, since it aims at no less than the creation of a universal language, expressed by means of 'marks, which should signifie things, and not words'. Wilkins acknowledges his debt to his contemporary linguists, especially in respect of the account of pronunciation which forms a comparatively small part of the *Essay*. Wallis, he says, 'seems to me, with greatest accurateness and subtlety to have considered the philosophy of articulate sounds.' Wilkins, too, describes the functions of the speech organs and gives a general classification of the sounds articulated by them; his treatment of consonants is in fact more satisfactory than that of Wallis. He claims that the 34 letters which he proposes for his alphabet are sufficient 'to express all those articulate sounds which are commonly known and used in these parts of the world'. In his account of the values of the letters, reference is made not only to European sound systems but also to such little known languages as Armenian, Arabic, Chinese and Japanese.

Any account of seventeenth-century phoneticians should include the name of Christopher Cooper. Though he did not achieve the great European reputation of Wallis, he is considered by many to be the greatest English phonetician of the century. His work on English pronunciation was first published in 1685 (*Grammatica Linguae Anglicanae*), with an English edition appearing in 1687 (*The English Teacher*, or *The Discovery of the Art of Teaching* and *Learning the English Tongue*). A schoolmaster rather than a member of the Royal Society, Cooper was less concerned than many of his contemporaries with the establishment of universal systems. His aim was to describe and give rules for the pronunciation of English for 'Gentlemen, Ladies, Merchants, Tradesmen, Schools and Strangers', rather than to devise a logical system into which the sounds of English and other languages might be fitted. Moreover, he deals with the spelling of English as it exists and does not seek to reform it. The first section of his book is concerned with the description of speech sounds ('The Principles of Speech') and the second part gives rules for the relation of spelling and pronunciation in different contexts. Cooper describes the organs of speech and names those

---

[2] Wallis's own symbols are here replaced by IPA equivalents, but it is not always clear from Wallis's description which sounds are intended: thus, his description of *ch* and *gh* would seem to indicate [x] for both, though in the system one would expect *gh* to mean [ɣ]

sections of the upper speech tract which are mainly responsible for the articulation of the 'breath': 'guttural, lingual, palatine, dental, labial, lingua-palatine, lingua-dental.' Those sounds in the production of which the airstream is 'straitned or intercepted' are consonants (classified as semi-vowels, aspirated, semimutes, and mutes), while those in which the airstream is 'freely emitted through the nostrils or the lips' are vowels. He notes that voice, 'made by a tremulous concussion of the larynx,' is a characteristic of vowels, semi-vowels, and semi-mutes. His classification of vowels is in terms of *lingual, labial,* and *guttural* categories, a somewhat confusing distinction being made between the English long and short vowels. Diphthongs are defined properly as 'a joyning of two vowels in the same syllable, wherein the power of both is kept'. His consonantal classification, with IPA equivalents here, shows: labial sounds, subdivided into semi-vowels [w,v,m], aspirated [ʍ,f,m̥], semi-mute [b], mute [p]; *lingual* sounds, subdivided into semi-vowels [z,ʒ,ð,n,l,r,j], aspirated [ʃ,θ,n̥,l̥,r̥,ç], semi-mute [d], mute [t]; *guttural* sounds, subdivided into semi-vowels [ɣ,ŋ,h], aspirated [x,ŋ̊,h], semi-mute [g], mute [k]. The second part of the work, dealing with the pronunciation of various English spelling forms, provides more specific information about the pronunciation of English than is to be found in the work of any other writer in this period. Numerous examples are given, e.g. more than 300 cases of the *-tion* suffix pronounced with [ʃ]; words are listed which have either the same pronunciation with different spellings or the same spellings with different pronunciation; and rules are given for the accentuation of words.

It will be seen from the mention of these few names, chosen from the many who were writing on matters of pronunciation in the seventeenth century and omitting those who were composing spelling books and grammars for foreigners, compiling lists of homophones, and devising systems of shorthand, that there was at this time a surge of scientific and analytical interest in speech and pronunciation such as was not to be repeated until the nineteenth century. It is true that the judgements made were largely intuitive, but this was to remain the case in phonetic research until the second half of the nineteenth century. In their theoretical approach, however, many of these early writers show a preoccupation with classification, systematization, and problems of distribution which is paralleled in the activities of modern linguists.

6.1.4   Eighteenth Century: Johnson, Sheridan, Walker, Steele

The spirit of general scientific inquiry into speech which characterized a large proportion of the phonetic work of the seventeenth century had, by the eighteenth century, lost much of its original enthusiasm. Prescriptive grammars containing rules for pronunciation continued to be produced in large numbers and provide us with information concerning the contemporary forms of pronunciation; shorthand systems, too, which show an undiminished popularity, necessitated the analysis of English into its constituent sounds. Yet the main achievement of the century lies in its successful attempt to fix the spelling and pronunciation of the language. Dictionaries had been published in the seventeenth century, but the works having the main stabilizing and standardizing influence on the language were to be the dictionaries of Samuel Johnson (1755),

Thomas Sheridan (1780), and John Walker (1791), the last two writers being particularly concerned with the standardization of pronunciation. John Walker, whose dictionary is called by the *Dictionary of National Biography* 'the statute book of English orthoepy', exerted a great influence on the teaching of English not only in this country but also in America. Moreover, he pays considerable attention in his work to the analysis of intonation, treated but perfunctorily by most earlier writers. About the same time Joshua Steele published his *Prosodia Rationalis* (1775–9), in which is presented a system of notation capable of expressing pitch changes, stress, and rate of delivery. (Steele is celebrated for his detailed analysis of a soliloquy delivered by David Garrick.)

We have, in fact, been dealing up to now with two types of work on pronunciation, which, especially in the eighteenth century, came to be confused: on the one hand, and in the minority, the books which laid emphasis on description, analysis, and classification; on the other, the books which were mainly normative and continue the tradition of 'rhetoric'. That part of rhetoric known as 'elocution' originally referred to the style and form of speech, 'the garnishing of speech', but in the eighteenth century the term was increasingly applied to the method of delivery. It was not until the nineteenth century that a clear distinction was made between the aesthetic judgments upon which elocution largely relies and the objective descriptive statements which form the basis of phonetic analysis. Until such a distinction was explicitly made, advances in phonetic techniques have to be disentangled from a mass of irrelevant opinion.

6.1.5   Nineteenth Century[3]: Pitman, Ellis, Bell, Sweet

In the nineteenth century the English traditional preoccupation with phonetic notation and the simplification of English spelling continued. Isaac Pitman (1813–97), whose system of shorthand is so widely used today, and Alexander J. Ellis (1814–90), concerned at the difficulties which our spelling presented to English children as well as to foreigners, devised an alphabet *Phonotype*, which conformed to a phonetic analysis of English and yet remained based upon the Latin characters. They were supported by the Phonographic Society and published a journal which eventually (1848) was named the *Fonetic Jurnal*. Ellis, however, developed other types of alphabet, notably *Glossic*, which is essentially an adaptation of traditional spelling, and *Palaeotype*, which used conventional letter shapes but in a great variety of type, so that fine shades of sound could be symbolized. This latter alphabet was put to good use by Ellis in his historical and dialectal studies; but not only is the precise value to be attached to a letter not always easily determined—because of the method of reference to sounds in languages—but also the complexity of the system renders it difficult for the reader to assimilate. Ellis's work on notation, however, largely inspired the 'Broad' and 'Narrow' Romic transcriptions of the great Henry Sweet (1845–1912). In 1867 Alexander Melville Bell, father of Alexander Graham Bell (the inventor of the telephone), published his book *Visible Speech*, whilst a lecturer on speech in the University of London. This remarkable work set out to classify all the sounds capable of

---

[3] See MacMahon (1998), and Collins and Mees (1999)

being articulated by the human speech organs and to allot a systematic and related series of symbols to the sounds. The unfamiliarity of the invented symbol shapes was no doubt responsible for the fact that this means of notation has never been widely used in purely phonetic work, but its value was for many years demonstrated, especially in America, as a system applied to the teaching of the deaf.

Although, in referring to these writers, emphasis has been laid on their contribution to the development of phonetic transcription, their published work covers every aspect of speech activity. Bell's interests, in his 49 publications, lay mainly in the field of elocution and the description of articulatory processes. But Ellis and Sweet applied the techniques of phonetic analysis both to the description of contemporary pronunciation and also to the whole field of historical phonological investigation. Ellis, in fact, will be chiefly remembered for his massive work, *On Early English Pronunciation*, published in five volumes between 1869 and 1889. In these volumes Ellis traces the history of English pronunciation and, at the same time, contributes descriptive phonetic studies of contemporary dialects. It is not surprising that a work of such enormous scope should since have been found to be inadequate in many respects, but it cannot be denied that Ellis was a great pioneer in the application of objective techniques to the description of past and present states of the language. Although his assessment of the value of many grammarians from the sixteenth century onwards was often faulty, he initiated a study of their work which has continued unabated to this day. Henry Sweet, a greater phonologist and scholar, applied stringent phonetic techniques to all his work, so that, whether it be a question of phonetic theory or the history of English or the description of a language such as Welsh or Danish, his basic approach and the majority of his conclusions remain valid today. He belongs as much to the twentieth century as to the nineteenth and his influence is clearly to be seen in the work of Daniel Jones, who dominated British phonetics in the first half of the last century.

This brief and selective outline goes some way towards revealing a line of phonetic inquiry which has been continuous in England from the sixteenth century to the present day. The techniques for describing speech and language have become progressively more objective, modern instrumental methods for physiological and physical investigation (now supported by digital computers) providing the latest stage in the process. A problem confronting linguists today concerns the correlation of concrete data, which is being accumulated in great detail in computer databases, with abstract linguistic realities, many of which have for centuries been implicit in the work of writers on language.

6.2 *Sound Change*

The language spoken in England has undergone very striking changes during the last 1,000 years, which have affected every aspect of the language, its morphology, syntax, and vocabulary as well as its pronunciation. Old English[4] is so

---

[4] The following abbreviations will henceforward be used: OE—Old English (up to approximately AD 1100); ME—Middle English (approx. 1100–1450); eModE—early Modern English (approx. 1450–1600); PresE—Present-day English; AN—AngloNorman; OF—Old French

different from present-day English from every point of view that it is unintelligible to the modern Englishman either in its written form or in a reconstructed spoken form; Chaucer's poetry presents difficulties in print and, when read in what is presumed to be the pronunciation of the fourteenth century, offers a sound pattern which it is not easy for the modern listener to interpret; even Shakespeare, though phonetically not far removed from ourselves, raises problems of syntax and meaning.

The pronunciation of a language seems to be subject to a continuous and inevitable process of change. Indeed, it would be surprising if a means of communication, handed on orally from one generation to another, showed no variation over the centuries. It is not difficult to find examples of changes which are taking place in our own times, e.g. the final vowel in words like *city* has become closer and tenser, and the vowel in *sad* has become more open, amongst young people in the south of England today than they were in the pronunciation of older people. A change of a different kind—the use of another phoneme in a class of words—is illustrated by the case of words such as *poor* and *sure*; these tend to be said by the older generation with /ʊə/, whereas the younger generation much more commonly uses /ɔː/. At any given moment, therefore, we must expect several pronunciations to be current, representing at least the older, traditional, forms and the new tendencies.

Today there are a number of reasons why we might expect these processes of change to operate less rapidly. The fact that communication throughout the whole country is easy, the spread of universal education and the resultant consciousness of the printed word, the constant impact of broadcasting with its tacit imposition of a standard speech, these are all influences which are likely to apply a brake to change in pronunciation. They are, however, factors which have operated only in comparatively recent times. In former stages of the development of English, there was no nationwide mass influence likely to lead to stability and levelling. Printing, it is true, has been with us for 400 years, but the wide dissemination of books, as of education, is a modern development. Indeed, as we have seen, the spelling of English, even in printed books, was not finally standardized until the eighteenth century. With such freedom from restraint, especially before the eighteenth century, it was not unexpected that there were considerable changes of pronunciation.

6.2.1   Types of Change

(1) The most important kind of change tends to affect a phoneme in all its occurrences. Such changes, not usually being set in motion by any immediate, outside influence, are in this sense independent; they are called INTERNAL ISOLATIVE changes. Thus, the ME realization of the phoneme in a word such as *house* had the sound [uː], which has generally become [aʊ] in modern English; similarly, the ME vowel phoneme having a value of the [aː] type, as in a word such as *name*, is in most cases realized as a kind of [eɪ] in PresE. Changes of this type apply particularly to the English vowel system, which underwent a remarkable evolution of values, known as the GREAT VOWEL SHIFT, during the centuries preceding the modern period.

(2) Another kind of change is that which is brought about by the occurrence of phonemes in particular contexts—a dependent change, called INTERNAL COMBINATIVE. Thus, the phoneme in *mice*, having now the sound [aɪ], results from an earlier [iː] by means of an isolative change; but this [iː] sound in [miːs] arose as a result of a combinative process of VOWEL HARMONY, or i-mutation, through the stages [muːsi], [myːsi] > [miːs], where the change [uː] > [yː] can be explained by the fronting of [uː] under the influence of the [iː] of the following syllable. Such a combinative change belongs to OE, but a more recent change of this type is exemplified by words such as *swan*. This word was probably pronounced [swan] or [swæn] in about 1600, but the [w] sound has rounded and retracted the vowel to give the modern form [swɒn]. The large majority of earlier [w]+[a] sequences have now given [w]+[ɒ], or [ɔː], by reason of this combinative change affecting this particular sound sequence, e.g. *want, quality, war, water* etc.

(3) Some changes are neither independent nor dependent upon the phonetic context; they may be said to be EXTERNAL to the main line of evolution. Thus, it was fashionable in Elizabethan times to pronounce words such as *servant* and *heard* with [ær] or [ar], perhaps originally a dialect form, rather than with [ɛr], the regular form of development; these words, with some exceptions such as *clerk*, have reverted to the normal development of ME [ɛr] > [ɜː] rather than [ɑː]. It was also fashionable to pronounce the termination -*ing* as [ɪn], only now retained as a special form of affectation or in some dialects. Such changes, involving a change of distribution of phonemes among words and morphemes, do not affect the phonemic system of the language. The introduction of foreign words may, however, at least temporarily and in the speech of a restricted number of individuals, disturb the number of phonemes or their distribution as regards position in the word. Thus, if the French word *beige* is used in English with the pronunciation /beɪʒ/, we have a case of a final /ʒ/ previously unknown in English words; or again, if *restaurant* is pronounced with any kind of nasalized vowel in the last syllable, the possibility of a new kind of vocalic opposition is introduced into the language. However, such foreign borrowings generally tend to conform to the English system: words with a final French /ʒ/, such as *prestige, camouflage* etc., may be realized in the English form with /dʒ/ and a word with a nasalized vowel like *restaurant* will be normalized to /ˈrestərɒŋ/, /ˈrestərɒnt/ or /ˈrestrənt/ etc.

(4) In addition to changes of quality, there have also to be taken into account changes involving LENGTH and ACCENTUAL PATTERN. Thus, the vowel in words such as *path, half, pass*, still short 300 years ago, is now long in the south of England. Or again, the vowels in *good, book* and *breath, death*, once long, are now relatively short. Changes of accent are particularly striking in the case of words which have come into the language from French: in ME, words such as *village* or *necessary* retained their accent on the penultimate syllable—/vɪˈlaːdʒə/ and /nɛsɛˈsaːrɪə/. Now, the accent has shifted to an earlier syllable, together with associated changes of quality—/ˈvɪlɪdʒ/, /ˈnesəsrɪ/ (the latter may retain the ME pattern in American English). Later borrowings, or those in less common use, often retain the French accentual pattern—thus, *hotel* or *machine*, with accent on the final syllable, whereas, if they had conformed to the English system, we might have had such modern forms as /ˈhəʊtl/ and /ˈmætʃɪn/ or /ˈmeɪtʃɪn/, in the same way that the thoroughly anglicized form of *garage* gives /ˈgærɪdʒ/. (See §7.4 on current changes.)

6.2.2 Rate and Route of Vowel Change

The English vowels have been subject to more striking changes than have the consonants. This is not surprising, for a consonantal articulation usually involves an approximation of organs which can be felt; such an articulation tends to be more stable in that it is more easily identified and transmitted more exactly from one generation to another. Changes in the consonantal system comparatively rarely involve a modification of sound (an example of such a modification would be the affrication, for combinative reasons, of the OE palatal plosives [c,ɟ] to [tʃ,dʒ] as in *church* < OE *cirice* and *bridge* < OE *brycg*). Far more common is the type of distributional change involving the conferment of phonemic status on an existing sound (e.g. [v,ð,z], allophones of /f,θ,s/ in OE, later obtain contrastive, phonemic, significance), or the disappearance of an allophone (e.g. post-vocalic [x] and [ç] in words such as *brought* and *right* were largely lost in the south of England by the seventeenth century), or the insertion of an existing phoneme in a particular class of words (e.g. the initial /h/ in words of French origin such as *herb*, *homage*). Whether it is a question of consonantal change, loss, or addition, it is usually possible to explain the type of modification which has taken place and the approximate period during which it occurred.

A modification of vowel quality will, however, result from very slight changes of tongue or lip position and there may be a series of imperceptible gradations before an appreciable quality change is evident (or is capable of being expressed by means of the Latin vowel letters). It is particularly difficult to assess rate and phonetic route of change in the case of those internal independent vowel changes which affect a phoneme throughout the language. It is known, for instance, that the modern homophones *meet* and *meat* had in ME different vowel forms, approximately of the value [eː] and [ɛː]. The [eː] vowel of *meet* became [iː] by about 1500 and it might be postulated that by a process of gradual change the [ɛː] of *meat* first closed to [eː] and then, by the eighteenth century, coalesced with the [iː] in *meet*. The available evidence, however, suggests that the change [ɛː] > [iː] may not have been either simple or gradual, but that two pronunciations existed side by side for a long period (the conservative [ɛː] beside another form [iː] which had resulted from an early coalescence with the *meet* vowel). In other vowel changes, it may be agreed that the change was gradual, but it is difficult to date precisely the stages of development. Thus, the modern /aɪ/ of *time* results from a ME [iː] value; it is clear that the change has been one of progressive, widening, diphthongization, but there may have been a period of incipient diphthongization when there was hesitation between the pure vowel [iː] and some such diphthong as [ɪi] or [əi]. It is well to remember, therefore, that at any particular time in history there are likely to be a number of different, coexistent, realizations of vowel phonemes, not only as between regions but also between generations and social groups. An example of such variety in modern English is provided by the vowel at the end of *city*, which in the south of England may be rendered as [ɪ] by the older generation and something more like [i] by the younger people. The speech of any community may, therefore, be said to reflect the pronunciation of the previous century and to anticipate that of the next.

6.2.3 Sound Change and the Linguistic System

It is convenient to study sound change in terms of the development of particular phonemes or sounds, but it is misleading to ignore the relationship of the sound units to the system within which they function and which may, in fact, not be changing. In other words, although there may be considerable qualitative changes, the number and pattern of the terms within the system may show relative stability. The ME /iː/ phoneme, for instance, is now realized as [aɪ], but there is still a phonemic opposition which contrasts words such as *time, team, tame, term, tomb* etc., and, in any case, a new phoneme /iː/ has emerged in words of the *team* type. On the other hand, the system may change because a sound, without itself changing, may receive a new, phonemic, value, e.g. the sound [ŋ] has always existed in English as a realization of /n/ followed by the velars /k/ or /g/, but when the final /g/ in a word like *sing* was no longer pronounced, /ŋ/ contrasted significantly with /n/ and /m/, e.g. *ram, ran,* and *rang*.

Since the system of our language consists of a framework of significant oppositions by means of which we communicate, it may be assumed that there is a tendency for the system to remain stable, the loss of an opposition involving a possibility of confusion. In fact, of course, the redundancy of English is such that some degree of neutralization of phonemes is easily tolerated: thus, today, few speakers in the south of England distinguish *saw* and *sore* by means of an opposition /ɔː/–/ɔə/, yet the loss of the /ɔə/ diphthong is no impediment to communication. An example of an earlier coalescence of vowel phonemes is that illustrated by the homophony of *meet* and *meat*. On the other hand, new oppositions may emerge in the language, e.g. the phonemes /v,ð,z,ŋ/, as we have seen. Nevertheless, despite the adjustments in the number of phonemes which have taken place, the history of the English sound system displays, over the last 1,000 years, a considerable degree of stability.

Though the relationships within the system may tend to remain stable, a change of phonetic realization of any phoneme is likely to have qualitative repercussions throughout the system. Such a disturbance may be observed in modern English. The phonetic relationship of the vowel phonemes in *set* and *sat*, in one type of pronunciation, is of a front vowel between close-mid and open-mid to a front vowel between open-mid and open. If, however, the vowel of *sat* has a closer articulation than that described, that of *set* must be raised, too. A limit of raising is imposed by the presence of *sit* and *seat*, for it is not possible to raise the vowel of *sit* to any extent without danger of confusion with that of *seat*, unless the latter vowel becomes strongly diphthongal. (It may be objected that a quantitative as well as qualitative difference distinguishes /iː/ from /ɪ/; but, in the examples given—*seat* and *sit*—the phonetic context imposes a quantity on /iː/ which is practically the same as that of /ɪ/). If /ɪ/ were too close to the region of /iː/, the opposition would be maintained only by realizing /iː/ as fully long at the expense of the shortening influence of the final /t/ (or by a process such as diphthongization). Alternatively, if the vowel phoneme of *sat* is realized as a front open vowel, as in many English regional dialects, the vocalic area in which the phoneme of *set* can be realized becomes more extensive; in fact, in those kinds of English where this occurs, the vowel in *set* tends to be open-mid variety. Such considerations of the phonetic relationship of phonemes have a relevance in the historical, DIACHRONIC, study of English. In ME there were, for instance, four long vowels in the front region—/iː,eː,ɛː,aː/. By 1600 /iː/ had diphthongized and the remaining vowels closed up. Such a movement may have been caused by pressure upwards from /aː/ or by the creation of an empty space brought about by the diphthongization of the pure vowel /iː/.

Although, therefore, it is often convenient in diachronic studies to investigate the development of individual phonemes in terms of the quality of their realization, it is clear that many sound changes can be explained only by reference to a readjustment of the phonetic relationships of the phonemes of the system as a whole. Moreover, any particular point in the development of the sound system of a language is not simply to be considered as a stage in the process of change of a number of sound units but rather as the presentation of the functioning of a system at a certain historical moment. The primary significance of the sounds of modern English is their function in the system of today; in the same way, the English sounds of 1600 are to be viewed in terms not only of their past and future forms but also of their contemporary, SYNCHRONIC, relationships and functions.

Some sound changes are, indeed, the result of an influence which applies to the system as a whole. Those drastic changes of vowel quality known as the Great Vowel Shift mainly affect vowels in accented syllables. But vowels in most unaccented syllables (especially those in word-final positions) have undergone, in the last thousand years, an equally striking, though different, type of change. Sweet called OE the period of full endings, *stanas* being realized as ['staːnɑs]; ME, the period of levelled endings, when *stones* was pronounced ['stɔːnəs]; and eModE and later English, the period of lost endings, when *stones* is [stoːnz], [stəʊnz]. There is, therefore, a general tendency for all unaccented vowels to shorten (if long) and to gravitate towards the weak centralized vowels [ɪ] or [ə], or sometimes [ʊ], if not to disappear altogether. This fact accounts for the high frequency of occurrence of [ɪ] and [ə] in PresE and for the complete elision of many vowels in unaccented syllables in rapid colloquial speech, e.g. *suppose* [spəʊz], *probably* [prɒbblɪ].

6.2.4   Sources of Evidence for Reconstruction

Whether our aim is to reconstruct the phonological system of English at any particular moment in history or to estimate the nature of the development affecting particular phonemes, it is necessary to establish the sound values which were used in the pronunciation of the language—relative values in the case of the system, absolute values as far as possible in the case of sound development. An investigation of the phonological structure of PresE would have to include direct observation of its phonetic features. For this purpose, future generations will have the benefit of recordings of the speech of today. Obviously this type of evidence cannot be used for the reconstruction of past states of the spoken language. The further back we go into history the scantier the evidence of spoken forms becomes. Our conclusions will, therefore, be based on information mostly of an indirect kind; yet such is the agreement generally amongst the various types of evidence that the broad lines of sound change can be conjectured with reasonable certainty.

(1) *Theoretical paths of development*—If, in dealing with the changing realization of a particular phoneme, we can be reasonably sure of its sound value at two points in history, we can, from our knowledge of phonetic possibilities and probabilities, infer theoretically the intervening stages of development. We can, of course, be sure of the pronunciation of PresE. If, then, the evidence suggested unequivocally that, for instance, the vowel in *home* was pronounced as [ɑː] in OE, the development to be described and accounted for would be [ɑː] > [əʊ]. It is likely that the articulation has always involved the back, rather than the front, of the tongue; the change has clearly meant a closing of the tongue position, to which at some stage there has been added a gliding (diphthongal) movement. We might, therefore, postulate such developments as [ɑː>ɑʊ>oʊ>əʊ] or [ɑː>ɔː>oː>oʊ>əʊ]. The available evidence will then confirm or refute the hypothesis—in this case the second solution being more in keeping with the information. Such recognition of phonetic probabilities will always be implicit in the tracing of change. It must be considered unlikely that [ɑː] on its way to [oʊ] or [əʊ] would have passed through a stage of front articulation, without any combinative influence. Nevertheless, the possibility of a type of change which is not the most probable theoretically must never be excluded. The rounded close-mid back ME [ʊ] developed by the nineteenth century to an unrounded open-mid centralized back [ʌ]; and in the London area this vowel has now become more open and more front [ä]. Yet, at the same time, there is a tendency to make the vowel in *sad* more open. There is here a potential conflict and the future development of these vowels is uncertain. It would, therefore, be dangerous to predict, merely according to phonetic probabilities, the way our present sound system will develop.

(2) *Old English*—It is most important in an investigation of the development of English sounds over the last thousand years that the pronunciation of OE should be established with some certainty. If this can be done, we shall have a 'starting point' for the phonetic route of change to PresE. The term Old English, however, spans a period of some 400 years from about AD 700 to AD 1100. Moreover, the invasion of the Angles, Saxons, and Jutes in the fifth and sixth centuries introduced four separate varieties of English: the Angles, in the Midlands, north-east England, and the south of Scotland, using types of English known as MERCIAN and NORTHUMBRIAN (or, in general terms, ANGLIAN); the Saxons, in the south and south-west, using the WEST SAXON dialect; and the Jutes, settling mainly in the region of Kent and using a dialect called KENTISH. Of the four dialects, West Saxon, which was to become a kind of standard language, is the one about which most is known from the extant texts. In its later form—that in use between about AD 900 and AD 1100—it is referred to as Classical OE.

The broad lines of the pronunciation of this language can be conjectured from a comparison of the development of the other members of the West Germanic group of languages to which it is related. But by far the most explicit evidence concerning its sounds is to be inferred from the alphabet in which it is written. The earlier runic spelling was replaced by a form of the Latin alphabet. This alphabet was probably introduced into the country in the seventh century by Irish missionaries. It can be assumed, therefore, that the sounds of OE were represented as far as possible by the Latin letters with their Latin values, with some modifications of an Irish kind. A great deal is known about the pronunciation of Vulgar Latin, whose sound system had much in common with that of modern

Italian. If an Italian, knowing no English, were today asked to write down with his own spelling the PresE pronunciation of the word *milk*, [mɪɫk], he would have no difficulty in representing the first sound, which he could spell as <m>; the vowel [ɪ] might, however, seem to him to resemble the sound he would write in Italian as <e> rather than as <i>; the 'dark' [ɫ] would appear to have a back vowel glide accompanying it, requiring a spelling such as <ol>; and, since he has no <k> letter, he would spell the final [k] as <c>. His transcription of the word might, therefore, be *meolc*, which is, in fact, a West Saxon spelling of the word now written *milk*. This is a fortuitous example and must not be taken to suggest that OE was pronounced in the same way as PresE. But it does demonstrate that OE spellings, which may appear to be very different, are often less surprising when we keep in mind the Latin values originally attached to the letters.

Sometimes the simple forms of the Latin alphabet were evidently inadequate for representing the English sound: thus, the joined form <æ> was used to symbolize a sound between C[a] and C[ɛ]; the sounds [θ] and [ð] were written in the earlier manuscripts as <th> initially and <d> medially and finally in a word, and later as <ð> or the rune <þ> regardless of the sound's position in the word or its voiced or voiceless quality; the rune <ƿ> frequently replaced the earlier <u> or <uu>. The vowel values of the OE system were particularly difficult to represent with the five Latin vowel letters. Sometimes the spelling used hesitated between two letters: thus, the vowel of *mann*, probably of a C[ɑ] or [ɒ] quality, was written either with <a> or <o>, indicating a vowel between the unrounded open central value of the Latin letter <a> and the rounded open-mid to close-mid back value of <o>. Unaccented vowels, too, already beginning to be obscured and levelled, presented a problem to the scribes, the Latin alphabet offering no way of showing a central vowel of the [ə] type. Unaccented <æ,e,i> soon began all to be written as <e> and unaccented <a,u,o> later tended to be used indifferently, indicating that the vowel distinction was being lost. A diphthong such as the one written as *ea* must probably be interpreted as a glide to a central [ə] quality.

Quantity is often shown in the case of vowels by doubling the letter or by the use of an accent mark and in the case of consonants by doubling the letter. The accent in a word is also sometimes shown by the use of a mark; but, in any case, it is agreed, from a comparison of the West Germanic languages, that the word accent in OE fell generally on the first syllable of words, with the exception of certain compounds.

The written form of OE provides us, therefore, with considerable information concerning the language's pronunciation; we have a working hypothesis from which to begin our investigations. The study of later forms of English will often, in fact, confirm that the OE pronunciation postulated from the spelling and the comparison of Germanic languages is the only one from which later forms can be expected to have developed.

(3) *Middle English*—Spelling forms can also help us to deduce the pronunciation of the ME period, roughly AD 1100–1450. Generally speaking, it may be said that the letters still had their Latin values and that those letters which were written were meant to be sounded. Thus, the initial <k> in a word such as *knokke* was still pronounced and the vowel in *time* would have an [i] quality. This persistence of Latin values in spelling was no doubt due to the influence of the Church,

which was still the centre of teaching and writing, and the absence of a thoroughly standardized spelling accounts for its predominantly phonetic character. However, English spelling was modified by French influences. Notably, the French <ch> spelling was introduced to represent the [tʃ] sound in a word such as *chin* (formerly spelt *cinn*), where the new spelling form indicates no change of pronunciation; in addition <ou,ow>, represents the sound [u], formerly written <u>, e.g. *hous*, in OE *hus*. The simple <u> spelling was retained to express both the French sound [y] in words like *duke* and *fortune* and the OE short [u] sound, though this latter sound is often written as <o>, especially when juxtaposed to letters of the <w,m,n> type, e.g. *wonne* rather than *wunne*, to avoid confusion between the letter shapes.

Rhymes, too, have their value, especially as, in this period, they are likely to have been satisfactory to the ear as well as to the eye—in the whole of Chaucer's work, for instance, there are very few rhymes which appear to involve the pairing of different vowel sounds. Nevertheless, evidence from rhymes is valueless unless it is possible to be certain, from other sources of evidence, of the pronunciation of one member of the pair. Thus, the Chaucerian rhyme *par cas :: was*, because we can be sure that the French word *cas* had a vowel of the [a] quality, is evidence to confirm the view that the [w] of *was* had not yet retracted and rounded the vowel to [ɒ] and, the final <s> in the two words being still likely to represent [s], that the word was probably pronounced [was].

Again, words imported from French can give us information concerning the timing of sound changes. Thus, French words such as *age* and *couch*, which we know from French sources had [aː] and [uː] at the time of their introduction into English, fell in with the English vowel development [aː] > [eɪ] and [uː] > [aʊ] in words like *name* and *house*; we can conclude, therefore, that at the time the French words came into the language the [aː] and [uː] vowels had not begun their change.

Moreover, after the ME period, as we shall see, a great deal of direct evidence is available to us, so that our conjectures from about 1500 onwards can be made with considerable certainty. We may often, therefore, be able to deduce from our knowledge of pronunciation in the sixteenth century the stage probably reached in the ME period in the development of a sound from OE. The OE [iː] sound in *time*, for example, was beginning to be diphthongized generally very early in the sixteenth century. It is reasonable to suppose (even if other evidence to support the theory did not exist) that *time* still had a relatively pure [iː] for much of the ME period.

Finally, the metre of verse reveals the accent of words. It is for this reason that we know that French words, in Chaucer's verse, generally retained their original accentual pattern, e.g. *courage* [kuˈraːdʒə], and that the accent shift in these cases is a phenomenon of at least late ME.

(4) *Early Modern English*—The same sources of evidence which we have already considered remain available for the eModE period, roughly AD 1450–1600. The introduction of printing brought standardization of spelling and already the spoken and written forms of the language were beginning to diverge. But individuals, especially in their private correspondence, often used spellings of a largely phonetic kind, in the same unsophisticated and logical way that children still do. If a modern child writes *He must have gone* as *He must of gone*,

he is only representing the phonetic identity of the weak forms of *have* and *of* ([əv]), an identity which he will learn to ignore when he adopts the conventional spelling distinction. In the same way, if fifteenth- and sixteenth-century spellings show the word *sweet* occasionally written as *swit*, it may be assumed that this original ME [eː] was by now so close that it could be represented by <i> with its Latin value. Or again, the spelling form *sarvant* instead of *servant* reflects an open type of vowel in the first syllable which was current throughout the eModE period in such words. Moreover, the conventional adoption of an unphonetic spelling can sometimes provide us with positive evidence as to its value: thus, when words like *delight* (formerly *delite*) began to be spelt with <gh>, this spelling form <gh> clearly no longer had the consonantal fricative value which it had formerly represented in *light*, since there never was a consonantal sound between the vowel and final [t] in *delight*. We may conclude, therefore, that <gh> no longer had its former phonetic significance in words such as *light*. Care must, of course, be taken to identify the increasing number of learned or technical spellings adopted by printers. The initial letter group <gh> in *ghost* (OE *gast*) indicates no change in pronunciation—*goose* was also sometimes spelt *ghoose* in this period. Again, spellings which aim at revealing the etymology (true or false) of a word must usually be discarded as phonetically valueless, e.g. *debt, island*. Thus from the writings of individuals some general indications concerning sound changes may be gathered and used to supplement evidence derived from other sources.

Rhymes, too, continue to be useful as complementary evidence. A rhyme such as *night :: white* confirms the view that post-vocalic <gh> no longer had a consonantal value; or again, *can :: swan* suggests that the rounding of [a] after [w] had not yet taken place. Yet, just as in the case of ME, rhymes must be treated with caution, more particularly as eye-rhymes were doubtless beginning to become more prevalent. There is, however, in Elizabethan literature, additional evidence afforded by the frequent use of puns, which usually rely for their effect upon similarities, if not identities, of phonetic value. Shakespeare, for instance, plays on the phonetic identity of pairs such as *suitor, shooter* (both capable of being pronounced [ʃuːtər]) and *known, none* (both [noːn]); such puns suggest that the pronunciation of the two words was commonly sufficiently close to make an immediate impression upon an audience.

The most important and fruitful evidence for this period is, however, of a direct kind. It is provided by the published works of the contemporary grammarians, orthoepists, and schoolmasters, some of whom have been mentioned in §6.1. They are of unequal value and their statements have often to be interpreted in the light of other evidence; yet they provide us with the first direct descriptive accounts of the pronunciation of English. From the sixteenth century onwards, our conclusions rely more and more on their descriptive statements and less on clues of an indirect kind. Sometimes there appears to be a conflict between the phonetic probabilities, the statements of grammarians, and evidence from other sources. Frequently the solution must be that there existed at any time a variety of current pronunciations, resulting from differences of dialect, generation, fashion, and place in society, in the same way that a description of PresE (even that of a restricted area such as the south of England) would have to take into account a large number of variants.

The following representative systems are conjectures of one possible set of phonemes current in the period in question.

6.2.5 Classical Old English Sound System

Vowels
iː,ɪ; yː,y uː,ʊ
eː,ɛ oː,ɔ
æː,æ
ɑː ɑ (allophone [ɒ] before nasal consonants)
[ə] occurs in certain weakly accented syllables

Diphthongs ɛːə,ɛə; eːə,eə

Consonants
p,b,t,d,k,g (allophone [ɣ])
tʃ,dʒ
m,n (allophone [ŋ] before velar consonants)
l,r
f,θ,s (medial allophones [v,ð,z])
ʃ,h (allophones [x,ç])
j,w

Consonants may be long or short.

The spellings *hn, hl, hr, hw* may be interpreted as phoneme sequences /h/+/n,l,r,w/; alternatively, if it is assumed that *h* is here an indication of voiceless [n̥,l̥,r̥,w̥], these four sounds may be counted as contrastive, i.e. of phonemic status.

Text (St John, Chapter 14, verses 22, 23)

22 juːdas kwæθ toː hɪm. næs nɑː seː skarɪɔt. drɪçtən, hwæt ɪs jəwɔrdən θæt θuː wɪlt θeː sylfnə jəswʊtɛlijən ʊs næs mɪddanɛərdə.

23 seː hæːlənd ɒndswɑrɔdə ɒnd kwæθ hɪm; jɪf hwɑː meː lʊvɑθ heː hɪlt miːnə spræːtʃə ɒnd miːn fædər lʊvɑθ hɪnə ɒnd weː kumɑθ toː hɪm ɒnd weː wyrkɪɑθ ɛərdʊŋstoːwə mɪd hɪm.

Authorized Version

22 Judas saith unto him, not Iscarioth, Lord, how is it that thou wilt manifest thyself unto us, and not unto the world?

23 Jesus answered and said unto him, If a man love me, he will keep my words; and my Father will love him, and we will come to him, and make our abode with him.

6.2.6 Middle English Sound System

Vowels
iː,ɪ uː,ʊ
eː oː
ɛː,ɛ ɔː,ɔ
aː,a ɑː
[ə] occurs in unaccented syllables.

Diphthongs ɛi,(æi),ɔi,iu,(eu),ɛu,ɔu,(ɑu)

Consonants
p,b,t,d,k,g,tʃ,dʒ
m,n (allophone [ŋ] before velar consonants)

l,r
f,v,θ,ð,s,z,ʃ,h (allophones [x,ç])
j,w (allophone [ʍ] after /h/)

Text (from the *Prologue to the Canterbury Tales*)[5]
hwan θat aːprɪl, wɪθ hɪs ʃuːrəs soːtə
θə druxt ɔf martʃ haθ pɛrsəd toː ðə roːtə,
and baːðəd ɛːvrɪ væin ɪn swɪtʃ likuːr
ɔf hwɪtʃ vɛrtiu ɛndʒɛndərd ɪs θə fluːr,
hwan zɛfɪrʊs ɛːk wɪθ hɪs sweːtə brɛːθ
inspiːrəd haθ ɪn ɛvrɪ hɔlt and hɛːθ
θə tɛndər krɔppəs, and ðə jʊŋgə sʊnnə
haθ ɪn ðə ram hɪs halvə kʊrs ɪrʊnnə,
and smaːlə fuːləs maːkən melɔdiːə
θat sleːpən aːl ðə nɪçt wɪθ ɔːpən iːə—
sɔː prɪkəθ hɛm naːtiur ɪn hɪr kʊraːdʒəs—
θan lɔːŋgən fɔlk toː goːn ɔn pɪlgrɪmaːdʒəs.

6.2.7   Early Modern English Sound System

Vowels	iː,ɪ	uː,u
	eː	oː,ɤ
	ɛː,ɛ	
	æ	ɒː,ɒ

/eː/ was probably /iː/ or /ɛː/ in certain types of pronunciation
[a] and [aː] occur as contextual variants of /æ/ and /ɒː/
[ə] occurs in unaccented syllables

Diphthongs   əi,əu,iu(or ju),eu,ou,ɔi,ui,ɛi
Consonants   p,b,t,d,k,g,tʃ,dʒ
m,n,ŋ
l,r
f,v,θ,ð,s,z,ʃ,ʒ (later, in medial positions), h
j,w (allophone [ʍ] after /h/)

Text (Macbeth, Act II, Scene 1)
nəu oːər ðə wʏn haːf wʏrld
neːtər siːmz ded, ənd wɪkɪd dreːmz əbjuːz
ðə kʏrtɛind sliːp: wɪtʃkraft sɛlɪbreːts
peːl hɛkəts ɒfərɪŋz: ənd wɪðərd mʏrdər,
əlarəmd bəi hɪz sɛntɪnəl, ðə wʊlf,
huːz həulz hɪz watʃ, ðʏs wɪθ hɪz stɛlθɪ peːs,
wɪθ tarkwɪnz rævɪʃɪŋ strəidz, tuːərdz hɪz dɪzəin
muːvz ləik ə goːst. ðəu sjuːr[6] ənd fɛrm-sɛt ɛrθ

---

[5] The type of transcription given here is slightly archaic for Chaucer's pronunciation, e.g. long consonants were probably lost in later ME and words such as *and, that*, would have had a weak vowel

heːr nɒt məi stɛps, hwɪtʃ wɛi ðɛi wɔːk, fər feːr
ðəi vɛrɪ stoːnz prɛːt əv məi hwɛːrəbəut,
ənd tɛːk ðə prɛzənt hɒrər frəm ðə təim,
hwɪtʃ nəu sjuːts[6] wɪð ɪt.

6.2.8 Present English Sound System

Vowels	iː,ɪ		uː,ʊ
	e	ɜː	
	æ	ʌ	ɔː
			ɑː,ɒ

[ə] occurs in unaccented syllables

Diphthongs eɪ,əʊ,aɪ,aʊ,ɔɪ,ɪə,eə,ʊə
Consonants p,b,t,d,k, g
　　　　　　 tʃ,dʒ
　　　　　　 m,n,ŋ
　　　　　　 l,r
　　　　　　 f,v,θ,ð,s,z,ʃ,ʒ,h
　　　　　　 j,w

6.2.9 Modifications in the English Sound System

(1) *Distribution of phonemes*—The similarities of the systems given above may obscure the fact that the same sound, especially as far as the vowels are concerned, may occur in different categories of words according to the period. Thus [uː], now in *food*, occurred in OE in words such as *town*; [iː], now in *team*, occurred in OE in *time*. The following summary shows some of the most strik-ing changes affecting the vowel quality used in particular types of word:

	OE	ME	eModE	PresE
time	iː	iː	əi	aɪ
sweet	eː	eː	iː	iː
clean	æː	ɛː	eː (or [iː])	iː
stone	ɑː	ɔː	oː	əʊ
name	ɑ	aː	ɛː	eɪ
moon	oː	oː	uː	uː
house	uː	uː	əu	aʊ
love	ʊ	ʊ	ɣ	ʌ

(2) *Vowel changes*—Several trends become apparent from a study of quality changes:

(a) OE long vowels have closed or diphthongized; on the other hand, PresE [əʊ] and [eɪ] show signs of monophthongization.

---

[6] Alternatively, [ʃ] or [ʃj] for [sj]

(b) Certain phonemic qualitative oppositions have coalesced, e.g. OE /eː/ and /æː/; the originally separate diphthongs of *day* and *way*; the diphthong of *know* with the originally pure vowel of *no*; the diphthongs of *day*, *way* with the former pure vowel of *name*; OE /yː,y/ with /iː,ɪ/.

(c) Short vowels, with the notable exceptions of the OE /ɑ,æ/ (and the short diphthong /ɛə/) in open syllables, and ME /ʊ/, have remained relatively stable.

(d) Rounded front vowels have been lost, e.g. OE /yː,y/ and earlier /øː,ø/.

(e) The loss of post-vocalic [r] in the eighteenth century gave rise to the PresE centring diphthongs /ɪə,eə,ʊə/, the pure vowel /ɜː/ and introduced /ɑː,ɔː/ into new categories of words (*cart, port*).

(f) Vowels under weak accent have increasingly been obscured to [ə] or [ɪ], or have been elided.

(g) Changes of quantity have affected certain phonemes in particular contexts or sets of words, e.g. lengthening of OE /ɑ,æ,ɛə/ in open syllables and of ME /a/+/f,θ,s/; and shortening of ME /oː/ in words like *good, book, blood*, and of ME /ɛː/ in words such as *breath, death, head*.

(3) *Consonant changes*—Changes in the consonantal system are less striking, but the following may be noted:

(a) Double (or long) consonants within words were lost by late ME; certain other consonant clusters ceased to be tolerated, e.g. /hl,hr,hn/ by ME and /kn,gn,wr/ in the eModE period; post-vocalic /r/ was lost in much of the south-east of England in the eighteenth century.

(b) Allophones of certain phonemes have been lost, e.g. the [ɣ] allophone of /g/ in late OE and the [x,ç] allophones of /h/ in eModE.

(c) New phonemes have emerged, e.g. /tʃ,dʒ/ in OE, /v,ð,z/ in ME, and /ŋ,ʒ/ in eModE; in addition, /h/ is used initially in words of French origin where, origi-nally, no [h] sound was pronounced (*habit, herb, humble* etc.).

7

Standard and Regional Accents

7.1 *Standards of Pronunciation*

The British are today particularly sensitive to variations in the pronunciation of their language. The 'wrong accent' may still be an impediment to social intercourse or to advancement or entry in certain professions. Such extreme sensitivity is apparently not paralleled in any other country or even in other parts of the English-speaking world. There are those who claim, from an elocution standpoint, that modern speech is becoming increasingly slovenly, full of 'mumbling and mangled vowels' and 'missing consonants'. Alexander Gil and others made the same kind of complaint in the seventeenth century. There is, in fact, no evidence to suggest that the degree of obscuration and elision, is markedly greater now than it has been for four centuries. Of more significance—social as well as linguistic—is the attitude which regards a certain set of sound values as more acceptable, even more 'beautiful' than another. Judgements of this kind suggest that there is a standard for comparison; and it is clear that such a standard pronunciation does exist, although it has never been explicitly imposed by any official body. A consideration of the origins and present nature of this unofficial standard goes some way towards explaining the controversies and emotions which it arouses at the present day.

7.2 *The Emergence of a Standard*

It is clear that the controversy does not centre on the written language: the spelling of English was largely fixed in the eighteenth century; the conventions of grammatical forms and constructions as well as of the greater part of our vocabulary have for a long time been accepted and adhered to by the majority of educated English speakers. Indeed, the standardization of the written form of English may be said to have begun in the ninth and tenth centuries. But there has always existed a great diversity in the spoken realizations of our language, in terms of the sounds used in different parts of the country and by different sections of the community. On the one hand, the sounds of the language always being in process of change, there have always been at any one time disparities between the speech sounds of the younger and older generations; the speech of the young is traditionally characterized by the old as slovenly and debased. On the other hand, especially in those times when communications between regions were poor, it was natural that the speech of all communities should not develop either in the same direction or at the same rate; moreover, different parts of the country might be exposed to different external influences (e.g. foreign invasion) which might influence the phonetic structure of the language in a particular area. English has, therefore, always had its regional pronunciations in the same way that other languages have been pronounced in a variety of ways for basically geographical reasons. Yet, at the same time, especially for the last five centuries, there has existed in this country the notion that one kind of pronunciation of English was preferable socially to others; one regional accent began to acquire social prestige.[1] For reasons of politics, commerce, and the presence of the Court, it was the pronunciation of the south-east of England, and more particularly to that of the London region, that this prestige was attached.

The early phonetician John Hart notes (1570) that it is 'in the Court and London speaches, where the general flower of all English country speaches are chosen and read. And though some would say it were not so, reason would we should graunt no lesse: for that unto these two places, do dayly resort from all towns and countries, of the best of all professions, as well of the own landsmen, as of aliens and straungers . . .'.[2] Puttenham's celebrated advice in the *Arte of English Poesie* (1589) recommends 'the usual speech of the Court, and that of London and the shires lying about London within 60 miles and not much above . . . Northern men, whether they be noblemen or gentlemen, or of their best clerks, [use an English] which is not so courtly or so current as our Southern English is'.[3] Nevertheless, many courtiers continued to use the pronunciation of their own region; we are told, for instance, that Sir Walter Raleigh kept his Devon accent. The speech of the Court, however, phonetically largely that of the London area, increasingly acquired a prestige value and, in time, lost some of the local characteristics of London speech. It may be said to have been finally fixed, as the speech of the ruling class, through the conformist influence of the public schools of the nineteenth century. Moreover, its dissemination as a class pronunciation throughout the country caused it to be recognized as characteristic not so much of a region as of a social stratum. With the spread of education, the situation arose in which an educated man might not belong to the upper classes and might retain his regional characteristics; on the other hand, those eager for social advancement felt obliged to modify their accent in the direction of the social standard. Pronunciation became, therefore, a marker of position in society.

7.3   *The Present-day Situation: RP*

(1) Some prestige is still attached to this implicitly accepted social standard of pronunciation. Often called RECEIVED PRONUNCIATION (RP),[4] the term suggesting

---

[1] See in particular Mugglestone (1995)
[2] See reprint of Hart (1570) in Danielsson (1955: 234)
[3] See edition of Puttenham (1589) by Willcock and Walker (1936: 145)
[4] The earliest recorded use of the term 'Received Pronunciation' is in Ellis (1869). See discussion in Gimson (1984) and in MacMahon (1998)

that it is the result of a social judgement rather than of an official decision as to what is 'correct' or 'wrong', it became more widely known and accepted through the advent of radio and television. The BBC used to recommend this form of pronunciation for its announcers mainly because it was the type which was most widely understood and which excited least prejudice of a regional kind. Indeed, early attempts to use announcers who had a mild regional accent used to provoke protests even from the region whose accent was used. Thus, RP often became identified in the public mind with 'BBC English'. But, over the last 20 years, both the BBC and other national radio and TV channels have been increasingly tolerant of the accent of broadcasters. Nevertheless, in their choice of newsreaders, the national TV and radio channels still use predominantly RP speakers, even though they may be speakers of a type of 'Regional RP' as discussed in (4) below.

(2) Certain types of regional pronunciation are, however, firmly established. Some, especially Standard Scottish English (SSE), are accepted; others, particularly the popular forms of pronunciation used in large towns such as Liverpool and Birmingham, are generally characterized as ugly by those (especially of the older generations) who do not use them. This rejection of certain sounds used in speech is not, of course, a matter of the sounds themselves: thus, [paɪnt] may be acceptable if it means *pint*, but 'ugly' if it means *paint*. It is rather a reflection of the social connotations of speech which, though they have lost some of their force, have by no means disappeared. Indeed, RP itself can be a handicap if used in inappropriate social situations, since it may be taken as a mark of affectation or a desire to emphasize social superiority.[5] Speakers of RP have themselves become aware of the fact that their type of pronunciation is one which is used by only a very small part of the English-speaking world. An American pronunciation of English, for instance, is now familiar in Britain; this was not the case in the 1930s when the first sound films were shown, an American pronunciation then being considered strange and even difficult to understand.

(3) Within RP, those habits of pronunciation that are mostly firmly established tend to be regarded as 'correct' whilst innovation tends to be stigmatized. Thus conservative forms tend to be most generally accepted, sometimes even by those who themselves use other pronunciations. Where the accentual patterns or the phonemic structure of words is concerned, this attitude may result in a speaker's use of the conservative variant in a formal situation and the use by the same speaker of a less well-established variant in more casual speech, e.g. the avoidance of /verɪˈfaɪəbl/ (*verifiable*) and /ˈdʒʊərɪŋ/ (*during*) in more formal speech and their replacement with the more conservative /ˈverɪfaɪəbl/ and /ˈdjʊərɪŋ/. It may be of interest that the pronunciation /ˈdʒʊərɪŋ/ with initial coalescent assimilation was noted as long ago as 1913 by Robert Bridges in his *Tract on English Pronunciation*. Nevertheless, there is still some resistance to accepting such coalescence word-initially in accented syllables (see section (5) below).

Where realizational variation (below the level of the phoneme) is affected, most speakers are unaware of their own changing speech patterns. Objections to

---

[5] For a summary of experiments on the social evaluation of RP using the matched-guise technique, see Giles *et al.* (1990)

the use of the glottal stop are often made, its use being popularly associated with Cockney speech, and yet its occurrence as a realisation of preconsonantal /t/ is increasingly frequent within the speech of the middle and younger generations of RP speakers. (See section (5) below and §9.2.8.)

(4) Even within RP there are some areas and many individual words where alternative pronunciations are possible. It is convenient to distinguish three main types of RP: General RP, Refined RP, and Regional RP.[6] The last two types require some explanation. Refined RP is that type which is commonly considered to be upper-class, and it does indeed seem to be mainly associated in some way with upper-class families and with professions which have traditionally recruited from such families, e.g. officers in the navy and in some regiments. Where formerly it was very common, the number of speakers using Refined RP is increasingly declining. This may be because for many other speakers (both of other types of RP and of regional dialects) a speaker of Refined RP has become a figure of fun, and the type of speech itself is often regarded as affected. (The adjective 'Refined' has been deliberately chosen as having positive overtones for some people and negative overtones for others.) Particular characteristics of Refined RP are the realization of /əʊ/ as [ɛ̈ʊ], and a very open word-final /ə/ (and where [ə] forms part of /ɪə,eə,ʊə/) and /ɪ/. The vowel /ɜː/ is also pronounced very open, this time in all positions. The vowel /æ/ is often dipthongized as [ɛæ].

Although Refined RP reflects a class distinction and describes a type of pronunciation which is relatively homogeneous, Regional RP reflects regional rather than class variation and will vary according to which region is involved in 'regional'. (Hence, strictly speaking, we should talk of Regional RPs in the plural.) Some phoneticians, on the basis that part of the definition of RP is that it should not tell you where someone comes from, would regard the term 'Regional RP' as a contradiction in terms. Yet it is useful to have such a term as 'Regional RP' to describe the type of speech which is basically RP except for the presence of a few regional characteristics which go unnoticed even by other speakers of RP. For example, vocalization of dark [ɫ] to [ʊ] in words like *held* [heʊd] and *ball* [bɔʊ] a characteristic of Cockney (and some other regional accents) now passes virtually unnoticed in an otherwise fully RP accent. Or, again, the use of /æ/ instead of /ɑː/ before voiceless fricatives in words like *after*, *bath* and *past* (part of the Northern accent within England) may be similarly acceptable. But some other features of regional accents may be too stigmatized to be acceptable as RP, e.g. realization of /t/ by glottal stop word-medially between vowels, as in *water* (Cockney) or the lack of a distinction between /ʌ/ and /ʊ/ (Northern English).

The concept of Regional RP reflects the fact that there is nowadays a far greater tolerance of dialectal variation in all walks of life, although, where RP is the norm, only certain types of regional dilution of RP are acceptable. It remains true, however, that most manuals and dictionaries of the pronunciation of British English, like this book, are based almost entirely on RP.

RP, Refined RP, and Regional RP are not accents with precisely enumerable lists of features but rather represent clusterings of features, such clusterings varying from individual to individual. Thus there are not categorial boundaries

---

[6] cf. Wells (1982: 280–3 and 297–301)

between the three types of RP nor between RP and regional pronunciations; a speaker may, for example, generally be an RP speaker but have one noticeable feature of Refined RP.

(5) Special mention must be made of London Regional RP, because, under the name of 'Estuary English', it has provoked much discussion in the press. As mentioned under (4), London Regional RP is a modification of RP towards Cockney. The vocalization of dark [ɫ] to [ʊ] has already been noted as one of the features of this form of Regional RP. The name Estuary English was first used because such a pronunciation was thought to have spread outwards from London along the Thames estuary into Essex and north Kent. But claims have been made that this type of pronunciation is spreading not only into rural areas all around London (i.e. the 'Home Counties') but also into urban areas remote from London, e.g. Milton Keynes, Norwich, Bristol, Hull, Manchester, Liverpool, Newcastle, and Glasgow. If confirmed (and the evidence at the moment is largely hearsay)[7] Estuary English would be competing with the Regional RPs of these cities. Estuary English is said to be being adopted by those wishing to avoid the stigma of RP as 'posh' and by upwardly mobile speakers of local dialect. It is often characterized among younger speakers as having 'street credibility' or 'streetcred', i.e. as being fashionable. The phonetic features of Estuary English are discussed under the section on London English below (§7.6.3).

(6) RP has traditionally been the type of pronunciation taught to learners of English as an L2 and that most commonly described in books on the phonetics of British English. But it has to be recognized that the role of RP in the English-speaking world has changed very considerably in the last century. Over 320 million people now speak English as a first language;[8] of this number native RP speakers form only a minute proportion (the majority speak some form of American English). At least another 150 million use English in varying ways as an official language and in these cases it is usually a form of local pronunciation of English which predominates (e.g. in India). However, despite the discrepancy in numbers, RP continues for historical reasons to serve as a model in many parts of the world; if a model is used at all, the choice is still effectively between RP and General American. Most teaching textbooks describe one of these two types and, of the two, RP seems to be the more widely acceptable; certainly some form of British English is more generally referred to in Europe, in Africa, in the Indian subcontinent, and increasingly in other parts of Asia and in South America. In Chapter 13 some suggestions are made about the way in which the pronunciation of RP may be adapted to suit local needs.

7.4 *Current Changes within RP*

In this section we survey changes in General RP which have begun approximately in the last 70 years but which a number of speakers, either small or large, have not yet embraced.

---

[7] See bibliography and collection of documents, including press articles on the web page of University College, London: http://www.phon.ucl.ac.uk

[8] Figures from Crystal (1997: 54)

7.4.1   Changes Almost Complete

This involves pronunciations which are now typical of the large majority of speakers of General RP:

(1) The distinction between /ɔː/ and /ɔə/ is lost, e.g. *paw* and *pour* (or *pore*) are both /ɔː/.

(2) /j/ is lost following /l,s,z/, e.g. *luminous, suit*, and *exhume* are /ˈluːmɪnəs/, /suːt/, and /ɪgˈzuːm/.

(3) The diphthong /eə/ is realized monophthongally as [ɛː], e.g. *fare* and *tear* as [fɛː] and [tɛː].

(4) /r/ is realized as a post-alveolar approximant in all positions and not, as formerly, as a tap [ɾ] in intervocalic positions following an accented syllable, e.g. *very* and *error* as [veɹɪ] and [eɹə].

(5) /əʊ/ is now regularly realized as [əʊ] rather than the older realization as [oʊ], e.g. *over, boat* and *comb* as [əʊvə], [bəʊt], [kəʊm] rather than [oʊvə], [boʊt], [koʊm].

(6) /tj,dj/ in unaccented positions are regularly changed to /tʃ,dʒ/, e.g. *culture* [kʌltʃə], *soldier* [səʊldʒə].

7.4.2   Changes Well-established

This section describes pronunciations which are now typical of a majority of speakers of General RP:

(1) /ɪ/ in many unaccented syllables replaced by /ə/. For this change there is, besides age variation, affixal and lexical variation, e.g. the suffix *-ity* as in *quality* now usually has /ə/, the word *palace* is variable between /pæləs/ and /pælɪs/, whereas the word *pocket* is usually pronounced /pɒkɪt/. (See more detail in §8.9.2 below).

(2) /ɔː/ used in place of /ʊə/ in some, particularly monosyllabic, words, e.g. in *sure, poor, cure, moor, tour*. This change, like the last, is also lexically conditioned: some words, like monosyllabic *pure* as well as non-monosyllabic *curious, puerile, endure*, and *secure*, are less likely to have /ɔː/ while in others it is impossible, e.g. in *dour, gourd, lure, Ruhr*, and *Ure*. It is also impossible in words derived from /uː/ plus a suffix /ə/ like *doer, fewer, newer, two-er, viewer, sewer* (strictly speaking this last is not analyzable into root morpheme plus suffix).

(3) Final /ɪ/ replaced by /iː/ in words like *city, pretty, happy, nappy, witty, smutty, potty, putty, hearty, booty, dirty*. Recent editions of pronouncing dictionaries transcribe this with /i/[9] without the length marks, presumably to indicate that this final unaccented /i/ is often shorter than /iː/ elsewhere, cf. the final vowels in *city* and *settee*, and also that it may still often have the variant /ɪ/. In a phonemic analysis this final vowel could be ascribed either to /iː/ or to /ɪ/ or regarded as a neutralized form.

---

[9] See, for example, the two major pronouncing dictionaries of British English: Jones (1997) and Wells (2000)

(4) The quality of the vowel /æ/ becoming more open, i.e. it is close to C[a], e.g. in *mad, rat, flaccid, bang,* and *cap.* In this way it has become closer to the vowel used in such words in the north of England (see §7.6.4. below), although it retains greater length than the northern vowel.

(5) Pre-consonantal /t/ becoming [ʔ], e.g. *not very* [nɒʔ veɹi], although such glottalization is not acceptable before /l/, e.g. *little* [lɪʔl] is considered substandard.

(6) Loss of /j/ following /n/, *news* [nuːz]. This is already standard in the USA.

(7) Fronting of /uː/ to [ʉː], e.g. *soon* [sʉːn].

(8) Accented /tj,dj/ become /tʃ,dʒ/, e.g. *tune* /tʃuːn/, *endure* [ɪndʒʊə].

7.4.3   Recent Innovations

This section describes pronunciations which are now heard in General RP but are not yet typical of a majority of speakers:

(1) /ɪə/ /ʊə/ realized as [ɪː] and [ʊː], e.g. *beer* [bɪː], *sure* [ʃʊː]. The latter change competes with the replacement of /ʊə/ by /ɔː/ (see §7.5.2. (2) above).

(2) Unrounding as well as fronting of /ʊ,uː/ as [ɨ] and [ɨː], e.g. *good* [gɨd], *soon* [sɨːn] Fronting on its own of /uː/ has been common in RP rather longer (as in §7.4.2 (2) above).

(3) The over-frequent use of a 'checking' high rise on declarative sentences in conversational narratives, where some form of fall would previously have been expected, e.g. (the mark ´ indicates the high rise) 'I was at Heath´row yesterday. They've got a new duty-´free shop'. This was a new trend in Australia and New Zealand some 20 years earlier, and perhaps even before that in parts of the USA. How it has spread to Britain is a matter of some dispute; suggested strong influences have been the high number of Australasian shop assistants in London and the popularity of Australian soap operas on British television.

(4) The realization of /r/ without a tongue tip contact, i.e. = [ʋ] or [ɰ], *red* as [ʋed] or [ɰed]. This has been described as one of the features of Estuary English, but it seems more likely that it is general tendency within RP and not something particularly typical of the London area.

7.4.4   Innovations on the Verge of RP

There are some pronunciations which are standard in London Regional RP ('Estuary English') which must be considered as on the verge of being acceptable as part of General RP:

(1) Vocalization of dark [ɫ] as [ʊ] in a wide range of pre-consonantal positions and finally, e.g. *fill* [fɪʊ], *middle* [mɪdʊ].

(2) Use of [ʔ] before an accented vowel or before pause, e.g. *not even* [nɒʔ iːvn], *need it* [niːd ɪʔ], although before unaccented /ɪ,ə/ use of [ʔ] is still stigmatized as non-RP (and typical of Cockney) and is considered substandard, both intra-word and inter-word, e.g. *water* [wɔːʔə], *got a* [gɒʔə], *fit it* [fɪʔ ɪʔ].

7.5   *Comparing Systems of Pronunciation*

A comparison of two types of pronunciation will reveal differences of several kinds (as first discussed in §5.3.5 above):

(a) *systemic differences* (i.e. differences in PHONEME INVENTORY)—The system may be different, i.e. the number of oppositions may be smaller or greater, e.g. the RP /æ/–/ɑː/ opposition may not be present in those Ulster or Scottish forms which do not distinguish *Sam* and *psalm*; or when RP /aɪ/ homophones, as in *side* and *sighed*, are differentiated qualitatively or quantitatively, as in some types of Scottish English; or when the presence of /g/ after [ŋ] in a word such as *sing* deprives [ŋ] of its phonemic status (see §7.6.4);

(b) *distributional differences* (i.e. different phonotactic possibilities)—The system may be the same, but the phonetic context in which certain phonemes occur may be limited, e.g. in RP /r/ has a LIMITED DISTRIBUTION, being restricted in its occurrence to pre-vocalic position as in *red* or *horrid*. Accents which display this limited distribution of /r/ are referred to as NON-RHOTIC accents, whilst those in which /r/ has a full distribution (such as most American and Scottish accents) are termed RHOTIC. In the latter accents /r/ occurs pre-consonantally and pre-pausally as well as pre-vocalically, thus *part* and *car* will be pronounced /pɑːrt/ and /kɑːr/, whereas in non-rhotic accents the pronunciation will be /pɑːt/ and /kɑː/ respectively. (See §7.6.2 and §12.4.7).

(c) *lexical differences* (i.e. differences of LEXICAL INCIDENCE)—The system may be the same, but the occurrence or 'incidence' of phonemes in words is different, e.g. in those Northern forms which have the RP opposition /uː/–/ʊ/, but nevertheless use /uː/ in *book, took* etc. (see §8.9.9); or when /ɒ/ is used instead of /ʌ/ in *one, among* etc., though the opposition /ɒ/–/ʌ/ exists (see §8.9.5); or when the choice of phoneme is associated with the habits of different generations, e.g. /ɔː/ for /ɒ/ in *off, cloth, cross* etc. (see §8.9.7) or /eɪ/ for /ɪ/ in *Monday, holiday* etc.

(d) *realizational differences*—The system, i.e. the number of distinctive (phonemic) terms operating, may be the same, but the PHONETIC REALIZATIONS of the phonemes may be different: e.g. the RP opposition between the vowels of *bet* and *bat* is maintained, but the realization of both vowels is much more open than in RP (as in Northern English) (see §7.6.4), so that the sound of /æ/ may come near to Cockney /ʌ/ (see §7.6.3); or when, as in London Regional RP (or 'Estuary English'), an allophone [ʔ] in unaccented positions represents /t/ and often /k/ or /p/ (see §7.6.3); or when the syllable-final allophone of /l/ is [l] ('clear [l]') rather than [ɫ] ('dark [ɫ]') as in Welsh English and Irish English in the south of Ireland.

7.6   *Systems and Standards Other than RP (and their Influence on Regional RPs)*

The remainder of this book is a description of English set within the basic framework of RP, with some reference to variation in other dialects in the discussion of each of the RP phonemes. But there are a number of reasons why such particular differences should be drawn together to show the major overall differences between the phonemic system of RP and that of other major dialects of English. In this section we survey briefly differences between RP and five other systems: General American, Standard Scottish English, Cockney, Northern (England) English, and Australian English. We survey an American pronunciation because, as noted in §7.3, this is more frequently the standard model for learners of English as a second language in much of Asia and Latin America. We look at Scottish English because this is the type of pronunciation of English within the British Isles which is most frequently accepted as an alternative standard to RP. We survey Northern (England) English and Cockney because these are the areas (apart from Scottish) whose characteristic pronunciations are heard most widely within Britain and which often underlie regional forms of RP. We look at Australian English because this is typical of an English pronunciation of the southern hemisphere and may increasingly become the standard for a wider area rather than just Australia. Of course we could easily have made a case for the inclusion of other systems of pronunciation here (e.g. Caribbean English and Indian English); but since this is not primarily a book about varieties of English, a limit had to be put somewhere. Moreover there are now books which survey dialectal variation in English pronunciation in detail.[10] Where reference is made in this book to non-standard varieties of English, the type of pronunciation being referred to is the BASILECTAL variety of the area concerned, i.e. that used by lower socio-economic classes (and by middle socio-economic classes in informal situations).

7.6.1   General American

The traditional (although not undisputed) division of the United States for pronunciation purposes is into Eastern (including New England, and New York City, although this has pronunciation characteristics of its own), Southern (stretching from Virginia to Texas and to all points southwards), and General (all the remaining area). General American (GA) can thus be regarded as that form of American which does not have marked regional characteristics (and is in this way comparable to RP) and is sometimes referred to as 'Network English' (just as RP, not entirely justifiably nowadays, is sometimes referred to as 'BBC English'). It is the standard model for the pronunciation of English as an L2 in parts of Asia (e.g. the Philippines) and parts of Latin American (e.g. Mexico).

There are two major areas of systemic difference between RP and GA. Firstly, GA lacks the RP diphthongs /ɪə,eə,ʊə/ which correspond in GA to sequences of short vowel plus /r/, e.g. *beard, fare, dour* /bɪrd/, /fer/, /dʊr/. This reflects the allied distributional difference between RP and GA, namely that unlike in RP, where /r/ occurs only before vowels, GA /r/ can occur before consonants and before pause (GA is called a rhotic dialect and RP a non-rhotic dialect). Secondly, GA has no /ɒ/. Most commonly those vowels which have /ɒ/ in RP are pronounced with /ɑː/ in GA, e.g. *cod, spot, pocket, bottle*. But a limited subset has /ɔː/, e.g. *across, gone, often, cough, orange, porridge* (as can be seen from the examples,

---

[10] In particular Wells (1982), Foulkes and Docherty (1999), Trudgill (1999)

these frequently involve a following voiceless fricative). Moreover, for an increasing number of GA speakers (and most Canadians), not only do RP /ɒ/ and /ɑː/ fall together but /ɔː/ also falls in with this group; for such speakers *cod, calm,* and *cause* will have the same vowel.

The main difference of lexical incidence concerns words which in RP have /ɑː/ while in GA they have /æ/. Like the change from /ɒ/ to /ɔː/ this change commonly involves the context before a voiceless fricative, or alternatively, before a nasal followed by another consonant; thus RP /pɑːst/–GA /pæst/, RP /ɑːftə/–GA /æftər/, RP /plɑːnt/–GA /plænt/ (this difference from RP is of course the same as in the north of England). Allied to the pronunciation of /r/ in pre-consonantal positions mentioned in the previous paragraph, there is considerable re-alignment of vowels before /r/, so that *merry* and *marry* may be pronounced the same whilst *short* and *sport* may have different vowels (/ɔ/ in the former and [o] corresponding to RP /əʊ/ in the latter).

Differences of realization are always numerous between any two systems of English pronunciation and only the most salient will be mentioned. Among the vowels this includes the realization of the diphthongs /eɪ/ and /əʊ/ as monophthongs [eː] and [oː], hence *late* [leːt] and *load* [loːd]. Among the consonants, /r/ is either phonetically [ɻ], i.e. the tip of the tongue is curled further backwards than in RP, or else a similar auditory effect is achieved by bunching the body of the tongue upwards and backwards; /t/ intervocalically is usually a voiced tap in GA, e.g. *better* [berɚ] and may sometimes become [d] producing a neutralization between /t/ and /d/; and /l/ is generally a dark [ɫ] in all positions in GA, unlike RP where it is a clear [l] before vowels and a dark [ɫ] in other positions (see §9.7.1).

A wholesale change in the realization of the short vowels in GA is increasingly reported, sometimes called the 'Northern Cities Shift',[11] although it now seems more widely spread than this. The vowel principally affected by this shift is /æ/ which becomes closer, to [ɛ] or [ɛə], or even [e] or [eə]. This affects both those words like *sad* which have /æ/ in RP and those words like *after* where the GA /æ/ corresponds to /ɑː/ in RP.

7.6.2   Standard Scottish English (SSE)

There are nowadays taken to be three languages in Scotland: Gaelic, Scots, and (Scottish) English. Old English spread into the south and east of Scotland at much the same time as it spread through England and has continued in use as present-day Scots. A different type of English was re-introduced from the south of England in the eighteenth century but was subsequently much influenced by Scots; it is this that is now described as Scottish English. Most speakers in Scotland will slightly or considerably vary their style of speech between Scots and Standard Scottish English (SSE) according to different situations. The typical vowel system of Scottish English involves the loss of the RP distinctions between /ɑː/ and /æ/, between /uː/ and /ʊ/, and between /ɔː/ and /ɒ/. Thus the pairs *ant* and

---

[11] See Labov (1991)

aunt, soot and *suit, caught* and *cot* are pronounced the same. On the other hand, there may be a phonemic split corresponding to RP /e/; while most such words have a vowel of an [ɛ] quality, a small group of words have a vowel of an [ɛ̈] quality, e.g. *heaven, eleven, next*.

SSE also has no /ɪə,eə,ʊə/ because, like General American, it is rhotic, and *beard, fare*, and *dour* are pronounced as /biːrd/, /feɪr/=[feːɹ], and /duːr/=[dyːɹ]. Some speakers will also have different sequences of vowel plus /r/ corresponding to RP /ɜː/ in *bird, serve*, and *turn*; others have the same r-coloured schwa [ɚ] in such words. Moreover the lexical incidence of other vowels before /r/ may not correspond to RP: *short* and *sport* may have different vowels as in GA, *short* rhyming with *caught* but *sport* with *boat*.

The vowel in *fare* /feɪr/ above which we transcribed with the RP diphthong /eɪ/ is typically monophthongal [eː] (and of course would be transcribed as such if we were devising a phonemic transcription independently for SSE). The vowel /əʊ/ is also monophthongal [oː] (and again would be transcribed as such in an independent transcription) as in *coat* [koːt]; so the vowels in *fare* and *coat* are similar to those in General American. Moreover, the vowel common to *soot* and *suit* is not like either of the RP vowels in these words, but is considerably fronted to something like [ÿ], hence [sÿt]. More generally there is no systemic durational difference between long and short vowels, as there is in RP.

The chief differences from RP in the realization of the consonants lies in the use of a tap [ɾ], e.g. *red* [ɾed] and *trip* [tɾɪp], though there is variation between this and [ɹ] (the usual type in RP), the use of [ɹ] being more common in post-vocalic positions and generally more prestigious. The phoneme /l/ is most commonly a dark [ɫ] in all positions, *little* [ɫɪtɫ], and *plough* [pɫaʊ]. Finally, inter-vocalic /t/ is often realized as a glottal stop, e.g. *butter* [bʌʔɚ].

7.6.3 London English

We deal firstly with the basilectal speech of London, namely Cockney. Unlike General American and Standard Scottish English, Cockney is as much a class dialect as a regional one. In its broadest form the dialect of Cockney includes a considerable vocabulary of its own, including rhyming slang. But the characteristics of Cockney pronunciation are spread more widely through the working-class of London than is its vocabulary.

Unlike the previous two types of pronunciation there are no differences in the inventory of vowel phonemes between RP and Cockney and there are relatively few (compared with GA and SSE) differences of lexical incidence. There are, however, a large number of differences of realization. The short front vowels tend to be uniformly closer that in RP, e.g. in *sat, set*, and *sit*, so much so that *sat* may sound like *set* and *set* itself like *sit* to speakers from other regions. Additionally, the short vowel /ʌ/ moves forward to almost C[a]. Among the long vowels, most noticeable is the diphthongization of /iː/ (= [əi]), /uː/ (= [əu]), and /ɔː/ which varies between [ɔu] morpheme-medially and [ɔwə] morpheme-finally, thus *bead* [bəid], *boot* [bəut], *sword* [sɔu], *saw* [ɔwə]. Cockney also uses distinctive pronunciations of a number of diphthongs /eɪ/= [aɪ], /aɪ/= [ɑɪ], /əʊ/= [æʊ], and /aʊ/= [aː], e.g. *late* [laɪt], *light* [lɑɪt], *load* [læʊd], *loud* [laːd]. The last two vowels are close enough to cause considerable confusion among non-Cockney listeners, although the distinction is not usually neutralized. In two cases special allophones are used before dark [ɫ] (which itself = [ʊ]—see below): /əʊ/ = [ɒʊ] and /uː/ = [uː] (is monophthongal compared with the usual [ʊu]), e.g. *bowl* [bɒʊɫ], *fool* [fuːʊ]). Before the vocalized form of /l/ there is much neutralization, e.g. *field* and *filled* as [fɪʊd], *col* and *coal* as [kɒʊ], and *pull* and *pool* as [pʊʊ].

Among the consonants most notable are the omission of /h/ and the replacement of /θ,ð/ by /f,v/, e.g. *hammer* /ˈæmə/, *think* /fɪŋk/, *father* /ˈfɑːvə/. Dark [ɫ], i.e. /l/ in positions not immediately before vowels, becomes vocalic [ʊ], e.g. *milk* [mɪʊk], *middle* [ˈmɪdʊ]; /t/ is realized as a glottal stop following vowels, laterals, and nasals, e.g. *butter* [ˈbʌʔə], *eat it* [ˈiːʔ ɪʔ], *not that* [nɒʔ ˈðæʔ], *benefit* [ˈbenɪfɪʔ], *belt up* [beɫʔ ˈʌp]; there may be similar replacement of /p,k/ before a following consonant, e.g. *soapbox* [ˈsæʊʔbɒks], *technical* [ˈteʔnɪʔʊ] (in this last word [ʊ] as the realization of /l/ still counts as a consonant); and there is coalescence of /t,d/ +/j/ to /tʃ,dʒ/, e.g. *student* [ˈʃtʃuːdṇʔ], *during* [ˈdʒʊərɪŋ], but elision of /j/ following /n/, e.g. *news* [nuːz].

Cockney has historically been the major influence in the phonetic development of RP and, as has been outlined in §7.3(5) above, London Regional RP, i.e. a hybrid between General RP and Cockney, popularly called Estuary English, is now widely used in south-east England and may be spreading to other urban areas. The phonetic features of Cockney in Estuary English include the replacement of dark [ɫ] by [ʊ], e.g. *field* [fɪʊd]; the glottalization of /t/ preconsonantally, e.g. *not that* [nɒʔ ˈðæʔ] and increasingly word-finally before pause and before a following vowel, e.g. *not that* [nɒʔ ˈðæʔ], *eat ice* [iːʔ ˈaɪs]; the use of Cockney-type realizations of the diphthongs /eɪ,aɪ/ and Cockney-type allophones before /l/, e.g. *cold* [kɒʊʊd], *cool* [kuːʊ], and the coalescent forms of /tj,dj/ together with the elision of /j/ following /n/, e.g. *tune* [tʃuːn], *June* [dʒuːn], *new* [nuː].

Other Cockney sounds are less likely in Estuary English, e.g. /h/-dropping, monophthongization of /aʊ/, the wide diphthong in /əʊ/, fronting of /ʌ/, and the replacement of /θ,ð/ by /f,v/ (although informal reports have been made of this change in Liverpool, Manchester, and Glasgow).

Some other characteristics sometimes claimed for Estuary English appear not to be based in Cockney but may be changes more generally in progress in General RP: the realization of /r/ without a tongue tip contact, i.e. [ʋ] or [ɰ], and the replacement of /s/ by /ʃ/ where it is initial in consonant clusters, e.g. *stop, stare, industry, strain, obstruct* as [ʃtɒp], [ʃtɛə], [ˈɪndʌʃtriː], [ʃtreɪn], [əbˈʃtrʌkt].

One intonational characteristic of Cockney that seems to have spread into Estuary English and even more widely is the use of the 'unknown' tag interrogative. In this the speaker uses an interrogative tag with a falling tone (which usually expects the listener to know enough to agree with the speaker) in cases where the listener clearly has no relevant knowledge, e.g. 'I was woken up at 6.30 this morning; the postman came knocking on the door, didn't he?' (with a falling tone on *did*). A similar spreading usage is that of preposition and auxiliary verb accenting, 'I didn't do anything because there was nothing TO do', 'You couldn't have seen me in London because I haven't BEEN in London'.

7.6.4 Northern English

While there is relative homogeneity in a broad Cockney accent but much less so in General American and Standard Scottish English, the label 'Northern English' is even less homogeneous (strictly speaking the label should be 'Northern England English'). We use it here simply to identify those things which the disparate pronunciations systems in the north of England have in common (and we will also mention a few characteristics which are typical only of certain areas). The area we are talking about covers that area north of a line from the river Severn to the Wash and includes Birmingham. Within this area there was a traditional dialect distinction between the north and the south of a line joining the rivers Humber in the east and Ribble in the west. Such a distinction still remains in conservative rural dialects and is shown in features like /iː/ in *night* and /æ/ in *long*.

The major identifying feature of this area is the loss of the distinction between RP /ʊ/ and /ʌ/, the single phoneme varying in quality from [ʊ] to [ɤ]. So Northern English has no distinction between *put* and *putt*, *could* and *cud* and, for many speakers, between *buck* and *book* (although others may use /uː/ in the latter word). Hypercorrections are often made by those attempting Regional RP producing, for example, *sugar* [ˈʃʌgə], *pussy* [ˈpʌsɪ], *put* [pʌt]. Almost as identifying a characteristic is the change-over in lexical incidence from /ɑː/ to /æ/ in words with a following voiceless fricative (or a nasal followed by a further consonant), as in General American, e.g. *past* /pæst/, *laugh* /læf/, *aunt* /ænt/. Another type of lexical incidence concerns the occurrence of a full vowel in prefixes where RP has /ə/, e.g. *advance* /ædˈvæns/, *consume* /kɒnˈsjuːm/ *observe*, /ɒbˈzɜːv/. The short vowels are generally realized with more open qualities than RP, e.g. *mad* [mad] and the diphthongs /eɪ/ and /əʊ/ are commonly monophthongal [eː] and [oː] as in GA and SSE (indeed sometimes, as in Newcastle, the direction of the diphthong is reversed to [eə] and [oə]). Many areas of Northern English have a fronted articulation of both /uː/ and /ɑː/ (the distinction between /æ/ and /ɑː/ being carried by length alone). Vowel incidence in the final syllable of *city, pretty, usually* etc., varies between /iː/ in, for example, Liverpool, Hull and Newcastle, and /ɪ/ in Manchester and Leeds.

Other vowel changes (compared with RP) characteristic of particular areas include the loss of the /eə/–/ɜː/ distinction in Liverpool (the local accent is called Scouse) and its common realization as [œː], e.g. both *fare* and *fur* are pronounced [fœː]; a similar neutralization and realization of /eə/ and /ɜː/ in Hull where another notable feature is the monophthongization of /əʊ/ to [ɜː]; the realization of /aʊ/ as [uː] in broad Newcastle (where the local accent is called Geordie) while /uː/ itself becomes [ɪə], e.g. *about* [əˈbuːt], *boot* [bɪət]; and the use of a particularly close /ɪ/ in Birmingham, e.g. *pit* is almost [pit], where the distinction between *pit* and *peat* will depend on length alone.

Most notable among the consonants of Northern English is the realization of /r/ as [ɾ] in a number of conurbations, including Leeds, Liverpool, and Newcastle, and the lack of the RP allophonic difference between clear [l] and dark [ɫ], clear [l] being used in all positions in many areas, e.g. Newcastle, and dark [ɫ] in others, e.g. Manchester. In a quite extensive area from Birmingham to Manchester and Liverpool the RP single consonant /ŋ/ becomes [ŋg], e.g. *singing* ['sɪŋgɪŋg]. Also, in a number of urban areas, notably south-east Lancashire, /p,t,k/ in final position (i.e. before pause) are realized as ejectives.

7.6.5 Australian English

There is little regional variation in Australian English (ANE), the variation which does occur being largely correlated with social class and ranging from a broad accent all the way up to Regional RP. The broad accent described here shares many features with Cockney, but has of course a particular combination of these and other features which identify it.

Like Cockney there are no differences of phonemic inventory from RP and no extensive classes of word involved in differences of incidence. It is the realization of long /ɑː/ as [aː] which more than any other identifies ANE, e.g. *father* ['faːðə], *part* [paːt]. Words which in RP have /ɑː/ before clusters of nasal plus another consonant, e.g. *dance, advantage, chance*, vary between /æ/ and /ɑː/ (= [aː]) in ANE; pronunciations with [aː] are by some considered prestigious, by others affected. Like Cockney /iː/ and /uː/ are realized as [əi] and [əu] and the short front vowels are all closer than RP, although [ɪ] does not occur in unaccented positions, being replaced by /iː/ word-finally and by /ə/ in other positions, e.g. *city* ['sɪtiː], *cities* ['sɪtəz]. In its diphthongs ANE is again like Cockney in having /eɪ/= [aɪ] and /aɪ/= [ɑɪ], and in having a convergence of quality of /əu/ and /au/; however, diphthongs in /ə/ are monophthongized, so /ɪə/= [ɪː], *clear* [klɪː] (leading to an accumulation of three vowels, /iː/, /ɪ/, and [ɪː] in the close front area), /eə/=[ɛː] *fare* [fɛː] while /ʊə/ is either replaced by /ɔː/ as in *sure* or becomes disyllabic as in *sewer* ['suːə/.

Although ANE does drop /h/, it does not use glottal stop nor does it vocalize /l/, having dark [ɫ] in all positions.

A particular development in ANE (and in New Zealand) which has been the subject of much discussion recently, both in newspapers and in academic journals,[12] is the increasing use of a high rising tone on declarative clauses (where a fall would normally have been expected). The meaning of this tone and the reasons behind its increased use have also been much discussed (see also §7.4.3 above and §11.6.3 below).

---

[12] Guy *et al.* (1986); Britain (1992)

8

The English Vowels

8.1 The Distinctive Vowels

A large number of vowel sounds (either relatively pure or clearly gliding in nature) have a distinctive function in RP. Their oppositional nature may be established by the commutations possible in such series as those shown in Table 2.

/iː/	heed	feel	bead	pea	
/ɪ/	hid	fill	bid		except
/e/	head	fell	bed		
/æ/	had		bad		
/ɑː/	hard		bard	par	
/ɒ/	hod		bod		
/ɔː/	hoard	fall	board	paw	
/ʊ/	hood	full			
/uː/	who'd	fool	booed	pooh	
/ʌ/			bud		
/ɜː/	heard	furl	bird	purr	
/ə/					accept
/eɪ/		fail	bayed	pay	
/aɪ/	hide	file	bide	pie	
/ɔɪ/		foil	buoyed		
/əʊ/	hoed	foal	bode	po	
/aʊ/	how'd	foul	bowed	pow	
/ɪə/			beard	peer	
/eə/	haired		bared	pair	
/ʊə/				poor	

Table 2. *Contrasts in vowels established by commutation*

A general phonetic assessment of the qualities of syllabic vowels, in terms of the Cardinal Vowels (see §4.4.2 above), may be made from the following examples, in word-final and non-final positions:

Final	Non-final	Quality	Notation
I *Short*			
city	bid	centralized, raised [e]	ɪ
—	bed	between [e] and [ɛ]	e
—	bad	just above [a]	æ
—	bod	C[ɒ]	ɒ
—	hood	centralized, raised [o]	ʊ
—	bud	central, open-mid	ʌ
sit*ter*	*acc*ept	central, mid	ə
II *Long (relatively pure)*			
pea	bead	lowered [i] or [ɪi] or [ij]	iː
pooh	booed	lowered [u] or [ʊu] or [uw]	uː
par	bard	centralized [ɑ]	ɑː
paw	board	raised [ɔ]	ɔː
purr	bird	central, mid	ɜː
III *Long (diphthongal glides, with prominent first element)*			
(a) glide to [ɪ]			
pay	fail	lowered [e] → [ɪ] above	eɪ
pie	file	between [a] and [ɑ] → [ɪ]	aɪ
coy	foil	[ɔ] → [ɪ]	ɔɪ
(b) glide to [ʊ]			
bow (archery)	bowed	[ə] above → [ʊ] above	əʊ
bough	bowed	between [a] and [ɑ] → [ʊ]	aʊ
(c) glide to open-mid [ə]			
peer	beard	[ɪ] above → [ə] above	ɪə
pair	bared	[ɛ] → [ə]	eə
poor	moored	[ʊ] → [ə]	ʊə

Notes

(1) Most people will make a considerable difference of length between the vowels in *hat, had*, and *bad* when the words are said in isolation, the vowel in *bad* being nearly as long as any of the 'long' vowels. Nevertheless, this length is not a constant distinctive feature of the vowel, but is rather dependent upon the context or is characteristic of the pronunciation of particular words (see §8.9.4). Since the short vowel is the more common and because the distribution of [æ] is like that of the other short vowels, the vowel is included in the table of short vowels.

(2) The so-called pure vowels of *bee* and *do* frequently contain a glide between two distinct elements, especially in a final position. Nevertheless, because the qualities of the elements are phonetically closely related and because a non-gliding vowel is not uncommon or thought to be un-English, these two vowels may on phonetic grounds be included in the 'long, pure' list.

(3) Some (usually older) speakers of RP pronounce *saw* and *sore* differently, using a pure vowel in saw and a diphthong ([ɔə]) in *sore*. This type of pronunciation therefore possesses an extra phoneme /ɔə/.

(4) A vowel glide [ʊɪ] exemplified by words such as *ruin, fluid, suet,* is of extremely rare occurrence within one syllable, though it may occur as a reduced form of [uː]+the suffix *-ing,* i.e. in the case of the juxtaposition of two syllables, e.g. in *doing.* The sequence [ʊ]+[ɪ] may occur across word boundaries as a result of smoothing e.g. *two in* [tʊɪn]. Since this diphthong carries such a low distinctive weight, and since it may be analysed as disyllabic, it may be regarded phonemically as a sequence of /ʊ/ plus /ɪ/.

(5) Of the short vowels, it is to be noted that [ə] occurs only in unaccented syllables.

(6) Devoicing of vowels is common in unaccented syllables between voiceless consonants. This is most likely to occur with short vowels (particularly /ə/) and before voiceless plosives, e.g. the first syllables of *capitulate, circumference, potato, fatigue* and the second syllables of *footpath, quantity, guidebook.*

8.2   *Vowel Glides with a Non-Prominent First Element*

We find that the sounds (semi-vowels) [j] and [w] regularly occur in positions preceding most of the above basic vocalic elements:

[j+ɪ]	Yiddish	[w+ɪ]	wit
[j+e]	yet	[w+e]	wet
[j+æ]	yap	[w+æ]	wax
[j+ɒ]	yacht	[w+ɒ]	watch
[j+ʊ]	you (*weak form*)	[w+ʊ]	wood
[j+ʌ]	young	[w+ʌ]	won
[j+ə]	failure	[w+ə]	were (*unaccented*)
[j+iː]	yeast	[w+iː]	week
[j+uː]	youth	[w+uː]	woo
[j+ɑː]	yard	[w+ɑː]	waft (*one pronunciation*)
[j+ɔː]	yawn	[w+ɔː]	wall
[j+ɜː]	yearn	[w+ɜː]	word
[j+eɪ]	yea	[w+eɪ]	way
[j+aɪ]	—	[w+aɪ]	wide
[j+ɔɪ]	yoicks	[w+ɔɪ]	quoit
[j+əʊ]	yeoman	[w+əʊ]	woe
[j+aʊ]	yowl	[w+aʊ]	wound
[j+ɪə]	year	[w+ɪə]	weir
[j+eə]	(Yare)	[w+eə]	wear
[j+ʊə]	lure	[w+ʊə]	—

Since [j] and [w] are often purely vocalic from a phonetic standpoint, being rapid vocalic glides from [i] and [u] positions, it is possible to consider their combination with other vowels as constituting:

(a) a rising diphthong, in the case of [j] or [w] followed by a short vowel or long, relatively pure, vowel, i.e. vowel glides in which the second element rather than the first is the more prominent;

(b) a triphthong, in the case of [j] or [w] followed by a vocalic glide, i.e. a vowel glide in which there are three vocalic elements, the central one being most prominent.

Nevertheless, since such combinations affect almost all our previously established basic vowels and glides, it would add enormously to our inventory of basic vowels if we were to include these combinations in our list. Moreover, these [j] and [w] elements function very much as if they were consonants, marginally rather than centrally in a syllable, and, indeed, in cases such as the [j] in *tune* or the [w] in *queen* tend to be voiceless and to have the friction which is phonetically characteristic of a consonant. For these reasons, it is more convenient to treat initial [j] and [w] as separate from the vocalic nucleus of the syllable and to include them in the list of consonants.

Note

It is possible, in the same way, to express the brief [ɪ] and [ʊ] elements occurring post-centrally in the diphthongal glides as consonantal /j,w/ following a simple syllabic element. Thus, if [iː] and [uː] are interpreted as glides and [ʊɪ] similarly included, the following statement may be made: [iː]=/ij/; [eɪ]=/ej/; [aɪ]=/aj/; [ɔɪ]=/ɔj/; [ʊɪ]=/ʊj/; [əʊ]=/əw/; [aʊ]=/aw/; [uː]=/uw/, with, in addition, the following possibilities of /j/ or /w/ preceding and following the central syllabic element: /jij,wij,jej,wej,waj,jɔj,wɔj,jəw,wəw,waw,juw,wuw/. In the present treatment of RP vowels, however, such post-central [ɪ,ʊ] elements are regarded as vocalic rather than consonantal because:

(i) they do not have a distribution after all vocalic elements as general as that which we find in the case of pre-central /j,w/;

(ii) they are in RP very weakly articulated (compared with pre-central /j,w/) and may correspond to monophthongal pronunciations in many other accents, cf. [eɪ] and [eː] or [ɛː];

(iii) they have none of the fricative (phonetically consonantal) allophones characteristic of pre-central /j,w/ following /p,t,k/.

8.3   *Glides to* [ə]

Similarly, glides to [ə] are treated here as composite vocalic units, since in general RP [ə] combines with a syllabic vowel element only after [ɪ,ɛ,ʊ] and may with some RP speakers be realized merely as an extension of the preceding syllabic vowel element.

8.4   *Vowel Length*

8.4.1   Phonetic Relationships

There are phonetic relationships between short and long vowels in English, as illustrated by the following words:

bid and *bead*	/ɪ–iː/
good and *food*	/ʊ–uː/
cad and *card*	/æ–ɑː/
cod and *cord*	/ɒ–ɔː/
(for)ward and *word*	/ə–ɜː/

Notes

(a) Only in the case of /ə/–/ɜː/ can there be said to exist an opposition solely of length and even in this case it has to be stated that /ə/ occurs only in unaccented syllables, whereas /ɜː/ can occur in syllables carrying primary or secondary accent.

(b) In the other cases the opposition between the members of the pairs is a complex of quality and quantity; and of the two factors it is likely that quality carries the greater contrastive weight. Indeed, in the particular case of the *cad/card* opposition, both vowels may be equally long.

(c) In a transcription which sets out to show explicitly certain phonetic characteristics, it would seem advisable to indicate especially the qualitative opposition, at the same time noting quantity by means of the length mark.

(d) Such insistence on purely phonetic characteristics, as compared with what is phonemically relevant, is justified when variations of vowel length are taken into consideration. In accented syllables the so-called long vowels are fully long when they are final or in a syllable closed by a voiced consonant, but they are considerably shortened when they occur in a syllable closed by a voiceless consonant. Thus:

/iː/ in *beat* is only about half as long as the /iː/ of *bee* or *bead* and may, in fact, be of approximately the same length (duration) as the /ɪ/ vowel of *bid*;

/uː/ in *boot* is only about half as long as the /uː/ of *do* or *food* and has about the same duration as the /ʊ/ vowel in *good*;

/ɔː/ in *caught* is only about half as long as the /ɔː/ in *cord* or *saw* and has about the same duration as the /ɒ/ in *cod*.

The length of /ɜː/ and /ɑː/ varies in the same way before voiceless and voiced, although the length relationships to /ə/ and /æ/ are more complex because /ə/ only occurs in unaccented syllables, and because of the varying length of /æ/ mentioned in §8.1, note (1).

(e) The same considerable shortening before voiceless consonants applies also to the diphthongs, cf.

play, played, plate
row, road, wrote
tie, tide, tight
cow, loud, shout
boy, noise, voice
fear, fears, fierce
scare, scares, scarce

(f) Since voiced /m,n,ŋ,l/ do not have voiceless counterparts, the variation of length in the preceding vowel does not apply when they close a syllable (/ŋ/ only closes syllables containing a short vowel).

(g) One study[1] showed the duration of English vowels in different phonetic contexts as follows (measured in csec in accented monosyllables):

	Word-final	+voiced C	+nasal C	+voiceless C
Short vowels		17.2	13.3	10.3
Long vowels	30.6	31.9	23.3	16.5
Diphthongs		35.7	26.5	17.8

(i) /æ/ is not included here in the category of short vowels, because of the special length often associated with it (see §8.1, note (1) and §8.9.4), but is classified separately as 'neutral'. The following are the measurements for /æ/: +voiced fricative, 25.2 csec; +voiced plosive, 21.6 csec; +nasal, 19.6 csec; +voiceless fricative, 16.5 csec; +voiceless plosive, 15.0 csec.

(ii) An example of the relationship of two vowels phonetically paired (/iː/–/ɪ/) shows the following typical descending durations: /iː/+voiced fricative, 36.0 csec; /iː/+voiced plosive, 28.5 csec; /iː/ final (not including words like *city*, which vacillate in RP between final /ɪ/ and /iː/), 28.0 csec; /iː/+nasal, 19.5 csec; /ɪ/+voiced fricative, 18.6 csec; /ɪ/+voiced plosive, 14.7 csec; /iː/+voiceless fricative, 13.0 csec; /iː/+voiceless plosive, 12.3 csec; /ɪ/+nasal, 11.0 csec; /ɪ/+voiceless fricative, 8.3 csec; /ɪ/+voiceless plosive, 7.3 csec.

Thus, it will be seen that /iː/ is typically shorter in a word such as *seat* (12.3 csec.) than /ɪ/ in a word such as *hid* (14.7 csec.).

(h) The difference between the long and the short vowels of English is sometimes alternatively referred to as an opposition between tense and lax, reflecting the fact that the short vowels are articulated with less muscular tension. Sometimes also the difference is related to the distinction between Advanced Tongue Root (+ATR) and Retracted Tongue Root (+RTR) (or non-Advanced Tongue Root, –ATR), which is commonly used to distinguish different sets of vowels in a number of African languages (e.g. Igbo); no confirming instrumental evidence has been put forward to support such different tongue root positions.

8.4.2   Morphophonemic Alternations

Another type of length relationship is that between the vowels in the root morpheme of cognate words. Thus the root morpheme *divin* in *divine* and *divinity* displays a relationship (called a MORPHOPHONEMIC ALTERNATION between the long vowel /aɪ/ and the short vowel /ɪ/). Originally this was an alternation between a short and a long vowel of the same quality, the alternation resulting from the different rhythmic structure of the two words (it will be noted that the shorter words generally have the long vowel and the longer words the short vowel). So in the case of the morpheme *divin* the alternation was between long [iː] and short [i]. However, historically, the long vowels underwent the Great Vowel Shift (see §6.2.1), so that the correspondences are no longer between vowels of the same quality. The change in vowel is sometimes accompanied by a change in the

---

[1] Wiik (1965)

position of the accent, e.g. *im`ply–impli`cation.* The relationship between pairs of vowels has remained productive, so that some recently imported words fall into the same patterns, e.g. *`microscope–micro`scopic* under (d) below. Five types of alternation are common:

(a) /aɪ/–/ɪ/ *divine–divinity, wise–wisdom, wide–width, five–fifty, type–typical, derive–derivative, sublime–sublimation, suffice–sufficient, divide–division, precise–precision, bible–biblical, wild–wilderness, reconcile–reconciliation, vice–vicious, recite–recitation, vile–villainy, deride–derision;*

(b) /iː/–/e/ *hero–heroine, serene–serenity, athlete–athletic, sheep–shepherd, intervene–intervention, extreme–extremity, obscene–obscenity, supreme–supremacy, compete–competitive, sincere–sincerity, discrete–discretion;*

(c) /eɪ/–/æ/ *sane–sanity, exclaim–exclamatory, chaste–chastity, volcano–volcanic, profane–profanity, urbane–urbanity, explain–explanatory, grateful–gratitude;*

(d) /əʊ/–/ɒ/ *mediocre–mediocrity, joke–jocular, diagnose–diagnostic, microscope–microscopic, neurosis–neurotic, episode–episodic, phone–phonic, nose–nostril, globe–globular, atrocious–atrocity, mode–modular;*

(e) /aʊ/–/ʌ/ *pronounce–pronunciation, profound–profundity, abound–abundant, south–southern, found–fundamental.*

Although such alternations are common, it is also the case that the short or the long vowel is often generalized to both forms, e.g. *desire–desirable, denote–denotation, promote–promotion.*

8.5   *Transcriptions of English Vowels*

The principles underlying the construction of a set of symbols to represent the phonemes of a language were discussed in §5.4, where we noted that even basing ourselves on one phonetic alphabet (in this case, the IPA) it was possible to arrive at different sets of symbols. The main reason for this difference lies in the degree of application of the principle of Romanization, i.e. the degree to which symbols giving phonetic detail about the most frequent allophone are replaced by their nearest Roman symbols, e.g. /r/ for /ɹ/ in *red.* The transcription of vowels in this present book does not carry the Romanization principle very far, i.e. it continues to show the phonetic quality of vowels in its choice of symbols; thus for example, using the Romanization principle, we could replace the /ɒ/ in *pot* by /o/ since we are not already using the latter symbol elsewhere, but this is not done because we wish to show that RP /ɒ/ is a rounded open vowel. The sort of transcription of vowels used here is called comparative phonemic (see §5.4) because it seeks to be phonetically explicit for the purposes of comparing English with other languages.

Variation in the sets of symbols which have been used to represent RP vowels has ranged from the comparative phonemic of the present book to a simple phonemic transcription where the Romanization principle is fully implemented. Such a simple phonemic system has been popular at various times and uses /iː,i,e,a,aː,o,oː,u,uː,ʌ,ə,əː,ei,ai,oi,ou,au,iə,eə,uə/ for the 20 vowels listed in §8.1. A variation on these symbols uses double letters instead of the length mark to indicate long vowels, e.g. /aa/ instead of /aː/ in *card*. Almost all other transcriptions of RP vowels represent some degree of Romanization lying between this fully Romanized transcription and the comparative phonemic of the present book. Only a few variations represent other factors; for example /e/ in *set* is sometimes transcribed by /ɛ/; this represents a judgement about the quality of the vowel, implying that it is nearer C3 than C2 (see further under §8.9.3) as does variation in the transcription of the first element of /əʊ/ as /oʊ/ (or, more commonly, /ou/), which again is a deliberate attempt to represent a different pronunciation (see under §8.10.4).

Transcriptions of English vowels in books on linguistics, phonology, and phonetics published in North America show further differences from those published in Britain. Firstly, of course, differences in pronunciation between RP and GA are represented (GA has no /ɒ, ɪə, eə, ʊə/ (see §7.6.1)), and secondly, in the representation of monophthongal realizations of the vowels in *play* and *goat* as /e/ and /o/ (which enforces the representation of the equivalent of RP /e/ in *set* as /ɛ/). Otherwise differences between British and American ways of transcribing vowels represent different traditions. Hence length in GA may be indicated by a macron, e.g. /ū/ rather than /iː/ and the second element in closing diphthongs is shown as /j/ or /w/, e.g. /aj/ for /aɪ/ and /əw/ for /əʊ/ (this usage was discussed in §8.2).

In conclusion, the transcription of the vowels of RP used in this book is clearly of the comparative phonemic sort. It uses vowel symbols which are to some extent indicative of the usual qualities of those vowels. Thus the short vowels /ɪ,æ,ɒ,ʊ,ə/ are given different symbols from the long vowels /iː,ɑː,ɔː,uː,ɜː/ to show that they are different in quality as well as length. At the same time the length mark is still used with the long vowels. Such a transcription is of course redundant in indicating a difference between pairs of phonemes in two ways, quality

Pure vowels				
	F1		F2	
	Male	*Female*	*Male*	*Female*
/iː/	275	319	2221	2723
/ɪ/	382	432	1958	2296
/e/	560	645	1797	2287
/æ/	732	1011	1527	1759
/ʌ/	695	813	1224	1422
/ɑː/	687	779	1077	1181
/ɒ/	593	602	866	994
/ɔː/	453	431	642	799
/ʊ/	414	414	1051	1203
/uː/	302	339	1131	1396
/ɜː/	513	650	1377	1593

Table 3. *Formant frequencies for RP (relatively) pure vowels (in citation form)*

Diphthongs								
	First component				*Second component*			
	F1		*F2*		*F1*		*F2*	
	Male	*Female*	*Male*	*Female*	*Male*	*Female*	*Male*	*Female*
/eɪ/	587	581	1945	2241	413	416	2130	2204
/aɪ/	734	822	1117	1275	439	359	2058	2591
/ɔɪ/	477	428	824	879	443	334	1924	2520
/əʊ/	537	545	1266	1573	379	380	1024	1267
/aʊ/	780	901	1368	1538	372	403	1074	1088
/ɪə/	382	399	2096	2514	578	417	1643	1846
/eə/	538	691	1864	2210	655	751	1594	1883
/ʊə/	426	420	1028	1157	587	485	1250	1258

Table 4. *Formant frequencies for RP diphthongs (in citation form)*

Pure vowels				
	F1		*F2*	
	Male	*Female*	*Male*	*Female*
/iː/	280	303	2249	2654
/ɪ/	367	384	1757	2174
/e/	494	719	1650	2063
/æ/	690	1018	1550	1799
/ʌ/	644	914	1259	1459
/ɑː/	646	910	1155	1316
/ɒ/	558	751	1047	1215
/ɔː/	415	389	828	888
/ʊ/	379	410	1173	1340
/uː/	316	328	1191	1437
/ɜː/	478	606	1436	1695

Table 5. *Formant frequencies for RP (relatively) pure vowels in connected speech*

and length. Yet it is considered important to use a transcription which reflects the fact that these factors are assumed to be equally important in maintaining the contrasts between the vowels.

8.6 *Acoustics of RP Vowels*

Figs 8 and 9 show spectrograms of the RP relatively pure vowels and diphthongs respectively. Tables 3 and 4 give average values in RP for the first and second formants of RP pure vowels and diphthongs in citation form (in monophthongal words, mostly in the frame h–d); while Table 5 gives the same information for

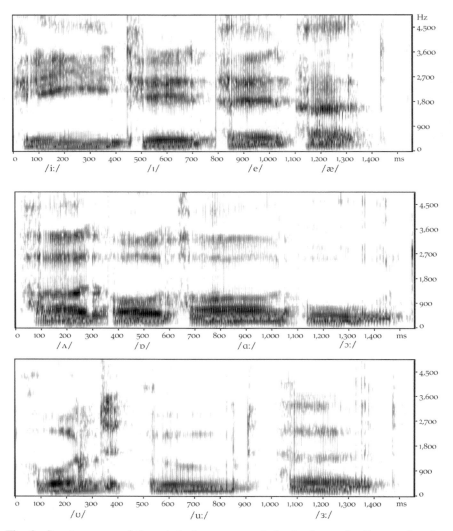

Fig. 8. *Spectrograms of the relatively pure vowels in the frame /h–d/ as spoken by a male speaker of RP.*

the RP pure vowels in connected speech. The values in Table 3 are averages from eight male and eight female speakers; those in Table 4 are averages from three males and three females; while those in Table 5 are from ten males and ten females.[2] Even though all the informants were speakers of RP, some showed

---

[2] Values for Tables 3 and 5 are taken from Deterding (1990, 1997). Those in Table 4 were computed in the Phonetics Laboratory, Department of Linguistics, University of Manchester; details can be obtained from the author

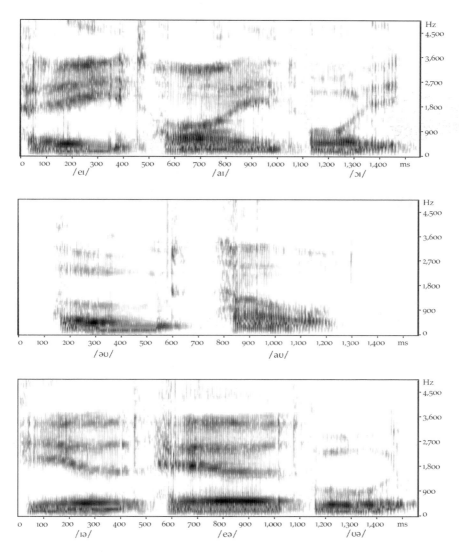

Fig. 9. *Spectrograms of the diphthongs in the frame h–d as spoken by a male speaker of RP.*

a slight influence from other accents: in particular, in Table 3 one male and one female showed slight London influence; in Table 4, two males and one female again showed similar influence from the London region; in Table 5 one speaker showed similar influence from the north of England. The spread of values from which the averages are computed is in general greater for the females than for the males. There are no figures for /ə/, whose quality varies greatly according to phonetic environment, and whose average values may be taken to be equivalent

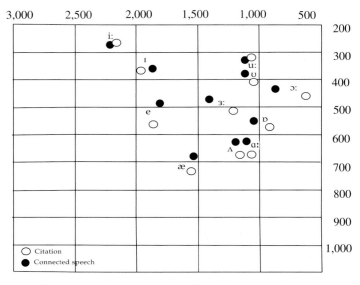

Fig. 10. *Formant frequencies for RP pure vowels said in citation from and in connected speech (male speakers).*

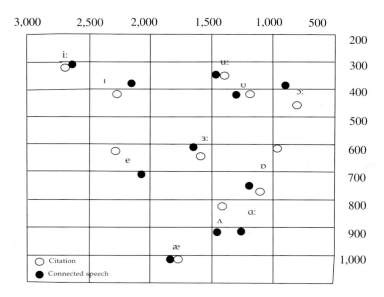

Fig. 11. *Formant frequencies for RP pure vowels said in citation from and in connected speech (female speakers).*

to those for /ɜː/. A comparison of the values for citation forms and those for connected speech shows that the values for connected speech represent vowels considerably less peripheral (more centralized) in articulatory terms. This can be seen from Figs 10 and 11 which compare the values for pure vowels in citation form and in connected speech on vowel quadrilaterals, one for the male speakers and one for the female speakers. These figures also demonstrate the much higher formant values for female speakers.

8.7   *Learning of Vowels*

8.7.1   Acquisition of Vowels by Native Learners

A striking fact about children's acquisition of their first language is that the vowel system, even one as complicated as that of English, is complete far earlier than the consonant system. In most children the full range of vowel phonemes is being produced by the age of two and a half years (2;5) and in many cases earlier. Because of the fast speed of development it is impossible to be very precise about any regular sequence of acquisition. During the period of babbling (approximately the latter half of the first year of life) an open vowel of the [a] type predominates and this continues into the first words (which usually occur around the age of 0;9–1;6). Vowels maximally differentiated from [a] (= /æ/) are likely to occur next, e.g. /iː/ and /uː/. Otherwise it is predictable that among the last vowel distinctions to be acquired will be those which are articulatorily closest together, e.g. /e/ vs /æ/ vs /ʌ/, /iː/ vs /ɪ/, /uː/ vs /ʊ/, /ɔː/ vs /əʊ/.

8.7.2   Advice to Foreign Learners

Many foreign learners come from backgrounds where their L1 has only five vowels, e.g. Greek, Hindi, Japanese, Spanish, and most Bantu languages. Russian also has five vowel phonemes though there is a great deal of variation within these phonemes, and some varieties of Italian have five, although seven is the more common. Five is the largest category of vowel system in the world's languages with those with six vowels and seven vowels being the next two most common.[3] In whatever way the vowels of English are counted (i.e. even counting some or all of the diphthongs as sequences of short vowel plus semi-vowel (= consonant)), the English system is one of the less common and more complex types. It is therefore completely predictable that most foreign learners will have trouble attaining the vowel system of any variety of English, including RP. Difficulty is most predictable in those areas where vowels are closest within the vowel space; thus confusions are very likely within any of the following groups: /iː,ɪ/, /e,æ,ʌ/, /ɒ,ɑː,ɔː/, /uː,ʊ/. These confusions and others may be reinforced or induced by English spelling or by the use of the Roman alphabet in the spelling of other languages: the letter <o> may represent a vowel around C[o] in the L1

---

[3] Maddieson (1984: 126) estimates 21.5% as having five vowels, 13.6% six vowels, 10.7% seven vowels, with only 4.1% having over 17

and hence the English diphthong /əʊ/ may be given a quality which leads to confusion with /ɔː/. The presence of an <r> in the spelling of /ɪə,eə,ʊə/ may lead to the pronunciation of a short vowel plus an /r/. In many languages the letter <a> commonly represents a vowel between C4 and C5; hence it may be given that quality in English, leading to confusions between /æ/ and /ʌ/. Because of such difficulties with the RP vowel system, foreign learners may need to set the more attainable target of Minimum General Intelligibility (see §13.6).

8.8   *Description of the Vowels*

In the following detailed descriptions the RP vowel phonemes will be treated in a sequence based upon their quality relationships, i.e.

/iː,ɪ,e,æ,ʌ,ɑː,ɒ,ɔː,ʊ,uː,ɜː,ə/
/eɪ,aɪ,ɔɪ,əʊ,aʊ/
/ɪə,eə,ʊə/

The treatment of each vowel will include:

(1) Illustrations of the common spellings associated with each vowel, together with words illustrating the main allophonic variants. Such variation principally concerns length variations occasioned by the shortening of vowels before voiceless consonants; a feature which is most obviously apparent in long vowels and diphthongs. Quality variation shows up principally before dark [ɫ]. Additionally in this section words are given to highlight relationships with auditorily adjacent vowels.

(2) An articulatory description and an assessment of quality in relation to the Cardinal Vowels. (In all cases, unless otherwise stated, the soft palate will be assumed to be in its raised position, the vocal folds vibrating, and the tongue tip behind the lower teeth.) Remarks on distributional features in the word and syllable.

(3) Indications of some of the chief variants—both within RP and regionally. These are also shown on vowel diagrams, on which the General RP realizations are marked with a *.

(4) Remarks on the principal historical sources of the vowel.

(5) Difficulties encountered by foreign learners, with appropriate advice.

8.9   *(Relatively) Pure Vowels*[4]

8.9.1   /iː/

(1) *Examples*
    ee—tree, cheese, canteen
    e—complete, be, these
    ea—leaf, reason, sea

---

[4] In the vowel diagrams * indicates principal RP realizations. For meanings of abbreviations in the sections on chief sources see §6.2

ie—piece, field, siege
ei, ey—seize, key, receive
i—machine, police, prestige, suite
(*Note* /iː/ in 'quay, people'.)

Spellings in <e>, <e..e>, and <ee> have a lexical frequency of 64%, those in <ea> have a lexical frequency of 20%, and those in <i>, <i..e> and <ie> 11%. The text frequencies are 64%, 25% and 7% respectively.

Long [iː]—see, seed, seen; fee, feed, fees
Reduced [i]—seat, feet, piece, lease, beef, reach
Compare [iː], [i]—bead, beat; seize, cease; leave, leaf; liege, leash; Eden, eaten
[ɫ] following—feel, meal, field, eels
Variation between /iː/–/ɪ/ *finally*—city, lady, sloppy, happy, charity, memory

(2) *Description*—The front of the tongue is raised to a height slightly below and behind the front close position; the lips are spread; the tongue is tense, with the side rims making a firm contact with the upper molars. The quality is nearer to C[i] (with the glide mentioned below) than to C[e]. /iː/ does not normally occur in a syllable closed by /ŋ/.

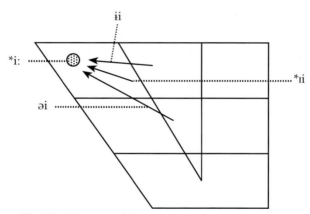

Fig. 12. *Variants of* /iː/.

(3) *Variants*[5]—The vowel is often noticeably diphthongized, especially in final positions. A slight glide from a position near to [ɪ] is common amongst RP speakers, being more usual than a pure vowel. Any glide having a starting point in the central area is, however, dialectal, that is, characteristic of a regional accent; a glide of the type [ɨi] is characteristic of the local pronunciation of Liverpool and Birmingham, whereas a lower central starting point may be heard in Cockney (and Refined RP) and many other dialects. The use of a pure vowel in a final

---

[5] On all the figures for vowels the principal RP realizations are marked with a *

position is also typical of Refined RP. In Standard Scottish English, this vowel generally does not have the length characteristic of RP and is not, therefore, subject to the same tendency to diphthongization.

Among many speakers of RP /iː/ is increasingly used finally in words like *city, lady, sloppy, happy* etc. See further under (3) and (5) for /ɪ/ below.

(4) *Chief sources*—(a) Many of the words now said with /iː/ have had this vowel since at least 1500; these are frequently spelt with *ee* or *ie*. Such words are those which in OE had a long vowel in the region of C[e] (*cheese, sleeve*); or had developed C[eː] from a diphthong [eːə] (*deep, thief*); or from a more open vowel near C[ɛː] (*deed, needle*); or from [øː] (*geese, green*), or from a lengthening of [ɪ] in an originally open syllable (*week*) or [ɛ] before [ɫd] (*field*). Some other words represent a development from OF [ie] through AN [eː] (*siege, niece, grief*).

Foreign words with [iː], adopted after the English [iː] vowel from the above sources had become established, fell in with the usual pronunciation of *ee* in English and sometimes changed their spelling from *i* to *ee* (*esteem, canteen; machine, routine*).

(b) Another group of words, frequently spelt now with *ea*, finally developed [iː] at about the end of the seventeenth century. Their chief origins are: an OE long vowel in the region of C[ɛː] (*sea, leave, teach*); an OE diphthong [ɛːə] (*leaf, stream, east*); an OE short [ɛ] lengthened in originally open syllables (*meat, eat*); and, in addition, a large number of words from OF [ai,ɛi] through AN [ɛː] (*please, eager, season, peace*).

(5) *Advice to foreign learners*—This vowel should give little difficulty to foreign learners, all of whom will have in their language a vowel of approximately the same quality. Their own vowel may not have the diphthongization which is typical of RP, but they should attempt to imitate this glide only with caution, since any exaggeration will sound dialectal. More important is the reduction of length before voiceless consonants, as exemplified above, since the differentiation between two words such as *seize* and *cease* is achieved more by the variation of the vowel length than by the quality of the final consonant. The reduced form of the vowel should, however, remain relatively tense and not be confused with [ɪ].

8.9.2   /ɪ/

(1) *Examples*
  i—fifth, rich, sit, with
  y—city, rhythm, symbol
  e—pretty, needed, wicket, wicked, except, careless, houses
  ie—ladies, cities
  a—village, private
  (*Note* 'build' /bɪld/, 'Sunday' /ˈsʌndɪ/ (and the other days of the week), 'business' /ˈbɪznɪs/, 'women' /ˈwɪmɪn/, 'minute' (n.) /ˈmɪnɪt/, 'England' /ˈɪŋɡlənd/.)

Spellings in <i> have a lexical frequency of 61%, those in <y> have a lexical frequency of 21%, and those in <e> one of 16%. The text frequencies are almost identical.

Compare [iː], /ɪ/—feel, fill; seen, sin; bead, bid
[i], /ɪ/—least, list; reach, rich; sheep, ship; week, wick; feet, fit
[iː], [i], /ɪ/—seed, seat, sit; league, leak, lick; seized, ceased, cyst
[ɫ] *following*—will, hill, milk, built, film, kiln
Variation between /iː/–/ɪ/*finally*—city, lady, sloppy, happy, charity, memory

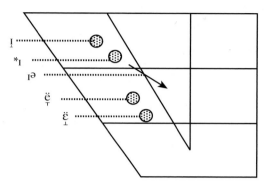

Fig. 13. *Variants of /ɪ/.*

(2) *Description*—The short RP vowel /ɪ/ is pronounced with a part of the tongue nearer to centre than to front raised just above the close-mid position; the lips are loosely spread; the tongue is lax (compared with the tension for /iː/), with the side rims making a light contact with the upper molars. The quality is that of a centralized C[e]=[ë]. /ɪ/ may occur in all positions in the word.

The degree of closeness and centralization varies according to the accentual force falling upon the vowel and its position in the word (cf. the realizations of /ɪ/ in the word *visibility*, those of syllables 1 and 3 being near to the sound described above, those of syllables 2 and 4 being somewhat more centralized, and that of the final syllable showing considerable variation from lower than close-mid (and even open-mid for Refined RP) at one extreme to something well above close-mid at the other). Indeed, in such final unaccented positions, e.g. in *city, lady, memory, coffee*, /ɪ/ is increasingly replaced by a short variety of /iː/ by many speakers. (The contrast between /ɪ/ and /iː/ is in any case neutralized in word-final position, so no ambiguity arises from such pronunciations.) The latest editions of standard pronouncing dictionaries transcribe such words with [i] and thus avoid equating it either with /ɪ/ or /iː/.[6]

A trend towards /ə/ in non-final unaccented syllables, traditionally having /ɪ/, is becoming increasingly noticeable among RP speakers of the middle and younger generations.

(a) In some terminations, /ə/ is now more common than /ɪ/, e.g.
-ity: /-əti/ rather than /-ɪti/ as in *sincerity, quality* etc.
-itive: /-ətɪv/ rather than /-ɪtɪv/ as in *positive, fugitive* etc.

---

[6] Jones (1997); Wells (2000)

-ily: /-əlɪ/ rather than /-ɪlɪ/ (especially after /r/) as in *merrily, primarily* and also *easily, happily* etc.

-ate: often /-ət/ rather than /-ɪt/ as in *fortunate, chocolate* etc. (Words such as *magistrate, candidate* sometimes also have /-eɪt/ as a third possibility).

-ible: /-əbl/ (as for *-able*) rather than /-ɪbl/ as in *possible, visible* etc.

-em: /-əm/ rather than /-ɪm/ or /-em/ as in *problem, system, item* etc.

(b) In the case of other weak syllables, both /ɪ/ and /ə/ are heard from RP speakers, e.g. *-ess*: /-ɪs/ or /-əs/ as in *useless, goodness* (/-əs/ being preferred by the younger generation); in cases where *-ess* is strongly felt as a feminine suffix, e.g. *goddess* /-es/, may be used.

-ace: /-ɪs/ or /-əs/ as in *necklace, palace, preface*, with an increasing tendency to /-əs/.

(c) In other cases, /ɪ/ remains dominant, e.g. *-age*: predominantly /-ɪdʒ/ in *manage, village* etc. (Recent French borrowings such as *barrage, camouflage* etc., tend to have /-ɑː(d)ʒ/.)

-et: predominantly /-ɪt/ especially following /k,g,tʃ,dʒ/ as in *pocket, target, hatchet, budget* etc. However, the endings *-let, -ret* often have /-ət/, as in *bracelet, scarlet, claret, garret* etc.

be: /ɪ/ is more common than /ə/, as in *begin, between, become* (though in *believe, belong, behave* etc., /ə/ is often heard).

(*Note* Although *se-*, as in *sedition, select*, may sometimes have /sə-/ rather than the more usual /sɪ-/, *de-*, as in *deposit, deny, desire*, . . . etc., is almost invariably with /dɪ-/)

In the preceding cases, no significant oppositions between /ɪ/ and /ə/ were involved. Where an opposition exists, it might be expected that there would be some pressure to retain the /ɪ/–/ə/ distinction, as in the inflected forms *offices* /-ɪz/ v. *officers* /-əz/ or *chatted* /-ɪd/ v. *chattered* /-əd/. The neutralization of this opposition is typical of several non-RP forms of English, but the opposition is still generally maintained by RP speakers. On the other hand, potential oppositions between /ɪ/ and /ə/ in pairs such as *effect, affect* and *except, accept* are commonly lost in favour of /ə/.

(3) *Variants*—Some Refined RP speakers—especially those using the type of speech which has the [ë] variety in unaccented syllables—will diphthongize /ɪ/ towards [ə] particularly in accented monosyllables, e.g. in *big, did, thin, wish* etc.

Regionally the use of a very close /ɪ/(=[i̇]), occurring in all positions, should be noted as particularly characteristic of Birmingham speech. As noted in the previous section word-final /ɪ/ has now generally been replaced by a shortened form of /iː/ (=[i]) in RP; this has also happened regionally throughout the south of England and the Midlands, while in the north the cities are divided between the two possibilities, with Liverpool and Newcastle having /iː/ and Manchester and Leeds having /ɪ/.

(4) *Chief sources*—As is the case with many of the PresE short vowels, /ɪ/ has shown considerable stability since OE. The OE forms of words such as *ship, quick, give, drink, this, smith* etc., probably had vowels similar in quality to that of RP /ɪ/. PresE /ɪ/ also derives from OE [iː] (*wisdom, bliss*); from OE [y] (*king, kiss, bridge*); from OF [i] (*rich, simple, mirror, prison*). In addition, OE or OF [e]+nasal consonant has often given PresE /ɪ/ (*England, string, ink, chimney*).

In unaccented syllables many new cases of /ɪ/ have arisen, notably from [ɛ] in suffixes such as *-es, -ed, -ness, -less, -est* (*horses, waited, kindness, hopeless,* *biggest*); from formerly accented syllables with [ɛ] or [aː] (*hostess, prophet, village, Highgate, orange*); from [ɛ] in prefixes and in unaccented medial syllables (*describe, enquire, despite, before, declare, expect, elegant, benefit*); from earlier diphthongs (*forfeit, sovereign, fountain, journey*).

(5) *Advice to foreign learners*—It is very important that a proper qualitative relationship should be maintained between /iː/ and /ɪ/. Many languages have a short variety of [i], e.g. French, Italian, but one which is likely to be too tense and close for the English /ɪ/; others, e.g. Polish, Russian, have a centralized type of [ɪ] which has too much of an [ə] quality for English; still more, e.g. German, have a type of [ɪ] near to the English variety but yet often still too tense. Speakers of those languages which possess a vowel of the C[e] type (which is approximately on the same level as the English /ɪ/) should modify this sound in the direction of [ə]; alternatively, a [y] sound, as in French *but*, said with relaxed spread lips, will come near to the English /ɪ/ as in *bit*.

Of equal importance is the quantitative relationship of /iː/ and /ɪ/. Once the correct quality of /ɪ/ has been acquired, most learners can distinguish *bead* [biːd] from *bid* [bɪd], where the distinction is a complex of quality and quantity. But an opposition of the sort *beat* [bit]–*bit* /bɪt/, where the difference of vowel length is insignificant, is more difficult. Three types of vowel should, therefore, be practised: close, tense, long [iː] (*bead*); close, tense, short [i] (*beat*), and the half-close, lax, short [ɪ] (*bit, bid*), as in the comparative examples given in (1) above.

Less commonly there may be confusion between /ɪ/ and /e/, e.g. by speakers of Arabic, when the advice should be to make /ɪ/ more like a very short form of /eɪ/.

The fact that /ɪ/ occurs very frequently in unaccented syllables should also be noted, since an unreduced vowel in the weak syllables of words such as *village, waited, fountain, describe* may seriously deform the accentual pattern. The learner may use either [i] (i.e. a shortened from of /iː/) or /ɪ/ for the ending <y> in *pity, ability, memory* etc.

8.9.3 /e/

(1) *Examples*
  e—bed, set, went
  ea—breath, dead, head
  a—many, Thames
  (*Note* the following words with /e/—'says, said, bury, Geoffrey' /ˈdʒefrɪ/, 'Leicester' /ˈlestə/, 'friend', 'ate' /et/, 'again' /əˈgen/ or /əˈgeɪn/.)

The lexical frequency of the spelling <e> for /e/ is 96% and that of <ea> 3%; the text frequencies are 84% and 6% respectively.

  Compare /ɪ/, /e/—sit, set; tin, ten; will, well; disk, desk
  /iː/, /ɪ/, /e/—neat, knit, net; reach, rich, wretch; reed, rid, red; feel, fill, fell
  [ł] *following*—well, sell, else, health, elm, held

(2) *Description*—For the short RP /e/, the front of the tongue is raised between the close-mid and open-mid positions; the lips are loosely spread and

are slightly wider apart than for /ɪ/; the tongue may have more tension than in the case of /ɪ/, the side rims making a light contact with the upper molars. The quality lies between that of C[e] and that of C[ɛ]=[ȩ,] or [ɛ̢]. /e/ does not occur in final, open, syllables, although in word-final position in Refined RP and in some dialects the quality of /ɪ/ may encroach on that of /e/.

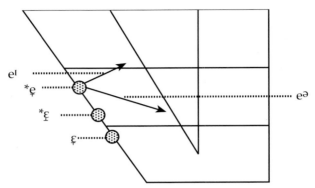

Fig. 14. *Variants of /e/.*

(3) *Variants*—The general RP variety of /e/ tends to be closer to C[ɛ] than to C[e]. An /e/ with a quality approaching C[e] is typical of Refined RP, as is a diphthong from this position in the direction of /ə/, e.g. *men, said, get* pronounced as [meᵊn, seᵊd, geᵊt]. Such diphthongization is often characterized as 'affected'.

A closer variety of /e/ is also heard in Australia, and in Cockney, where it may additionally involve a glide towards [ɪ]. This is particularly apparent where /e/ is in its longer form before voiced consonants, e.g. *bed, leg* [beᶦd, leᶦg]. A more open type of /e/ at or slightly below C[ɛ] is used in the north of England.

(4) *Chief sources*—The majority of PresE /e/ forms can be traced to: OE [ɛ] (*bed, neck, edge, best*); shortened OE [eː] (*fed, met*); OE [eːə] (*theft, friend*); OE [æː] (*let, ever, flesh*); eModE shortening of ME [ɛː] (*bread, death, deaf*); OE [y] (*bury, merry*)—the Kentish [ɛ] form having been adopted; OF [ɛ] (*debt, press, accept, second, member*). Some modern /e/ forms previously vacillated between /e/ and /æ/ (*then, when, any, many*); others derive from a former [ɛi] (*Leicester, said, says*).

(5) *Advice to foreign learners*—This vowel may present difficulties to those foreign learners whose native language possesses two types of /e/, usually of C[e] and C[ɛ] qualities. A foreign learner may in such cases equate English /e/ with one or other of his own vowels; this risks confusion with /ɪ/ if a C[e] quality is used, e.g. by Arabic speakers, or with /æ/ if a C[ɛ] quality is used, e.g. by Cantonese, German, and Hindi speakers. He should therefore aim to produce a vowel intermediate between the two qualities.

8.9.4 /æ/

(1) *Examples*
  a—hand, lamp, macho, marry, rash, sat

(*Note* /e/ in 'plaid, plait, reveille, timbre (or tamber)'.)
99% of spellings of /æ/ are with <a>.
Compare /e/, /æ/—pet, pat; peck, pack; said, sad; ten, tan; lend, land; merry, marry
/ɪ/, /e/, /æ/—bid, bed, bad; big, bed, bag; tin, ten, tan; miss, mess, mass
[æː] (before /b,d,g,dʒ/) and [æ]—cab, cap; bad, bat; bag, back; badge, batch
[ɫ] *following*—alphabet, shall (accented form), balcony, scalp

(2) *Description*—The mouth is more open than for /e/; the front of the tongue is raised to a position midway just above open, with the side rims making a very slight contact with the back upper molars; the lips are neutrally open. This vowel has become more open recently, previously being nearer to C[ɛ] where now it is now close to C[a]. Only tradition justifies the continuing use of the symbol 'æ' for this phoneme. Since the vowel /ʌ/ has had a tendency over a somewhat longer period to move forward towards C[a], this may occasionally result in a neutralization of /æ/ and /ʌ/. More often, however, the lowering of /æ/ has resulted in a retreat of /ʌ/ towards the central region.

This traditionally short vowel is now generally longer in RP than the other short vowels /ɪ,e,ʌ,ɒ,ʊ/. Such lengthening is particularly apparent before voiced consonants, e.g. in *cab, bad, bag, badge, man*; /æ/ in these contexts is almost equivalent to the long vowels, so *badge* /bædʒ/ and *barge* /bɑːdʒ/ have vowels of similar length. Moreover, some RP speakers in the south of England appear to have a contrast between short /æ/ and long /æː/ which shows up in a limited number of minimal pairs like *jam* (to eat) (and probably also *jamb*) as [dʒæm] and *jam* (of traffic) [dʒæːm]. Potential minimal pairs involve *land* (n) and *land* (vb), *banns* and *bans*, and *champ* (= *champion*) and *champ* (at a bit).

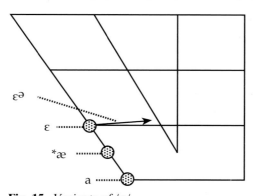

Fig. 15. *Variants of /æ/.*

(3) *Variants*—Speakers of Refined RP and older speakers of General RP generally have a closer variety of /æ/ almost at the level of C[ɛ] which may also be diphthongized to [ɛə], hence *bad, bag* as [bɛəd, bɛəg] or [beˑd, beˑg] (cf. similar diphthongization of /ɪ/ and /e/): such speakers may also produce /æ/ with considerable constriction in the pharynx, the tongue itself having more tension than is the case for /e/.

Like /e/, this vowel will generally be produced closer in Australian English and in Cockney, speakers in both areas having a vowel around C[ɛ]; Cockney may also have a diphthongization to [ɛ°] (like Refined RP; indeed a closer realization of the three front vowels is typical of Australian, Cockney, and Refined RP!). The north of England generally has a fully open pronunciation [a] like RP, but is noticeably different from RP in not having the length associated with this vowel in RP; in this area /æ/ is no longer than the other short vowels. Also in the north of England, words which have /ɑː/ plus a voiceless fricative or nasal plus another consonant in RP are pronounced with /æ/, hence *past, after, bath, dance* /pæst, ˋæftə, bæθ, dæns/; this also applies to Australian English (although indeterminately to the nasal plus consonant words) and to General American, where such words are also prone to raising to [ɛ]. It should also be noted that Scottish English generally has no distinction between /æ/ and /ɑː/, thus the words *cam* and *calm* will have the same vowel (of intermediate length) between C[a] and C[ɑ].

(4) *Chief sources*—PresE /æ/ derives regularly from: OE [ɑ] (*man, cat*); OE [æ] (*sad, back, apple*); OE [ɛːə] (*shadow, shank*); shortened OE [ɑː] (*hallow*) or OE [æː] (*ladder, mad*)—this shortening being earlier than that of the *death* type where ME [ɛː] > eModE [ɛ]; Scandinavian [ɑ] (*flat, anger*). Also regularly from OF [a] (*lamp, manner, passage*) and occasionally from OF [au] (*salmon, savage*). Most earlier sequences of the type [wa-] have given [wɒ-] or [wɔː-] (*watch, quality, water*); /æ/ is, however, retained in some cases, especially when a velar consonant follows (*wag, wax, twang*).

(5) *Advice to foreign learners*—The main difficulty for all those whose own languages have a less complex vowel system than English lies in the establishment of the qualitative oppositions /ɪ/–/e/–/æ/–/ʌ/. The opposition /e/–/æ/ may be emphasized by making use of the length component of RP /æ/ in certain contexts, e.g. in *men, man; bed, bad*. Where length may not be so distinctive, e.g. in *net, gnat*, learners should be careful not to make /æ/ like the typical <a> vowel in those languages which only have one (central) vowel in the open region (e.g. in those languages, like many in the Bantu group, which only have a five or seven vowel system). /æ/ must be kept fully front and, if necessary, above C[a] to avoid confusion with /ʌ/ and even /ɑː/ (e.g. by Arabic speakers).

8.9.5　/ʌ/

(1) *Examples*
　　u—cut, drug, dull, sun, yuppie
　　o—son, come, among, one, done, month, colour, monkey, mother, nothing, Monday, onion, London, oven
　　ou—country, southern, couple, enough, young
　　oo—blood, flood
　　oe—does
　　(*Note* many earlier *u* spellings have been changed to *o*, especially in the vicinity of *u, m, n, w, v*, e.g. in 'love, some, won' etc.)

Spellings in <u> have a lexical frequency of 91%, those in <o> a lexical frequency of 7%, and those in <ou> 2%. The text frequencies, because of the high frequency of some words in <o>, are rather different at 63%, 27%, and 8% respectively.

Compare /æ/, /ʌ/—cat, cut; lamp, lump; match, much
/ɑː/, /ʌ/—cart, cut; barn, bun; march, much
/ɒ/, /ʌ/—cot, cut; fond, fund; wander, wonder
/ɜː/, /ʌ/—curt, cut; fern, fun; turf, tough
[ɬ] *following*—dull, result, pulse, bulge, bulb

(2) *Description*—The short RP /ʌ/ is articulated with a considerable separation of the jaws and with the lips neutrally open; the centre of the tongue is raised just above the fully open position, no contact being made between the tongue and the upper molars. The quality is that of a centralized and slightly raised C[a]=[ä] (the IPA symbol for a vowel in this region is [ɐ]; /ʌ/ is kept partly for traditional reasons and partly because a more back vowel is used in many dialects). /ʌ/ does not occur in final, open, syllables.

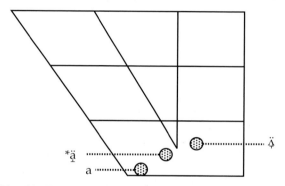

Fig. 16. *Variants of /ʌ/.*

(3) *Variants*—Refined RP has a variety of /ʌ/ which is more of a back vowel (=[ɐ̈]). Cockney has a vowel further forward and more open, approaching C[a]. In the north of England there is no contrast between /ʌ/ and /ʊ/, so that *put* and *putt* are pronounced the same; the vowel in such cases is generally closer to the quality of RP /ʊ/ and thus it can be said that NE has no /ʌ/. Some Regional RP speakers from the north of England (see §7.6.4) may, in adopting /ʌ/, use the vowel in words which even in RP have /ʊ/, e.g. *butcher* /ˈbʌtʃə/, *cushion* /ˈkʌʃn̩/, *sugar* /ˈʃʌgə/. Most such hypercorrections involve words written with the letter <u>; the spellings <oo, ou>, seem to block pronunciations with /ʌ/, e.g. in *shook* and *should*. This is connected to the fact that a number of words spelt with <ook> are pronounced with the long vowel /uː/ in the north of England, e.g. *look, cook, book* /luːk, kuːk, buːk/. Also in the north of England the morpheme *one* is pronounced /wɒn/ rather than /wʌn/, e.g. /ˈsʌmwɒn, ˈnəʊwɒn/. Alternation between these vowels /ʌ/ and /ɒ/ may also be heard within RP in words where the letter <o> is followed by a nasal consonant, e.g. *accomplish, combat, comrade, conduit, constable, Montgomery*.

(4) *Chief sources*—PresE /ʌ/ is the regular development of the ME rounded close-mid centralized back [ʊ]. This in turn derives from OE and OF sources: OE [ʊ] (*sun, love, nut, ugly*); shortened OE [uː] (*us, husband, utter, enough, scum*); OE [y] (*blush, much, such*); OF [u] (*cousin, touch, dozen, colour, cover*) and OF [u] or [o] before a nasal consonant (*number, sum, front, uncle, comfort, money*); OF [y] (*just, judge, public, study*). The ME [ʊ] sound has, in those words where we now have /ʌ/, i.e. [ä], been lowered and has lost its lip-rounding. The unrounded stage appears to have been reached by or during the seventeenth century in the London region, though at that time the lowering may not have been very considerable, i.e. a centralized variety of C[ɤ]. An open-mid stage (probably somewhat fronted from true back) may be postulated for the eighteenth century, with the quality C[ʌ̈] typical of the nineteenth century, the tongue position being by the end of the century rather below open-mid. Thus, PresE /ʌ/ is the result of qualitative changes greater than those which have affected any other short vowel. Further progress into the front region is likely to be inhibited by the presence of /æ/, unless the lengthening of /æ/ becomes general, in which case /ʌ/ may fulfil the function of a short open front vowel opposed to both /æː/ and /ɑː/.

It is to be noted that some PresE /ʌ/ forms have developed from a ME [oː] (*flood, blood, done, month, glove, mother*). ME [oː] must have shortened in time for it to develop, as ME [ʊ] ([o] being similar in quality to [ʊ]), to PresE /ʌ/. The words *one, none*, should regularly give PresE /əʊn, nəʊn/, this being the normal development of ME [ɔː]; this regular sound change is attested into the seventeenth century and is retained in the PresE form of the compound *alone*. The modern RP form with unrounded /ʌ/ derives from a shortened, raised ME vowel, preceded in the case of *one* by a glide [w], originally considered a vulgarism; the vowel of *none* results from an analogy with that of *one*.

(5) *Advice to foreign learners*—Most languages possess a vowel of the [a] or [ä] type; this sound will be spelt <a> if the Roman alphabet is used. The English /ʌ/ should be related to this quality and, indeed, good results can often be obtained in teaching by transcribing the English vowel as /a/ rather than with the traditional /ʌ/ symbol. In this way prejudice induced by the frequent orthographic spelling with <u> or <o> is avoided; if the quality thus obtained is too fronted, it may be modified in the direction of /ɑː/. A proper qualitative distinction should be maintained between the vowels in words such as *match, much, march; ban, bun, barn; hat, hut, heart*. There should be no lip-rounding such as might produce a type of front open-rounded [œ] or confusion with lip-rounded /ɒ/ (common among Arabic speakers).

8.9.6   /ɑː/

(1) *Examples*
   a—Bach, pass, after, bath, Inkatha, tomato, father, branch, camouflage, morale
   ar—part, car, march
   ear—heart, hearth
   er—clerk, Derby, sergeant

al—calm, palm, half
au—aunt, laugh
(*Note* in borrowings from French in which the French *-oir* [waːr] is realized in English as /wɑː/, e.g. 'reservoir', 'repertoire', 'memoir'.)

The lexical frequency of /ɑː/ as <ar> is 60% (text frequency also 60%) and that of <a> without <r> 32% (text frequency 34%). Many of the simple <a> spellings involve a following voiceless fricative where the /ɑː/ was originally short (and remains as /æ/ in General American and in Northern English).

Long—bar, far, farm, large, hard
Reduced—dart, last, raft, lark, arch

Compare [ɑː], [ɑ]—card, cart; parse, pass; carve, calf; large, larch
/ɑː/, /ʌ/—cart, cut; harm, hum; march, much; lark, luck; dance, dunce
[ɬ] *following*—snarl, gnarled, Charles

(2) *Description*—This normally long vowel is articulated with a considerable separation of the jaws and the lips neutrally open; a part of the tongue between the centre and back is in the fully open position, no contact being made between the rims of the tongue and the upper molars. The quality is nearer to C[ɑ] than to C[a]. Although there is a difference of length according to whether it occurs in a syllable closed by a voiceless or voiced consonant, the shortening effect of a closing voiceless consonant is not as marked as for other long vowels; thus, whereas the reduced [i] of *beat* may be of similar length to the /ɪ/ of *bit* the reduced [ɑ] of *cart* is somewhat longer than the short /ʌ/ of *cut*. /ɑː/ does not normally occur before /ŋ/.

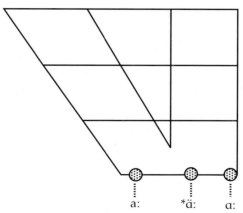

Fig. 17. *Variants of /ɑː/.*

(3) *Variants*—A variety of /ɑː/ retracted near to the quality of C[ɑ] is typical of Refined RP, whereas a quality near to C[a] is typical of Australian English and in much of south-west England as well as in some cities in the north of England,

e.g. Liverpool, Manchester, and Leeds. In some parts of the south-west, where the short vowels are in general lengthened, the fronting of /ɑː/ may thus lead to neutralization between /ɑː/ and /æ/.

Where an /ɑː/ is followed in RP by a voiceless fricative or by a nasal plus a second consonant, General American, Australian English and the north of England have /æ/, e.g. in *laugh, pass, branch, advance*. In many dialects, including General American and that of south-west England, RP /ɑː/ corresponds in a number of words to /ɑː/+/r/ (indicated by an <r> in the spelling), e.g. in *car, card, large* (such dialects, having /r/ in positions other than before a vowel, are called RHOTIC, see §7.4). This also applies to Standard Scottish English but here in addition the remaining instances of RP /ɑː/ fall together with /æ/ and there is thus no contrast between these words, *cam* and *calm, Pam* and *palm* being pronounced equivalently.

Although RP /ɑː/ followed by a voiceless fricative or a nasal plus second consonant generally corresponds to /æ/ in northern English, the reverse is not true, that is, there are examples where RP itself has /æ/ in these contexts, e.g. *passage, finance, gas, romance*. In such words hypercorrections may sometimes be heard from speakers of Regional RP, e.g. /pɑːsɪdʒ, fɪnɑːns, gɑːs, rəʊmɑːns/. In a number of other words RP is undecided; thus *lather, transfer, elastic, plastic* are words in which either /æ/ or /ɑː/ may be heard. In some words a pronunciation with /ɑː/ rather than /æ/ is typical of Refined RP, e.g. in *gymnastic* and *Atlantic*.

(4) *Chief sources*—Of the many sources of RP /ɑː/, the following are the most important:

(a) through loss of post-vocalic /r/ in the eighteenth century, short [a] or [æ] > /ɑː/ (*charm, march*); the [a] or [æ] in question may often result from ME [ɛ] (*far, star, heart*) as well as from an earlier French [ɛ] (*farm, clerk, sergeant*);

(b) lengthening of [a] or [æ]>/ɑː/, due to the following fricative (especially /f,θ,s/), incipient at the end of the seventeenth century (*staff, after; path, bath; pass, ask, cast; father, rather*);

(c) reduction of OF [ã]>ME [ɑu]>[ɒː]>/ɑː/ (*aunt, branch, command, chant*);

(d) reduction of ME [ɑu] and late ME loss of [ɫ]>/ɑː/ (*half, calf, palm, balm*);

(e) approximations of foreign values in more recent borrowings—mainly from French and Italian (*charade, moustache, memoir, sonata, tomato, drama, saga*).

It should also be noted that a new /ɑː/ is appearing in PresE, resulting from the smoothing of the sequences [aɪə] and [aʊə] (*fire, tower*)—see §8.11.

(5) *Advice to foreign learners*—Many languages do not have a qualitative opposition, in the relatively open region, of the English /æ/—/ɑː/ type. The retracted nature of RP /ɑː/ should be insisted upon to distinguish it from /æ/ and its length to distinguish it from /ɒ/ (a common confusion among Arabic speakers). Retraction may be achieved by getting learners to open the mouth more widely.

In addition, in the case of words in which /ɑː/ is shown in the spelling by vowel letter <r>, the temptation to pronounce any kind of [r] should be overcome (except when word-final /r/ may link to a following word beginning with a vowel). It is helpful to consider such post-vocalic <r> letters simply as a mark of length for the preceding vowel. French learners should be careful not to use undue nasalization in words of French origin which suggest modern French forms, e.g. *branch, plant* etc.

8.9.7 /ɒ/

(1) *Examples*
   o—dock, bonk, dog, holiday, sorry, gone
   a (*following* /w/)—was, what, swan, want, watch, quality, squash, quarrel
   ou, ow—cough, trough, Gloucester, knowledge
   au—because, sausage, laurel, Austria, Australia, cauliflower, bureaucracy
   (*Note* /ɒ/ in 'yacht'.)

Spellings in <o> have a lexical frequency of 95% and those in <a> a lexical frequency of 4%. The text frequencies are 92% and 6% respectively.

   Compare /ɒ/, /ɑː/—lodge, large; cot, cart; cough, calf; impossible, impassable
   /ɒ/, /ɔː/—cod, cord; don, dawn; stock, stalk
   [ɫ] *following*—doll, involve, revolver, solve

(2) *Description*—This short vowel is articulated with wide open jaws and slight open lip-rounding; the back of the tongue is in the fully open position, no contact being made between the tongue and the upper molars. The quality is that of an open lip-rounded C[ɑ], i.e. secondary C[ɒ], /ɒ/ does not occur in a final, open syllable.

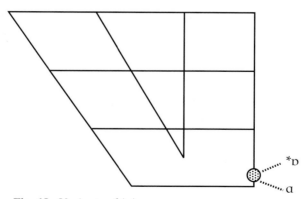

Fig. 18. *Variants of /ɒ/.*

(3) *Variants*—The realization of /ɒ/ varies very little within RP. A small number of words prefer /ɔː/ in Refined RP, e.g. *off, cloth, across.* (This also applies to Cockney). There is also little variation within Britain, such variation as there is generally involving unrounding to [ɑ] as in south-west England; in such cases /ɒ/ and /ɑː/ may be kept apart only by length (although, as noted under /ɑː/ above, /ɑː/ often = [aː]). In General American the contrast between /ɒ/ and /ɑː/ is lost,

both *bomb* and *balm* being pronounced with a vowel similar to RP /ɑː/. However, a smaller group of words with /ɒ/ in RP take /ɔː/ in General American, a group similar to but larger than that already mentioned for Refined RP above (largely involving words with a following voiceless fricative or a nasal), e.g. *across, soft, gone*. In SSE almost all words with RP /ɒ/ fall together with /ɔː/, the quality being nearer to the latter RP vowel; thus *cot, caught; not, nought; nod, gnawed* etc. will all be pronounced with /ɔː/. In other cases RP /ɒ/ corresponds to Scottish /ɔː/ while RP /ɔː/ corresponds to /ɔː/ plus /r/ (Scottish English generally being rhotic), hence *cod* /kɔːd/ but *cord* /kɔːrd/.

(4) *Chief sources*—PresE /ɒ/ derives regularly from OE [ɔ] (*dog, cock, song, long*) and OF [ɔ] (*offer, lodge, jolly*), and occasionally from shortened OE [oː] (*blossom, soft*). It is likely that the short [ɔ] of OE and ME was somewhat closer than PresE [ɒ], the more open type of articulation having been reached at the end of the eModE period. Between the sixteenth and eighteenth centuries, many words, having [ɔ] in ME, were pronounced with [a] or [æ], e.g. in *God, strop, stop, plot*. This pronunciation, typical during those centuries of both fashionable and vulgar London speech, is now retained only in the forms *strap* and *Gad* (exclamation).

ME short [a] preceded by [w] is often rounded to [ɒ] (*what, watch, was, want, quality*), a change which appears to have become established during the seventeenth century. The rounding has not taken place when a velar consonant follows, e.g. in *wag, wax, swagger, twang*, nor in the word *swam*.

Shortening of ME [ɔː] has taken place in words such as *gone, shone* (though the regular development with [oː] was still used in the seventeenth century); monophthongization and shortening has affected the ME forms of *knowledge, sausage* etc. The lengthened form of ME [ɔ] before /f,θ,s/ appeared in the second half of the seventeenth century and is used in some varieties today (see under (3) above). /ɒ/+nasal consonant occasionally represents [ɒ̃] in recent French borrowings, e.g. *restaurant, fiancé* /ˈrestrɒnt, frˈɒnseɪ/.

(5) *Advice to foreign learners*—Short back open vowels occurring in other languages often differ from the English /ɒ/ in that either they are somewhat closer or more centralized, or are pronounced with stronger lip-rounding. The extremely open nature of the English vowel can be emphasized by relating it to /ɑː/ in words such as *part, large, calf* and adding shortening and lip-rounding (although the lip-rounding must only be slight). The shortness of /ɒ/ also keeps it distinct from /ɔː/. Confusions between the three vowels /ɒ,ɑː,ɔː/ are common, e.g. by Cantonese, Hindi and Spanish speakers.

8.9.8   /ɔː/

(1) *Examples*
    ar, or—war, quart, cord, horse, sword, born
    ore—before, more
    our—court, four
    oar, oor—oar, board, door, floor
    au, augh—fault, cause, daughter
    a—all, talk, salt, water

aw—saw, lawn, jaw, yawn, awesome
ou—bought, ought
(*Note* /ɔː/ in 'broad' and 'sure, pure, cure' with alternative /ʊə/.)

Spellings involving an <r> have a lexical frequency of 43% and a text frequency of 39%. Those not involving an <r> have a lexical frequency of 57% and a text frequency of 61%. Among the spellings involving an <r>, <ar>, <or>, and <ore>, account for 35% of the overall lexical frequency (25% text frequency) and <our> 4% overall (8% text). Among the spellings not involving an <r>, <au>, and <augh> account for 27% of the overall lexical frequency (11% text frequency), <a> (chiefly before <l>) accounts for 15% of the overall lexical frequency (34% text frequency), and aw> for 12% lexical frequency (9% text frequency).

Long [ɔː]—saw, war, born, board, dawn
Reduced [ɔ]—sort, ought, horse, chalk, quart
Compare [ɔː], [ɔ]—saw, sort; war, wart; board, bought; saws, sauce
/ɒ/ /ɔː/—cod, cord; don, dawn; stock, stork
/ʊ/ /ɔː/—put, port; could, cord; bull, ball
/əʊ/, /ɔː/—code, cord; cold, called; bone, born
[ɫ] *following*—all, ball, bald, walled, halt, false

(2) *Description*—This relatively long RP vowel is articulated with medium lip-rounding; the back of the tongue is raised between the open-mid and close-mid positions, no contact being made between the tongue and the upper molars. The quality lies between C[ɔ] and C[o], i.e. [ɔ̝] or [o̞]. /ɔː/ does not normally occur before /ŋ/.

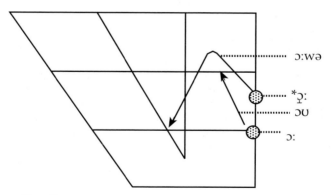

Fig. 19. *Variants of /ɔː/.*

(3) *Variants*—Until relatively recently there was a contrast between /ɔː/ and /ɔə/ in RP, so that *saw* and *sore* were pronounced differently. Nowadays this contrast is generally not made, except by some older speakers. A number of words which formerly had only /ʊə/ in RP have now acquired an alternative pronunciation with /ɔː/, e.g. *sure, poor, your.*

Words which formerly had /ɔə/ are often words derived from [ɔ] or [ɔ:] plus /r/, as reflected in the spelling; rhotic dialects like General American and Scottish English will therefore have a shorter vowel plus /r/ in words like *horse, cord, war*. In non-rhotic dialects other than RP, /ɔə/ may nevertheless be kept distinct from /ɔ:/, e.g. in some parts of the north of England. In Standard Scottish English /ɔ:/ covers both RP /ɔ:/ and RP /ɒ/, no contrast being made between these two vowels; thus *cot* and *caught* are pronounced the same. However, a number of pairs of words are still kept apart by the presence of /r/, e.g. *cod* /kɔːd/ *cord* /kɔːrd/. There is also no distinction between /ɔ:/ and /ɒ/ in General American. Words which have /ɒ/ in RP usually have /ɑ:/ in GA but a minority have /ɔ:/, e.g. *across, trough, coffee*. The quality of the vowel in General American is generally more open (= [ɔ̞:]) than in RP. In general, dialectal variation in /ɔ:/ is small; most notable is the diphthong or triphthong of Cockney, where /ɔ:/ = [ɔʊ] in morpheme-non-final positions, but [ɔwə] in morpheme-final positions, *board* [bɔʊd] but *bored* [bɔwəd].

(4) *Chief sources*—The tendency of PresE RP /ɔ:/ to become closer is a continuation of a historical closing process. Many instances of modern /ɔ:/ result from a ME diphthong [ɑu], which is likely to have had a variant ˈɑ:]. This diphthong or open vowel derives in turn from: OE open vowel+velar or labial consonant sequences, e.g. [ɑ]+[w] (*thaw*), [ɑ]+[ɣ] (*law*), [æ:]+[x] (*taught*), [ɑ]+[v] (*hawk < hafoc*); an earlier OE [ɑ] with [ʊ] glide before [ɫ] (*all, call, fall*) and with later (approximately seventeenth-century) loss of [ɫ] (*talk, walk*); OF [ɑ̃] or OF [ɑ]+[u] or [o] sequences (*cause, autumn, sauce, haunt, lawn*) or sometimes as a reduction of [ɑ]+[v] (*saunter, laundry*). ME diphthong [ɔu] is also often realized in PresE /ɔ:/; this ME form derives from OE [ɔ]+[x] (*bought, wrought*), from OE [o:]+[x] (*thought, brought, daughter*) and from OE [ɑ:]+[x] (*ought*).

In addition, in the same way that ME [a] preceded by [w] generally gives modern /ɒ/, [w] has also rounded ME [a] or [a:] to /ɔ:/ during the seventeenth century (*water, quart, warn, warm*). Finally, a large number of instances of RP /ɔ:/ result from the loss of post-vocalic /r/ in the eighteenth century (*horse, lord, source, forth*) via such stages as [ɔə] or [oə]. This change has levelled several ME vowel distinctions, e.g. ME [ɔ]+/r/ (*short, horse*), ME [ɔ:]+/r/ (*force, board*), and ME [o:] or [u:]+/r/ (*sword, fourth, floor, mourn, pour*); such lowering and monophthongization of earlier [uə] is also extended by some speakers to words such as *sure, poor*.

(5) *Advice to foreign learners*—In many countries a type of /ɔ:/ is taught which is rather more open than the general RP variety described above and which can no longer be said to be typical of RP. The slightly higher tongue position should be accompanied by closer lip-rounding. Many languages have a vowel in the region of C[o]; this latter sound may serve as a starting point for acquiring RP /ɔ:/, the tongue and lip positions being relaxed until the correct quality is reached.

The spelling forms of /ɔ:/ often cause difficulty. No <r> should be pronounced where it occurs in the spelling of words such as *port, sort, lord, more*, except when, in a word-final position, it is used as a link with a following word beginning with a vowel, e.g. *pour out* /pɔːrˈaʊt/. Words having /ɔ:/ and spelt with <au, aw, ou>, e.g. *taught, saw, ought*, are often wrongly given a [ɔu] or [ou] type of diphthong. The monophthongal nature of /ɔ:/ should be insisted upon, especial care being taken to keep a proper distinction between /ɔ:/ and /əʊ/ in pairs such as *caught, coat; saw, sew*.

8.9.9 /ʊ/

(1) *Examples*
 u—butcher, cellular, cushion, full, put, sugar
 oo—book, good, wood, wool
 o—bosom, wolf, woman
 ou—could, courier, should, would
 (*Note* 'Worcester' /ˈwʊstə/, 'worsted' (cloth) /ˈwʊstɪd/.)

Spellings in <u> have a lexical frequency of 54% (text frequency 32%), and those in <oo> a lexical frequency of 35% (text frequency 64%).

 Compare /ʊ/, /uː/—full, fool; wood, wooed
 /ʊ/, /ɔː/—could, cord; wood, ward
 [ɫ] *following*—full, pull, wool, wolf

(2) *Description*—The short RP vowel /ʊ/ is pronounced with a part of the tongue nearer to centre than to back raised just above the close-mid position; it has, therefore, a symmetrical back relationship with the front vowel /ɪ/; the tongue is laxly held (compared with the tenser /uː/), no firm contact being made between the tongue and the upper molars. There is a increasing tendency for this vowel to be unrounded; if the lips are rounded at all, a close but loose rounding is involved. The quality is that of a centralized C[ɤ] or [o]=[ö] or [ÿ]. Unrounding is particularly noticeable in the common word *good* [gö̞d] or [gÿ̞d], and also in *should, could,* and, to a lesser extent, *would*. (The unaccented forms of these last three words very often have /ə/ rather than /ʊ/.) This vowel occurs in both accented and unaccented syllables, being present in the accented syllable of a relatively small number of words, though some of these are of common occurrence, e.g. *put, good, look, would*. /ʊ/ does not occur in word-initial positions nor before final /ŋ/ and finally only in a (nowadays relatively rare) unaccented form of *to* /tʊ/ and *you* /jʊ/.
 (3) *Variants*—Apart from variation in rounding, little striking variety is found in RP realizations of /ʊ/. In some words there is a variation between /ʊ/ and /uː/, e.g. *room, groom, broom, tooth*, the commoner phoneme being /uː/.

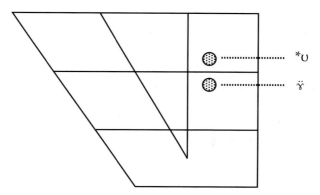

Fig. 20. *Variants of* /ʊ/.

Throughout the north of England no contrast is made between /ʊ/ and /ʌ/, a vowel in the region of /ʊ/ occurring for both the RP vowels (see §§7.6.4 and 8.9.5). A form of [ʏ̈] represents /ʊ/ in some northern regional speech, e.g. *butcher* [ˈbʏ̈tʃə]; and again, in some northern speech, many words spelt with *oo* have /uː/, e.g. *cookery book*. In SSE the opposition /ʊ/–/uː/ is neutralized, a centralized [ü] being used for both, so that *pull* and *pool* have a similar vowel quality.

(4) *Chief sources*—As we have seen ME short [ʊ] has a regular development to PresE /ʌ/. A number of cases of ME [ʊ], however, whether from OE sources (*full, bull, wolf, wool, wood*) or from OF sources (*push, butcher, pulley*), have retained their [ʊ] quality; the presence of a preceding labial consonant may be said to account for the retention of a lip-rounded vowel, but there are several cases where /ʌ/ has developed despite a labial consonant (*butter, bud, pulse*). In another group of words, PresE /ʊ/ derives from a ME [oː] which regularly gives PresE /uː/ (*food, moon*); such words are *good, foot, stood, book, look*, for which alternative pronunciations with /uː/ or /ʊ/ existed into the seventeenth century. The northern pronunciation with /uː/ in many such words (mentioned above) retains the closer form.

(5) *Advice to foreign learners*—The difficulty of /ʊ/ is similar to that of /ɪ/, i.e. just as the vowels /iː/ and /ɪ/ presented three oppositions involving complexes of quality and quantity, [iː]–[i]–[ɪ], so /ʊ/ has to be distinguished from /uː/ sometimes by quality alone (*foot–boot*), sometimes by quality and quantity (*good–food*). The quality of /ʊ/ must be kept quite distinct from that of the reduced form of /uː/; if a vowel of the quality of C[o] occurs in the learner's own language, this may be used as a starting point for learning English /ʊ/—essentially a centralized C[o]. Thus, in the case of French learners, for instance, the vowel in *foot* may be usefully related to the French vowel in *faute* and the English vowel acquired by relaxing the whole articulation. Relating /ʊ/ and C[o] in this way underlines the fact that /ʊ/ is not a kind of [u] sound. If the centralization of /ʊ/ is not sufficient, the starting point may be a central [ə] modified in the direction of [o]. The opposition between /ʊ/ and fully long /uː/ is less difficult once the distinction /ʊ/—reduced /uː/ is established (see following section for comparative exercises).

8.9.10   /uː/

(1) *Examples*
    u—rude, June, Susan, crucial
    oo—food, soon, moon, spoon
    o—do, who, move, lose
    ou—group, soup, wound (n.), through
    ew—chew, flew, askew
    ue, ui, oe—blue, juice, shoe
    (*Note* in many cases of the spelling *u, eu, ew, ue, ui*, /uː/ is preceded by /j/, e.g. 'music, duke, neuter, new, few, hue, argue, nuisance, beauty'; in some words, both /uː/ and /juː/ are heard, e.g. 'suit, enthusiasm'.)

The lexical frequencies (text frequencies in brackets) of the principal spellings of /uː/ are <u> 42% (27%), <oo> 33% (39%), <o> 7% (15%), <ew> 5% (9%), and <ou> 8% (7%).

Long [uː]—two, blue, food, move
Reduced [u]—boot, fruit, hoof, group, douche, hoop
Compare [uː], [u]—shoe, shoot; rude, root; lose, loose; use (v.), use (n.); nude, newt; Jews, juice
[uː], /ʊ/—food, good; pool, pull
[u], /ʊ/—boot, foot; loop, look
[ɫ] *following*—cool, rule, schools, fooled

(2) *Description*—RP long /uː/ is a close back vowel, but the tongue raising is relaxed from the closest position and is somewhat centralized from true back; its relationship with /ʊ/ is similar to that between /iː/ and /ɪ/, the articulation of /uː/ being tense compared with that of /ʊ/, though no firm contact is made between the tongue and the upper molars. The lips tend to be closely rounded; there is a tendency, less common with /uː/ than with /ʊ/, towards unrounding. The quality is that of a relaxed, slightly lowered and centralized C[u]. /uː/ does not normally occur before /ŋ/.

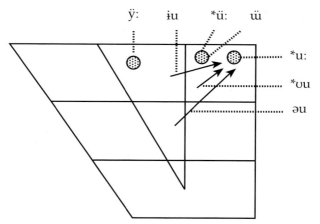

Fig. 21. *Variants of* /uː/.

(3) *Variants*—There is some variation in the realization of this vowel within RP. Two variants within General RP are (i) a more centralized vowel [ü] or [ʉ] or [ʉ̈], and (ii) a short diphthong [ʊu] or [ʉʉ̈] (this being particularly common in final position (*do, shoe, who*). A fully back and round C[u] is typical of Refined RP. Considerable centralization of /uː/ is present following /j/ in all types of RP, e.g. in *youth, beauty, cute*, as is a more monophthongal and back [uː] before [l], e.g. in *tool, school, rule*.

Increased fronting and diphthongization is characteristic of a number of other dialects. Cockney has diphthongs of the type [əʉ̈] and [ïʉ̈] with little, if any, lip-rounding. Diphthongization of the former variety is also typical of Australian English. As mentioned under the section on /ʊ/, SSE loses the contrast between /uː/ and /ʊ/, the common vowel being in the region of [ü] or [ÿ]; in some cases the lip-rounding may be only slight, so that the distinction between /uː/ and /ɪ/

in, for example, *room* and *rim*, may be minimal. Fronting of this vowel in varying degrees is also common in much of the north of England.

(4) *Chief sources*—PresE /uː/ derives regularly via ME [oː] from OE [oː] (*doom, soon, to, tool, goose*); Scandinavian [oː] (*root, boon*) and OE [ɑː] preceded by [w] (*womb, whom, two*); also from OF [oː] (*fool, prove, proof*). *o* and *oo* are, therefore, the typical spelling forms of the regular development to [uː], which was reached by about 1500. Certain French words with [uː] (*ou* spelling), introduced after the change [uː]>[ɑʊ] had begun, i.e. after about 1400, retained their [uː] quality (*route, routine, group, soup*). In many cases, too, especially in those words where the French accent on the last syllable has been kept, French *-on* (= probably [õ]) has given English /uː/ with a spelling change to *oo* (*platoon, balloon, saloon, typhoon*).

PresE /juː/ derives from many sources. The chief of these are:

(a) ME [iu], [eu] or [yː] < OE [i] + [w] (*Tuesday, hue*), < OE [eːə]+[w] (*you, knew*), < OF [iu] (*adieu, lieu*), < OF [eu] (*due, view*), < OF [y] (*duke, accuse, deluge*), < OF [ui] (*suit, pew, nuisance*). It is likely that in these cases a ME falling diphthong [iu] changed the relative prominence of its elements to give [juː] in the sixteenth century (a variant with [yː] perhaps remaining in some kinds of English);

(b) ME [ɛu] < OE [ɛːə] or [æː]+[w] (*few, dew, hew*); and < later French (post-1400) [ɛu] (*feud, neuter*). This ME diphthong closed to [eu] by eModE (still being kept separate from [ju]) and finally coalesced with [juː] in the late seventeenth century.

(5) *Advice to foreign learners*—The quality of this vowel should cause no difficulty to most learners, many of whom will have a close back rounded vowel in their own language. A pure vowel of this kind will usually be suitable in English, though too energetic lip-rounding should be avoided. The typical RP centralization or diphthongization should be imitated only with caution, since any exaggeration of the movement will produce an effect which may be judged dialectal. The centralization of /uː/ following /j/ need not be consciously aimed at. Those learners, such as Norwegians, who have a centralized [ü] in their own languages, should avoid using this sound in English because of its dialectal connotations. The unrounded back vowel of Japanese may involve considerably more lip spreading than the newer unrounded realization of English /uː/ and Japanese learners of English should introduce some lip-rounding.

More difficult is the relationship of fully long [uː], reduced [u] and short [ʊ] as in *food, boot*, and *foot*. It should be noted, for instance, that *use* (v.) [juːz̪] differs from *use* (n.) [jus] more by the length of the vowel than by the quality of the final consonant, and that the difference between the vowels of *boot* ([u]) and of *foot* ([ʊ]) may lie as much in their quality than in their length.

8.9.11   /ɜː/

(1) *Examples*
   er, err—her, serve, err, perfect

ur, urr—turn, church, nurse, purr, cursor
ir, yr—sir, bird, first, girl, myrtle, myrrh
w + or—word, world, work, worse
ear—earth, heard
our—journey, courtesy, scourge
(*Note* /ɜː/ in 'colonel' /ˈkɜːnl/, 'milieu' /miːlˈjɜː/.)

With very few exceptions the spellings of /ɜː/ involve a vowel letter and a following <r>. The lexical frequencies of the principal sequences (text frequencies in brackets) are: <er(r)> 54% (39%), ur(r) 24% (17%), ir(r) 11% (18%), or(r) 4% (17%), and <ear> 4% (8%).

Long [ɜː]—fur, burn, bird, urge
Reduced [ɜ]—first, earth, worse, church
Compare [ɜː], [ɜ]—cur, curt; heard, hurt; surge, search; purrs, purse; Thursday, thirsty; serve, surf
[ɫ] *following*—earl, curl, world, girls

(2) *Description*—RP /ɜː/ is articulated with the centre of the tongue raised between close-mid and open-mid, no firm contact being made between the tongue and upper molars; the lips are neutrally spread. The quality is, therefore, remote from all peripheral Cardinal Vowel values.

The quality of /ɜː/ often coincides with that of /ə/, the difference between the two being only one of length. Since /ɜː/ usually occurs in accented syllables and /ə/ in unaccented syllables, this might suggest that the two vowels be treated as accented and unaccented allophones of the same phoneme. However, there are clear cases where /ɜː/ occurs in unaccented syllables and is not reducible to /ə/, e.g. in *commerce* /ˈkɒmɜːs/, cf. *commas* /ˈkɒməz/, and indeed most speakers have a minimal pair between *foreword* /ˈfɔːwɜːd/ and *forward* /ˈfɔːwəd/. Moreover, most words which have /ɜː/ in their citation form do not reduce this vowel to /ə/ when they occur unaccented in connected speech, e.g. *Now its my turn, he said* (but note that *were, her*, and *sir* can be reduced to /ə/).

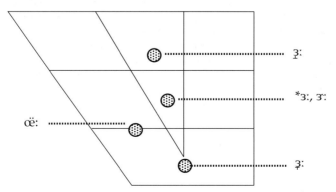

Fig. 22. *Variants of /ɜː/.*

(3) *Variants*—/ɜː/ being the only accented vowel in the central area, there is considerable individual variation in its realization, with variations from close-mid to open-mid. A pronunciation somewhat below open-mid is characteristic of Refined RP. Such a pronunciation comes close to the usual RP position for /ɑː/; however, speakers of Refined RP generally use a retracted variety of /ɑː/ to ensure the vowels keep their distance.

In most cases /ɜː/ is derived from an earlier sequence of vowel plus /r/ and in General American and in south-west England this shows up in r-colouring of this vowel, often symbolized as [ɝ]. This *r*-colouring is produced by slight retroflexion of the tip of the tongue or by contraction of the body of the tongue. In SSE a sequence of vowel (usually [ɪ,e,ʌ,ʊ]) plus /r/ is retained; hence this dialect has no /ɜː/ in its phonemic inventory. In broad varieties of Tyneside /ɜː/ falls together with /ɔː/ so that *burn* and *born* may be pronounced the same. There is considerable variation in the quality of /ɜː/ in other dialects, notable being a close variety (=[ɹ]) in Australian English and in Birmingham, and a rounded variety (=[œ̈]) in Liverpool, where the contrast between /ɜː/ and /eə/ is lost, *fur* and *fare* being pronounced the same.

(4) *Chief sources*—The great majority of cases of PresE /ɜː/ derive from: ME [ɛ]+/r/ (*virtue = vertue, earth, heard, fern*) or ME [ɪ]+/r/ (*shirt, birth, myrrh*); or ME [ʊ]+/r/ (*word, journey, spur*). ME [ɛ], [ɪ], and [ʊ] (> [ʌ] with loss of lip-rounding) all centralized before final /r/ or /r/+consonant, so that the pronunciation [ər] for all three was incipient in the London region in the sixteenth century and general in the late seventeenth century, though contemporary grammarians still often insisted upon the earlier vowel quality, especially in the case of ME [ɛ] and [ʊ] words. With the loss of /r/ in post-vocalic positions in the eighteenth century, the PresE central long /ɜː/ was reached. Some attempts to reproduce the French [œːr] in final accented syllables have also resulted in /ɜː/, e.g. *connoisseur* /kɒnəˈsɜː/; *liqueur* /lɪˈkɜː/ (also /lɪˈkjʊə/); *amateur* /ˈæməˈtɜː/ (also /ˈæmətə, ˈæmətjə, ˈæmətʃə, ˈæmətjʊə/).

(5) *Advice to foreign learners*—It is comparatively rare to find a long central vowel such as /ɜː/ in other languages. Some languages, however, possess somewhat centralized front rounded vowels of the [ø] and [œ] types, e.g. Dutch, French, German, and the Scandinavian languages. These are unacceptable for RP because of the lip-rounding. An articulation with spread lips should, therefore, be insisted upon, keeping the same position with spread lips for words such as *fur, bird, learn* as for *fee, bead, lean*. Lip-spreading is particularly important after /w/, e.g. in *word, world, work* etc. In addition, the quality must be of a central rather than fronted kind, though some latitude may be allowed as far as the degree of raising of the tongue is concerned.

Since nearly all cases of /ɜː/ occur in words having an <r> in the spelling, care must also be taken to avoid post-vocalic /r/ (except as a liaison form as in *stir up* /stɜːrˈʌp/) or any retroflexion of the tongue such as would produce /r/-colouring.

8.9.12   /ə/

(1) *Examples*—/ə/ may be spelt with most vowel letters and their combinations, e.g. *i* (poss*i*ble), *e* (gentlem*e*n), ɑ (wom*a*n), *o* (*o*blige), *u* (s*u*ppose), *ar* (partic*u*lar), *er* (moth*er*), *or* (doct*or*), *ou* (fam*ou*s), *our* (col*our*), *ure* (fig*ure*) etc.

The lexical and text frequencies of the most frequent spellings of /ə/ (excluding those function words with strong and weak forms) are: <a> 30% (35%), <o> 24% (19%), <e> 13% (13%), and <er> 12% (15%).

/ə/ is most frequently in opposition either with zero vowel, e.g. *about, bout; waiter, wait*, or with unaccented /ɪ/, e.g. *affect, effect; accept, except; razors, raises; grocers, grosses; mitre, mighty; waiter, weighty; sitter, city; battered, batted.*

/ə/ is normal in common unaccented (weak) forms of words such as *a, an, the, to, for, but, and* etc. (see §11.3).

(2) *Description*—/ə/ has a very high frequency of occurrence in unaccented syllables. Its quality is that of a central vowel with neutral lip position, having in non-final positions a tongue-raising between open-mid and close-mid, e.g. in '*alone, fatigue, decorative, afterwards*' etc.; in the vicinity of the velar consonants /k,g/ and /ŋ/, however, the tongue may be slightly more raised and retracted, e.g. 'long ago' /ˈlɒŋəˈɡəʊ/. But in final positions, e.g. in 'mother, doctor, over, picture, China', the vowel may be articulated in the open-mid central position (=[ɐ̈]). The acoustic formants of /ə/ are, therefore, likely to be similar to those for /ɜː/ or /ʌ/ according to the situation.

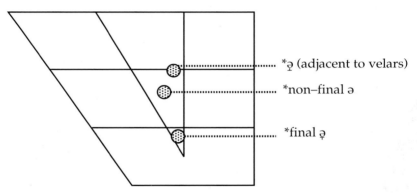

the velars)
                                           *ə̞ (adjacent to velars)

*non–final ə

*final ə̞

Fig. 23. *Variants of /ə/.*

(3) *Variants*—As is the case for /ɜː/, /ə/ has no qualitative opposition within the central area of vowel articulation, so that considerable variation is possible within this region. In particular, as has been stated, the quality of final /ə/ tends to be of a more open kind. In Refined RP, final /ə/ will be below open-mid (=[ɐ]) and may even approach /ɑː/) so that the two vowels in *father* become similar.

Many examples of /ə/ derive from sequences of vowel plus /r/ (usually shown in the spelling, e.g. *waiter, doctor, colour, figure*. In rhotic dialects this original /r/ may be reflected in *r*-colouring of the schwa (=[ɚ]) as in General American and south-west England, or may correspond to sequences of a full vowel (usually short) plus /r/, as in Scottish English.

(4) *Chief sources*—As the great variety of spellings indicates, /ə/ may represent the reduced (obscured, 'schwa') form of any vowel or diphthong in an unaccented position. This reduction of unaccented vowels has been a feature of

the English sound system for over a thousand years. Since our spelling of vowels is based on the Latin vowel letters, our written language has always concealed these obscurations of quality. But it is evident from confusions in the use of vowel letters that such reductions were taking place in unaccented syllables even in OE. Thus, OE letters <æ,e,i> in unaccented syllable are very often confused, probably indicating a sound [ë]; *o* and *u*, too, are often interchanged, though remaining separate from *a* representing [ɑ]. By the eleventh century all these major distinctions of weak [ɛ], [ʊ], and [ɑ] tend to be confused, especially in unaccented final syllables, no doubt with an obscuration in the direction of [ə]. This tendency continued in the ME period, so that by the middle of the fifteenth century the vowels of unaccented syllables probably showed much the same kind of obscuration (towards [ə] or [ɪ]) as in PresE. Thus, fifteenth-century spellings such as *disabey, Bishap, tenne a clocke, sapose,* seem to indicate a vowel of the [ə] type.

Accentual patterns in ME, especially in words taken over from French, were often not the same as now, so that a syllable which was accented in ME has now not only lost its accent but in some been reduced to schwa. Thus, *adversary* was pronounced [advɛr`saːrɪ] in ME, whereas today the accent has moved to the first syllable and the vowel in the third syllable has been reduced or lost altogether, giving /ˈædvəsərɪ/ or /ˈædvəsrɪ/. In general, however, Shakespeare's English can be taken as having [ə] where PresE has it, e.g. in words such as *second, among, palate, father, colour, vulgar, measure* (in these last cases [ə]+[ɹ]) and even in the last syllable of words like *follow,* where RP has restored /ˈfɒləʊ/. In some words a pronunciation with the full vowel was kept into the seventeenth century and is often reflected in differences between General American and RP, cf. RP *temporary* /ˈtempərərɪ/ (or `temprərɪ, `tempɪɪ, /ˈtemprɪ/) with GA /tempərˈerɪ/. In the north of England a number of prefixes still keep the full vowel, e.g. *advance* /æd`vaːns/, *conflict* /kɒn`flɪkt/, *observe* /ɒb`zɜːv/.

(5) *Advice to foreign learners*—The quality of this vowel, including the two main allophones described in (2) above, does not usually present difficulties to the foreign learner, provided that he remembers that English /ə/ has no lip-rounding and is extremely short. Moreover, when /ə/ is spelt with vowel + <r>, the learner should avoid pronouncing any kind of [r] sound, except when in final positions an /r/ is pronounced as a link to a following word beginning with a vowel, e.g. *mother and father* /mʌðər ən `faːðə/.

When occurring in final positions, e.g. in *supper, sofa, actor,* the quality of /ə/ should not be too open or too long. There is a tendency by some learners, e.g. Hindi and Bantu speakers, to equate final /ə/ with /aː/.

In particular, the learner should note those syllables of a word containing /ə/, remembering that /ə/ is a sound which occurs very frequently in English and that correct obscuration of the unaccented syllables of a word is as much a part of the word's accentual pattern as the full vowels on the accented syllables. In this connection, the learner may gain greater familiarity with the occurrence of /ə/ by reading English texts transcribed phonetically and by himself making a phonetic transcription of connected English. Particular attention should be paid to the use of [ə] in the weak forms of function words like *the* /ðə/, *has* /həz/, *for* /fə/, *from* /frəm/ etc. (see §11.4).

8.10   *Diphthongal Vowel Glides*

The sequences of vocalic elements included under the term 'diphthong' are those which form a glide within one syllable. They may be said to have a first element (the starting point) and a second element (the point in the direction of which the glide is made). The RP diphthongs have as their first element sounds in the general region of [ɪ,e,a,ə,ʊ] and for their second element [ɪ,ʊ,ə] (but see §8.2). The following generalizations refer to all the RP diphthongs:

(1) Most of the length and stress associated with the glide is concentrated on the first element, the second element being only lightly sounded (see §§8.12.1, 8.12.3 for the exceptional cases of /ɪə,ʊə/); diphthongs of this type are said to be 'falling'.

(2) They are equivalent in length to the long (pure) vowels and are subject to the same variations of quantity, e.g. *plays* [pleːɪz], *place* [pleɪs]. The reduced forms show a considerable shortening of the first element.

(3) They are particularly susceptible to variation regionally and socially. Even within RP, considerable variation is possible in both elements.

(4) No diphthong occurs before /ŋ/, except where word-final /n/ is assimilated to /ŋ/ in connected speech (see §12.4.5).

(5) With the exception of /ɔɪ/, the RP diphthongs principally derive from earlier pure vowels.

8.10.1   /eɪ/

(1) *Examples*
   a—ape, late, make, lady, waste, base
   ai—waist, rail, aim, rain
   ay—day, may, crayon
   ei, ey—eight, veil, weigh, rein, they, whey
   ea—great, steak, break
   (*Note* 'gauge' /geɪdʒ/, 'gaol' /dʒeɪl/, 'fete' /feɪt/, 'suede'/sweɪd/ and French words in -e, -er, -et, -ee, pronounced with final /-eɪ/, e.g. 'cafe', 'foyer', 'dossier', 'saute', 'fiancé', 'ballet', 'sachet', 'purée', 'matinée'.)

The lexical frequency of spellings in <a>, chiefly <a..e> is 82%, those in <ai> 10%, and those in <ay> 4%. The corresponding text frequencies are 65%, 12%, and 18% respectively.

   Long [eːɪ]—day, made, game, gaze
   Reduced [eɪ]—eight, late, face, safe, ache
   Compare [eːɪ], [eɪ]—played, plate; ray, race; way, waist; save, safe
   /e/, /eɪ/—bet, bate; fell, fail; chess, chase; west, waist
   [ɫ] *following*—male, pail, failed, sails

(2) *Description*—The glide begins from slightly below the close-mid front position and moves in the direction of RP /ɪ/, there being a slight closing

movement of the lower jaw; the lips are spread. The starting point is, therefore, [ẹ] (somewhat closer than RP /e/ of *bet*.) Before [ɫ], the [ɪ] element is often absorbed into the [ə] or [ʊ] glide on to [ɫ], e.g. *sail* [seˀɫ].

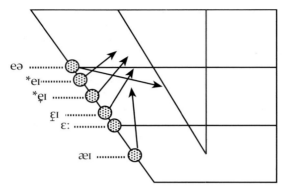

Fig. 24. *Variants of* /eɪ/.

(3) *Variants*—Although the quality mentioned under (2) is the most common in RP, nevertheless there is considerable variation in the starting point. Older speakers may have a starting point nearer to C[e], whereas in Refined RP a more open starting point nearer to C[ɛ] is common, as is a monophthongal [ɛː].

An even more open starting point (=[æɪ]) is usual in Cockney. When /eɪ/ is produced as openly as this, /aɪ/ has its starting point retracted so that *fate* [fæɪt] is kept distinct from *fight* [fɑɪt]. A similar movement of these two vowels occurs in Australian English. This change of /eɪ/ and /aɪ/ is often part of a more general change known as the 'Southern diphthong shift', typical of London, Birmingham, and the south and midlands of England, whereby /iː/=[əɪ], /eɪ/=[aɪ], /aɪ/=[ɑɪ] or [ɔɪ], and /ɔɪ/=[oɪ] (the accent of Birmingham is more usually similar to the north of England).

Many other regional realizations of /eɪ/ have a monophthongal [eː], e.g. Standard Scottish English and General American. Northern English may have [eː] or [ɛː] and some areas may have a split between [eː] in *late* and *main* and [ɛː] in *eight* and *straight*. In many parts of north-east England, notably Tyneside, there is a centring movement giving [eə].

(4) *Chief sources*—The main sources of PresE /eɪ/ are ME [aː] and [æɪ] or [ɛɪ]. Of these, ME [aː] develops from: OE [æ] or [ɑ] lengthened in an open syllable (*name, ape, raven, ale*) or from Scandinavian words with a similar vowel (*gate, take*); OF [aː] (*male, nature, cave, state*); earlier OF [au] (*chamber, change, strange, safe*). This ME [aː] was closed in the eModE period to [ɛː] and, perhaps, in some pronunciations, to [eː]. (Note the pronunciation of words such as *great, steak, break*—with ME [ɛː]—which have /eɪ/ in PresE instead of the more usual /iː/ deriving from this ME vowel.)

ME [æɪ] or [ɛɪ] develops from: OE [æ]+[j] (*day, again*); OE [æː]+[j] (*grey, clay*), OF [ai] (*pay, chain*); OE [ɛ]+[j] (*way, play*); Scandinavian [ei] (*they, swain*); OF [ei] (*faith, obey*). It will be seen that the ME diphthong of the type [ɛɪ] results from a coalescence of two earlier distinct diphthongs of the types [æi], [ai] and [ɛi], [ei], from both English and French sources. In many cases the modern spelling reflects the origins, e.g. *vain* as against *vein*, but often the spelling has been changed, e.g. *way* < [ɛi], *grey* < [æi]. The coalescence of the two earlier diphthongs took place at the end of the ME period, producing a glide of the [ɛi] or [æi] type. The evidence suggests that this glide was monophthongized in the eModE period, though the diphthongal pronunciation continued to be recommended by the earlier grammarians. The new monophthong was of the [ɛː] type, thus coalescing with [ɛː] < ME [aː].

In the seventeenth century, therefore, a pure vowel [ɛː] was probably used in both classes of words, though careful speakers might still use a diphthong in the second group. The general diphthongization of this [ɛː] is likely to have begun in the eighteenth century, developing towards a glide of the present type.

In addition, a number of words of more recent importation today have /eɪ/ in imitation of the French [e] or [ɛ], e.g. *fiancé, soirée, ballet, bouquet, beige, crêpe*.

(5) *Advice to foreign learners*—Foreign learners should give sufficient length to the first element of this diphthong, making the correct reduction of quantity in the appropriate contexts. Care should also be taken that the quality remains within the permitted RP limits, i.e. preferably slightly more open than C[e] and not as open as C[ɛ]. The second part of the diphthong should be only lightly touched on and should never reach the region of fully close [i]. For those who do not have a diphthong in this area, e.g. Arabic, French and German speakers, there may be a tendency to substitute a pure vowel around [eː]. This is a realization of this phoneme in many accents of English, e.g. Scottish English and General American. It is an acceptable substitute for the diphthong provided the sound is kept long; if it is shortened, there is danger of confusion with /ɪ/ or /e/.

8.10.2 /aɪ/

(1) *Examples*
  i—time, write, bite, climb, design
  ie—die, lie, pie, tried
  y, ye—cry, dry, by, dye, type, tyrant, cycle, asylum, anodyne
  igh—high, light, fight, might, right, bright, sight
  (*Note* /aɪ/ in 'eye, height, either, (also /iːðə/), neither (also /niːðə/), eider, aisle, buy, maestro'.)

The lexical frequency of spellings of /aɪ/ as <i> and <i..e> (non-finally) and <y> <ye> <ie> (finally) is 82%, for <y> (non-finally) 9%, and for <igh> 4%. The corresponding text frequencies are 80%, 2%, and 13%.

  Long [aːɪ]—fly, die, mine, hide, eyes
  Reduced [aɪ]—fight, like, ice, ripe
  Compare [aːɪ], [aɪ]—tie, tight; tidal, title; eyes, ice; riding, writing
  [ɫ] *following*—mile, aisle, piles, mild

(2) *Description*—The glide of RP /aɪ/ begins at a point slightly behind the front open position, i.e. [ä], and moves in the direction of the position associated with

RP /ɪ/, although the tongue is not usually raised to a level closer than [ë]; the glide is much more extensive than that of /eɪ/, the closing movement of the lower jaw being obvious. The starting point may be similar to the articulation used in RP /ʌ/ (see §8.9.5). The lips change from a neutral to a loosely spread position. Before [ɫ] the [ɪ] element is often absorbed into the [ə] or [ʊ] glide on to the [ɫ], e.g. *pile* [paːᵊɫ].

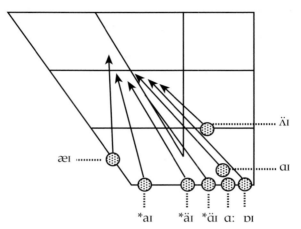

Fig. 25. *Variants of /aɪ/.*

(3) *Variants*—Variants commonly used in the realization of this diphthong comprise mainly in differences of starting point of the glide. Since RP /eɪ/ is realized between the limits [eɪ] and [ɛɪ], /aɪ/ cannot, while remaining contrastive, have a first element closer than C[ɛ]. Those RP speakers who use the closest form of /eɪ/ will probably have a type of [æɪ] glide for /aɪ/, whereas those whose /eɪ/ is nearer to [ɛɪ] may realize /aɪ/ with a more retracted type of [a] or fronted [ɑ]. In Refined RP a very back starting point is most common, and this may sometimes involve the eliminating of the glide, leaving [ä], which may be only marginally differentiated from /ɑː/ realized as C[ɑ].

In Cockney also /aɪ/ has a back starting point to give [äɪ], as indeed has Australian English, although in this case there may be rounding to [ɒɪ] (see this realization as part of the Southern diphthong shift under /eɪ/ above). In different parts of the north of England, all varieties of starting point from front to back may be heard. In an extensive area of south-west and south-central England a closer starting point may be heard (=[əɪ]). In Scottish English many speakers have a distinction between a morpheme-non-final realization [aɪ] and a morpheme-final [ʌ̈ɪ], thus *tied* [taɪd] but *tide* [ʌ̈ɪd]. In the so-called mid-Atlantic pronunciation used by pop singers, *I* and *my* are generally reduced to [ä], following the open monophthongal pronunciation of this vowel in the southern USA.

(4) *Chief sources*—PresE /aɪ/ derives regularly from ME [iː], whose main sources are: OE [iː] *(ice, like, time, life)*; OE lengthened [ɪ] *(child, find, wild)*; OE or Scandinavian [yː] *(hide, mice, kind, sky)*; OE [eː] or [ɛː]+[j] *(fly, lie, dye, eye)*; OE [eː] + [ç] *(light, night)*; OF [iː] *(fine, arrive, licence, price)*. The pure vowel [iː]

probably diphthongized by the beginning of the sixteenth century, the first element following a central route with increasing opening: [ɪi] in the late ME (cf. PresE diphthongization of /iː/), [əɪ] in the sixteenth and early seventeenth centuries, [ʌɪ] (where [ʌ] has an open-mid back to central value) in the late seventeenth and eighteenth centuries, and a variety of [aɪ] from the late eighteenth century.

(5) *Advice to foreign learners*—Apart from observing the proper reductions of quantity in syllables closed by a voiceless consonant, foreign learners should avoid over-retraction of the quality of the first element, so as to remain within the limits of the RP vowel and avoid confusion with /ɔɪ/. Many languages have a vowel in the region [ä] and this is generally a suitable starting point. Care should also be taken not to glide to too close a position, i.e. to the C[i] area, such as is reached in diphthongs of this type in many languages.

8.10.3 /ɔɪ/

(1) *Examples*
   oi—boil, noise, point, voice
   oy—boy, oyster, toy, voyage.
   (*Note* 'buoy' /bɔɪ/.)

The lexical frequency of spellings in <oi> is 71%, and that of <oy> 29%. The text frequencies are 62% and 38%.

   Long [ɔːɪ]—boy, noise, void, coin
   Reduced [ɔɪ]—voice, joist, joint, choice
   Compare [ɔːɪ], [ɔɪ]—noise, voice; joys, joist
   [ɫ] *following*—soil, coiled, boils

(2) *Description*—For RP /ɔɪ/ the tongue glide begins at a point between the open-mid and open back positions and moves in the direction of /ɪ/, generally not reaching a level closer than [e̞]. The tongue movement extends from back to centralized front, but the range of closing in the glide is not as great as for /aɪ/; the jaw movement, though considerable, may not, therefore, be as marked as in the case of /aɪ/. The lips are open rounded for the first element, changing to neutral for the second. Before [ɫ] the [ɪ] element is often absorbed into the [ə] or [ʊ] glide on to the [ɫ], e.g. *oil* [ɔːᵊɫ].

It will be noted that this is the third diphthongal glide towards an [ɪ] sound; it is, however, the only glide of this type with a back starting point (if the case of [ʊɪ], as in *ruin* (see §8.1 Note (4)) is discounted). To this extent, /ɔɪ/ may be considered asymmetrical in the RP diphthongal system.

(3) *Variants*—Refined RP unrounds, raises, and centralizes the starting point, so that we have [ʌ̈ɪ]. This produces a cluster of unrounded back open vowels or diphthongs: /ɑː/=[ɑ̈ː], /ɜː/=[ɑ̈ː], /aɪ/=[ɑ̈ɪ], /ɔɪ/=[ʌ̈ɪ] and /aʊ/=[ɑ̈ᵒ], the cumulative effect of which is the so-called 'plummy' effect associated with this accent.

A number of dialects have a starting point closer than that of RP, i.e. something between close-mid and open-mid, e.g. Cockney, Australian English,

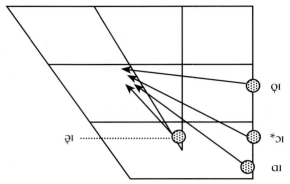

Fig. 26.   *Variants of /ɔɪ/*

and Scottish English. A phonemic merger between /ɔɪ/ and /aɪ/ is typical of many West Indian accents; thus there is, for example, no difference between *buy* and *boy*.

(4) *Chief sources*—PresE /ɔɪ/ derives mainly from OF sources with [ɔɪ] (*choices, noise*), [oɪ] or [ʊɪ] (*boil, point*). In ME some words, now with /ɔɪ/, were pronounced with [ʊɪ]; a regular development of this latter diphthong's first element would result in eModE [ɤɪ] or [əɪ]. Confusion was, therefore, possible between words containing this glide and those containing [əɪ]< ME [iː], now with /aɪ/. We find, in fact, that some PresE /ɔɪ/ words have [ʊɪ] in eModE (*boil, coin, point, join*) and that, in some cases, there is confusion with PresE /aɪ/ words, e.g. *boil* rhyming with *bile*. Such pronunciations were current in educated English until late in the eighteenth century and since then have occurred in regional forms of speech.

(5) *Advice to foreign learners*—This diphthong does not present very great difficulties to foreign learners, provided that, in addition to the appropriate variations of quantity, the quality of the first element lies between the sounds of RP /ɔː/ and /ɒ/ and that the glide does not extend beyond the close-mid front level, i.e. [ë].

8.10.4   /əʊ/

(1) *Examples*
   o—so, old, home, both, folk, bimbo, clone, zero, trombone
   oe—toe, doe, sloe, foe, hoe, cocoa, oboe
   ow—know, blow, hollow, pillow, sparrow, meadow, bungalow
   oa—oak, road, foal, toast, soap, hoax, loaf, reproach
   ou—soul, though, shoulder, boulder, soldier
   (*Note* /əʊ/ in 'mauve, brooch, beau, sew, don't, won't, plateau, bureau, chauffeur, gauche')

The lexical frequency of spellings of /əʊ/ as <o>, <o..e>, and <oe> together is 85%, that of <ow> 7%, and that of <oa> 5%. The corresponding text frequencies are 75%, 18% and 4%.

Long [ɘːʊ]—go, toe, home, road, pose
Reduced [əʊ]—goat, rope, oak, post, both
Compare [ɘːʊ], [əʊ]—robe, rope; toes, toast; grows, gross; road, wrote; cold, colt
/əʊ/, /ɜː/—foe, fur; own, earn; goal, girl; oath, earth; coat, curt; foam, firm
/əʊ/, /ɔː/—so, saw; pose, pause; bold, bald; load, lord; boat, bought; choke, chalk
/əʊ/, /ɜː/, /ɔː/—foe, fur, four; bone, burn, born; woke, work, walk; coat, curt, caught; coal, curl, call
[ɫ] *following*—hole, roll, old, moult, bolt, poles

(2) *Description*—The glide of RP /əʊ/ begins at a central position, between close-mid and open-mid, and moves in the direction of RP /ʊ/, there being a slight closing movement of the lower jaw; the lips are neutral for the first element, but have a tendency to round on the second element. The starting point may have a tongue position similar to that described for /ɜː/.

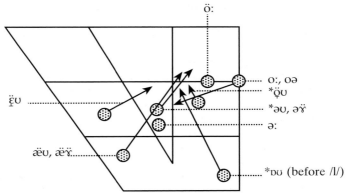

Fig. 27. *Variants of* /əʊ/.

(3) *Variants*—Older speakers of RP commonly use a rounded first element, i.e. [o̞ʊ]. Refined RP uses a type of diphthong where an unrounded first element is produced further forward, i.e. between close-mid and open-mid and centralized from front, giving [ɪ̈ʊ]. Alternatively, an unrounded central first element may be lengthened and the second element weakened, i.e. [ɜː] so that there may arise for a listener a confusion between /əʊ/ and /ɜː/ (especially where [ɫ] follows, e.g. *goal* and *girl*, where a weak [ʊ] element may be taken as the glide onto dark [ɫ]).

/əʊ/ is regularly kept in RP in unaccented syllables where other dialects reduce to /ə/, e.g. in *window* /wɪndəʊ/, *fellow* /feləʊ/; such pronunciations are generally considered substandard by RP speakers. In unaccented syllables in some other words a careful pronunciation produces an allophone [o], e.g. in *obey, phonetics*, although /ə/ is more common. The reduction of /əʊ/ to /ə/ may produce colloquial speech homophones which are distinct in a more formal style, e.g. *ferment* (v.), *foment*—both /fəˋment/, *hypertension, hypotension*—both /haɪpəˋtenʃn/.

Dialectally there is considerable variation in this vowel. Cockney has [æʊ] or even [æ̈ɏ], with unrounding spreading to the second element; this realization is near to Refined RP [ɛ̈ʊ], although Cockney often has more pharyngealization than RP. The lower and more front pronunciation of /əʊ/ in Cockney keeps it apart from the realization of /uː/ as [əʊ], see §8.9.10 above. Regional RP of the London region may have the unrounding but not the fronting of Cockney, i.e. [əɏ]. Cockney also has a considerably different allophone of /əʊ/ before [ɫ], that is [ɒʊ], and this allophone is also typical of London Regional RP.

Australian English has a very similar spread of allophones for this allophone to Cockney. Many other dialects have a relatively pure vowel around C[o]; this applies to SSE, to GA, and to much of the north of England, although north-west England (particularly Tyneside) may have a reversed diphthong [oə].

(4) *Chief sources*—PresE /əʊ/ derives chiefly from ME [ɔː] or ME [ɔu]. Of these, ME [ɔː] has the following main sources: OE [ɑː] (*no, go, home, loaf, ghost*); OE [ɛə] or [æ]+[ld] (*old, told, cold*); OE [ɔ] in open syllables (*over, open, nose, hope*); OF accented [ɔ] (*robe, rose, coat, toast, gross*). This pure vowel had probably reached a quality near C[oː] in the sixteenth and seventeenth centuries.

ME [ɔu] derives mainly from: OE [ɑː] or [ɔ]+[w] or [ɣ] (*know, blow, soul, snow, own, dough*); OE [oː]+[w] (*glow, flow, row*). This diphthong probably reached the stage [ou] by the seventeenth century, with an alternative pronunciation [oː]. The coalescence with [oː]< ME [ɔː] took place in the seventeenth century and the new [oː] was diphthongized to [ou] in the eighteenth and nineteenth centuries, to give PresE /əʊ/.

/əʊ/ is also used in PresE in imitation of French [o] or [ɔ] in more recent importations, such as *beau, hotel, bureau*.

(5) *Advice to foreign learners*—It is advisable to learn /ɜː/ first and to modify /ɜː/ by adding lip-rounding to the end of the vowel. Thus, *fur* may be modified to *foe*, *girl* to *goal*, *burn to bone* etc. In this way, the diphthong will be kept distinct from /ɔː/ (see comparative examples in (1) above). In addition, proper prominence must be given to the first element and reduction of the total length of the glide made in the appropriate contexts.

Many foreign learners will use a pure vowel around C[o], e.g. speakers of Arabic, French, German, Italian, and Spanish. This is the realization of this phoneme in many accents of English. There is no objection in principle to this but the danger is then of confusion with /ɔː/. For this reason, for those aiming at an RP pronunciation, it is worthwhile attempting the diphthong in the way outlined above.

8.10.5   /aʊ/

(1) *Examples*
   ou—house, sound, out, council, ground, blouse, doubt
   ow—allow, cow, town, crowd, owl, browser, growl, powder

The spellings <ou> and <ow> together have a lexical frequency 96% and a text frequency of 99%.

Long [aːʊ]—how, loud, town, cows
Reduced [aʊ]—shout, about, mouse, mouth
Compare [aːʊ], [aʊ]—allows, a louse; found, fount; mouth (v.), mouth (n.);
loud, lout
[ɫ] *following*—cowl, foul, owls

(2) *Description*—The glide of RP /aʊ/ begins at a point between the back and
front open positions, slightly more fronted than the position for RP /ɑː/, i.e. C[ä],
and moves in the direction of RP /ʊ/, though the tongue may not be raised higher
than the close-mid level, i.e. [ö]. The glide is much more extensive than that used
for /əʊ/ and is symmetrically opposed to the front glide of /aɪ/. The lips change
from a neutrally open to a weakly rounded position.

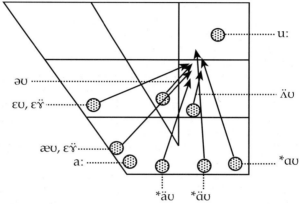

Fig. 28. *Variants of* /aʊ/.

(3) *Variants*—The RP diphthong /aʊ/ is in opposition in the back region with
/əʊ/; if the latter has a starting point in the central area below close-mid, the starting point of /aʊ/ cannot be raised to any extent without the possible loss of
contrast between words such as *tone* and *town*. RP variants, therefore, involve
particularly the fronting or retraction of the starting point rather than its raising.
Considerable latitude is permitted between the values C[a] and C[ɑ]; for many
speakers, the first element of /aɪ/ and /aʊ/ may in fact be identical. Since, however,
several popular regional forms of speech (especially in the London region) have
typically a first element in the C[a] or [æ] areas, reaction amongst careful speakers causes the diphthong to have a more retracted starting point, sometimes
reaching C[ɑ]. In Refined RP the [ɑ] element is extra long, especially in those
contexts in which the diphthong has its fully long form, with a weak glide involving comparatively little raising of the tongue and little, if any, lip-rounding; *loud*
and *lard* may, therefore, be distinguished only by a slight movement at the end
of the vowel.
In Cockney, the first element may be of the [ɛ] or [æ] varieties. It would appear
that with such a glide there would be risk of confusion with the Cockney realization of /əʊ/ as [æʊ] or [äʏ], as between words such as *now* and *no*; in fact, the

starting point used for /əʊ/ may be more open than that of /aʊ/, e.g. *no* [näẙ], *now* [nëʊ]. Even if the two starting points are on the same level, however, the diphthongs are kept phonetically separate by the greater centralization of the first element of /əʊ/ and also, in some cases, by the closer end-point reached in /əʊ/ as compared with that of /aʊ/: [ä̈ẙ], [äẙ], [äʊ] or [ä̈ü] for /əʊ/ as against [æɔ̈] or [ɛɔ̈] for /aʊ/. Alternatively, /aʊ/ may be realized as a long, relatively pure vowel of the [a] type, e.g. *town* [taːn]. The realizations of /əʊ/ in Australian English are once again similar to those in Cockney, although the monophthongal variant does not seem to occur. In Scottish English and in Northern English, where /əʊ/ is realized as [oː], the starting point of /aʊ/ may be raised to give [əʊ] or [ẍʊ]. Also some speakers of these dialects may have [uː] as a realization of /aʊ/. Generally, but not always, the contrast between /aʊ/ and /uː/ is not lost, since /uː/ is realized as [ÿː] in Scottish English, and [ɪə] in those parts of the north of England (mainly the north-east) where the [uː] realization of /aʊ/ occurs. In Scottish English realization with [uː] in words like *town, mouse, about, house* etc., is typical only of broad accents.

(4) *Chief sources*—RP /aʊ/ has origins and development in the back vowel area similar to those of RP /aɪ/ in the front. PresE /aʊ/ derives regularly from ME [uː], whose main sources are: OE [uː] (*cow, house, mouth*); lengthened OE [ʊ] (*ground, found*); OE [ʊ] or [oː]+[w] or [ɣ] (*fowl, bow, bough*); OF or Anglo-Norman [uː] (*allow, powder, couch, count, mountain*). Diphthongization of the pure vowel begins in the fifteenth century ([ʊu]) and the first element is progressively lowered by a central route ([əʊ] or [ẍʊ]) during the sixteenth and seventeenth centuries, there being no confusion with the development ME [ɔː] or [ɔu]>[oː] or [ou]>PresE /əʊ/. The more open first element of /aʊ/ must have become established during the eighteenth and nineteenth centuries.

In some types of Northern and Scottish English the diphthongization (by the Great Vowel Shift) was not completed, the original [uː] being sometimes retained, e.g. *house* [hu(ː)s] or [hy(ː)s]. The pure vowel [uː] is also sometimes retained in RP in the vicinity of bilabial consonants, e.g. in *wound* ('to injure'), *droop, stoop*; in other cases, ME [uː] was shortened and gives PresE /ʌ/ (*plum, crumb, thumb*).

The present spelling forms <ou, ow> for /aʊ/ result from the French influence on the language. OE /uː/ was spelt with *u*, but this letter had a different value in French, [y]; by ME, therefore, the French spelling *ou* or *ow* for the sound [uː] was generally used.

(5) *Advice to foreign learners*—Just as for /aɪ/, foreign learners should be careful to use a correct first element, i.e. a variety which is not so fronted or raised as to be dialectal; a starting point too near to C[ɑ] is also to be avoided, being part of the nowadays very marked Refined RP (see §7.3(4)). The first element should be the most prominent and the second element only lightly touched on, the tongue closing to a position not higher than close-mid, i.e. [ö].

8.11   *Diphthongs* + [ə]

All the preceding diphthongal glides /eɪ,aɪ,ɔɪ,əʊ,aʊ/ are FALLING (i.e. have decreasing prominence, indicated by a longer first element and not to be confused with the falling pitch of intonation) and CLOSING (i.e. gliding from a more open to a closer position); three of them, /aɪ,ɔɪ,ɑʊ/, require an extensive movement of the tongue. All may be followed by [ə] within the word, either as an inseparable part of the word, e.g. *Noah, fire, choir, iron, hire, society, our, sour, tower* /nəʊə, faɪə, kwaɪə, aɪən, haɪə, sə`saɪətɪ, aʊə, saʊə, taʊə/ or as a suffix (morpheme) appended to the root, e.g. *greyer, player, slower, mower, higher, drier, employer* /greɪə, pleɪə, sləʊə, məʊə, haɪə, draɪə, ɪm`plɔɪə/ or, sometimes, as a separable element internal in a composite form, e.g. *nowadays* /`naʊədeɪz/. In such cases, a third vocalic element [ə] may, in slow speech, be added to the two elements of the diphthongal glide; but there is a tendency in General RP spoken rapidly and particularly in Refined RP (even spoken slowly) to omit the second ([ɪ] or [ʊ]) element, especially when [ə] is not felt as a separable morpheme. This process is sometimes known as SMOOTHING.

(1) [aɪə]→[aːə] in General RP, e.g. in *fire, tyre, choir, society, hire, shire, byre, lyre, liable*, and also in cases where [ə] may be considered as a separable suffix, e.g. *higher, shyer, buyer, liar*.
(2) [aʊə]→[ɑːə] in General RP, e.g. in *our, shower, flower, coward, nowadays*.

It will be seen that the reduction of the phonetic sequences [aɪə, aʊə] to [aːə, ɑːə] results in a phonemic opposition relying on a distinction between [aː] and [ɑː]. It is natural that such a tenuous qualitative difference should be levelled out, with the result that both original [aɪə] and [aʊə] are frequently reduced to a diphthongal glide whose first element is a central open vowel. Several new homophones are produced in this way, e.g. *tyre, tower; shire, shower; sire, sour*.

In addition, in Refined RP the diphthongal pronunciations thus produced are sometimes further reduced to a long monophthong, i.e. [aːə]→[aː] and [ɑːə]→[ɑː]. If [aː] and [ɑː] are kept distinct, there is nevertheless confusion between [ɑː] < [aʊə] and /ɑː/, resulting in homophones such as *shower, Shah; tower, tar*. A more extensive levelling (criticized as an affectation in RP, but also as a Cockney vulgarism, and also present in other accents, e.g. Liverpool) reduces both [aːə]

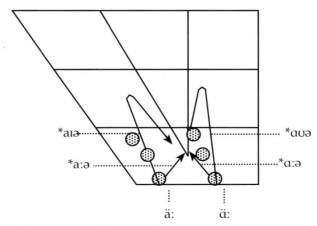

Fig. 29. *Variants of* /aɪə, aʊə/.

and [ɑːə] to [ɑː], so that homophones of the type *shire, shower, Shah; tyre, tower, tar; byre* (or *buyer*), *bower, bar*, are produced, all with /ɑː/. The most likely situation in RP at the moment seems to be a levelling of the two triphthongs to a single diphthong, usually [aːə], but not the further reduction to a monophthong and no loss of the contrast with /ɑː/.

(3) [eɪə]→[eːə] in General RP, e.g., in *player, greyer, conveyor, layer*. In these examples, in which it is a question of /eɪ/+ an /ə/ suffix, the resultant diphthong is frequently levelled with the /eə/ of *there, rare* etc. Thus, homophones such as *prayer, pray-er; lair, layer*, are produced (see §8.12.2 for reduction /eə/ to [ɛː]).

(4) [əʊə]→[əː]=/ɜː/ in General RP, levelling frequently occurring between *mower, slower*, and *myrrh, slur* (with /ɜː/).

(5) [ɔɪə]→[ɔːə] in General RP, as in *employer, enjoyable, buoyant, joyous*. In these cases the [ɔː] element of the diphthong is qualitatively distinct from the value associated with /ɔː/, since it has a tongue position not higher than open-mid. Thus, *drawer* ('one who draws') with /ɔː/+/ə/ may have a closer initial vowel element than the starting point of the glide in the reduced form of *coir*, with [ɔ̞ːə].

(6) Some speakers distinguish between sequences of diphthong + /əl/, usually in the case of terminations spelt -*el*, -*al*, e.g. *trial, towel, royal*, and sequences of diphthong + /l/, e.g. *tile, owl, toil*. However, the first sequence, containing three vocalic elements, may be reduced to a centring diphthong; and, in the case of the second type of sequence, an [ə] (or [ʊ]) glide is present before [ɫ], so that a similar triphthongal glide reducible to a centring diphthong is produced. Thus, /eɪ,aɪ,aʊ,ɔɪ/ followed by either /l/ or /əl/ tend to be realized as [eːə, aːə, ɑːə *or* ɑːʊ, ɔːə], the examples given above being perfect rhymes. In the case of /əʊ/ (=[əʊ])+[ɫ], the [ʊ] element of the diphthong may be retained, both because it is reinforced by the glide on to [ɫ] and also in order to maintain the distinction /əʊ/–/ɜː/ as in *pole, pearl*. In London Regional RP (= Estuary English) it is also likely that /əʊ/ before /l/ as in *pole* will be produced with the contextual allophone [ɒʊ] and the quality of the beginning of the diphthong will thus keep such words distinct.

(7) There is some suggestion that smoothing may be more likely where the triphthong is within one morpheme rather than when two morphemes are involved, e.g. that smoothing is more likely in *flour* and *hire* than in *flower* and *higher*. However, it is certain that smoothing is possible across morpheme boundaries and indeed it may occur across word boundaries where a word-final diphthong followed by word-initial /ə/, e.g. *they are* [ðeːə] or [ðɛːə], rhyming with *there; go away* ['ɡəːəˋweɪ]=/ɡɜːˋweɪ/; *buy a house* [baːəˋhaʊs]; *now and then* [naːənˋðen]; *boy and girl* [bɔːənˋɡɜːl].

(8) The weakness of the final elements of diphthongs is also demonstrated by their instability before vowels other than [ə]. Thus, in the case of /eɪ,aɪ,ɔɪ/, when /iː/ or /ɪ/ follow (i.e. a vowel articulation at or closer than the end-point of the diphthongal glide), the [ɪ] second element of the diphthong may be lost, e.g. in *playing, way in, they eat it, highest, hyena, buy it, try each, annoying, the boy easily*; the [ɪ] element may also be absorbed before other vowels, e.g. in *way up, by all means, they understand, toy engine*, though some glide in the direction of [ɪ] is likely to be made when the following vowel has a quality near to that of the first element of the diphthong (especially of the wide diphthongs /aɪ,ɔɪ/), e.g. in *may end, my uncle, the boy often* etc. In the case of /əʊ,aʊ/, absorption of the [ʊ] element before /ʊ/ or /uː/ rarely arises, since a following /ʊ/ or /uː/ is unusual. But

absorption of the [ʊ] element of the narrow diphthong /əʊ/ frequently occurs before other vowels, e.g. in *go easy, glowing, no end, go off, know all, show up*, though when /ɜ:/ follows some movement towards [ʊ] and lip-rounding normally takes place, e.g. in *so early*. Loss of the [ʊ] element of /əʊ/ does not, in pre-vocalic positions, lead to confusion with /ɜ:/, since /ɜ:/ in such a position will normally be realized with a linking /r/, cf. *slow it* /ˈsləʊ ɪt/ or /ˈslɜ: ɪt/ and *slur it* /ˈslɜːr ɪt/. In the case of /aʊ/, loss of the [ʊ] element may also occur before vowels other than [ə], e.g. in *allow each, vowing, how else, now or never*, but when the following vowel has an open quality similar to that of the first element of /aʊ/ some tongue movement towards [ʊ] and lip-rounding normally takes place, e.g. in *how are they, plough up, how odd*. This tendency to absorb the second element of diphthongs before other vowels is a feature which is more marked in Refined RP than General RP. A more careful pronunciation of sequences of diphthong following vowel may involve the presence of a linking [j,w], e.g. *plough up* [plaʊʷʌp], *way in* [weiʲɪn], but this linking [j,w] is never as prominent as phonemic /j,w/, cf. *three ears* vs *three years* and *two-eyed* vs *too wide* (see further under §12.4.7).

(9) A similar weakening of the monophthongs /u:/ and /i:/ sometimes occurs across syllable boundaries. /u:/ may be replaced by /ʊ/ and /i:/ by /ɪ/ before vowels in phrases such as *two in the morning* /tʊ ɪn ðəˈmɔːnɪŋ/ and *three o'clock* /θrɪ əˈklɒk/. It is possible in a word such as *ruin* to regard the pronunciation /ˈrʊɪn/ as a version of /ˈruːɪn/ exhibiting smoothing. (Alternatives in careful speech may again involve the use of linking [j,w], e.g. [tuːʷɪn ðə ˈmɔːnɪŋ].)

(10) There are difficulties of analysis into syllables related to the smoothing of triphthongs. The diphthongs which form the first part of triphthongs are clearly monosyllabic, i.e. they involve only one peak of prominence. But when a /ə/ is added, this produces a sequence with two peaks of prominence and hence two syllables. When the triphthongs are smoothed, the sequences are again reduced to one syllable.

(11) *Advice to foreign learners*—Foreign learners should be aware of this tendency to reduction of vowel sequences, in order that they may understand colloquial English. They will observe that such reduced forms are normal among many educated speakers. Nevertheless, like most changes of pronunciation, these reductions are often condemned as vulgarisms—frequently by those who use them and are not aware of the fact. Foreign learners should, therefore, avoid the extreme forms of reduction, e.g. [aː] and [ɑː] for [aɪə] and [aʊə], and [ɜː] for [əʊə]. But the levelling to [aːə], [ɑːə], [eːə], and [ɔːə], described above, may be taken to be current and permissible. Certainly such pronunciations are preferable to sequences containing an exaggerated [ɪ] or [ʊ] element, i.e. [j] or [w], giving [ajə], [ɑwə], [əwə], [ejə], [ajə], etc.

8.12 *Centring Diphthongs* /ɪə,eə,ʊə/

8.12.1 /ɪə/ (See Fig. 30.)

(1) *Examples*
  er, ere—material, hero, zero, here, austere, interfere, sincere
  ear, eer—dear, fear, year, nuclear, career, sneer, deer

ia—material, brilliant, media, industrial, familiar, ruffian
ea—idea, cochlea, pancreas, nausea, diarrhoea, area
eu, eo—museum, theological, creosote
ie—soviet, spaniel, fierce, salient, thirtieth etc.
io, iou—period, million, chariot, axiom, opinion, previous
iu—medium, stadium, union, tedium, delirium
(*Note* 'weird' [wɪəd].)

The lexical frequency of the principal spellings involving an <r> are <er> and <ere> together 10%, <ear> 7%, and <eer> 5% (text frequencies 12%, 28%, and 4% respectively). The lexical frequencies of the principal spellings without an <r> are <ia> 31% and <ea> 6% (text frequencies 10% and 12%). As can be seen there are a large number of less frequent spellings.

Long [ɪːə]—dear, here, cheer, beard
Reduced [ɪə]—pierce, fierce
Compare [ɪːə], [ɪə]—fears, fierce
[ɫ] *following*[7]—real

(2) *Description*—The glide of RP /ɪə/ begins with a tongue position approximately that used for /ɪ/, i.e. close-mid and centralized from front, and moves in the direction of the more open variety of /ə/ when /ɪə/ is final in the word; in non-final positions, e.g. in *beard, fierce*, the glide may not be so extensive, the quality of the [ə] element being of a mid type. The lips are neutral throughout, with a slight movement from spread to open.

In unaccented syllables the sequence [ɪ]+[ə][8] may not always constitute the falling diphthong described, i.e. prominence may not always be on the first element. Thus the [ɪ] element may be the weaker of the two, giving a rising diphthong and being almost equivalent to [j], cf. the two [ɪ] + [ə] sequences in both syllables of *period, serious*, [ˈpɪərï ə d] or [ˈpɪərjəd] and [ˈsɪərï ə s] or [ˈsɪərjəs]. Thus a falling diphthong is usual in *reindeer* and a rising diphthong in *windier*.[9] The glide of the rising type [ɪ̆ə] is often used when the [ə] represents a suffix with morphemic status, e.g. *easier, carrier*, in which case [ɪ] and [ə] are conveniently treated as a hiatus of vowels in two syllables with a variant monosyllabic pronunciation [jə]. Increasingly, a closer vowel is to be heard in such words, i.e. [ˈiːzɪə], [ˈkærɪə], which may be interpreted as /ˈiːzɪːə/, /ˈkærɪːə/, an interpretation which supports the view that there is vowel 'hiatus' between two syllables. Such a solution may also be applied to cases of a rising diphthong where there is no morpheme boundary as commonly heard in *billiards* and *hideous*, e.g. [ˈbɪlɪədz], [ˈhɪdɪəs], to be interpreted as /ˈbɪlɪːədz/ and /ˈhɪdɪːəs/ (alongside their monophthongal variants /ˈbɪljədz/ and /ˈhɪdjəs/.

---

[7] This solitary example of /ɪə/ + [ɫ] may be taken as a variant of /iː/ + [ɫ] (cf. also *ideal*). It is possible to pronounce *real* with /iː/ in the same way as *meal, feel* etc.; /ɪə/, however, seems to be more common in this particular word, cf. *reel* /riːl/, *rill* /rɪl/
[8] Jones (1954)
[9] Andrésen (1957)

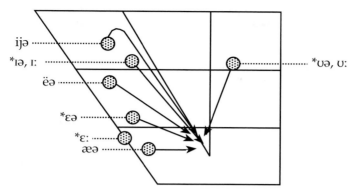

Fig. 30. *Variants of final* /ɪə, eə, ʊə/.

(3) *Variants*—Increasingly pronunciations with a monophthong [ɪː] can be heard within General RP. (This type of pronunciation has been common in Australian English for some time.) In some kinds of Refined RP, and especially when /ɪə/ is accented and final, a different type of rising diphthong may be heard, the quality often being near to the phonetic quality of /ɜː/ or even /ɑː/. Thus, *here, dear*, may become /hjɜː, djɜː/ or /hjɑː/(=[çɑː]) /djɑː/. The form with /ɑː/ is usually characterized as an affectation.

Rhotic dialects like General American and Standard Scottish English have no /ɪə/, having /ɪ/ or /iː/+/r/ in those words which have an <r>in the spelling. In Cockney a glide from a relatively close to an almost open position may be heard, sometimes with an intervening [j], i.e. [ïjä].

(4) *Chief sources*—PresE /ɪə/ results generally from ME [eː]+[r] (*here, hear, dear, weary, appear, clear*) and from early ME [ɛː]+[r] (*ear, shear, fear, beard*). In the sixteenth and seventeenth centuries some variation existed between [iːɹ] and [eːɹ], but by the seventeenth century [iːɹ] was predominant; [ɹ] was lost and replaced by [ə] in the eighteenth century. In those cases where no *r* occurs in the spelling, e.g. *idea, idiom, museum*, the [ə] element derives from the juxtaposition of two vowels with reduction of the second.

(5) *Advice to foreign learners*—Foreign learners should avoid using a first element which is too close, i.e. /ɪ/ should be used rather than /iː/. Because of the <r> in the spelling, many foreign learners may use the nearest vowel plus /r/. They should know that to native speaker ears this gives the impression of an American pronunciation. Although the <r> should not be pronounced finally or before a consonant, it should be remembered than an /r/ link is regularly made before a following vowel, initial either in a bound or a compounded morpheme, e.g. *hearing* /ˈhɪərɪŋ/ (cf. /hɪə/), *car auction* /ˈkɑːr ɔːkʃn/, or initial in the next word of the group, e.g. *hear and there* /hɪər ən ˈðeə/, *area of it* /ˈeərɪər əv ɪt/.

8.12.2   /eə/ (See Fig. 30.)

(1) Examples
   ar, are—rarity, care, share, aware, parent, welfare, librarian, scarce
   air—air, chair, affair, despair, impair, eclair
   ear—bear, pear, wear, tear (v.), swear
   cf. hare, hair; fare, fair; stare, stair
   (*Note* spellings with <aer> as variant of <air> in 'aerobic, aerial, aeroplane'
   etc. Also with /eə/, 'heir, their, there, mayor, prayer, compere, premiere,
   sombrero'.)

Spellings as <ar> and <are> together have a lexical frequency of 64 %, those as
<air> 15%, and those as <ear> 6%. (Text frequencies are 59%, 28%, and 10%.)

   Long [eːə]—pair, there, chairs, cared
   Reduced [eə]—scarce
   Compare [eːə], [eə]—scares, scarce
   (No cases of /eə/+[ɫ].)

   (2) *Description*—The glide of RP /eə/ begins in the open-mid front position,
i.e. approximately C[ɛ], and moves in the direction of the more open variety of
/ə/, especially when the diphthong is final; where /eə/ occurs in word-medial
position, the [ə] element tends to be of a mid [ə] type. The lips are neutrally
open throughout. (See §8.11 for the reduction of /eɪ/+/ə/ to /eə/.)
   (3) *Variants*—Nowadays a long monophthong [ɛː] is a completely acceptable
alternative in General RP. Refined RP keeps the diphthong but has a more open
starting point, giving [æə̞].
   Rhotic dialects like General American and Standard Scottish English have no
/eə/, this diphthong usually corresponding to /eɪ/ or /e/ plus /r/. Most dialects of
the north of England prefer a monophthongal pronunciation. In Liverpool the
contrast between /eə/ and /ɜː/ is lost, with the resulting single phoneme being
realized as a vowel centralized from C[ɛ] and rounded, i.e. [œː]. In Cockney the
starting point of this diphthong is closer, giving [eə̞]. The opposition between /eə/
and /ɪə/ does not occur in the West Indies and in New Zealand, neutralizing on
/eə/ in the former and on /ɪə/ in the latter.
   (4) *Chief sources*—PresE /eə/ derives from three ME sources: ME [aː]+[r]
(*care, hare, mare*); ME [ɛi] or [æi]+[r] (*their, air, hair, fair*); ME [ɛː]+[r] (*bear,
there, where, swear*). We have seen (§8.10.1 (4)) that ME [aː] and [æi] tended to
coalesce into [ɛː] in eModE and they in turn are confused by the seventeenth
century with the descendent of ME [ɛː] when followed by [r]. It is likely that all
words with PresE /eə/ were pronounced with [ɛːɹ] (or perhaps [eiɹ]) in the seventeenth century. The diphthongal glide to [ə] results from the loss of post-vocalic
[ɹ] in the eighteenth century.
   (5) *Advice to foreign learners*—See the comments in section (5) of the
previous section about the effect produced by pronouncing an /r/ in this
diphthong. The post-vocalic <r> of the spelling forms can be pronounced as a
linking form when a following word begins with a vowel, e.g. *pair of shoes*
/peər əv `ʃuːz/, or when a vowel occurs in the following syllable of the same

word, e.g. *care* /keə/, but *caring* /ˈkeərɪŋ/. Since a monophthongal pronunciation of /eə/ is now common, a suitable realization of this phoneme can be achieved starting from /e/ and adding length and opening the mouth somewhat.

8.12.3 /ʊə/ (See Fig. 30.)

(1) *Examples*

    oor—poor, moor, boor
    our—tour, dour, gourd, amour, tournament, bourgeois
    ure—pure, endure, cure, sure, abjure, secure
    ur—curious, spurious, during, security, insurance, furious
    ue, ua—cruel, fluent, puerile, actual, mutual, usual, gradual, annual
    (*Note* with /ʊə/ 'jewel, incongruous, pleurisy, arduous'.)

Common spellings with an <r> involve <oor>, <our> and <ure> (and <ur> in word-medial position). Where there is no <r> in the spelling the most frequent spellings are <ue> and <ua>.

(2) *Description*—RP /ʊə/ glides from a tongue position similar to that used for /ʊ/ towards the more open type of /ə/ which forms the end-point of all three centring diphthongs with, again, a somewhat closer variety of [ə] when the diphthong occurs in word-medial position. The lips are weakly rounded at the beginning of the glide, becoming neutrally spread as the glide progresses.

In the same way that the sequence [ɪ]+[ə] may constitute a rising diphthong, the sequence [ʊ]+[ə] may also, in unaccented syllables, have the prominence on the second element, e.g. in *influence, valuable, vacuum, jaguar* etc., the first element often weakening to [w]. In many cases of such sequences, [ŭə] represents a realization of a final unaccented /uː/+morpheme /ə/, e.g. *rescuer*, /ˈreskjuː/+/ə/ → [ˈreskjŭə].[10]

(3) *Variants*—/ɔə/ having coalesced with /ɔː/ for most RP speakers, the pattern of centring diphthongs is rendered asymmetrical, there being only one back glide of this type opposed to the two front glides. As a result, the first element of /ʊə/ can be lowered considerably without risk of confusion. Thus several words with /ʊə/, which have a pronunciation [ʊə] for some RP speakers, are given by others a glide [ɔə], e.g. in *poor, sure*. This glide [ɔə] may in turn be levelled with the realization of /ɔː/. So *Shaw, sure, shore*, still pronounced by some /ʃɔː,ʃʊə,ʃɔə/, are levelled by many others to /ʃɔː/ for all three words; or again, *you're* (most frequently with /ʊə/) may be realized as /jɔː/, i.e. identical with *your*. It is to be noted, however, that such lowering or monophthongization of /ʊə/ is rarer in the case of less commonly used monosyllabic words such as *dour, gourd*. The [ʊə] or [uə] derived from /uː/ plus /ə/, as in *rescuer*, is not subject to alternation with /ɔː/. Words with a preceding /j/, e.g. *cure, curious, puerile, secure, endure, bureau*, are also generally not involved in such alternation, although in Refined RP the /ʊə/

---

[10] As with /ɪə/ (see §8.12(2)) this sequence may be realized as a closer short vowel, thus [ˈreskjuə]

in such words may be subject to monophthongization with both lowering and unrounding, giving [ӛː].

An alternative development in RP is a monophthongization of /ʊə/ to [uː], which is kept distinct from /ɔː/. The same development occurred somewhat earlier in Northern English, in Cockney and in Australian English, although in all these accents there is often merger with /ɔː/ with a quality nearer to [ɔː] In those kinds of English like General American and Standard Scottish English, in which /r/ occurs before consonants and before a pause, the /ʊə/ of RP usually corresponds to an /uː/ or /ʊ/ plus /r/ where there is an <r> in the spelling.

(4) *Chief Sources*—PresE /ʊə/ derives generally from an earlier vowel or diphthong+[r], e.g. < ME [oː] or [ɔː]+[r] (*moor, poor, boor*); < ME [uː]+[r] (*mourn,* for those RP speakers who use /ʊə/ rather than /ɔː/)—it is to be noted that most cases of pure vowel+[r] have been lowered to /ɔː/, e.g. *fourth, floor, court* (see §8.9.8 (4)); and < ME [iu] or [ɛu]+[r] or morpheme [ər] (*sure, pure, fewer*). In these cases the [ə] element developed with the loss of [ɹ] in the eighteenth century. Sometimes, however, /ʊə/ arises from the juxtaposition of /uː/ or /ʊ/ and another vowel which has weakened to [ə] (*influence, truant, virtuous, jewel*).

(5) *Advice to foreign learners*—Care should be taken to use a first element of a close-mid kind rather than a quality resembling that of /uː/. Alternatively, /ʊə/ may be pronounced as a monophthong, achieved by lengthening /ʊ/. In addition, the spelling <r> should not be pronounced, except when an /r/ link is made before a following vowel, either occurring initially in the next word, e.g. *poor old* man /pʊər əʊld ˈmæn/, or before a prefix or the second element of a compound, e.g. *tour* /tʊə/ but *touring* /ˈtʊərɪŋ/, *cure* /kjʊə/ but *cure-all* /ˈkjʊərɔːl/. See section §8.12.1(6) above for comments about the effect of producing the post-vocalic /r/ in all positions.

8.13   *Vowels in Syllables without Primary Accent*

With the principal exception of /ə/, which occurs only in unaccented syllables, we have so far dealt mainly with vowels in accented syllables. In polysyllabic words one syllable is pronounced with a PRIMARY ACCENT (the principal exponent of accent being pitch prominence—but see Chapter 10 for more on the phonetic exponents of accent). Table 6 illustrates the occurrence of vowels in a selection of situations other than that of primary accent—in words containing from two to five syllables. The first column, *Remote preceding*, shows vowels in a place more than one syllable before the the primary accent; the second, *Adjacent Preceding*, vowels immediately preceding the accent; the third, *Adjacent Following*, vowels immediately following the accent; and the fourth, *Remote Following*, vowels in a place more than one syllable after the accent.

Notes

(1) One of the syllables before that having the primary accent may carry a SECONDARY ACCENT (marked by pitch prominence, like primary accent). This may be on the Remote Preceding or the Adjacent Preceding, e.g. *referee* /ˈrefəˈriː/, *canteen* /ˈkænˈtiːn/. Any vowel except /ə/ may form the centre of a syllable with secondary accent.

	Remote preceding	Adjacent preceding	Adjacent following	Remote following
Reduced				
/ɪ/	ina`bility	e`ffect	`sorry	`apathy
/ʊ/	superi`ority	silhou`ette	`ambulance	`neighbourhood
/ə/	conside`ration	a`llow	`mother	`character
Short				
/e/	refe`ree	Sep`tember	`prefect	`architect
/æ/	maga`zine	can`teen	`syntax	`caravan
/ʌ/	subjec`tivity	sul`phuric	`product	`aqueduct
/ɒ/	poli`tician	Oc`tober	`diphthong	`catalogue
Long				
/iː/	precon`ceive	aes`thetic	`phoneme	`obsolete
/ɑː/	arti`san	sar`castic	`placard	`reservoir
/ɔː/	audi`bility	au`gust	`record	`corridor
/uː/	super`sede	Ju`ly	`nephew	`residue
/ɜː/	perpen`dicular	ur`bane	`expert	`universe
Diphthongs				
/eɪ/	phrase`ology	a`orta	`detail	`magistrate
/aɪ/	bio`logical	mi`nute (adj.)	`missile	`civilize
/ɔɪ/		employ`ee	`convoy	`celluloid
/əʊ/	photo`graphic	No`vember	`window	`episode
/aʊ/	counte`ract	out`rageous	`compound	`eiderdown
/ɪə/	superi`ority	theo`logical	`frontier	`overseer
/eə/	varia`bility	where`by	`fanfare	`underwear
/ʊə/	neuro`logical	cu`rator	`contour	`manicure

Table 6. *Vowels in syllables without primary accent*

(2) Some of the remaining syllables (i.e. those not carrying a primary or secondary accent) have a FULL VOWEL (i.e. one other than /ɪ/, /ə/ or /ʊ/) at their centre, e.g. *window*. Such syllables have a degree of prominence (sometimes called a weak accent) lesser than that produced by the pitch prominence of primary and secondary accent.

(3) Other syllables not containing a pitch prominence have a REDUCED VOWEL, i.e. /ɪ/, /ə/ or /ʊ/. These are the three short vowels with a central or centralized quality and are the least prominent syllables.

The present relationship of vowel quality and accentuation arises from the various conflicting phonological influences to which English has been exposed over the last 1,000 years. As a general rule, weak accent in OE led to the obscuration of short vowels and the shortening of long vowels. By ME, however, new long vowels or diphthongs under relatively weak accent emerged as a result of vocalization of earlier consonantal articulations, e.g. [iː] < OE [ɪ]+[ɡ] or [j] (*holy*), [əu] deriving from an intrusive [o] or [ɔ] before [ɣ] or [w] (*follow*). Moreover, words of French origin such as *empire, increase* (n.), while shifting their primary accent back to the first syllable, kept the full vowel quality in the final syllable or, in the case of polysyllables such as *justify, temporary*, retained a full vowel on a syllable following the primary accent. In words of the *temporary, secretary* type, American English, for instance, keeps a full [e] vowel, as was the case in English up to the eighteenth century, whereas in present RP the former [e] or [ɛ:] is reduced to [ə] or elided. As a result of influences of this kind, full vowels were found in eModE in a number of situations where to-day qualitative weakening is once again the rule,[11] e.g. *certain, bargain*, with [eɪ] in the final syllable; *history, majesty, tragedy*, and *merrily*, with [əɪ] finally; and *emperor, saviour*, with [əur] finally.

8.14   *Frequency of Occurrence of RP Vowels*

In colloquial RP, /ə/ (10.74%) and /ɪ/ (8.33%) clearly emerge as the vowels having the highest text frequency. This is to be expected, since /ə/ is the most common vowel in unaccented syllables in a language which has a high proportion of unaccented syllables, and /ɪ/ has a high frequency of occurrence in both accented and unaccented syllables. The frequency of occurrence of each RP vowel as given in Fry (1947) is shown in Table 7. Frequency of occurrence measured by other authors in both RP and in American English[12] (in so far as similar measurements can be made, given that /ɒ,ɪə,eə,ʊə/ do not occur in General American and /ʌ/ is not always given phonemic status) produces the same top five /ə,ɪ,e,aɪ,iː/, a second group of three /eɪ,əʊ,æ/ and a bottom six of /uː,ʊ,ɑː,aʊ,ɔɪ/ with /ɔɪ/ always last.

	%		%
ə	10.74	ɔː	1.24
ɪ	8.33	uː	1.13
e	2.97	ʊ	0.86
aɪ	1.83	ɑː	0.79
ʌ	1.75	aʊ	0.61
eɪ	1.71	ɜː	0.52
iː	1.65	eə	0.34
əʊ	1.51	ɪə	0.21
æ	1.45	ɔɪ	0.14
ɒ	1.37	ʊə	0.06
Total all vowels: 39.21%			

Table 7. *Text frequencies of vowels in RP (from Fry, 1947)*

[11] For an account of vowels in unaccented syllables in eModE see Dobson (1957)
[12] See French *et al.* (1930), Carterette and Jones (1974), Mines *et al.* (1978), Knowles (1987)

9

The English Consonants

9.1 *The Distinctive Consonants*

It is possible to abstract from a continuous utterance of English by means of a process of commutation (see §5.3) 24 distinctive units which are consonantal both in terms of their position in syllables (see §5.6) and also, in the majority of cases, in terms of their phonetic nature (i.e. they have, at least in some of their realizations, articulations involving the obstructions or narrowings which produce, acoustically, a noise component—see §4.2).

These 24 consonantal phonemes are classified in Table 8 in two general categories:

(a) Those articulations in which there is a total closure or a stricture causing friction, both groups being typically associated with a noise component (OBSTRUENTS); in this class there is a distinctive opposition between voiceless and voiced types.

(b) Those articulations in which there is only a partial closure or an unimpeded oral or nasal escape of air; such articulations, typically voiced, and frequently frictionless, i.e. without a noise component (SONORANTS), may share many phonetic characteristics with vowels.

	Plosive	Affricate	Fricative	Nasal	Approx.
Bilabial	p,b			m	(w)
Labiodental			f,v		
Dental			θ,ð		
Alveolar	t,d		s,z	n	l
Post-alveolar					r
Palato-alveolar		tʃ,dʒ	ʃ,ʒ		
Palatal					j
Velar	k,g			ŋ	w
Glottal			h		

Table 8. *The distinctive consonants of English*

Notes

(1) In some types of RP it may be necessary to include the labial-velar voiceless fricative [ʍ] as a phoneme, e.g. in words like *which, what, whether*, but for most RP speakers these words are pronounced with a /w/.

(2) In practical teaching it may sometimes be convenient to treat /tr/ and /dr/ as distinctive affricates as well as /tʃ/ and /dʒ/ (see §9.3).

(3) The glottal stop [ʔ] has been excluded, since it is not phonemically distinctive in RP; its use as a reinforcement for vowels and its allophonic association with /p,t,k/ will be treated in §9.2.8.

It will be seen from Table 8 that:

(a) the plosive and nasal phonemes fall into three contrastive groups as far as the place of articulation is concerned, i.e. bilabial, alveolar, and velar;

(b) the affricates, lateral, and /r/ phonemes have an alveolar basis;

(c) the fricatives have five areas of articulation, i.e. labiodental, dental, alveolar, palato-alveolar, and glottal.

These basic areas of articulation, convenient for labelling the phonemes, will need to be extended when the various allophonic realizations are discussed, but in any particular context the number of oppositions involving the place of articulation will remain unchanged; thus, the allophones of /t/ may be dental or post-alveolar, and the allophones of /k/ may be palatal, without constituting additional distinctive areas of articulation, since such variants are conditioned by the context.

Class A: Obstruents

9.2   *Plosives*

The complete articulation of a pulmonic egressive plosive, or stop, consonant consists of three stages:

(1) the CLOSING stage, during which the articulating organs move together in order to form the obstruction; in this stage, there is often an on-glide (a TRANSITION) audible in a preceding sound segment and visible in an acoustic analysis as a characteristic curve of the formants (see §9.2.2 below) of the preceding sound;

(2) the COMPRESSION stage, during which lung action compresses the air behind the closure; this stage may or may not be accompanied by voice, i.e. vibration of the vocal folds;

(3) the RELEASE stage, during which the organs forming the obstruction part rapidly, allowing the compressed air to escape abruptly (i.e. with an explosion, hence 'plosive'); if stage (2) is voiced, the vocal fold vibration will continue in stage (3) if a vowel follows; if stage (2) is voiceless, stage (3) may also be voiceless (aspiration) before silence or before the onset of voice (as for a following vowel), or stage (3) may coincide with the onset of vocal fold vibration, as when a voiceless plosive is followed without intervening aspiration by a vowel; again, an off-glide (TRANSITION) associates the plosive with a following sound.

Since a condition of plosive articulation is that the whole of the speech tract behind the primary closure should form a chamber sealed to the escape of air, and since the primary closures for the English plosives are normally made in the oral cavity, it follows that the soft palate is held in its raised position in the compression stage and usually also during the closing stage (the exception being when a nasal consonant precedes).

9.2.1 The Phonetic Features of English Plosives

The RP plosive phonemes comprise three pairs: /p,b/; /t,d/; /k,g/. Table 9 illustrates oppositions in word-initial, medial, and final positions.

	/p/	/b/	/t/	/d/	/k/	/g/
Initial	pole	bowl	toll	dole	coal	goal
Medial	riper		writer	rider		
			bitter	bidder	bicker	bigger
	caper	caber	cater			
		rubber		rudder		rugger
	lopping	lobbing			locking	logging
Final	rip	rib	write	ride	rick	rig

Table 9. *Minimal oppositions among English plosives*

These oppositions may be realized by means of one or several of the following phonetic features:

(1) *Place of articulation*—/p,b/, generally bilabial; /t,d/, generally alveolar; /k,g/, generally velar.
(2) *Force of articulation*—/p,t,k/ tend to be pronounced with more muscular energy and a stronger breath effort than /b,d,g/; the former are known as relatively strong or fortis, the latter as relatively weak or lenis.[1]
(3) *Aspiration*—The voiceless series /p,t,k/, when initial in an accented syllable, are usually accompanied by aspiration, i.e. there is a voiceless interval consisting of strongly expelled breath between the release of the plosive and the onset of a following vowel, e.g. *pin, tin, kin* [ˈpʰɪn, ˈtʰɪn, ˈkʰɪn]. When /l,r,w,j/ follow /p,t,k/ in such positions, the aspiration is manifested in the devoicing of /l,r,w,j/, e.g. in *please, pray, try, clean, twice, quick, pew, tune, queue*; some devoicing may also occur in relatively unaccented situations, e.g. *apricot, atlas, applicant, heckler, buckram, vacuum* etc. In other positions, i.e. preceding a vowel in an unaccented syllable and finally, such aspiration as may occur is relatively weak, e.g. /p/ in *polite, lip*; in absolute final positions, i.e. preceding silence, /p,t,k/

---

[1] Lower intraoral pressure for /b,d,g/ was reported by Subtelny *et al.* (1966) and Malécot (1968).

may have no audible release (see §9.2.4(1)). Where a plosive follows /s/ within the same syllable the distinction between /p,t,k/ on the one hand and /b,d,g/ on the other is neutralized (see §5.3.4); the resulting plosives are unaspirated (i.e. similar to /b,d,g/ in all other positions), although they have no voicing in the compression stage (similar to /p,t,k/ in all other positions); only the apparent fortis nature of these articulations suggests a preferred transcription of *spin, stop, skin* as /spɪn,stɒp,skɪn/ rather than /sbɪn,sdɒp,sgɪn/.[2] This is confirmed by sequences of /s/ plus /p,t,k/ which cross morpheme or word boundaries where the aspiration of /p,t,k/ may be lost but where nevertheless a distinction may remain between /p,t,k/ and /b,d,g/ based on strength of articulation alone, cf. *discussed* vs *disgust*.

(4) *Voicing*—The voiced series /b,d,g/ may have full voice during their second stage when they occur in positions between voiced sounds, e.g. in *labour, leader, eager, windy, rub out, read it, egg and, to be, to do, to go*. In initial and especially in final positions, i.e. following or preceding silence, /b,d,g/, while remaining lenis, may be only partially voiced or completely voiceless, e.g. in *bill, done, game, cub, lid, bag*. In these positions /b,d,g/ are realized as [b̥,d̥,g̥], vocal fold vibration beginning only in the last portion of the compression stage in initial position, and finishing in the first portion of the compression stage in final position (or having no voicing at all in this stage). Even in the intervocalic positions mentioned at the beginning of this section /b,d,g/ may sometimes be subject to devoicing, particularly where a word boundary is involved.[3] It has also been claimed that, even when vocal cord vibration is not present, glottographic and laryngoscopic studies show that whisper-like narrowing is present.[4]

Aspiration and voicing in syllable-initial position can together be regarded as involving differences in Voice Onset Time (or VOT), i.e. the interval between the release burst and the onset of voicing. VOT differences, and the voicing of [d] in other positions, are shown schematically in Table 10. Note that an initial fully devoiced [d̥] as in *done* has approximately the same VOT value as an initial unaspirated [t] as in *stun*. VOT values for aspirated voiceless stops are generally around 40–75 ms, whereas VOT for voiced plosives varies from a much smaller positive value or has a negative value (i.e. voicing starts before the point of plosion). VOT in voiceless plosives has been shown to increase as the place of articulation moves from labial to velar.[5]

(5) *Length of preceding sounds*—When the RP plosives occur finally in a syllable, their value is determined largely (since the voicing factor is not strongly operative) by the length of the syllable which they close. It is a feature of English (and to varying extents universally in languages) that syllables closed by voiceless

---

[2] Wingate (1982) also shows that the fundamental frequency of the following vowel equates with /p,t,k/ rather than /b,d,g/

[3] Suomi (1976, 1980) reported only 11 out of 144 instances of interruptions in the voicing of voiced plosives in word-medial position compared with 76 out of 213 such interruptions in word-final plosives preceding a vowel. Docherty (1992) found interrupted voicing in the compression stage in 97% of word-initial voiced plosives following vowels and in 46% of word-final voiced plosives preceding vowels.

[4] Catford (1977:112)

[5] See Docherty (1992), Volaitis and Miller (1992)

l	i:	d̥			final devoiced [d̥]
l	i:	d	ə		medial fully voiced [d]
		d	ʌ	n	partially voiced [d̥] (negative VOT)
	s	t	ʌ	n	unaspirated [t] (zero VOT)
		t	ʌ	n	aspirated [tʰ] (positive VOT)

Table 10. *VOT differences in English (underlining indicates voicing) in 'lead, leader, done, stun, ton'*

consonants are considerably shorter than those which are open, or closed by a voiced consonant.[6] We have seen in the chapter on vowels that this variation of length is particularly noticeable when the syllable contains a 'long' vowel or diphthong, cf. the fully long vowels or diphthongs in *robe, heard, league* (closed by voiced /b,d,g/) with the reduced values in *rope, hurt, leak* (closed by voiceless /p,t,k/). Preceding consonants, notably /l,n,m/, are also shortened by a following /p,t,k/, especially when the consonants are themselves preceded by a short vowel, e.g. compare the relatively long /l/ in *killed, Elbe,* /n/ in *wand,* and /m/ in *symbol* with the reduced varieties in *kilt, help, want, simple.* A phonemic transcription of *rope, robe,* as /rəʊp, rəʊb/ is, therefore, to be interpreted as indicating that the words are distinguished not only or even primarily by a difference of the final consonant, but rather by a complex of quantitative and qualitative contrasts extending over the whole of the coda of syllables. The same effect of reduction also operates when /p,t,k/ occur medially in a word, cf. the length of /aɪ/ in *rider, writer,* although in this situation voicing throughout the compression stage is also likely to be present in /b,d,g/ as another cue to the voiced series.

(6) *Summary*—The RP plosives may, therefore, be said to be distinguished—

(a) by means of a three-term series in respect of place of articulation—bilabial vs alveolar vs velar;
(b) at each point by a phonological feature labelled 'voice' which phonetically consists of a complex of phonetic features, each feature being more prominent in certain positions:

(i) aspiration operates where /p,t,k/ are in syllable-initial position. It is most apparent initially in accented syllables, cf. *pole* vs *bowl.* This aspiration is much less apparent initially in unaccented syllables, particularly those preceding accented syllables. So in *potato* we have three degrees of aspiration: most following the plosion of the /t/ of the second syllable, much less for the /t/ of the third syllable, and even less for the initial of /p/. Indeed /p,t,k,/ in pre-accent unaccented positions like the /p/ in *potato* are auditorily almost indistinguishable from /b,d,g/;
(ii) shortening of vowels and sonorants operates where /p,t,k,/ are in syllable-final position, cf. *rope* vs *robe, kilt* vs *killed*;

---

[6] Peterson and Lehiste (1960) found vowels up to one and a half times as long preceding voiced consonants as preceding voiceless consonants

(iii) full voicing of /b,d,g/, i.e. voicing throughout the compression stage, applies only in word-medial positions between voiced sounds (in other positions voicing usually occurs only at the very beginning or end of the compression stage when adjacent to a voiced sound), cf. *rabid* vs *rapid*. This phonetic feature of voicing may operate in addition to the features of length and (lack of) aspiration in (i) and (ii) above; so in *sordid* the /d/ will be preceded by a unshortened vowel of the same length as in *sword*, (and will of course have no aspiration) as well as having voicing through the compression stage (i.e. it is behaving in all ways as an 'intersyllabic' consonant).

(7) *Advice to foreign learners*—Particular attention must be paid to the aspiration of /p,t,k/ when these phonemes occur initially in accented syllables. If a word such as *pin* is pronounced [pɪn], instead of [pʰɪn], there is the danger that the English listener may understand *bin*, since he interprets lack of aspiration as a mark of the voiced /b/. The danger is particularly great for speakers of those languages, e.g. many in the Romance and Slav groups, where oppositions between pairs of plosives rely purely upon presence or absence of voice. Although Hindi speakers have a phonemic distinction between /p,t,k/ and /pʰ,tʰ,kʰ/, they tend to identify English /p,t,k/ with their unaspirated series.

The aspiration cue for /p,t,k/ should also be retained, when /p,t,k/ are followed by /l,r,j,w/, by the devoicing of these latter, e.g. compare *plight, try, crate, tune, twelve*, with *blight, dry, great, dune, dwell*.

Speakers of some other languages, e.g. Cantonese, German, and Russian, neutralize the oppositions between /p,t,k/ and /b,d,g/ in syllable-final positions, using only voiceless plosives. Such speakers should concentrate on the vowel preceding the plosive, remembering that vowels and sonorants are shortened before /p,t,k/ while keeping their full length before /b,d,g/ so, for example, the /iː/ of *beat* is shortened compared with the same vowel in both *bee* and *bead*.

9.2.2   Acoustic Features of English Plosives

Perceptual cues, capable of being expressed in acoustic terms, may be provided by all three stages of plosive articulations, so that it is possible to distinguish: (1) plosives from other consonants, (2) /p,t,k/ from /b,d,g/, (3) the bilabial, alveolar, and velar types.

(1) Plosives differ from other consonants mainly in the stage corresponding to the articulatory 'hold'. This part of the consonant is generally characterized acoustically by a perceptible period of silence throughout the whole spectrum or, in the voiced /b,d,g/, an absence of energy except at a low frequency as in (2).

(2) /b,d,g/ may be distinguished from /p,t,k/ by means of a low frequency component present in the former, i.e. voice; such a 'voice bar' is generally below 250 Hz. For /p,t,k/ there is also usually a higher onset or offset in fundamental frequency to a following or from a preceding vowel.[7] Moreover, there is likely

---

[7] Ohde (1984)

to be a marked rising bend of F1 of the adjacent vowel in the case of /b,d,g/, which is not as marked in the case of /p,t,k/.[8] However, as we have seen, /b,d,g/ may often be voiceless, in which case they are distinguished from /p,t,k/—initially, by the comparatively weak burst of noise associated with the onset of the release stage and by the longer VOT characterizing /p,t,k/; finally, by their influence on the duration of the preceding sounds; medially, by the longer closure period (absence of energy) required for /p,t,k/.[9] Although there is a tendency for the longer length of the vowel before /b,d,g/ and the longer closure for /p,t,k/ to produce a similar overall vowel plus consonant duration, the sequences of vowel plus /b,d,g/ is usually somewhat longer.[10]

(3) Cues to the distinction between bilabial, alveolar, and velar plosives are provided by the frequency of the noise burst at the onset of the release stage together with characteristic bends of F2 and F3 (called FORMANT TRANSITIONS) towards following vowels and from preceding vowels.[11] Before [a][12] bilabial /p,b/ have MINUS TRANSITIONS, i.e. transitions which start from and go to a point (called a LOCUS) lower than the steady-state formants for the vowel, while alveolar /t,d/ have PLUS TRANSITIONS, i.e. transitions which start from and go to a higher locus. Velar /k,g/ have a plus transition for F2 and a minus transition for F3. The formant transitions accord with the location of the noise bursts associated with the various places; low for bilabials (maximum around 800 Hz), high for alveolars (maximum around 4000 Hz) and intermediate for velars (maximum around 2,000 Hz). See Fig. 31 for a diagram of formants and bursts before [a] and Fig. 32 for spectrograms of /b,d,g/ before /aɪ/.

The outline of noise bursts and formant transitions given in the preceding paragraph applied to cases with a following or preceding /a/. There is, however, considerable variation when other vowels are involved. This applies particularly to the velars (and, to a lesser extent, the alveolars) and reflects the different articulation of these consonants in different vocalic environments, e.g. before /i,ɪ,e/, /k,g/ may be considerably fronted and on the verge of being palatal [c,ɟ], and thus their noise bursts will approach those for /t,d/ and both F2 and F3 may have plus transitions.

Formant transitions do not extend fully from the formants of the vowel to a locus in the noise burst of the plosive, but merely point in the direction of the latter. Best recognition is achieved in synthetic speech if the first half of the transition from plosive to vowel consists of silence; if the transition is extended too far (so that the total period of voiced transition exceeds 30 ms) then glides of the type [j,w] may be perceived.

---

[8] Liberman *et al* (1958) and Stevens and Klatt (1974)
[9] Lisker (1957) showed that an intervocalic /b/ has an average duration of 75 ms while an intervocalic /p/ has an average of 120 ms. See also Malécot (1968) and Subtelny *et al.* (1966)
[10] See Laeufer (1996)
[11] Cooper *et al* (1952), Stevens and Blumstein (1978) and Lieberman and Blumstein (1988)
[12] As [a] is described as part of a seven-vowel systems in much American work, its quality is best assumed to be intermediate between RP /æ/ and /ɑː/

The VOT (aspiration) usual in /p/ is always shorter than that for /t,k/[13] and this may constitute an additional, although weak, cue to the recognition of the labial.

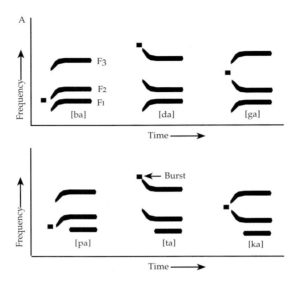

Fig. 31. *Formant transitions and bursts for the syllables [ba, da, ga, pa, ta, ka] (from Lieberman and Blumstein, 1988).*

9.2.3   Acquisition of Plosives by Native Learners

Plosives, along with nasals, are the first consonants to be acquired. They are the most frequent consonants in babbling (which occurs during the latter half of the first year), and occur regularly in the first words (which occur between 0;9 and 1;6). During early babbling labials and velars occur most frequently but in late babbling and early words it is more usually labials and alveolars which predominate, the velars being replaced by alveolars (although a minority of children may show a preference for velars). Like most consonants plosives are generally acquired first in syllable-initial positions; final plosives in adult words are often completely omitted in children's early words. In all languages it is the the plosive series with zero VOT (i.e. where voicing starts simultaneously with the release) which is acquired first: in English (see Table 10) this means that /b,d,g/ precede /p,t,k/. When /p,t,k/ are first differentiated from /b,d,g/, it is aspiration which is the main distinguishing cue; at first children may make an uncertain use of such aspiration,[14] either underaspirating (and hence the distinction not being

---

[13] Docherty (1992) finds word-initial /p/ having a VOT of around 40 ms and /t,k/ a VOT of around 60 ms
[14] Macken and Barton (1980)

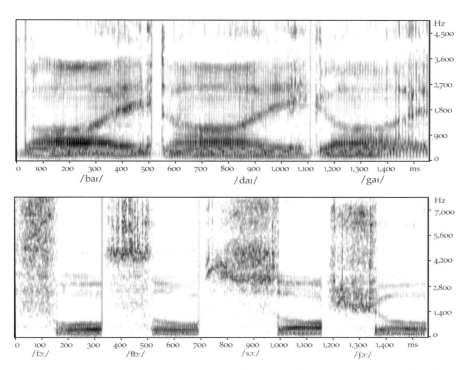

Fig. 32. *Spectrograms of /baɪ/, /daɪ/, /gaɪ/ and of /fɔː/, /θɔː/, /sɔː/, /ʃɔː/ as spoken by a male speaker of RP (the full length of /ɔː/ is not displayed).*

perceived by adult listeners) or overaspirating (and hence the plosives sounding as if they are being followed by an /h/).

9.2.4   The Release Stage of English Plosives

It is not always the case that plosives in English have a third stage[15] consisting of a sudden oral release of air, either in the form of aspiration or as an immediately following vowel. The main variants are:

(1) *No audible release in final positions*—In syllable-final positions (i.e. particularly before a pause), as in *map, mat, mack,* or *robe, road, rogue,* the closure stage may be maintained, the air compression becoming weak and the release being achieved by a gentle, delayed, and relatively inaudible opening of the oral

---

[15] Some writers, e.g. Arnold (1966), argue that this stage should be separated into a 'release' (an articulatory feature which is the converse of the 'closure') and a 'plosion' (an auditory feature)

closure; or the compressed air may be released nasally and relatively inaudibly by lowering the soft palate and delaying the separation of the organs forming the oral closure. When an audible third stage is missing, the plosive is sometimes termed 'incomplete'. The absence of an audible release stage entails the loss of the release noise burst as a cue to the identification of the plosive. Unreleased final bilabial, alveolar, and velar plosives will, therefore, be distinguished mainly by the transitional features of the preceding sound. The sensitivity of English listeners to such cues is proved by the high percentage of correct discrimination between pairs such as *mat, mack,* or *road, rogue,* presented without a context, even when the final plosive is not released. The voiceless series /p,t,k/ will, of course, be distinguished in final positions from the voiced series /b,d,g/ either by the reduction of length of the sounds preceding /p,t,k/ or by the presence of some voicing in /b,d,g/, or by a combination of both factors. The non-release of final plosives is a feature of colloquial RP. Careful speakers, however, tend to release such plosives audibly and those who, in ordinary conversational style, use the unexploded variety will often use an audible release in more formal circumstances. Velar stops are more prone to non-release than bilabial and alveolar stops.[16] (See further under §12.7 on stylistic variation.)

(2) *No audible release in stop clusters*—It is also a feature of most kinds of English that in a cluster of two stops (plosives or plosive+affricate) either within a word or at word boundaries, the first plosive has no audible release, e.g. in *dropped* (/p/+/t/), *rubbed* (/b/+/d/), *white post* (/t/+/p/), *good boy* (/d/+/b/), *locked* (/k/+/t/), *big boy* (/g/+/b/), *object* (/b/+/dʒ/), *great joke* (/t/+/dʒ/), *big chin* (/g/+/tʃ/). In those languages where plosives in such situations are released audibly, the result is an intervening [ʰ] in the case of voiceless plosives and an obscure vowel of the [ə] type in the case of voiced plosives. In English the closure for the second stop is made before the release of the first,[17] forming a further obstacle to the airstream if the second closure is at a more advanced point, e.g. /t/+/p/ in *white post*, or checking the air pressure if the second closure is at a more retracted point, e.g. /t/+/k/ in *white cat*. No separate release of the first plosive is made in cases of GEMINATION, i.e. sequences of identical stops, e.g. *top people, good dog, big girl*; in such cases one closing stage and one release stage are involved together with an approximately double-length compression stage. Much the same applies when plosives which are homorganic but different in voicing occur in sequence, e.g. *top boy, white dog, big car*; in these cases, cues to recognition of the voiced or voiceless series are provided by the onset or cessation of voice, by the aspiration of the voiceless series, and by the duration of preceding vowels or sonorants. It should also be noted that, in addition to the omission of an audible third stage of the first plosive in clusters, the first stage (onglide, transition) of the following stop is also inaudible. Thus, in sequences of three plosives, e.g. *wept bitterly* (/p/+/t/+/b/), *locked door* (/k/+/t/+/d/), *jogged by* (/g/+/d/+/b/), the central plosive has no audible first or third stage; when this position is occupied by /p,t,k/, the plosive is manifested only by a silence of a certain duration, i.e. the length of its second stage. Alternatively, the middle plosive in such sequences may be dropped completely (see §12.4.6).

---

[16] Byrd (1992b)
[17] For articulatory overlap in plosive clusters, see Byrd (1994)

(3) *Glottal reinforcement of final* /p,t,k/—It is increasingly typical of many types of British English that final /p,t,k/, in words such as *shop, shot, shock*, have the oral closure reinforced by a glottal closure [ʔ]. In some cases this glottal coincides in time with the oral closure, inhibiting much of the air pressure behind the oral closure, whether or not this latter is released audibly; in others the glottal closure may slightly anticipate the articulation of the oral obstruction so that the closing stage of a glottal closure is heard followed by the audible release of an oral plosive. In other, rarer, cases there may be some compression of the air between the glottal and oral closures by means of the raising of the larynx and a constriction of the pharyngeal cavity, resulting in a potential ejective release. In such a case the plosive is no longer glottally reinforced or glottalized but is instead produced using the egressive glottalic (or pharyngeal) airstream mechanism. This is rather more common in some dialects (e.g. south-east Lancashire) than in RP. In certain cases, too, [ʔ] may replace /p,t,k/, see §9.2.8.

(4) *Nasal release*—When a plosive is followed by a homorganic nasal consonant, either syllabic or initial in a following syllable, the release of air is normally effected not by a removal of the oral closure, which is retained, but by the escape of the compressed air through the nasal passage, opened by the lowering of the soft palate for the nasal consonant, e.g. /p/+/m/ *topmost*, /p/+[m̩] sometimes in *happen* [ˈhæpm̩], /b/+/m/ *submerge*, /b/+[m̩] sometimes in *ribbon* [ˈrɪbm̩], /t/+/n/ *chutney*, /t/+[n̩] *cotton*, /d/+/n/ *madness*, /d/+[n̩] *sudden*; and, more rarely, /k/+[ŋ̍] *thicken* [ˈθɪkŋ̍], /g/+[ŋ̍] *organ* [ˈɔːgŋ̍], *token* [ˈtəʊkŋ̍], *pagan* [ˈpeɪgŋ̍]. The same release takes place when the plosive and homorganic nasal occur at word boundaries, e.g. *cheap meat, robe mistress, not now, red nose* etc. (Since /ŋ/ does not occur initially in syllables, this last generalization does not apply to /k/ and /g/.)

A different kind of nasal release occurs when the nasal consonant following a plosive is not homorganic, e.g. in *cheap nuts, rub now, nutmeg, bad man, black magic, big nose, big man* etc. In these cases the plosive closure is not normally released until the articulatory movements for the nasal consonant, i.e. the second oral closure and the lowering of the soft palate, have been accomplished. Thus the plosion will be more or less inaudible, depending on which of the two closures is the fronter.

(5) *Lateral release*—The most frequent tongue contact for English /l/ being alveolar, the sequences /t/ or /d/+/l/ are homorganic (i.e. made at the same place of articulation). /t/ and /d/ in such situations are normally released laterally, i.e. one or both sides of the tongue are lowered to allow the air to escape, the tongue tip contact remaining. Such a release occurs whether the following /l/ is syllabic, e.g. in *cattle, medal*, or if it is initial in the next syllable or word, e.g. in *atlas, at last, regardless, bad light*. Such homorganic lateral release is to be distinguished from sequences of /p,b,k,g/+/l/, e.g. in *apple, up late, bubble, blow, rub lightly, tackle, clean, blackleg, glow, eagle, big lad*. In these cases, the partial alveolar contact for /l/ is made before or at the time of the release of the plosive and, in this sense, the escape of air is lateral; but since /p,b/ and /k,g/ may be released in a truly lateral way, i.e. by the removal of one or both sides of the bilabial or velar closure, the term 'lateral release' is best reserved in English for the homorganic alveolar + /l/ sequences. Such true lateral releases must be taken as typical of English usage, there being no intervening removal of the tongue contact on the alveolar ridge, such as would result in aspiration or an obscure vowel.

Pronunciations of the type [ˈlɪtʰɬ], [ˈmɪdˀɬ] for *little, middle*, are frequently to be heard in the speech of children.

(6) *Affrication and weakening of plosives*—If the release of plosive closures is not made rapidly, a fricative sound, articulated in the same area of articulation as the plosive, will be heard; plosives made with this slow, fricative release are said to be AFFRICATED. Common realizations of the English plosives /p,b,t,d,k,g/ might, therefore, be followed by brief fricatives of the types [ɸ,β,s,z,x,ɣ]. In some varieties of English the alveolars /t,d/ may frequently be heard in affricated form [tˢ,dᶻ]: in strongly accented positions, e.g. in *time, day*; in relatively weakly accented positions, e.g. in *waiting, riding*; and in final positions, e.g. in *hat, bed*. (Note that, in these last two examples, the forms [tˢ] and [dᶻ] differ from the realization of the plural terminations /t/+/s/ and /d/+/z/ mainly in the brevity of the friction associated with the affricated plosives.) Affrication is also occasionally also heard with the velar plosives, i.e. [kˣ] and [gˠ], e.g. in hesitant or emphatic speech in accented situations in words such as *come, good*, or, more commonly with /k/, in weakly accented or final positions, e.g. in *talker, talk*. /p/ and /b/ are rarely affricated.

It should also be noted that in rapid, familiar speech, where speed rather than articulatory precision is the aim, the closure of plosives is often so weak that the corresponding fricative sound, without a preceding stop, is produced, especially in weakly accented intervocalic positions. The following examples have been noted among educated speakers; *imported* [ɪmˋpɔːsɪd], *invaded* [ɪɲˋveɪzɪd], *baker* [ˈbeɪxə], *dagger* [ˈdæɣə] (this latter, on the stage, in the *Macbeth* 'dagger' soliloquy), and even *pepper* [ˈpeɸə], rubber [ˈrʌβə].

(7) *Advice to foreign learners*—All the foregoing variants of the hold and release stages of English plosives may be heard from RP speakers. A foreign speaker of English may be generally intelligible without adopting any of these features, such is the redundancy of information carried in the English utterance. But the foreign learner who aims at a near approximation to the speech of English natives should adopt the following features at least:

(a) Inaudible release of plosives preceding other plosives or affricates.

(b) Nasal release of plosives followed by a homorganic nasal, especially /t,d/+/n/, with avoidance of any intervening [ʰ] or [ˀ].

(c) Lateral release of /t,d/+/l/, also with avoidance of intervening [ˀ].

(d) Affrication of /p,t,k/ as a stage in learning aspiration of these plosives in strongly accented positions.

On the other hand, speakers of most varieties of Chinese have final /p,t,k/ unreleased or replaced by glottal stop so regularly that this may produce problems of intelligibility when introduced into English; such learners should practise releasing final /p,t,k/.

9.2.5   Bilabial Plosives

(1) *Examples*

/p/—*voiceless* (regularly spelt with <p> or <pp> but note 'hiccough' /ˈhɪkʌp/. Note also silent <p> in 'pneumonia, psychology, psalm, ptarmigan, receipt, cupboard, raspberry').

accented, aspirated—pin, pill, pain, appear, impatient; play, pray, pew
accented after /s/, *unaspirated*—spin, spill, Spain, spear; splay, spray, spew (but see §5.3.4)
weakly accented, relatively unaspirated—upper, capable, opportunity, gospel; simply, apricot, champion
syllable-final (often with no audible release)—cheap, lip, lap, shape, lisp, pulp, pump; upright, chaplain, upward
followed by another plosive, with no audible release—captain, topcoat, wiped, hop picker, top boy, top girl, top dog, ripe cheese
nasal release, followed by nasal consonant—topmost, happen, cheap meat
lateral release, followed by lateral consonant—apple, couple, please, up late

/b/—*voiced* (regularly spelt with <b> or <bb>. Note silent <b> in 'limb, lamb, bomb, thumb, comb, debt, subtle, doubt')

word-initial, partially devoiced—big, boast, banana, begin; blow, brain, beauty
between voiced sounds, fully voiced—rubber, labour, harbour, husband, symbol
final, fully devoiced—rib, ebb, sob, robe, bulb
followed by another plosive, with no audible release—obtain, rubbed, subconscious, sob bitterly, sub-prefect, rib cage, object
nasal release, followed by nasal consonant—submerge, robe mistress, ribbon
lateral release, followed by lateral consonant—bubble, blow, rub lightly

Compare

/p/, /b/—post, boast; peach, beach; rapid, rabid; dapple, dabble; sopping, sobbing; simple, symbol; cup, cub; rope, robe; plead, bleed; pray, bray; puke, rebuke; mopped, mobbed.

(2) *Description*—The soft palate being raised and the nasal resonator shut off, the primary obstacle to the airstream is provided by the closure of the lips. Lung air is compressed behind this closure, during which stage the vocal folds are held wide apart for /p/, but may vibrate for all or part of the compression stage for /b/ according to its situation in the utterance. The air escapes with force when the lip closure is released, unless the airstream has been blocked by a second closure at

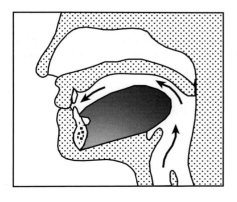

Fig. 33. *Section of* /p,b/.

a point behind the lips (as for a following /t/) or has been diverted through the nose by the lowering of the soft palate (as for /m/); when a lateral sound follows, the airstream will have a lateral escape round the point of alveolar closure.

In those cases where a bilabial plosive precedes a labiodental sound (/f,v/), as in *cup-full, obvious*, the stop is often made by a labiodental rather than a bilabial closure, in anticipation of the following fricative articulation, thus [ˈkʌpfʊl], [ˈɒbvɪəs]. Tongue movements involved in vowels or consonants adjacent to the bilabial stop are made independently of the lip closure, e.g. the /ɔː/ tongue position is maintained through the /b/ closure in *four balls* and the /l/ alveolar contact through the /p/ closure in *helpless*.

(3) *Variants*—No important variants of /b/ occur, except in respect of the amount of voicing in initial and final positions, full voicing in either position being rare. On the other hand, some speakers may also devoice in intervocalic positions, particularly across word boundaries. In the same way, the amount of aspiration given to /p/ varies between speakers, though the accented form will always tend to be more strongly aspirated than the unaccented form (see §9.2.1).

(4) *Chief sources*—PresE /p/ and /b/ develop regularly from the same OE phonemes (single and geminated) and from French /p/ and /b/. In some cases /b/ derives from earlier /p/, e.g. *lobster, pebble*, and /p/ from earlier /b/, e.g. *pudding, purse, gossip*.

(5) *Advice to foreign learners*—See general remarks in §§9.2.1 (7), 9.2.4 (7), and examples for practice in (1) of this section. Most languages have some sort of /p,b/ although they are notably absent in Vietnamese, and Arabic has no /b/.

9.2.6   Alveolar Plosives /t,d/

(1) *Examples*
/t/—*voiceless* (regularly spelt <t> or <tt>; sometimes with <th>, e.g. 'thyme, posthumous', and in many names, e.g. 'Thames, Thomas'; also <ed> in verbal past tenses and participles after voiceless consonants other than /t/, e.g. 'jumped, looked, laughed, guessed, pushed'. Note silent <t> in 'castle, hasten, soften, Christmas, mortgage'. Note also /ts/ as <z> <tz><zz> in 'scherzo, schizophrenia, quartz, blitz, pizza, intermezzo').

   accented, aspirated—take, tall, tone, attend, obtain; try, between, tune
   accented after /s/, *unaspirated*—steak, stall, stone (but see §5.3.4)
   weakly accented, relatively unaspirated—butter, letter, after, taxation, phonetic; entry, antler, outward
   syllable-final (often with no audible release)—beat, boat, late, past, sent, halt, tuft
   followed by another plosive with no audible release—outpost, hatpin, football, catgut, white tie, that dog, white chalk, great joke
   with homorganic nasal release—cotton, button, eaten, not now
   nasal release, followed by /m/—nutmeg, utmost, that man[18]
   with homorganic lateral release—little, cattle, atlas, at least

---

[18] If the alveolar plosive is articulated as such. See §9.2.8 and §12.4.5.

/d/—*voiced* (regularly spelt <d>, <dd>. Note elision of /d/ in 'sandwich, handsome, landscape, grandfather etc.')

> *word-initial, partially devoiced*—do, dog, double, date; dry, dwindle, duke
> *between voiced sounds, voiced*—leader, order, adorn, hiding, London, elder, under, middle, sundry, fiddler, endways
> *final, fully devoiced*—bid, mad, road, rubbed, bend, old, loved, bathed, raised, judged
> *followed by another plosive, with no audible release*—head boy, head girl, bad pain, red car, good dog, bedtime, good judge, good cheese
> *with homorganic nasal release*—sudden, madness, red nose
> *nasal release followed by* /m/—admit, road map
> *with homorganic lateral release*—middle, padlock, headless, badly, good luck

Compare

> /t/, /d/—town, down; latter, ladder; water, warder; written, ridden; metal, medal; fated, faded; sat, sad; wrote, road; kilt, killed; bent, bend; train, drain; twin, dwindle; tune, dune
> /t/, /θ/—tin, thin; taught, thought; eater, ether; fort, fourth; tent, tenth; welt, wealth
> /d/, /ð/—dough, though; day, they; den, then; udder, other; loading, loathing; breed, breathe; side, scythe

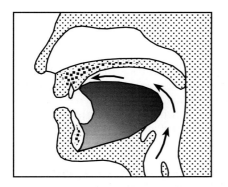
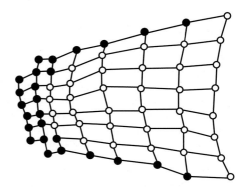

Fig. 34. *Section and palatogram of* /t,d/.

(2) *Description*—The soft palate being raised and the nasal resonator shut off, the primary obstacle to the airstream is usually formed by a closure made between the tip and rims of the tongue and the upper alveolar ridge and side teeth (although in a minority of speakers the blade of the tongue rather than the tip may be used).[19] Lung air is compressed behind this closure, during which stage

---

[19] Bladon and Nolan (1977)

the vocal folds are wide apart for /t/, but may vibrate for all or part of the compression stage for /d/ according to its situation in the utterance. The lip position for /t/ and /d/ will be conditioned by that of the adjacent sounds, especially that of a following vowel or semi-vowel, e.g. spread lips for /t/ in *teeth*, anticipatory lip rounding for /t/ in *tooth, twice*. The air escapes with force upon the sudden separation of the alveolar closure, unless the airstream has been blocked by a second closure either behind the alveolars (as for /k/) or forward of the alveolars (as for /p/), or unless it has been diverted through the nose by the lowering of the soft palate (as for /n/); if the release is lateral, only part of the alveolar obstruction is removed, the tongue-tip contact remaining. Nasal plosion will be heard in sequences of /t/ or /d/ plus /n/ and lateral plosion will be heard in sequences of /t/ or /d/ plus /l/.

The alveolar stop contact is particularly sensitive to the influence of the place of articulation of a following consonant. Thus, followed by /r/ as in *try, dry*, the contact will be post-alveolar [t̠,d̠] and followed by a /θ,ð/ as in *eighth, not that*, the contact will be dental [t̪,d̪]. In addition, word-final /t,d/ assimilate readily to /p,k/ and /b,g/, when followed by word-initial bilabial and velar consonants (see §12.4.5).The instability of alveolar articulations is further demonstrated by the ease with which /t/ or /d/ may be elided in consonantal clusters (see §10.8 for examples within words and §12.4.6 for examples at word boundaries).

(3) *Variants*—In addition to the general plosive variations commented on in §§9.2.1, 9.2.3, it should be noted that /t,d/ are especially liable to affrication and even replacement by the equivalent fricative in weakly accented situations, e.g. *time* [tˢaɪm], *important* [ɪmˈpɔːtˢənt].

Increasingly, /t/ in syllable-final positions is reinforced or replaced by a glottal closure unless a vowel or syllabic /n̩/ or /l̩/ follows, e.g. *late, want, cricket, outright, chutney*. (But even before a following vowel the use of [ʔ] for word-final /t/ before a following vowel is now acceptable as a form of London Regional RP (Estuary English), e.g. in *get off, got it, right order*.) An alternative pronunciation, voicing of /t/ to [d], is increasingly reported for a minority of RP speakers, e.g. in *British, hot enough, not unusual, fat or thin*.

Some RP speakers will also use [ʔ] to realize /t/ when syllabic [n̩] follows, e.g. *cotton, certain*. But the use of [ʔ] for /t/ preceding syllabic [l̩], and, more particularly in unaccented intervocalic word-medial positions, is typical of regional varieties of English (e.g. those of Cockney and Glasgow), as in *kettle, butter, later*; such pronunciations are not even acceptable as part of London Regional RP. (See §9.2.8 for further detail on [ʔ].)

The amount of aspiration associated with /p,t,k/ varies considerably across dialects, some, like Irish English and Welsh English, having more aspiration than RP, others, like Lancashire, having very little aspiration. Scottish English generally has little aspiration also, although in the Western Highlands, where Gaelic influence is strong, there is very strong aspiration. In General American /t/ in unaccented intervocalic positions (post-accentual) is generally realized as a tap [ɾ], e.g. in *butter, latter, put it*; for some speakers the closure may be long enough to produce neutralization with /d/. Similar realizations may be heard in South African English and in southern Irish English. Also in the unaccented intervocalic position following a short vowel and across a word boundary, /t/ may be realized as [ɹ] in a number of urban varieties of south Lancashire and west

Yorkshire, e.g. *get off* [geˈɹɒf]; in the same position in Cockney /t/ may be realized as a tap [ɾ] as an alternative to [ʔ]. In Indian English and among speakers of ethnic Indian origin /t/ will generally be realized as [t̪].

(4) *Chief sources*—PresE /t/ and /d/ derive from the same phonemes of OE (single and geminated) and from French introductions with /t/ and /d/. Some words, now spelt with <th> and pronounced with /θ/, had /t/ until eModE, e.g. *throne, orthography, diphthong, authority*. There are, in addition, many cases in PresE of established elision of an earlier /t/ or /d/, e.g. in *castle, hasten, Christmas, often, fasten, Wednesday, handsome*, in which words the /t/ or /d/ was probably sounded up to the seventeenth century. In other cases /t, d/ have been added to earlier French stems ending in /n/, e.g. *peasant, parchment, sound, astound*, and to certain English and French words after a voiceless fricative, e.g. *against, amongst, graft*. It should also be noted that the past tense and participle termination <ed> (earlier [əd]) of weak verbs assimilated to /t/ following voiceless consonants—other than /t/—on the loss of the intervening weak vowel, e.g. *wrapped, missed, annexed, pierced, blessed* etc.

(5) *Advice to foreign learners*—In addition to the general remarks in §9.2.1, 9.2.3, and the examples for practice given in (1) of this section, it is to be emphasized for foreign learners that the general articulation of /t,d/ is an alveolar one, made with the tongue tip raised. The corresponding phonemes of many other languages, e.g. Arabic, French, Italian, Portuguese, Spanish, have a dental rather than an alveolar point of contact. Those learners who carry over from their own language a dental articulation should practise the slightly affricated forms of /t,d/, i.e. [tˢ] [dᶻ] in words such as *time, day*. If the closure point remains dental, the affrication produced will be clearly of the [tθ], [dð] type. Those learners who, in their own language, have two varieties of stop closure made with the tongue tip, e.g. speakers of Indian languages, having dental and post-alveolar or retroflex varieties, should, if aiming at a British pronunciation, avoid using their retroflexed plosives in English, since these sound over-retracted to the English ear (unless of course they are aiming only at Minimum General Intelligibility as in §13.6); similarly they should also avoid using their dental /t,d/ for English /θ,ð/. Learners are often prone to omit /t,d/ before /s,z/ when followed by another consonant; this particularly applies to sequences where *is* is reduced by elision and assimilation to /s/, as in *it's, what's, that's* in, for example, *it's true, what's that, that's normal*, which should not be pronounced as /ɪs ˈtru/, /wɒs ˈðæt/, /ðæs ˈnɔːməl/.

9.2.7 Velar Plosives /k,g/

(1) *Examples*
/k/—*voiceless*

> *k*—king, kept, kettle, revoke, break, walk, bank, sky, monk, turkey
> *c*—carpet, cord, caught, crew, clique, disc, maniac, alcohol, circus
> *cc*—accused, occur, accommodation, account, occupy, occasion
> *q, qu, cqu*—cheque, conquer, unique, bouquet, liquor, mosquito, racquet
> (<qu> = /kw/ in 'quiet, quilt, queer, quest' and <cqu> = /kw/ in 'acquire')

ch—stomach, chemist, choir, chorus, chaos, echo, orchid, character
ck—chicken, neck, buttocks, hemlock, mackerel, creaky, tacky

(*Note* silent <c>or<k>in 'muscle, knew, knit'.)

accented, aspirated—come, car, kin, incur, according; cry, clean, quick, queue
accented after /s/, unaspirated—scum, scar, skin (but see §5.3.4)
weakly accented, relatively unaspirated—income, baker, talking, biscuit, anchor; secret, duckling, equal, dockyard
syllable-final (often with no audible release)—leak, duck, rock, choke, bank, bulk, desk
followed by another plosive, with no audible release—locked, blackboard, thick dust, black cat, dark grey, deckchair, lockjaw
nasal release, followed by nasal consonant—acknowledge, dark night, thicken (sometimes /ˈθɪkŋ/), black magic
lateral release, followed by lateral consonant—buckle, clean, close, blackleg

/g/—*voiced*

g—go, gourd, good, geese, grow, glum, agree, congratulate, dragon
gg—egg, waggon (also wagon), aggravate, aggressive
gh—ghost, dinghy, ghastly, spaghetti
gu, gue—rogue, guilt, vague, guitar, guy, guard, guess, league

(*Note* silent <g> silent in 'gnaw, gnat, diaphragm, sign, reign'.)

word-initial, partially devoiced—go, geese, guess, girl; glass, grass
between voiced sounds, voiced—eager, hunger, figure, ago, begin, eagle, juggling, angry, anguish, argue
word-final, fully devoiced—dog, leg, rogue, vague
followed by another plosive, with no audible release—rugby, begged, bagpipes, wagtail, big game, eggcup, big jaw, big chin
nasal release, followed by nasal consonant—dogma, ignore, quagmire, big man, drag-net, organ grinder
lateral release, followed by lateral consonant—bugle, struggle, glow, wriggling, dog lead

Compare

/k/, /g/—cap, gap; coat, goat; clue, glue; decree, degree;
bicker, bigger; stacker, stagger; lacked, lagged; ankle, angle; hackle, haggle; pick, pig; back, bag; duck, dug; crate, great

(2) *Description*—The soft palate being raised and the nasal resonator shut off, the primary obstacle to the airstream is formed by a closure made between the back of the tongue and the soft palate. Lung air is compressed behind this closure, during which stage the vocal folds are wide apart for /k/, but may vibrate

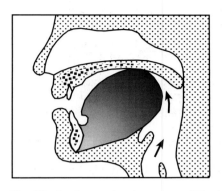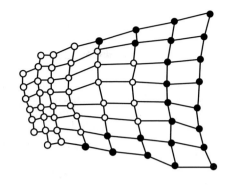

Fig. 35. *Section and palatogram of* /k,g/ + /iː/.

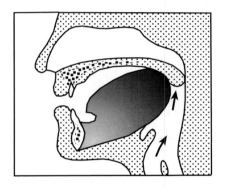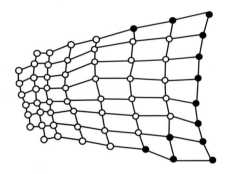

Fig. 36. *Section and palatogram of* /k,g/ + /ɑː/.

for all or part of the compression stage for /g/ according to its situation in the utterance. The lip position will be conditioned by that of adjacent sounds, especially following vowels or semi-vowels, e.g. spread lips for the plosives in *keen, geese*, and somewhat rounded lips for the plosives in *cool, goose, quick*. The air escapes with force upon the sudden separation of the linguo-velar closure, unless the airstream has been blocked by a second closure forward of the velum (as for /p/ or /t/), or has been diverted through the nose by the lowering of the soft palate (as for /ŋ/); when a lateral sound follows, the airstream will have a lateral escape round the point of alveolar closure.

The velar stop contact is particularly sensitive to the nature of an adjacent vowel (especially a following vowel). Thus, when a front vowel follows, e.g. /iː/ in *key, geese*, the contact will be made on the most forward part of the soft palate and may even overlap on to the hard palate; when a back vowel follows, e.g./ɒ/ in *cot, gone*, the contact on the soft palate will be correspondingly retracted; a contact in the central region of the soft palate is made when a vowel of a central type follows, e.g. /ʌ/ or /ɜː/ as in *come, gun, girl* (see Figs. 35, 36).

(3) *Variants*—The actual extent of advancement or retraction of the velar closure will depend upon the exact quality of the vowels of an individual; if /iː/ has a very front and tense articulation, the /k,g/ closures will in turn be near palatal, i.e. [c,ɟ] (noted by John Wallis in the seventeenth century as <ky, gy>), whereas, if /ɒ/ is of the most back and open variety, the velar closure will be of the most retracted kind. (For other variations affecting all plosives, see §§9.2.1, 9.2.3.) Since the initial clusters /kl,gl/, as in *clean, glean*, are not in opposition with /tl,dl/ which do not occur initially, a substitution of /tl,dl/ for /kl,gl/ in such positions may occasionally be heard both in RP and in other forms of English.

(4) *Chief sources*—PresE /k,g/ derive from the same phonemes in OE (in single and geminated forms) and in French introductions. Some English forms with /k/ (spelt with <c> or <ck>) as in *pocket, carpenter*, derive not from the affricates usual in Central French (*pochette, charpentier*) but from the plosive equivalents of northern French dialects. Again, some early French borrowings with <qu> retain the original /kw/ pronunciation, e.g. *quit, squadron*, where modern French has lost the /w/ element (cf. the later borrowing *bouquet*). Occasionally, a learned *c* spelling has been introduced with a resultant /k/ pronunciation, e.g. *perfect, subject* (note that in *victuals*, despite the introduction of a <c> in the spelling, no /k/ is pronounced). The phoneme /g/ is sometimes spelt <gu> before <e, i> in words of English origin, e.g. *guest, guilt*, by analogy with words of central French origin such as *guide, guerdon*. /k,g/ initially before /n/ (*know, gnaw*) were finally lost late in the seventeenth century; /g/ following /n/ was lost in the south of England, e.g. in *sing, rung* etc., in the seventeenth century, though it is kept intervocalically in certain words, e.g. *finger, longer, single*, and in all positions in many dialects of the north-west Midlands (see §9.6.3 for the origins of /ŋ/).

(5) *Advice to foreign learners*—Note the general remarks in §§9.2.1, 9.2.3, and the examples for practice given in (1) of this section. French learners should be particularly careful not to over-palatalize /k,g/ both before and after front vowels; Spanish learners should avoid reducing intervocalic /g/ to a fricative [ɣ] or pronouncing initial /g/ (especially before a back vowel) as [gw] or [w].

9.2.8   Glottal Plosive [ʔ]

(1) *Description*—In the case of the glottal plosive (stop), the obstruction to the airstream is formed by the closure of the vocal folds, thereby interrupting the passage of air into the supraglottal organs. The air pressure below the glottis is released by the sudden separation of the vocal folds. The compression stage of its articulation consists of silence, its presence being perceived auditorily by the sudden cessation of the preceding sound or by the sudden onset (often with an accompanying strong breath effort) of the following sound. The plosive is voiceless, there being no vibration of the vocal cords. Because the position of the vocal folds is not that associated with other voiceless sounds (i.e. with wide open vocal cords), an alternative viewpoint regards [ʔ] as neither voiceless nor voiced. Nevertheless where [ʔ] substitutes for /p,t,k/ in English, it has the usual effect of voiceless plosives in shortening preceding vowels. The articulation of [ʔ] must be distinguished from that type of glottalization or laryngealization which involves

tension in the laryngeal region and either an excessively slow rate of vibration of the vocal folds ('creaky voice') or a vibration of the false vocal folds situated just above the true vocal folds ('ventricular voice' or 'harsh voice').[20] In the production of these latter sounds, often heard in the lowest pitches of intonation and associated with weak intensity (though sometimes with muscular tension, e.g. at the lower level of the fall–rise tone) or on almost any pitch level in certain affected voice qualities, there is no total closure of the vocal folds. Nor is there compression between the glottal and oral closures which would produce ejectives (see §4.3.9).

It is clear from the description given above that there is no acoustic manifestation of the glottal plosive other than the abrupt cessation or onset of the adjacent sounds.

(2) *Usage*—The glottal plosive, though frequently used by RP speakers, is not a significant sound in the RP system. A distinction must be made between (a) the regular occurrence of glottal reinforcement in RP, (b) extended use of reinforcement in RP, (c) use of glottal replacement in RP, and (d) more extensive use of glottal replacement in other dialects.

(a) *Regular glottal reinforcement in RP*[21]—[ʔ] serves regularly for many RP speakers as a syllable boundary marker, when the initial sound of the second syllable is a vowel. Thus, a hiatus of vowels belonging to different syllables (especially when the second vowel is accented), may in careful speech be separated by [ʔ] instead of being joined by a vocalic glide, e.g. *co-operate, geometry, reaction* [kəʊˈʔɒpəreɪt, dʒiːˈʔɒmətriː, riːˈʔækʃən], and even when the second vowel is weakly accented, e.g. *day after day* [deɪ ˈʔɑːftə ˈdeɪ]. This usage of [ʔ] is extended amongst careful speakers to those cases where there is a possibility of an intrusive /r/ (see §12.4.7) at a point of vowel hiatus, e.g. in *law and order, drama and music*; the glottal marker is in turn applied by some speakers (and in the teaching of singing) in cases where a regular linking /r/ is permissible, e.g. in *later on, far off, four aces*.

Finally, any initial accented vowel may be reinforced by a preceding glottal stop when particular emphasis is placed on the word, whatever the preceding sound, e.g. in *It's* [ʔ] *empty, I haven't seen* [ʔ] *anybody, She's* [ʔ] *awfully good*; or again, any vowel, initial in an accented morpheme, may receive this glottal reinforcement, e.g. It's *un* [ʔ] *eatable, such dis* [ʔ] *order*.

(b) *Extended glottal reinforcement in RP*—As was pointed out in §9.2.4, in RP (although not in Refined RP) /p,t,k/ and also /tʃ/ may be reinforced by a glottal closure which generally precedes it. The closing and release of such a glottal closure take place just before the closures for the mouth closure, so that phonetically the glottal closure and the oral closure are in a sequence just like other sequences of plosives. As such the closing stage of the oral closure and the release stage of the glottal closure are masked in the overlapping of the two closures. This type of reinforcement occurs in syllable-final position where a vowel, nasal, or lateral precedes and where a pause or a consonant follows (and,

---

[20] Catford (1964, 1977), Laver (1980)
[21] Christophersen (1952), O'Connor (1952), Andrésen (1958, 1968), Higginbottom (1965), Roach (1973)

for /tʃ/, where a vowel follows as well). Reinforcement is more likely to occur at the end of an accented syllable. Some examples where glottal reinforcement may occur are: for /p/, *reap, limp, help, apt, stop me*; for /t/, *beat, bent, melt, atlas, at last*; for /k/, *beak, bank, baulk, chocolate, back down*; for /tʃ/, *rich, bench, searched, teaching, wretched, search me, reach it*.

(c) *Glottal replacement in RP*—Some RP speakers replace syllable-final /p,t,k/ by [ʔ] when a consonant follows, no oral closure being made. Such a glottal closure most commonly replaces /t/ when the following consonant is homorganic, i.e. /t,d,tʃ,dʒ,n,l,r/ as in *that table, get down, that chair, great joke, witness, not now, Scotland, at least, that ring* but [ʔ] is also heard for /t/ before other non-syllabic consonants, e.g. in *football, gatepost, cat-call, catgut, not mine, nutmeg, Catford, not for me, not very, what thing, out there, outset, great zeal, nutshell, outright, cart-wheel, not yet, not here, boathouse*. Some RP speakers may also replace the first (plosive) element of the affricate /tʃ/ e.g. in *coach, much, catch, couch*. Use of [ʔ] to replace /t/ in other positions, i.e. before the syllabic [n̩] and [l̩] and before words beginning with vowels was until recently stigmatized as non-RP but is now acceptable in London Regional RP, e.g. in *cotton, little, eat an apple, bat and ball*. Use of [ʔ] for /t/ word-medially intervocalically, as in *water*, remains stigmatized as non-RP.

The replacement of final /p,k/ by [ʔ] is much less frequent among RP speakers and occurs only when the following consonant is homorganic, e.g. *soap powder, cap badge, back garden, bookcase*.

(d) *Glottal replacement in other dialects*—In some dialects (particularly Cockney) glottal replacement occurs in the same positions as RP, although more frequently, but also occurs in a wider number of contexts. Word-medially and intervocalically a /t/ following an accented vowel may be replaced by [ʔ], e.g. in *daughter, butter, Saturday, Waterloo, writing, potato* [pəˈtæɪʔə], *salty, wanted*. In rapid speech the glottal closure is likely to be very weak, so that the /t/ in such positions may border on being elided.

In Cockney glottal replacements of /p,k/ also occur in similar situations, e.g. in *supper, paper, cup of tea* [kʌʔə ˈtˢəɪ], *lucky, joker, he doesn't like it* [əɪdə̃ʊʔˈlaɪʔɪʔ], but there appears to be a greater tendency to retain a bilabial or velar closure. In cases of /-mpl,-ntl,-ŋkl/, as in *simple, mental, uncle*, if the nasal consonant is articulated, the [ʔ] used for /p,t,k/ is likely to be accompanied by the already formed bilabial, alveolar, or velar closure; if, however, as often happens in Cockney speech, /-ɪm,-en,-ʌŋ/ are realized as [ĩ,ẽ,ʌ̃], the following stop may be only glottal. [ʔ] may also occasionally replace the fricative /f/ in Cockney, especially in the phrase *half a*, e.g. *half a minute* [ɑ:ʔ ə ˈmɪnɪʔ]. It should also be noted that, initial /h/ often being elided, vowels thus rendered initial may have glottal emphatic reinforcement applied to them, especially in hiatus with a preceding vowel, e.g. *I hate him* [ɑɪ ˈʔæɪ ʔɪm], *we haven't* [wɪ ˈʔævn̩ʔ].

Glottal replacement and glottal reinforcement are used in similar ways in East Anglia, Bristol, Glaswegian and Tyneside,[22] intervocalic (post-accentual) replacement being generally marked as characteristic of broad varieties of accents (sometimes referred to as 'basilectal'). Tyneside is unique in realizing glottal

---

[22] Wells (1982)

reinforcement in intervocalic positions by post-glottalization, e.g. *water* [watʔə], *keeper* [kiːpʔə], *speaker* [spiːkʔə].

(3) *History*—Since it would appear that [ʔ] has never been a significant sound in English, it is not to be expected that its stylistic use should have been described in detail by the early grammarians. It is, however, mentioned in the seventeenth century[23] as a feature of the onset of initial vowels and, in works dealing with singing technique, has traditionally been described as the 'hard attack'. But the substitution of [ʔ] for a voiceless plosive in regional speech is not explicitly mentioned until the nineteenth century and it is only in recent years that the phenomenon of reinforcement has been explicitly noted. Lack of descriptive evidence concerning this non-significant sound is not, however, a reason for assuming that [ʔ] is a feature of only recent occurrence in English speech. But the fact that glottal reinforcement and glottal replacement are generally absent from Australian English, which shares many features with Cockney and hence might be assumed to have been derived principally from earlier London speech, might suggest that the glottal characteristics of Cockney have arisen in the last 200 years.

(4) *Advice to foreign learners*—Many languages use [ʔ] to re-inforce word-initial vowels but some do this much more regularly and frequently than English, e.g. German. Speakers should therefore generally avoid this type of re-inforcement. They should also be aware that use of glottal replacement between vowels, either within words or across word boundaries, is more typical of London Regional RP (Estuary English) than of General RP.

9.3 *Affricates*

(1) *Definition*—The term 'affricate' denotes a concept which is primarily of phonetic importance. Any plosive whose release stage is performed in such a way that considerable friction occurs approximately at the point where the plosive stop is made, may be called 'affricative'. In English, apart from the exceptional affrication mentioned in §9.2.3(6), only /t,d/ may have this type of release, namely in /tʃ,dʒ,tr,dr,ts,dz,tθ,dð/.

(2) *Phonemic status*—From a functional or distributional point of view these compound sounds may be considered either as single phonemic entities or as sequences of two phonemes. The choice of phonemic solution will depend upon the purpose of the analysis, but the following factors may be taken into account:

(a) *The distribution of the sound sequence*, in particular in the following positions: word-initial, word-final, and word-medial with different syllable assignments. A sound sequence which has a general distribution and shows an opposition in word-medial position between CLOSE-KNIT realizations and DISJUNCT realizations (i.e. with the elements in separate syllables or morphemes) may be treated as a complex phonemic entity.

---

[23] Abercrombie (1948)

	Word-initial	Word-final	Word-medial close-knit	Word-medial disjunct
/tʃ/	chap	patch	butcher	lightship
/dʒ/	jam	badge	aged	
/tr/	tram		mattress	footrest
/dr/	dram		tawdry	handrail
/ts/		cats	curtsey (?)	outset
/dz/		roads	Pudsey (?)	
/tθ/		eighth		
/dð/		(width)		

Table 11. *Distribution of homorganic sequences of plosive plus fricative*

Table 11 shows that /tʃ,dʒ/ best fulfil these conditions, occurring in all positions with a medial distinction between close-knit and disjunct. /tr,dr/ also have a distinction between close-knit and disjunct in medial position but do not occur in final position. /ts,dz/ do not occur initially (except in rare foreign words) and only doubtfully in close-knit medial situations. /tθ,dð/ have an occurrence restricted to the final position in very few words.

Close-knit and disjunct sequences of /t,d/ plus /ʃ,ʒ/ or /r/ involve different phonetic characteristics. In the case of /t/ plus /ʃ/, and /d/ plus /ʒ/, the fricative is shorter in close-knit sequences: thus the friction in *butcher* is of shorter duration that the friction in *lightship*. For sequences /t/ or /d/ plus /r/, the /r/ is fricative (although of course made in a different position from /ʃ,ʒ/) in close-knit sequences but approximant in disjunct sequences: additionally the /r/ is devoiced following /t/.[24] Thus the /r/ in *mattress* is fricative and voiceless while the /r/ in *footrest* is approximant and voiced. Medial close-knit sequences can be regarded as involving the two sounds within one syllable[25] while the disjunct sequence involves a syllable boundary between the two sounds.

(b) *Possibilities of commutation of the elements.*

(i) The elements of /tʃ/ may be commutated within the same syllable as follows: word-initially, the stop, commutates only with zero, cf. *chip, ship* while the fricative commutates with /r,j,w/ and zero, cf. *chip, trip, twin, tune, tin*; word-finally the stop commutates with /l/ or zero, cf. *watch, Welsh, was* while the fricative commutates with /s/ or zero, cf. *catch, cats, cat*; and word-medially the stop commutates with zero, cf. *matches, mashes* while the fricative commutates with

---

[24] The different length of friction as between the fricative element of an affricate and a fricative following a plosive is shown by a comparison of the affricated /t/ in *cat* [kætˢ] and the longer friction of the plural form *cats* /kæts/ or between *ratchet* /rætʃɪt/ and *rat shit* /ræt ʃɪt/. Dialectal affrication of /t,d/ is, however, more common initially (where /t,d/ + /s,z/ is rare) than finally, being inhibited in final positions by the risk of confusion with the inflected forms

[25] In words like *mattress* /tr/ may be analyzed as one complex unit having ambisyllabic status (see §5.5.2)

/r/ or zero, cf. *enchants, entrance* (v.), *marcher, martyr* (syllable boundaries are assumed to occur in the following words: *welshing, pinching, outward, atlas, chutney*).

The elements of /dʒ/ have a more restricted possibility of commutation owing to the rarity of syllable initial /ʒ/. Word-initially only the fricative commutates, with /r,j,w/ and zero, cf. *jest, dressed, dune, dwell, dam*; word-finally again only the fricative commutates, with /z/ or zero, cf. *hedge, heads, head*; word-medially the stop commutates with zero, cf. *ledger, leisure,* and the fricative commutates with /r/ and zero, cf. *orgy, Audrey, larger, larder.*

Thus the possibilities of commutation are restricted in the case of the elements of /tʃ/ to zero (and occasionally /l/) for the stop, and to zero, /r,w/ and /s/, according to the situation, for the fricative. The commutability of the elements of /dʒ/ is also restricted, i.e. with zero in the case of the stop, and with zero, /r,j,w/ or /z/, according to the situation, in the fricative. Moreover, /tʃ/ is in opposition to /dʒ/ as a complex in all positions (see §9.3.1 for examples).

(ii) /tr,dr/, on the other hand, have considerable possibilities of commutation especially in the first element: in the case of /tr/, cf. *try, cry, pry, fry, rye; true, shrew, drew, grew, threw, brew; tree, three, tea; trill, chill, twill; troop, tune; train, chain*; in the case of /dr/, cf. *drew, true, crew, grew, brew, threw, shrew, rue, do, due, Jew; dry, fry, pry* etc.

On the basis of commutability, therefore, /tr,dr/ are more reasonably to be considered as consisting of separable elements than /tʃ,dʒ/.

(c) *Glottalization*—/tʃ/ is liable to glottal reinforcement before vowels as in [tiːʔtʃɪŋ] where /p,t,k/ are, within RP, generally subject to reinforcement only when a consonant follows; and to glottal replacement of the [t] element alone as in [kəʊʔʃ]. Both facts suggest that the [ʃ] element of /tʃ/ is in some sense the 'following consonant' which allows glottalization of the preceding [t]. Contrary to sections (a) and (b) above, section (c) argues for an analysis of [tʃ] as always a sequence of [t] + [ʃ].

(d) *Native speakers' reaction*—It seems that the native speaker does not regard /tʃ,dʒ/ as composite sounds, i.e. composed of distinctive elements. He is likely, for instance, to consider that *chip, catch,* consist of three parts in the same way as *tip, ship,* or *cat, cash*; or again, *jam, badge,* as structures equivalent to *dam, bad.* (It is, of course, true that PresE /tʃ,dʒ/ derive in many cases from earlier (OE or OF) plosives [c] or [ɟ], as well as from a coalescence of /t/ or /d/+/j/—see §9.3.1—but this is irrelevant in any consideration of the present structure of the language.) On the other hand, /tr,dr/ are not normally regarded as anything but sequences of /t,d/+/r/ and, in many dialects where the /r/ has a tap or trill realization, there is no question of affrication.

(e) *Speech errors*—Any of the elements of a consonantal cluster may be involved in a speech error, e.g. *play the game* →/peɪ ðə ˈɡleɪm/, *came to a stop* →/skeɪm tu ə ˈstɒp/ (Sometimes an error will involve a transposition, sometimes just an addition). In this respect /tr,dr/ behave like clusters, e.g. *caught the tram* →/krɔːt ðə ˈtæm/, whereas /tʃ,dʒ/ are never involved in such errors; we do not, for example, get errors like *ring the changes* →/trɪŋ ðə ˈʃeɪndʒɪz/.[26]

---

[26] Fromkin (1971)

(f) *Conclusion*—The criteria above on balance clearly suggest taking /tʃ,dʒ/ as phonemic affricates (despite the contrary evidence from glottalization). On the other hand, of the other phonetic affricates only /tr,dr/ have some evidence favouring a uniphonemic analysis (i.e. the distinction between close-knit and disjunct), but even for these sequences the evidence is nowhere near as strong as for /tʃ,dʒ/. Accordingly, only /tʃ,dʒ/ are here analyzed as unit phonemes.

(3) *Acoustic features*—The acoustic features of affricates are those appropriate to stops (see §9.2.2) and fricatives (see §9.4.1). Since, however, the release stage is fricative, the most essential perceptual cues will be provided by the transition between the preceding vowel and the stop and by the explosive onset of the friction. Nevertheless, in the case of /tʃ,dʒ/, the transition will not necessarily be that which is typical of the alveolar plosives, since the stops of /tʃ,dʒ/ will be of a palatalized type; alternatively there may, in the case of /tʃ,dʒ/, be a brief intervening friction of the alveolar /s,z/ type before the [ʃ,ʒ] elements proper.[27]

9.3.1   Palato-alveolar Affricates[28] /tʃ,dʒ/

(1) *Examples*
/tʃ/—*voiceless*

>   *ch*—chain, choose, chunk, leech, pinch, achieve, rich, attach, much
>   *tch*—watch, fetch, wretched, aitch (the letter 'h'), bitch, butcher
>   *ti*—question, suggestion, navigation etc.
>   *tu*—nature, statue, furniture, virtuous, century, actual

(*Note* 'righteous, cello, concerto'.)

>   *word-initial*—cheese, chain, charge, charm, choke, cheer
>   *word-medial (intervocalic)*—feature, richer, wretched, orchard, butcher, nature, merchant
>   *(consonant preceding)*—gesture, posture, mischief, juncture, capture, lecture, pilchard, culture, adventure
>   *word-final*—wretch, catch, larch, porch, much, coach
>   *(consonant preceding)*—inch, conch, bench, branch, filch, mulch

/dʒ/—*voiced*

>   *j*—jam, jaw, job, juice, major, pyjamas, enjoy, eject, jostle
>   *g*—gem, magic, pigeon, fragile, cage, imagine, village

---

[27] Strevens (1960)

[28] In the latest versions of the chart of the International Phonetic Alphabet (see Table 1) the fricatives [ʃ,ʒ], and hence by implication the affricates [tʃ,dʒ], are labelled 'post-alveolar'. In this book the former label 'palato-alveolar' is retained as more closely indicating the palatalized alveolar articulation of these sounds. The term 'post-alveolar' is kept for RP /r/ (= [ɹ]) which is simply labelled 'alveolar' on the new chart (see further under §9.7.2)

dg—midget, lodge, judge, edge, fridge, badge, budge
dj—adjacent, adjective, adjunct, adjacent

(*Note* 'soldier, suggest, exaggerate, grandeur, arduous'.)

word-initial—gin, jest, jar, jaunt, Jew, jerk, joke, joist, jeer
word-medial (intervocalic)—midget, ledger, margin, fragile, urgent, orgy, adjacent, agenda, major
(consonant preceding)—avenger, danger, stringent, soldier, Belgian, bulges, object
word-final—ridge, edge, large, dodge, judge, huge, age, doge, gouge
(consonant preceding)—bilge, bulge, hinge, sponge, change

Compare

/tʃ/, /dʒ/—chin, gin; chest, jest; choose, Jews; choke, joke; cheer, jeer; catches, cadges; nature, major; a venture, avenger; riches, ridges; leech, liege; larch, large; perch, purge; lunch, lunge; cinch, singe; beseech, besiege

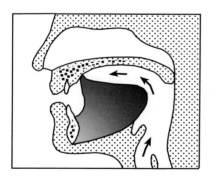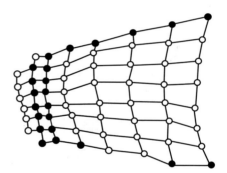

Fig. 37. *Section and palatogram of* /tr,dr/.

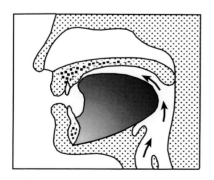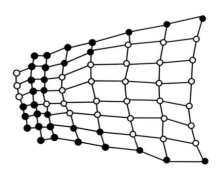

Fig. 38. *Section and palatogram of stop phase of* /tʃ,dʒ/.

(2) *Description*—The soft palate being raised and the nasal resonator shut off, the obstacle to the airstream is formed by a closure made between the tip, blade, and rims of the tongue and the upper alveolar ridge and side teeth. At the same time, the front of the tongue is raised towards the hard palate in readiness for the fricative release. The closure is released slowly, the air escaping in a diffuse manner over the whole of the central surface of the tongue with friction occurring between the blade/front region of the tongue and the alveolar/front palatal section of the roof of the mouth. During both stop and fricative stages, the vocal folds are wide apart for /tʃ/, but may be vibrating for all or part of /dʒ/ according to the situation in the utterance. (/dʒ/ shares the features of devoicing in initial and final positions exhibited by plosives, see §9.2.1(4), and fricatives, see §9.4(3). /tʃ,dʒ/ differ from plosives in that they never lose their fricative release stage. The lip position will be conditioned by that of adjacent sounds, especially that of a following vowel (cf. the greater lip-rounding of /tʃ/ in *choose* in relation to that of *cheese*), though with some speakers a certain amount of lip protrusion is always present.

In addition, it should be noted that the voiceless /tʃ/, when final in a syllable has the same effect of reducing the length of preceding sounds as was noted for /p,t,k/ (see §9.2.1(5)); comparatively full length of preceding sounds is retained before /dʒ/. This effect must be taken as the primary perceptual cue to the /tʃ/–/dʒ/ opposition in final positions.

(3) *Variants*—No important variants of /tʃ,dʒ/ occur, except in the matter of the degree of lip-rounding used. Some very careful speakers, however, use /t/ and /d/+/j/ in words which otherwise frequently have /tʃ/ or /dʒ/ e.g. *gesture, culture, virtue, statue, righteous, fortune, literature, question, posture, Christian, soldier, grandeur*. Potential oppositions between medial /tʃ,dʒ/ and /tj,dj/ are rare, but compare *verger* with /dʒ/, and *verdure* with /dj/. In the case of /t,d/+<u>, both the palato-alveolar affricate and /t/ or /d/+/j/ may be heard, e.g. in *actual, punctual, mutual, obituary, individual, gradual, educate*. Some speakers omit the stop element in the clusters /ntʃ,ndʒ/ in word-final positions as in *pinch, French, lunch, branch, paunch, hinge, revenge, challenge, strange, scrounge* etc., and also medially as in *pinching, luncheon, avenger, danger* etc.

(4) *Chief sources*—PresE /tʃ,dʒ/ derive from: early OE [c] and [ɟ] (*child, chin, kitchen, teach, church, edge, bridge*), this change being accomplished by the late OE period; OF [tʃ,dʒ] (*chief, chair, chamber, choice, merchant, branch, judge, major, age, village, change*); a coalescence of medial /tj/ or /dj/ (*nature, virtue, question, creature, grandeur, soldier*)—this latter change was not general until the early eighteenth century; a number of eighteenth-century coalesced forms have now reverted to a stop +/j/ or [ɪ] sequence, e.g. *piteous, bestial, tedious, odious*.

(5) *Acquisition by native learners*—The affricates /tʃ,dʒ/ are, along with the fricatives and /r/, among the consonants which are acquired later rather than earlier (often not until the age of four). It might be expected that, being composed of a homorganic sequence of plosive plus fricative, their acquisition would depend on the prior acquisition of the plosives and fricatives of which they are composed. However, this does not always seem to be the case; in particular the fricative /ʒ/ may be of later occurrence than the affricate /dʒ/, perhaps due to its comparative low frequency of occurrence in the adult language. Like most consonants the affricates are used first in syllable-initial positions, and are often

omitted in final position in early words. Before they are correctly produced in initial position, they are frequently replaced by /t,d/.

(6) *Advice to foreign learners*—Some languages do not have /tʃ,dʒ/, e.g. French and Portuguese, and will replace them with /ʃ,ʒ/, or, in the case of Greek which has no /ʃ,ʒ/ either, with the affricates /ts,dz/. Good starting points for learners from such languages are the clusters /tj,dj/; moving the tongue forward while producing these sequences will often produce the required effect. Learners from some other languages (especially Scandinavians) are apt to articulate /tʃ,dʒ/ with too much lip spreading and overpalatalization, producing sounds resembling [tç,dʝ]; these, too, should move the tongue forward. Some languages have only /tʃ/, e.g. Arabic, German, Russian, and Spanish, and replace the one with the other; weakening /tʃ/ will generally produce /dʒ/ in such cases. Particular attention should also be paid to the shortening of sounds preceding syllable final /tʃ/, the examples in (1) of this section providing practice for this feature. In sequences of two affricates like *which chair, Dutch cheese, large jar*, it is acceptable to omit the plosive element of the first affricate, e.g. /wɪʃ ˋtʃeə/, /dʌʃ ˋtʃiːz/, /lɑːʒ ˋdʒɑː/; however it is not acceptable to omit the fricative element.

Although only /tʃ,dʒ/ are here considered as unit phonemes, special attention should nevertheless be given to the sequences /tr,dr/ (see Fig. 37) because of the nature of the retracted [t̠,d̠] used before /r/, the friction associated with the /r/ in these sequences, and the devoicing of /r/ following /t/. Foreign learners should take care not to confuse /tʃ/ and /tr/ and /dʒ/ and /dr/ as in the minimal pairs *cheese, trees; chip, trip; chap, trap; chew, true; chain, drain* and *jest, dressed; jaw, draw; Jew, drew; jam, dram*.

9.4 Fricatives

In the articulation of a fricative consonant, two organs are brought and held sufficiently close together for the escaping airstream to produce local air turbulence; fricatives are, therefore, like plosives and affricates, characterized by a noise component. This turbulence may or may not be accompanied by voice. There is an on- or off-glide in respect of an adjacent sound (manifested acoustically by formant transitions), most appreciable if the adjacent sound is a vowel.

The RP fricative phonemes comprise four pairs /f,v,θ,ð,s,z,ʃ,ʒ/ and /h/. [x], a voiceless velar fricative, occurs exceptionally in some speakers' pronunciation of Scottish words such as *loch*; for [ɸ,β,s,z,x,ɣ] occurring as the fricative element of affricated plosives, see §9.2.4(6), and for the fricative allophones of /r,l,j,w/, see §9.7.

Table 12 illustrates oppositions, especially between members of the fricative pairs, in word-initial, word-medial, and word-final positions.

These oppositions may be realized by means of one or several of the following phonetic features:

(1) *Place of articulation*—/f,v/—labiodental; /θ,ð/—dental; /s,z/—alveolar; /ʃ,ʒ/—palato-alveolar; /h/—glottal. Such a series must be considered to be relatively complex. The existence, in particular, of place oppositions between the dental, alveolar, and palato-alveolar areas of articulation necessitates a precision of

	Initial	*Medial*	*Final*
f	feel	proofing	leaf
v	veal	proving	leave
θ	thigh	earthy, ether	wreath
ð	thy	worthy, either	wreathe
s	seal	racer	peace
z	zeal	razor	peas
ʃ	sheet	fission, Confucian	niche
ʒ	gigolo	vision, confusion	rouge
h	heat	behave	

Table 12. *Fricatives in different word positions*

articulation in English which is not required in many other languages. Thus, for example, the lack of palato-alveolar fricative phonemes in Spanish permits the retraction of articulations in the alveolar region (e.g. /s/), whereas the absence in French and many other languages of dental fricative phonemes allows a dental-ized quality in the alveolar articulations, which if introduced into English, is liable to cause confusion with /θ,ð/ or to produce a 'lisping' fricative which is consid-ered socially undesirable. This reflects the fact that [s,z], whether alveolar or dental, are made with a configuration of the tongue which allows the air to escape along a groove, whereas /θ,ð/ use a flatter configuration where the air escapes through a slit. /ʃ,ʒ/ are made with flat blade and tip but with grooving further back, although even this grooving is not as deep as that for /s,z/.[29] These differ-ence in configuration are at least as important as the difference places of artic-ulation.

(2) Force of articulation—Within the four pairs, /f,θ,s,ʃ/ tend to be pronounced with relatively more muscular energy and stronger breath force than /v,ð,z,ʒ/;[30] the former are FORTIS, the latter LENIS. /h/ is normally fortis in character, but may have a lenis allophone (see §9.4.6).

(3) *Voicing*—Like the voiced plosives and affricates, /v,ð,z,ʒ/ tend to be fully voiced only when they occur between voiced sounds, e.g. in *cover, other, easy, leisure, a van, all that, by the zoo*. In initial and (especially) in final positions, the voiced fricatives may be partially or almost completely devoiced,[31] e.g. initially in *van, that, zoo* (i.e. with silence preceding) only the latter part of the friction is likely to be voiced, and finally in *leave, breathe, peas, rouge* /ruːʒ/ (i.e. with silence following) the friction is typically voiceless, though the consonant remains lenis—[v̥,ð̥,z̥,ʒ̥]. Additionally, some devoicing of the voiced series may even occur in intervocalic position. The voiceless series remains completely voiceless in all positions. /h/, however, occurring only in word-initial and word-medial situations, though voiceless in an initial position, may have some voicing medially between voiced sounds, e.g. *anyhow*.

---

[29]   Stone (1990), Stone *et al.* (1992)
[30]   Subtelny *et al.* (1966), Malécot (1968)
[31]   Haggard (1978), Docherty (1992)

(4) *Length*—When /f,θ,s,ʃ,v,ð,z,ʒ/ occur finally, the perception of voiceless or voiced consonants is largely determined by the length of the sounds which precede them.[32] /f,θ,s,ʃ/ have the effect of reducing the length of the preceding vowel (particularly a long vowel or diphthong) and of /l,m,n/ interposed between the vowel and the fricative, cf. *fife, loath, place, leash, self, fence* with *five, loathe, plays, (liege), selves, fens* etc. The same reduction in the length of vowels, nasals and laterals is operative when the voiceless fricatives occur in a medial position, cf. *proofing, proving; earthy, worthy; racer, razor; fission, vision.* While they shorten the vowels and continuant consonants which precede them, voiceless fricatives are themselves longer than their voiced equivalents.[33]

Summary—The RP fricatives may, therefore, be said to be phonetically distinguished:

(a) by means of a five-term series in respect of place of articulation—labio-dental v. dental v. alveolar v. palato-alveolar v. glottal, and
(b) at each of the first four points of articulation, by a complex of factors including force of articulation (which applies in all positions), voicing (which applies principally word-medially between voiced sounds), and by the length of preceding vowels, consonants and laterals within the same syllable.

(5) *Advice to foreign learners*—A distinction between five places of articulation is rare in the world's languages[34] and learners will have to spend some effort to get the articulation at each place correct. Particular attention needs to be given to the precision of articulation required for the distinctions among dental, alveolar and palato-alveolar fricatives. Advice is given under each place of articulation below.

Learners should not attempt to rely only on voicing to make distinctions between the various pairs, but concentrate on the strength of the friction and the correct reductions in the length of vowels before the voiceless series. Additionally, many languages only have strong fricatives like [s] and [f], e.g. Malay, Norwegian and Thai, and learners from such backgrounds have to learn to produce a second series by weakening their articulation.

9.4.1 Acoustic Features of English Fricatives

In acoustic terms,[35] our perception of the various types of fricative (whose characteristic feature is a continuous noise component) appears to depend upon the following factors (for spectrograms, see Fig. 32):

---

[32] Denes (1955), Wiik (1965)
[33] Subtelny *et al.* (1966), Malécot (1968)
[34] Maddieson (1984: 43) found only 3.5% of the 317 languages in his survey had 11 or more fricatives
[35] Hughes and Halle (1956), Strevens (1960), Jongman (1989), Amerman and Parnell (1992), Scully *et al.* (1992), Stevens *et al.* (1992)

(1) *Extent and position of noise component*—Continuous noise in the spectrum is appropriate to articulatory friction regions:

alveolars	3,600–8,000 Hz
palato-alveolars	2,000–7,000 Hz
labiodentals	1,500–7,000 Hz
dentals	1,400–8,000 Hz
glottal	500–6,500 Hz

(2) *Intensity of noise component*—/s,ʃ/ have relatively high intensity; /f,θ,h/ relatively low intensity. The voiced series has an overall lower intensity than that of the voiceless series.

(3) *Low frequency component*—The voiced series may have a periodic low frequency component (voicing) which is absent in the voiceless series.[36] Voicing may also manifest itself in more extensive transitions of the first formant adjacent to voiced fricatives.[37]

(4) *Formant transitions*—Especially in the case of the low intensity labiodentals and dentals, much information regarding place of articulation comes from the nature of the adjacent vocalic glide. In the case of /h/ (often an anticipatory voiceless version of the following vowel), the spectral pattern is likely to mirror the formant structure of the following vowel.

(5) *Duration of fricative noise*—The friction of the voiced series is shorter than that of the voiceless series.

9.4.2   Acquisition of Fricatives by Native Learners

The fricatives constitute the largest area of difficulty for native learners in the area of consonant acquisition. The distinction of five places of articulation is particularly difficult: three of the places (dental, alveolar, palato-alveolar) depend on different and delicate adjustments of the tip/blade of the tongue and it is in this area that most of the difficulty occurs. The first fricative (generally /f/ or /s/) occurs later than plosives and nasals and, unlike them, may occur at first just as frequently in medial or final position as in initial position. The /s/ will often be misarticulated, sometimes only slightly, sometimes to the extent of being a lateral fricative [ɬ]. The distinction between the three apical/laminal pairs will, for many children, not be complete and/or correctly articulated until the age of five or six. The voiceless members of the pairs are generally acquired before the voiced members; this may be due to their higher frequency of occurrence in the adult language or to the greater perceptibility of the stronger friction in the voiceless series. Before any fricatives have been acquired, they may be replaced in initial position by the corresponding plosives, i.e. /f,v/→/p,b/, and /θ,ð,s,z,ʃ,ʒ/→/t,d/. Once /f/ and /s/ have been acquired, the voiced series may continue to be replaced by plosives, while /θ,ʃ/ are replaced by /s/. The glottal

---

[36] Stevens *et al.* (1992) found that an interval of at last 60 ms was necessary for an intervocalic fricative to be perceived as voiceless

[37] Stevens *et al.* (1992)

fricative /h/ (which of course is not paired) is very variable in acquisition, reflecting its varying presence in the fricative systems of different dialects and hence in the speech with which a child is surrounded.

9.4.3 Labiodental Fricatives /f,v/

(1) *Examples*
/f/—*voiceless*

>*f*—fork, friend, frame, funnel, fake, fat, fetish, fill, four, fog, fool
>*ff*—off, stuff, giraffe, cliff, afford, offend, coffee, suffer, effort, daffodil
>*ph*—physics, phonetics, diaphragm, epitaph, photograph
>*gh*—enough, rough, cough, draught, laugh

*(*Note *'sapphire'.)*

>*word-initial*—feet, fit, fat, father, fool, fail, photo
>*word-medial*—affair, defend, offer, tougher, loafer, suffer, selfish, comfort
>*word-final*—leaf, laugh, cough, stuff, roof, loaf, strife
>*in word-initial clusters*—fry, fly, few, sphere
>*in word-final clusters*—/fθ(s)/ fifth(s), /ft(s)/ raft(s), /mf(s)/ triumph(s)[38]
>/lf(s)/ wolf('s), /lft/ engulfed, /lfθ(s)/ twelfth(s), /fn(z,d)/ soften (s,ed), /fl(z,d)/
>baffle(s,ed), /fs/ coughs

/v/—*voiced*

>*v*—vine, vote, view, veal, veer, savage, seven, deliver, clever, ever, river, novel
>*ve*—live, active, wave, love, dove, glove, save
>(*Note* 'of', 'nephew' and slang 'civvy, bovver, navvy'.)
>*word-initial*—veal, vex, vat, vast, vain, vice, voice
>*word-medial*—ever, nephew, over, silver, cover, event, canvas
>*word-final*—leave, give, have, of, move, dove, grove
>*in word-initial clusters*—/vj/ view
>*in word-final clusters*—/vz/ loaves, /vd/ loved, /vn(z)/ oven(s), /lv(z,d)/
>solve(s,d), /vl(z,d)/ grovel(s,ed) etc.

Compare

>/f/, /v/—fine, vine; fat, vat; few, view; offer, hover; surface, service; laugher, larva; camphor, canvas; leaf, leave; proof, prove; safes, saves.

(2) *Description*—The soft palate being raised and the nasal resonator shut off, the inner surface of the lower lip makes a light contact with the edge of the upper teeth, so that the escaping air produces friction. The actual point of contact will vary somewhat according to the adjacent sound, e.g. in the case of a back strongly rounded vowel or of a bilabial plosive (*fool, roof, obvious*), the contact on the lower lip tends to be more retracted than in the case of a front spread vowel (*feel, leaf*). For /f/, the friction is voiceless, whereas there may be some vocal fold

---

[38] An epenthetic /p/ may be inserted, thus /ˈtraɪʌmpfs/. Cf. §9.4.5(3) and §10.8(3)

vibration accompanying /v/, according to its situation (see §9.4(3) above). The tongue position of an adjacent vowel will persist or be anticipated during the labiodental friction; in the case of intervocalic /f,v/, the tongue will articulate independently for the vowels or, if the vowels are similar, e.g. in *stiffest, giving,* will retain its position during the labiodental friction.

(3) *Variants*—No important articulatory variants for /f,v/ occur among RP speakers, although word-final /v/ may change to /f/ before a voiceless consonant initial in the following word, e.g. regularly in *have to* and more rarely in such sequences as *love to, have some* (see §12.4.3) or may, in familiar speech, be elided in the case of the unaccented form of *of, have,* e.g. in a *lot of money, I could have bought it* /ə lɒt ə ˈmʌnɪ, aɪ kəd ə ˈbɔːt ɪt/, where /ə/ is phonetically equivalent to the unaccented form of *are, a* (see §12.2).[39] In south-west England speech, the voiceless /f/ is often replaced by /v/ in word-initial position (e.g. in *fox, family, fourth*).

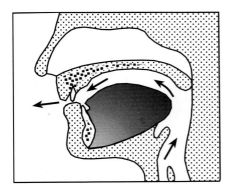

Fig. 39. *Section of* /f,v/.

(4) *Chief sources*—PresE /f/ derives from OE initial and final [f] (*foot, fowl, free, thief, leaf, wife*) and from OF [f] (*fine, fruit, profit, chief*). The spelling <ph> next to <th> (as in *diphthong*) was pronounced with /p/ rather than /f/ in eModE, and often spelt with <p>; such a pronunciation with a bilabial plosive is still widely heard. An earlier final [x] following a rounded vowel gave [f] by late ME (*dwarf, laugh, rough, cough*); in words such as *plough, dough, bough*, the PresE pronunciation derives from the inflected form in which [x] has been lost, as also in the final [xt] sequence (*ought, thought*). An irregular change [u]>[v]>[f] has taken place in the word *lieutenant*, though the regular development /l(j)uːˈtenənt/ is used in American English. The increasing use of /f/ in *nephew* is a spelling pronunciation, instead of the earlier, regular /v/.

PresE /v/ derives from OE /f/=[v] between voiced sounds (*love, devil, wolves, wives, driven*), from SW dialect initial OE [v] for [f] (*vat, vixen, vane*) and from OF [v] (*vain, very, cover, serve*).

---

[39] Note the accepted forms of *man-of-war, tug-of-war, o'clock, will-o'-the-wisp*, with /ə/ rather than /əv/ for *of*

(5) *Advice to foreign learners*—Some learners (particularly Indians) use too weak a contact for /v/, so that the friction is lost, giving the labiodental approximant [ʋ]; others (particularly Germans and Hungarians) use bilabial friction [β] instead of the labiodental sound. In both of these cases, there is a tendency to use the same sound for both /v/ and /w/. Care should, therefore, be taken to distinguish pairs such as *vine, wine; verse, worse; vest, west* etc., using friction between the lower lip and upper teeth for /v/. Many languages have only /f/, e.g. Cantonese and Malay, and need to attain /v/ by weakening the friction and paying attention to the length of preceding vowels.

9.4.4   Dental Fricatives /θ,ð/

(1) *Examples*
/θ/—*voiceless* (always spelt <th>)

> *word-initial*—thief, thick, thatch, thong, thought, thumb
> *word-medial*—ether, ethics, lethal, method, author, anthem, lengthy, atheist, athletic, deathly, worthless
> *word-final*—heath, smith, breath, path, cloth, earth, fourth, oath
> *in word-initial clusters*—three, throw, thew, thwart
> *in word-final clusters*—/θt/ earthed, /θs/ mouth's, /pθ(s)/ depth(s), /tθ(s)/ eighth(s), /fθ(s)/ fifth(s), /ksθ(s)/ sixth(s), /mθ/ warmth,[40] /nθ(s)/ month(s), /lfθ(s)/ twelfth(s), /ŋkθ(s)/ length(s), /lθ(s)/ health('s), /θl(z)/ Ethel('s), /θn/ earthen

/ð/—*voiced* (always spelt <th>)

> *word-initial*—there, this, then, the, though, thy, they
> *word-medial*—breathing, leather, gather, father, mother, northerly, southern, worthy, either, although
> *word-final*—seethe, with, soothe, lathe, clothe, writhe, mouth (v.)
> *in word-final*[41] *clusters*—/ðm(z)/ rhythm(s), /ðn(z)/ southern('s), /ðl(z)/ betrothal(s), /ðz/ clothes, /ðd/ writhed, /dð/ width (alternatively /wɪtθ/)

Compare

> /θ/,/ð/—thigh, thy; ether, breather; earthy, worthy; wreath, wreathe; mouth (n.), mouth (v.); oath, clothe.
> /θ/,/s/—thick, sick; thought, sort; thumb, sum; mouth, mouse; worth, worse
> /θ/,/t/—thick, tick; thought, taught; three, tree; heath, heat; both, boat; fourth, fort
> /ð/,/z/—seethe, seas; lathe, laze; clothe, close (v.); breathe, breeze
> /ð/,/d/—then, den; though, dough; there, dare; other, udder; worthy, wordy; seethe, seed; writhe, ride

(2) *Description*—The soft palate being raised and the nasal resonator shut off, the tip and rims of the tongue make a light contact with the edge and inner

---

[40] An epenthetic /p/ may be inserted, thus /wɔːmpθ/, Cf. §9.4.5(3) and §10.8(3)
[41] /ð/ does not occur in word-initial clusters

surface of the upper incisors and a firmer contact with the upper side teeth, so that the air escaping between the forward surface of the tongue and the incisors causes friction (such friction often being very weak in the case of /ð/). With some speakers, the tongue tip may protrude between the teeth; this is a commom type of articulation in American English. The tongue being relatively flat, the aperture through which the air escapes is in the nature of a slit rather than a groove, which produces fricative noise at a lower frequency than that associated with /s,z/. For /θ/ the friction is voiceless, whereas for /ð/ there may be some vocal fold vibration according to its situation (see §9.4(3) above). The lip position will depend upon the adjacent vowel, e.g. being spread for *thief, heath, these* etc., and somewhat rounded for *thought, truth, soothe* etc.

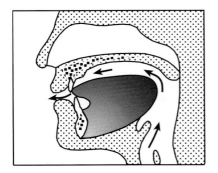 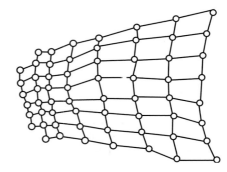

Fig. 40. *Section and palatogram of /θ,ð/.*

(3) *Variants*—No important RP variants of /θ,ð/ occur. Since /θ,ð/ offer difficulties of articulation when followed by /s,z/, they are sometimes elided in clusters, e.g. *clothes* /kləʊz/, *months* /mʌns/, or /mʌnts/. In sequences of the type /s,z/ followed by unaccented /ð/, as in *Is there any?, What's the time?*, the preceding alveolar articulation may influence the dental fricative in rapid speech—/ˈɪz zər enɪ, wɒts zə ˈtaɪm/. Again, in Cockney and in Southern American, the dental articulation may be replaced by labiodental, e.g. *throw it, Smith* /ˈfrəʊ ɪt, smɪf/, *mother, breathe in* /ˈmʌvə, briːv ˈɪn/. In these areas other alveolar articulations may also be heard for the weak /ð/, e.g. *all the way* /ɔːl də ˈweɪ/, *in the morning* /ɪn nə ˈmɔːnɪn/. In Southern Irish speech /θ,ð/ are often realized as dental plosives [t̪,d̪] but this does not generally lead to neutralization with /t,d/.

(4) *Chief sources*—PresE /θ/ derives from initial and final (including morpheme-final) OE [θ] (*think, throat, bath, tooth, earthly, worthless*), from OF [ð] (*faith*), from learned Greek forms (*theory, thesis*), and others which until ModE commonly had /t/ (*catholic, authority, theatre*).

PresE /ð/ derives from OE /θ/=[ð] between voiced sounds (*other, feather, breathes*). Note that of the English words where there is initial /ð/ rather than /θ/ (which is to be expected from the OE forms), e.g. *the, this, then, that, than, they* etc., most are words which are frequently medial and unaccented in an utterance.

(5) *Advice to foreign learners*—Most learners will have an L1 which does not have /θ,ð/ (although Arabic and European Spanish speakers do) and will usually

replace them with /t,d/, two exceptions being French and German which are more likely to replace by /s,z/, and Hindi speakers who use their /t̪,d̪/. Such pronunciations are to be avoided if at all possible. In particular, those words with /ð/ which are normally unaccented, e.g. *the, than, they* etc. should not be pronounced with /d/. The difficulty of /θ,ð/ lies not so much in their articulation, which most learners can perform correctly in isolation, as in their combination with other fricatives, especially /s/ and /z/. Learners should, therefore, practise with drills containing such combinations involving rapid tongue glides, e.g. /s+θ/ *this thing*, /k+θ/ *sixth*, /z+θ/ *his thumb*, /s+ð/ *pass the salt*, /z+ð/ *is this it?*, /θ+s/ *fifths*, /θ+s+ð/ *Smith's there*, /ð+z+ð/ *soothes them* etc., /s,z/ preceding /θ,ð/ in sequences like *what's that, is this, nice thing* should not be assimilated to /θ,ð/.

9.4.5   Alveolar Fricatives /s,z/

(1) *Examples*
/s/—*voiceless*

> *s, se*—so, single, sun, saw, bus, gas, stay, skin, snow, tense, lapse, goose
> *ss*—pass, kiss, class, cross, discuss, assist, cassette, embarrass, essential, waitress
> *c,ce*—receive, decide, exercise, council, niece, science, licence, advice, sauce
> *sc*—science, descend, acquiesce, scent, obscene
> *x* (=/ks/)—axe, climax, six, axle, reflex

(*Note* 'psychology, answer, sword, psalm, castle, etc.)

> *word-initial*—cease, sat, sample, soon, soap, sign, soil
> *word-medial*—pieces, losses, essay, axes, concert, escape, pencil, whisper, wrestler, excite, useless
> *word-final*—niece, farce, pass, puss, goose, famous, dose, ice, mouse, fierce, scarce
> *in word-initial clusters*—/sp/ spare, /st/ stain, /sk/ scarce, /sm/ smoke, /sn/ snake, /sl/ slow, /sf/ sphere, /sw/ swear, /spl/ splice, /spr/ spray, /spj/ spume, /str/ stray, /stj/ stew, /skr/ scream, /skj/ skewer, /skw/ square
> *in word-final clusters*—/sp(s,t)/, gasp(s,ed), /st(s)/ rest(s), /sk(s,t)/ ask(s,ed), /sm/ lissom, /sn(z)/ listen(s), /sns/ licence, /sl(z)/ muscle(s), /ns(t)/ mince(d), /nsl(z)/ pencil(s), /lst/ whilst, /snt/ decent, /ps(t)/ lapse(d), /mps(t)/ glimpse(d), /lps/ helps, /ts/ cats, /kts/ acts, /pts/ opts, /lts/ faults, /nts/ tents, /ls/ pulse, /fts/ drafts, /ks(t)/ tax(ed), /ŋks/ thanks, /lks/ milks, /mfs/ nymphs, /fs/ laughs, /θs/ fourths, /fθs/ fifths, /fθs/ twelfths, /nθs/ months, /ksθ(s)/ sixth(s), /tθs/ eighths, /dst/ midst, /mpts/ prompts, /stl(z)/ pistol(s), /tns/ pittance, /dns/ riddance, /vns/ grievance, /ʃns/ patience etc.

/z/—*voiced*

> *s,se*—bars, dogs, plays, news, rose, please, cruise, choose, praise, bosom, prison
> *ss*—scissors, possess, dessert, dissolve
> *z*—zoo, zeal, zero, zip, quiz, wizard

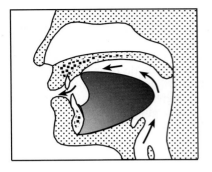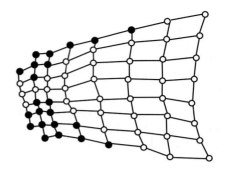

Fig. 41. *Section and palatogram of* /s,z/.

zz—dizzy, blizzard, buzz, buzzard, dazzle, jazz, nuzzle
x (=/gz/)—exact, anxiety, exaggerate, exempt, exhaust, exist, auxiliary

(*Note* 'xerox, xylophone, xenophobia'.)

> *word-initial*—zeal, zest, zinc, zoo, zone, zero
> *word-medial*—easy, hesitate, bazaar, bosom, hawser, lazy, thousand, palsy, pansy, husband
> *word-final*—fees, is, says, as, was, ooze, does, butchers, gaze, rose, cows, noise, ears, airs, tours
> *in word-final clusters*[42]—/bz/ ribs, /dz/ heads, /gz/ legs, /mz/ limbs, /nz(d)/ cleanse(d), /ndz/ hands, /ŋz/ rings, /lz/ holes, /vs/ caves, /ldz/ holds, /lvz/ valves, /lbz/ bulbs, /lmz/ films, /lnz/ kilns /ðz/ clothes, /zm(z)/ prism(s), /zn(z,d)/ emprison(s,ed), /zl(z,d)/ puzzle(s,d), /zd/ raised, /zml/ dismal, /plz/ apples, /blz/ bubbles /tlz/ battles, /dlz/ saddles, /klz/ buckles, /glz/ eagles, /tʃlz/ Rachel's, /dʒlz/ cudgels, /mlz/ camels, /nlz/ channels, /θlz/ Ethel's, /slz/ thistles, /vlz/ evils, /flz/ ruffles, /ʃlz/ officials, /tnz/ kittens, /dnz/ saddens, /fnz/ orphans, /vnz/ ovens, /snz/ hastens, /ʃnz/ oceans, /ʒnz/ visions, /ðnz/ heathens, /znt/ present, /mplz/ samples, /mblz/ symbols, /zndz/ thousands, /ndlz/ sandals, /ntlz/ lentils, /ŋklz/ uncles, /ŋglz/ angles, /stlz/ pastels, /mzlz/ damsels etc.

Compare

/s/, /z/—seal, zeal; sink, zinc; passing, parsing; fussy, fuzzy; racer, razor; peace, peas; loose, lose; use (n.), use (v.); gross, grows; place, plays; ice, eyes; house (n.), house (v.); scarce, scares; pence, pens; false, falls

(2) *Description*[43]—The soft palate being raised and the nasal resonator shut off, the blade (or the tip and blade)[44] of the tongue makes a light contact with the

---

[42] /z/ does not occur in an initial cluster apart from /zj/ in *zeugma* and *Zeus* (in which /zjuːgmə/ and /zjuːs/ alternate with /zuːgmə/ and /zuːs/).
[43] See Stone (1990) for the grooving of /s,z/
[44] Bladon and Nolan (1977) found a majority of speakers using a blade articulation

upper alveolar ridge, and the side rims of the tongue make a close contact with the upper side teeth. The airstream escapes by means of a narrow groove (cf. the slit associated with /θ,ð/ described in §9.4.4) in the centre of the tongue and causes friction between the tongue and the alveolar ridge. There is very little opening between the teeth. For /s/ the friction is voiceless, whereas for /z/ there may be some vocal fold vibration, according to its situation (see §9.4(3) above). The lip position will depend upon the adjacent vowel, e.g. spread for *see, zeal, piece, bees* etc., and somewhat rounded for *soon, zoo, loose, lose* etc. Some speakers make a light additional contact between the lower lip and the upper teeth, thus giving the sounds a secondary labiodental quality. A lisp, i.e. a substitution of /θ,ð/ for /s,z/ or a strongly dentalized version of /s,z/, is a common speech defect.

(3) *Variants*—Apart from the articulatory variants mentioned above, which are individual rather than social or regional, the voiceless /s/ is often replaced in word-initial position (e.g. in *seven, six, serve*) in south-west England by /z/. Before /r/, the approximation of the tongue to the alveolar ridge may be more retracted, e.g. in *horse-riding, newsreel*. Word final /s,z/ exhibit a readiness to assimilate before /ʃ,j/ (see §12.4.5).

Few RP speakers regularly maintain the distinction between /ns/ and /nts/ which is widespread in regional speech, e.g. distinguishing the final clusters in *mince–mints, tense–tents, assistance–assistants, dance–plants*, /nts/ tending to be used in all cases. This PLOSIVE EPENTHESIS, the insertion of /t/ between /n/ and /s/, results from the raising of the soft palate before the oral closure for /n/ is relaxed for the fricative /s/. Similarly, when /m/ or /ŋ/ precedes the /s/, an epenthetic plosive homorganic with the nasal may occur, e.g. *Samson* /ˈsæmsən/ → /ˈsæmpsən/, *Kingston* /ˈkɪŋstən/ → /ˈkɪŋkstən/, such variation being reflected in the spellings of proper names such as *Sam(p)son* and *Sim(p)son*.[45] /nz/ and /ndz/ are more frequently kept distinct by most RP speakers, e.g. in *wins–winds, tens–tends, fines–finds*, except in the most rapid speech when the /d/ may be elided.

Alternative pronunciations for words beginning /str-/ are commonly heard with /ʃtr-/, in, for example, *strawberries, string, strap*. This is evidently the influence of the retracted nature of the /t/ before the /r/.

(4) *Chief sources*—PresE /s/ derives from OE [s,ss] (*soon, sun, kiss, mice, wasp*) and from OF [s] (*sudden, strange, lesson, beast, pace, false*).

PresE /z/ derives from OE /s/=[z] between voiced sounds (*rise, wise, thousand, wisdom*) and from OF [z] (*zeal, easy, dozen, cause*). In addition, the weak termination [əs] gives [z], on the loss of [ə] by eModE, when following a voiced sound (*loves, dogs, lands, stones*); where the vowel is retained—as /ɪ/ or /ə/ in PresE— (after /s,z,ʃ,ʒ,tʃ,dʒ/), the [z] fricative form is also used in the weak ending (*passes, roses, rushes, touches, pages*). In the same way, words like *is, as, was, has, his*, which occur most commonly in weakly accented positions, were pronounced with final [z] by eModE. In French words, an earlier [s] occurring medially between

---

[45] Similar epenthesis may occasionally take place in sequences of nasals + other voiceless fricatives. The epenthetic plosive is always homorganic with the nasal., e.g. *confusion* /kəmpˈfjuʒn/, *convert* /kəmbˈvɜːt/ (= [kəᵐbvɜːt], *anthem* /ænθəm/ (=[æn̪θəm]), *mansion* /mæntʃən/

weakly accented and strongly accented syllables often > [z] (*resemble, possess, observe, disease, exact*); but many exceptions occur, perhaps for reasons of analogy of the spelling pronunciation or because the [s] is felt to belong to a separable prefix or to be initial in a common word preceded by a separable prefix (e.g. *assist, excite, dishonest, research*). In words where the medial fricative, especially final in the prefix *dis-*, precedes a voiced consonant, both /s/ and /z/ are heard, e.g. in *disdain, disgust*.

(5) *Advice for foreign learners*—In many languages, especially those where no dental fricatives exist, /s,z/ are articulated nearer to the teeth than the English varieties. Such a dentalized articulation is to be avoided in English because of the danger of confusion with /θ,ð/ (both in terms of the phonemic opposition involved and of the difficulties of alveolar/dental clusters). The more retracted articulation for /s,z/ should be practised in opposition with /θ,ð/ in pairs such as: *sing, thing; sort, thought; close* (v.), *clothe; sees, seethe; mouse, mouth; use* (n.), *youth*. On the other hand, those whose /s,z/ are often too retracted for English, e.g. Greeks, should practise oppositions between /s,z/ and /ʃ,ʒ/: *sin, shin; sort, short; lasses, lashes; Caesar, seizure; leased, leashed; mess, mesh*.

A large number of languages have /s/ but no /z/, e.g. Cantonese and Spanish. Learners from such backgrounds need to attain /z/ by a process of weakening and making vowels shorter before /s/, this being particularly important because /s,z/ occur so frequently in final positions. Hindi speakers have neither /s/ nor /z/; they should avoid substituting /ʃ,tʃ,dʒ/ and need to learn the tongue-tip articulation as completely new.

9.4.6   Palato-alveolar Fricatives /ʃ,ʒ/

(1) *Examples*
/ʃ/—*voiceless*

> *sh*—shoe, shed, shape, sham, sheep, wish, finish, brush, washer, ashes, publisher
> *ch, chs*—machine, chef, fuchsia, brochure, parachute, sachet, chateau, chalet
> *s, ss* +u—sure, sugar, censure, assure
> *-ti-, -si-, -sci-, -ci-, -ce-*—nation, mansion, mission, conscience, special, appreci-
> ate, ocean

(*Note* 'schedule, fascist, conscientious, luxury' (<x>=/kʃ/).)

> *word-initial*—sheet, shed, shop, sugar, charade, shout
> *word-medial*—Asia, bishop, ashore, mission, luscious, bushel, cushion, rashly,
> machine
> *word-final*—dish, cash, wash, push, douche, rush, finish, ruche
> *in word-initial clusters*[46]—/ʃr/ shrink
> *in word-final clusters*—/lʃ(t)/ welsh(ed), /ʃn(z,d)/, fashion(s,ed), /ʃnt(s)/
> patient(s), /nʃn(z,d)/[47] mention(s,ed), /ʃt/ pushed, /ʃlz,d)/ marshal(s,led); where

---

[46] /tʃ/, /dʒ/, having been treated as single complex phonemic entities, are not considered here as initial or final clusters

[47] An epenthetic /t/ may be inserted, thus /ˆmentʃn(z,d)/. See §9.4.5(3) and §10.8(3)

/n/ precedes final /tʃ/, e.g. in bench, lunch, some speakers use a final cluster /nʃ/, without the [t] stop.

/ʒ/—*voiced*

g—gigolo, genre
si—vision, allusion, conclusion, occasion, division
s, z, ss +u—measure, casual, usually, closure, leisure, measure, pleasure, seizure, azure
ge—beige, fuselage, dressage, garage, massage, sabotage, bourgeois, blanc-mange (=/bləˈmɒnʒ/) (alternative pronunciations with /dʒ/ are generally possible)

(*Note* 'regime'.)

word-initial—(in French loan words) gigolo, gigue, jabot, genre
word-medial—pleasure, leisure, usual, confusion, decision
word-final—prestige, barrage, rouge, beige, garage
in word-initial clusters—does not occur
in word-final clusters—/ʒn(z)/ vision(s), /ʒd/ camouflaged, /nʒd/ arrange(d)

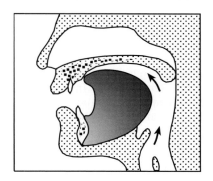 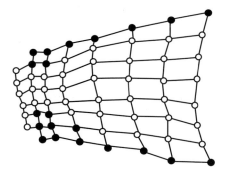

Fig. 42. *Section and palatogram of /ʃ,ʒ/.*

Compare

/ʃ/,/tʃ/—sheep, cheap; shore, chore; shoes, choose; leash, leech; dish, ditch; wash, watch
/ʒ/,/dʒ/—leisure, ledger; vision, pigeon
/ʃ/,/ʒ/—Aleutian (when pronounced /əˈluːʃn/), allusion; Confucian (when pronounced /kənˈfjuːʃn/, confusion.

(2) *Description*[48]—The soft palate being raised and the nasal resonator shut off, the tip and blade of the tongue make a light contact with the alveolar ridge, the front of the tongue being raised at the same time in the direction of the hard palate and the side rims of the tongue being in contact with the upper side teeth.

---

[48] See Stone (1990) for the grooving of /ʃ,ʒ/.

The escape of air is diffuse (compared with that of /s,z/), the friction occurring between a more extensive area of the tongue and the roof of the mouth. The articulation is also laxer than that of /s,z/ and what grooving there is is further back than that for /s,z/.[49] The palatalization effect (i.e. the [i]-ness caused by the raising of the front of the tongue) is less marked than in sounds of the [ʃ,ʒ] type in some other languages, indicating either that the front raising is less close or that the tongue as a whole is slightly more retracted. In the case of /ʃ/, the friction is voiceless, whereas for /ʒ/ there may be some vocal fold vibration according to its situation (see §9.4(3)). Some speakers use slight lip-rounding for /ʃ,ʒ/ in all positions; for others, lip-rounding is an effect of the adjacent vowel, e.g /ʃ/ of *shoe* tends to be lip-rounded, whereas /ʃ/ of *she* has neutral or spread lips.

(3) *Variants*—Apart from the degree of palatalization or lip-rounding used, no important articulatory variants occur. Medially in certain words, however, /ʃ,ʒ/ are not used by all speakers:

(a) especially before /uː/ or /ʊ/, there is often variation between /ʃ,ʒ/ and /s,z/+/j/, e.g. in *issue, sexual, tissue, inertia, seizure, casual, usual, azure* (cf. *assume* with /sj/ and *assure* with /ʃ/);

(b) a similar variation between /ʃ/ or /s/+/ɪ/ (or/j/)+vowel, e.g. *ratio, appreciate, negotiate*;

(c) the sequence /s,z/+/ɪ/ (or /j/)+ vowel is more commonly kept in words such as *hosier, axiom, gymnasium, Parisian* (note American English /pəˈrɪʒn/) and especially before the /ə/ comparative adjectival inflexion, e.g. *easier, lazier*;

(d) the lack of words distinguishable by /ʃ/ and /ʒ/ results in possible alternations between /ʃ/ and /ʒ/, e.g. in *Asia, Persia, transition, version*. In word-final position, where /ʒ/ exists only in comparatively recent French loanwords, e.g. *beige, rouge, prestige, garage* etc., a variant with /dʒ/ is always possible and is felt to be the fully anglicized form. It will be seen that /ʒ/, rare initially in a word, replaceable by /dʒ/ finally and sometimes varying with /ʃ/ medially, has a particularly weak 'functional load' in English.

(4) *Chief sources*—PresE /ʃ/ derives from OE [ʃ], earlier OE [s]+[k] or [c] (*ship, shadow, bishop, fish, English*); from OF palatalized [s] (*cushion, cash, radish, finish*); from a coalescence of /s/+/j/ or /ɪ/ finalized in the seventeenth century (*sure, sugar, ambition, ocean, special, patient*)—note that in the seventeenth and eighteenth centuries, several words at present with /sjuː/ were pronounced with /ʃ/ (*suit, supreme, assume*); from French /ʃ/ in words adopted after earlier French /tʃ/ had given /ʃ/ (*chemise, chic, machine, charlatan, moustache*).

PresE /ʒ/ derives from a coalescence of /z/+/j/ or /ɪ/ finalized in the seventeenth century (*occasion, measure, treasure, usual*), /ʒ/ being considered for a long time as a foreign sound; from French /ʒ/ in words adopted after earlier French /dʒ/ had given /ʒ/ (*prestige, rouge, beige, bijou*)—many of these words still retaining a foreign flavour.

(5) *Advice to foreign learners*—Many languages do not possess palato-alveolar fricatives, e.g. Cantonese, Greek, and Spanish; others have only /ʃ/. The usual

---

[49] See §9.4 (1) above

substitutes are /s,z/, although Hindi speakers substitute /dʒ/. Good results can generally be achieved by starting from /sj, zj/ and fronting the tongue. The weak character of /ʒ/ should be taught, although oppositions between /ʃ/ and /ʒ/ are rare.

Other languages have fricatives in this region but of a more strongly palatalized kind, e.g. German; a slight retraction of the tongue will often suitably 'darken' the quality of the friction.

9.4.7 Glottal Fricative /h/

(1) *Examples*—(Spelt <h> but note 'who, whom, whose, whore, whole'.) (*Note* <h> is not pronounced initially in *hour, honest, honour, heir, heiress*, medially in words such as *exhaust, exhilarate, exhibit, vehicle, vehement*, and in some final suffixes, e.g. *shepherd, Durham, Clapham* etc.)

>   *word-initial*—heat, hen, ham, hot, horse, who, hate, hoe, high, how, here, hair, halo, halibut
>   *word-medial*—ahead, behave, perhaps, behind, spearhead, anyhow, manhood, abhor, adhere

Compare

>   /h/+ vowel, initial vowel—heat, eat; hill, ill; hedge, edge; harbour, arbor; haul, all; hate, eight; hold, old; hear, ear

(2) *Description*—Since English /h/ occurs only in syllable-initial, pre-vocalic positions, it may be regarded as a strong, voiceless onset of the vowel in question. The air is expelled from the lungs with considerable pressure, causing some friction throughout the vocal tract, the upper part of which is shaped in readiness for the articulation of the following vowel (i.e. as regards the position of the tongue, lips, soft palate, and the configuration of the pharynx). Thus differing types of friction (patterns of resonance) will be heard for /h/ in the sequences /hiː/, /hɑː/, /huː/. With the onset of the vocal fold vibration of the vowel, the air pressure is reduced. There is no distinctive voiceless/voiced opposition such as characterizes the other English fricatives.

(3) *Variants*—Although /h/ functions in English essentially as a voiceless syllable-initial phoneme (in the same way that /ŋ/ occurs only in syllable-final positions), a few speakers use a voiced (or slightly voiced) allophone medially between voiced sounds when initial in an accented syllable, e.g. in words such as *ahead, perhaps, behind*, and less frequently in an unaccented syllable, e.g. in *anyhow*. In such pronunciations, the strong airstream of /h/ is accompanied by vocal fold vibration, the result being a kind of breathy vowel or voiced glottal fricative [ɦ].

In basilectal forms of most accents in England and Wales,[50] and in Australia, /h/ is lost, so that no distinction is made between RP minimal pairs such as *hill,*

---

[50] See Trudgill (1999)

ill; high, eye; hair, air. Usually in such speech, the /h/ words will behave as if they had an initial vowel, e.g. *a hill* /ən ˋɪl/, *the house* /ði: ˋaʊs/, but sometimes a trace of the boundary marking function of /h/ will be shown in the use of [ʔ], or at least a weak glottal constriction, e.g. *a hill* [ə ˋʔɪl], *the hospital* [ðə ˋʔɒspɪtl]. Overcorrections may also occur whereby forms of the article used before a vowel are not used and a weak glottal stop or glottal fricative is inserted, e.g. *an egg* [ə ˋʔeg] or [ə ˋʰeg], *the end* [ðə ˋʔend] or [ðə ˋʰend].

Such loss of /h/ is usually considered characteristic of uneducated speech, but certain function words (especially *have, has, had,* pronouns and pronominal adjectives) frequently lose /h/ in RP in unaccented, non-initial, situations in connected speech (see §11.3), e.g. *he pushed him on his back* /hi: pʊʃt ɪm ɒn ɪz ˋbæk/, *I could have hit her* /aɪ kəd əv ˋhɪt ə/.

Some older RP speakers treat an unaccented syllable beginning with an <h>, as in *historical, hotel, hysterical, hysterectomy,* as if it belonged to the special group *hour, honest* etc., i.e. without an initial /h/, e.g. *an historical novel.* Pronunciations with initial /h/ are, however, commoner, e.g. *a historical novel.* (For /h/+/j,w/, see §9.7.3.)

(4) *Chief sources*—OE had /h/ (=[h], [x], or [ç]), not only initially in a sylla-ble before a vowel, but also in initial clusters, e.g. /hn/ (*hnutu*), /hl/ (*hlaf*), /hr/ (*hreosan*), /hw/ (*hweol*), where the realizations may have been [n̥,l̥,r̥,w̥] or [xn,xl,xr,xw]; also in medial and post-vocalic positions, with palatal or velar fricative realizations, e.g. *hliehhan, ahte, heah.* Of these occurrences, PresE retains only initial /h/ before a vowel (see §9.7.5 for possible /hw/), e.g. *home, high, help, horse* etc. In addition, a new initial /h/ was introduced into English in some French words of Germanic origin, e.g. *hardy, haste, herald,* and also in a large number of French words of Latin origin, e.g. *herb, horror, habit, harass, heretic, hospital, host, humour* etc. In the case of this latter group, spelling with <h>, both in OF and ME, was erratic, probably representing an /h/-less pronun-ciation. In certain words (*hour, heir, heiress, honour, honest*), the /h/-less pronunciation has been kept despite the general adoption of the spelling <h>. In most other cases, the letter <h> began to be pronounced in late ME in these words of Latin (via French) origin, though in some the spelling <h> was not sounded as late as the eighteenth and nineteenth centuries, e.g. *herb, hospital, humble, humour.*

The general elision of /h/ in weak pronouns and auxiliary verbs probably dates at least from eModE, whereas the loss of /h/ in accented words, as in much regional speech in England and Wales, has existed for at least two centuries and has always been considered a vulgarism.

(5) *Advice to foreign learners*—Many languages do not possess a phoneme of the /h/ type. Speakers of these languages should, in learning English, practise the examples given in (1) above, making a correct distinction between words with initial /h/+ vowel and those with initial vowel, e.g. *hill, ill* etc.; they should also learn to elide the /h/ of *he, him, his, her, have, had, has,* when these words occur in weakly accented, non-initial, positions in the utterance.

Those learners who in their own language have no /h/ but do have a /x/, e.g. Spaniards and Greeks, should avoid using any velar friction in English, and should practise the English /h/ as a voiceless onset to the following vowel.

9.5   *Voiced and Voiceless as Phonological Categories*

It will be seen from the from the preceding sections that in various ways the members of the class /p,t,k,f,θ,s,ʃ,tʃ/behave similarly to each other and differently from their counterparts in the class /b,d,g,v,ð,z,ʒ,dʒ/. This difference has generally been labelled as one of voicing; however, it will also have been seen that the realization of the distinction between the two classes varies according to position. To summarize, (i) members of the voiceless series are indeed voiceless in all positions while those in the voiced series are potentially fully voiced only in word-medial positions between voiced sounds and are regularly devoiced in word-initial and word-final positions; (ii) the voiceless series /p,t,k/ are aspirated in syllable-initial positions (particularly in accented syllables), while voiced /b,d,g/ are unaspirated; (iii) the voiceless series cause a reduction in length in preceding vowels, nasals, and laterals while the voiced series has no such effect; (iv) the voiceless series are generally longer than their voiced counterparts; (v) the voiceless series are made with greater muscular effort and breath-force (and hence are referred to as fortis) while the voiced series are made with lesser effort and force (and are referred to as lenis).

Class B: Sonorants

Although voiceless fricative allophones of the following consonants occur, their most common realizations are voiced and non-fricative.

9.6   *Nasals*

(1) *Articulatory features*—Nasal consonants resemble oral plosives in that a total closure is made within the mouth; they differ from such plosives in that the soft palate is in its lowered position, allowing an escape of air into the nasal cavity and giving the sound the special resonance provided by the naso-pharyngeal cavity. Since the airstream may escape freely through the nose, nasal consonants are continuants; they differ, however, from continuants such as fricatives in that no audible friction is produced and from the fact that they are usually voiced, without significant voiced/voiceless oppositions. In many respects, therefore, being normally frictionless continuants, they resemble vowel-type sounds.

(2) *Acoustic features*[51]—Voiced nasal consonants have no noise component such as results from the burst of plosives or the friction of fricatives, nor the silence gap associated with plosives. Moreover the weak intensity of nasals (particularly in non-syllabic positions) and the considerable damping caused by the soft walls of the nasal cavity generally makes any formant structure difficult to identify. The key acoustic feature of all nasals is a low frequency 'murmur' below 500 Hz which precedes transitions to following sounds and follows transitions from preceding sounds. Moreover there is generally an absence of energy

---

[51] Liberman *et al.* (1954) and Malécot (1956)

around 1,000 Hz. Place of articulation is identifiable by the direction of the transitions to and from F2 and F3, these being the same as for the homorganic plosives (see §9.2.2(3)), i.e. minus transitions for /m/, slight plus transitions for /n/, and plus transition of F2 and minus transition of F3 for /ŋ/. More recent research has identified a key characteristic of labial vs alveolar nasals as being the relative proportion of energy present in two spectral bands ('barks'), 395–770 Hz for the labials and 1,265–2310 Hz for the alveolars.[52] Spectrograms of /m,n,ŋ/ in *ram, ran, rang* are shown in Fig. 43.

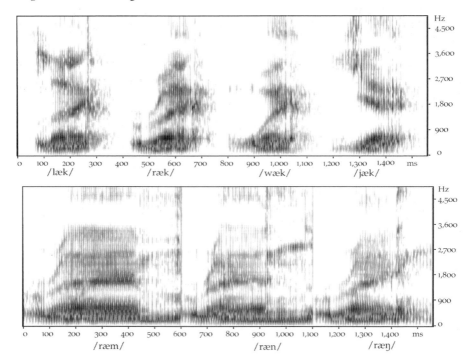

Fig. 43. *Spectrograms of* /læk/, /ræk/, /wæk/, /jæk/ *and of* /ræm/, /ræn/, /ræŋ/, *as spoken by a male speaker of RP.*

(3) *The English nasal consonants—*

(a) Three nasal phonemes correspond to the three oral plosive areas of articulation: *bilabial* /m/–/p,b/; *alveolar* /n/–/t,d/; *velar* /ŋ/–/k,g/. If, in the articulation of a nasal consonant, the nasal passage is blocked as, for instance, often happens during a cold, /m,n,ŋ,/ will be realized as /b,d,g/, e.g. *morning* /ˈbɔːdɪg/, *some nice*

---

[52] Kurowski and Blumstein (1984), Repp (1986), Kurowski (1989), Harrington (1994), Ohde (1994)

lemons /səb ˈdaɪs ˈlebədz/. Oppositions amongst the nasals may be illustrated as follows:

	Bilabial /m/	Alveolar /n/	Velar /ŋ/
Initial	might	night	—
Medial	simmer	sinner	singer
Final	sum	sun	sung

It will be seen that, since /ŋ/ does not occur initially in a word or morpheme, a complete series of oppositions is found only where the nasals occur in post-vocalic positions in the same syllable or morpheme.

(b) The vocalic nature of the nasals is underlined by the fact that they readily perform the syllabic function of vowels: most often /n/, e.g. *mutton* [ˈmʌtn̩]; less commonly /m/ e.g. *rhythm* [ˈrɪðm̩]; occasionally, with some speakers, /ŋ/, e.g. *bacon* [ˈbeɪkŋ̩].

(c) Although no opposition occurs between voiced and voiceless nasals in English, a somewhat devoiced allophone of /m/ and /n/ may be heard when a voiceless consonant precedes, e.g. *smoke, smart, topmost; snake, sneeze, chutney.* The distribution of /ŋ/ being restricted, it is only rarely—in a syllabic situation as in *bacon*—that a voiceless consonant precedes, with the consequent partial devoicing.

(4) *Acquisition of nasals by native learners*—Bilabial and alveolar nasals, along with plosives, are among the most frequent sounds in children's pre-linguistic babbling, and regularly occur in their first words. The velar nasal /ŋ/, limited in adult words to syllable-final position, is acquired later but is nevertheless among the first sounds to occur in post-vocalic positions. Voiceless bilabial and alveolar nasals can be heard in the speech of some children, replacing the clusters /sm-/ and /sn-/ of the adult language, e.g. *sneeze* [n̥iː], *smile* [m̥aɪl].

9.6.1 Bilabial Nasal /m/

(1) *Examples*

> *m*—morning, moon, gum, simple, number, amber, famine, damage, woman
> *mm*—summer, dimmer, dimming, committee, immense, immoral, programme, ammonite
> *mb*—comb, bomb, lamb, climb, crumb, womb, plumber, numb

(*Note* 'autumn, column, solemn, hymn'.)

> *word-initial*—meal, mat, march, move, mirth, make, mouse
> *following word-initial* /s/—smack, smock, smite, smoke, smear
> *word-medial*—demon, glimmer, lemon, salmon, among, gloomy, summer, sermon, commit, omen; jumper, timber, empty, comfort, hamlet, simple, symbol, dismal, camel, dimly, asthma
> *word-final*—seem, lamb, harm, warm, tomb, game; (in final clusters) worms, harmed, film(s), warmth, glimpse, prompt(s), nymph(s); (syllabic) rhythm(s), prism(s), lissom

(2) *Description*—The lips form a closure as for /p,b/; the soft palate is lowered, adding the resonance of the nasal cavity to those of the pharynx and the mouth chamber closed by the lips; the tongue will generally anticipate or retain the position of the adjacent vowel or /l/. Except when partially devoiced by a preceding voiceless consonant, e.g. initially—*smoke*, medially—*topmost*, finally—*happen*, /m/ is voiced. (Normal breathing through the nose with the lips closed may be described as a weak [m̥]; where, because of some organic defect, such as cleft palate, the nasal cavity cannot be shut off, /p/ may be realized as [m̥] and /b/ as [m].) When followed by a labiodental sound /f,v/, the front closure may be labiodental [ɱ] rather than bilabial, e.g. in *nymph, comfort, triumph, come first, circumvent, warm vest*. Additionally pronunciations of *infant, enforce, unforced* etc. with assimilation of [n] to [ɱ] can be regarded as having an allophone of /m/.

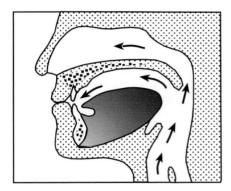

Fig. 44. *Section of* /m/.

In connected speech /m/ frequently results from a final /n/ of the citation form before a following bilabial, e.g. *one mile* /wʌm ˈmaɪl/, *more and more* /mɔːr əm ˈmɔː/, *ten pairs* /tem ˈpeəz/, *gone back* /gɒm ˈbæk/; sometimes /m/ is a realization of word-final /ən/ or /n̩/ following /p/ or /b/, e.g. *happen* /ˈhæpm̩/, *ribbon* /ˈrɪbm̩/, or, in context, *cap and gown* /kæp m̩ ˈgaʊn/ (see §12.4.5).

(3) *Variants*—There are no important regional or social variants of /m/ articulations.

(4) *Chief sources*—PresE /m/ derives from OE [m], [mm] (*man, hammer, swim, home*)—note [b] of [mb] was lost in word-final positions in ME in words such as *climb, lamb*, though kept medially as in *timber*, or inserted as in *thimble, bramble, slumber* before /l/ and /r/; from OF [m] (*master, family, solemn, sum*).

(5) *Advice to foreign learners*—This phoneme should present no difficulty.

9.6.2   Alveolar Nasal /n/

(1) *Examples*

  n—now, noon, number, nonce, new, keen, barn, bend, bent
  nn—funny, sinning, sinner, connect, annoy, innocent, innate, inn, innuendo
  gn—gnaw, gnash, gnu, gnat, sign, campaign, champagne, reign, alignment

kn—know, knee, knife, knob, knot, knowledge, acknowledge, knuckle, knickers

pn—pneumonia, pneumatic

(*Note* 'rendez-vous' /ˈrɒndeɪvuː/.)

> *word-initial*—neat, knit, net, gnat, knot, gnaw, none, nurse, name, know, near
> *following word-initial* /s/—sneeze, snatch, snore, snug, snake, snow, sneer
> *word-medial*—dinner, many, hornet, monitor, annoy; wonder, hunter, unless, unrest, answer, pansy, infant, invoice; chutney, madness, amnesty, walnut, fastener, evening
> *word-final*—mean, pen, gone, soon, learn, melon, down, coin; pint(s), pond(s), inch, hinge, final(s), pence, pens, month(s), kiln(s), rental(s), bundle(s), pencil(s), against
> *syllabic* /n/—cotton, sudden, often (=/ɒfn̩/), oven, earthen, southern, listen, dozen, mission, vision; maddening (or with non-syllabic /n/), reasonable (or with non-syllabic /n/ or /ən/), ordinary (or with non-syllabic /n/ or /ən/ or /ɪn/), southerner (or with /ən/)

(2) *Description*—The tongue forms a closure with the teeth ridge and upper side teeth as for /t,d/; the soft palate is lowered, adding the resonance of the nasal cavity to those of the pharynx and of that part of the mouth chamber behind the alveolar closure; the lip position will depend upon that of adjacent vowels, e.g. spread lips in *neat, keen*; neutrally open lips in *snarl, barn*; somewhat rounded lips in *noon, soon*. Except when partially devoiced by a preceding voiceless consonant, e.g. initially—*snug*, medially—*chutney*, finally—*cotton*, /n/ is voiced. (Where, because of an organic defect, such as cleft palate, the nasal cavity cannot be shut off, /t/ may be realized as [n̥] and /d/ as [n].) The place of articulation of /n/ is particularly liable to be influenced by that of the following consonant, e.g. when followed by a labiodental sound /f,v/, as in *infant, invoice, on fire, in vain*, /n/ may be realized as [ɱ]—and thus strictly speaking to be regarded as an allophone of the /m/ phoneme (see §9.6.1 above); /n/ before dental sounds /θ,ð/ is realized with a lingua-dental closure [n̪], as in *tenth, when they*—and sometimes when following /θ,ð/ (*earthen, southern*); before /r/, /n/ may have a post-alveolar contact, as in *unrest, Henry*; in addition, in context, word-final /n/ frequently assimilates to a following word-initial bilabial or velar consonant, being realized as /m/ or /ŋ/, e.g. *ten people, ten boys, ten men*, where the final /n/ of *ten* may assimilate to /m/, and *ten cups, ten girls*, where the final /n/ of *ten* may assimilate to /ŋ/ (see §12.4.5).

(3) *Variants*—There are no important regional or social variants of /n/ articulations.

(4) *Chief sources*—PresE /n/ derives from OE [n,nn] (*name, many, man, spin*); from OE [hn], [xn] or [ŋ] (*nut*)—by the twelfth century; from OE [kn,gn] (*know, knit, gnaw, gnat*)—by the late seventeenth century; from OF [n] (*noble, dinner, plain*); from OF palatal [ɲ] (*sign, reign, line, mountain, onion*). Note that sometimes earlier [n]>[nt,nd] (*pheasant, tyrant, ancient, sound, pound*); and that sometimes [n] of the indefinite article has become affixed to a noun beginning with a vowel (*newt, nickname*), or initial [n] of a noun has been lost through transference to the preceding indefinite article form (*adder, apron, umpire*).

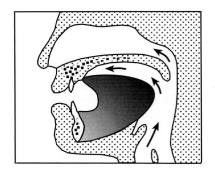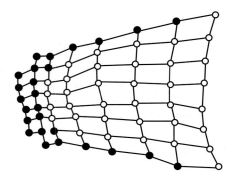

Fig. 45. *Section and palatogram of* /n/.

(5) *Advice to foreign learners*—Care should be taken that /n/, like /t,d/, is normally given an alveolar rather than a dental articulation (see practice examples in (1) above).

9.6.3   Velar Nasal /ŋ/

(1) *Examples*

> *ng*—sing, singer, singing, longing, tongue
> *n* +/k,g/—sink, anxious, uncle, ankle, bangle, income
> *word-medial*—singer, hanger, longing, anxiety
> *word-medial* +/g/—finger, anger, angry, hunger, strongest, language, single, angle, England, bungle, nightingale
> *word-medial* +/k/—tinker, anchor, banquet, monkey, donkey, conquer, wrinkle, ankle, uncle, anxious
> *word-final*—sing(s), hang(s, ed), wrong(s, ed), tongue(s, ed), among
> *word-final* +/k/—sink(s), rank(s, ed), conch (sometimes /kɒŋk/), chunk(s), monk(s), distinct, amongst (or with /ŋst/), strength (with /ŋkθ/, /ŋθ/, or sometimes /nθ/)
> *word-final syllabic*—(occasionally) bacon, taken, thicken, blacken, organ /ŋ/, or less commonly /n/, in words such as—income, conclude, encourage, concrete, bronchitis, engage, enquiry

Compare

> /ŋ/, /n/—sing, sin; rang, ran; hanged, hand; sung, sun; mounting, mountain; gong, gone; robbing, robin
> /ŋ/, /ŋk/—thing, think; rang, rank; sung, sunk; singing, sinking; hanger, hanker

(2) *Description*—A closure is formed in the mouth between the back of the tongue and the velum as for /k,g/ (the point of closure will depend on the type of vowel preceding, the contact being more advanced in *sing* than in *song*); the soft palate is lowered, adding the resonance of the nasal cavity to that of the pharynx and that small part of the mouth chamber behind the velar closure;

the lip position will depend upon that of the preceding vowel, being somewhat spread in *sing* and relatively open in *song*. /ŋ/ is normally voiced, except for partial devoicing in the possible, though uncommon, case of syllabic /ŋ/ in words such as *bacon, thicken*. (Where, because of an organic defect, such as cleft palate, the nasal cavity cannot be shut off, /k/ may be realized as /ɲ̊/ and /g/ as [ɲ].) Word-final /ŋ/ may result in context from citation forms of /n/, e.g. *ten cups* (see §12.4.5). Except in assimilations /ŋ/ occurs usually after the short vowels /ɪ,æ,ɒ,ʌ/; rarely after /e/.

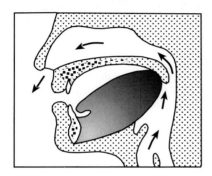 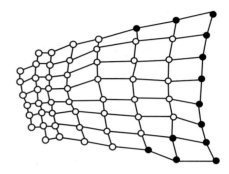

Fig. 46. *Section and palatogram of /ŋ/ in sang.*

(3) *Variants*—Earlier [ŋg] forms are retained, instead of RP /ŋ/, in many regional types of speech, notably in the north-west Midlands (e.g. Staffordshire, Derbyshire, Cheshire, and south Lancashire), e.g. *singing* [ˈsɪŋgɪŋg] for RP /ˈsɪŋɪŋ/. If /g/ is always pronounced in such situations, [ŋ] must be counted an allophone of /n/ rather than a separate phoneme.

In most regions where /n/ and /ŋ/ are in contrast (*sin, sing* being distinguished only by the final nasal), the *-ing* of the present participle varies between /ɪn/ and /ɪŋ/, such variation being dependent on both social and stylistic factors. /ɪn/ is used consistently by speakers at the lower end of the socio-economic spectrum and /ɪŋ/ at the top end, whereas speakers in intermediate classes often vary stylistically, using /ɪŋ/ in more formal speech (e.g. when reading aloud).[53]

In Cockney, in which /ŋ/ is phonemic (cf. *sin, sing*), the word *-thing* in compounds is often pronounced /-fɪŋk/ e.g. in *something, anything, nothing*; the verbal termination *-ing* may be /-ɪŋ/ or /-ɪn/ without /k/.

(4) *Chief sources*—PresE /ŋ/ occurs in words of OE origin (*sing, hunger, thank, tongue*) or of OF origin (*frank, rank, conquer, language*), following a short vowel. So long as [ŋ] occurred only before /k,g/, the nasal was an allophone of /n/. But with the loss of /g/ in the sequence [ŋg], /ŋ/ gained a phonemic significance, based on oppositions of the *sing, sin* type. Although loss of /g/ in [ŋg] may have occurred in popular dialects in late ME, it seems that the plosive (and allophonic

---

[53] See e.g. Trudgill (1974, 1999)

nature of [ŋ]) was retained in educated speech until the end of the sixteenth century. At first, in the late sixteenth and early seventeenth centuries, /g/ was elided only before consonants, the loss of /g/ in final [ŋg] before a vowel or a pause becoming general during the seventeenth century.

The pronunciation /-ɪn/ for the termination -*ing*, common in the sixteenth and seventeenth centuries, became a general feature of fashionable speech in the eighteenth century and has been retained today as a characteristic of an archaic form of RP (e.g. in *huntin', shootin', and fishin'*). It is to be noted that the sequence [ŋk] has not lost the plosive element and [ŋ] in such a situation could still be treated as an allophone of /n/, were it not for the emergence of /ŋ/ as a phoneme as a result of the reduction of [ŋg]>/ŋ/. The very restricted distribution of /ŋ/ in PresE is, therefore, imposed by the circumstances of its development.

(5) *Advice to foreign learners*—Many languages do not have /ŋ/ or have it only before /k,g/. Those learners whose own language has [ŋ] only as an allophone of /n/ before /k,g/, e.g. Arabic, Hindi, German, and Spanish, should avoid using /g/ (or more rarely [k]) in those cases where /ŋ/ occurs in English without a following plosive, especially in sequences where final /ŋ/ is followed by a vowel, e.g. in *singing, reading out, a long essay*. In practising, the nasal /ŋ/ should be given exaggerated length and sequences such as /ŋiː,ŋɑː/ repeated in order to obtain a succession of nasal + vowel without a plosive. Some other learners may substitute palatal /ɲ/, e.g. French and Spanish; while this does not lead to unintelligibility, it does give a strong foreign accent and should be avoided.

9.7   *Oral Approximants*

For this group of phonemes the airstream escapes through a relatively narrow aperture in the mouth without friction but with voice (apart from the allophones mentioned below). In many respects their articulatory and/or acoustic characteristics are sufficiently different to need a separate description under each phoneme. Nevertheless their distributional characteristics are very similar: (i) they appear in consonantal clusters in similar ways (a consonant plus /l,r,w,j/ is one of the two common types of two-consonant cluster (see §10.9.(1)) which occur syllable-initially in English (as in *play, broad, queen, pure*) the other being /s/ plus consonant); (ii) when they occur in such clusters they are all similarly devoiced if the preceding consonant is voiceless (e.g. /p,t,k/ produce devoicing in *clay, crawl, queer*, and *cure*).

9.7.1   Lateral Approximant /l/

(1) *Examples*

l—leave, droplet, deal, fault, middle, symbol, italic, polish, balance, salad, talent
ll—allow, collide, illegal, million, balloon, intelligent, parallel

(*Note* silent <l> in 'talk, would, could, should, half, calm, salmon, folk etc.'.) Note also divergent British and American spelling in 'travel(l)ing, dial(l)ing, signal(l)ing etc.'.

(a) *Clear* [l] (before vowels and /j/)
word-initial—leave, let, lock, look, late, loud, leer, lewd
in word-initial clusters—blow, glad, splice
word-medial—silly, yellow, alloy, collar, caller, pulley, foolish, sullen, sailor, island, oily, million, failure, allow, select; medley, ugly, nobly, gimlet, inlay, bachelor, specially (with [l] or [əl])
word-final, before following vowel or /j/—feel it, fall out, all over, will you

(b) *Devoiced clear* [l̥]:

Fully devoiced clear [l̥] (following voiceless plosives in accented syllables)—play, please, plant, apply, aplomb, clean, close, climb, click, acclimatize
Partially devoiced [l̞] (following voiceless plosives in unaccented syllables or across syllable boundaries)—placebo, aptly, butler, antler, ghastly, short loan, simplest, couplet, rope ladder, hopeless, sprinkler, clarinet, clandestine, dark lake
Partially devoiced [l̞] (following voiceless fricatives)—sloppy, slow, slink, gas leak, fling, flow, flick, flak, half life, earthly, wash load

(c) *Dark* [ɫ] (in all other positions)

word-final, after vowel—feel, fill, fell, canal, snarl, doll, call, bull, pool, dull, pearl, pale, pole, pile, owl, oil, royal, real, cruel
after vowel, before consonant—help, bulb, salt, cold, milk, filch, bilge, film, kiln, self, solve, health, else, bills; alpine, elbow, halter, elder, alchemy, almost, illness, alphabet, silver, wealthy, although, ulcer, palsy, Welsh, always
syllabic [ɫ̩]—table, middle, eagle, cudgel, camel, final, quarrel (or with [əɫ]), oval, easel, usual, spaniel (or with [-jəɫ]), equal, tumble, fondle, angle, doubled, tables, measles, finally (or with [-əl-]; cf. 'finely' with [l])
syllabic [ɫ̩], *partially devoiced following voiceless consonant*—apple, little, buckle, satchel, awful, parcel, special, simple, mantle, uncle, sinful, pistol (cf. gambling [l] or [ɫ] vs gambolling [ɫ̩])
variations in inflected forms of verbs having [ɫ] *in the uninflected form*—[ɫ], or [əl] (more rarely [l])—pommelling, tunnelling, cudgeling; [l] (more rarely [ɫ] or [əl])—fondling, doubling, circling, wriggling, settling, coupling, whistling, puzzling, scuffling, shovelling. Some speakers have minimal pairs dependent on the presence of clear [l] or syllabic dark [ɫ̩] or even non-syllabic dark [ɫ], cf. *coupling* [ˈkʌplɪŋ] (connecting device) vs [ˈkʌpɫ̩ŋ] or [ˈkʌpɫɪŋ] (joining); *gambling* [ˈgæmblɪŋ] vs *gambolling* [ˈgæmbɫ̩ŋ] or [ˈgæmbɫɪŋ]; *codling* [ˈkɒdlɪŋ] vs *coddling* [ˈkɒdɫ̩ŋ] or [ˈkɒdɫɪŋ].
possible syllabic [ɫ̩] occurring in pre-accentual positions or rarely in accented syllables—fallacious, believe, select, bullish, building (this last possibly with a clear syllabic [l̩].

(2) *Description*[54]
(a) *Articulatory and distributional features*—The soft palate being in its raised position, shutting off the nasal resonator, the tip of the tongue is in contact with

---

[54] See Stone (1990), Stone *et al.* (1992) for the articulation of /l/

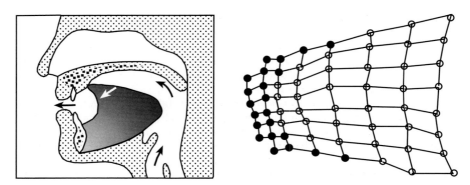

Fig. 47. *Section and palatogram of clear* [l].

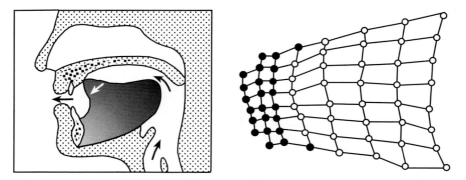

Fig. 48. *Section and palatogram of dark* [ɫ].

the upper teeth ridge, allowing the air to escape on both sides or, in the case of a unilateral tongue-rim closure on the upper side teeth, on one side. For clear [l], the front of the tongue is raised in the direction of the hard palate at the same time as the tip contact is made, thus giving a front vowel resonance to the consonant; this resonance is often of the [ë] type, but may be closer or more open according to the following vowel, cf. *leap, loop*. For dark [ɫ], the tip contact is again made on the teeth ridge, the front of the tongue being somewhat depressed and the back raised in the direction of the soft palate, giving a back vowel (or velarized) resonance; this resonance is often of the type [ö] or [ɤ]. The lips' position is influenced by the nature of the adjacent vowel, cf. *leap, feel* (with spread lips), *loop, pool* (with somewhat rounded lips); in the case of [ɫ], and especially [ɫ], there is, with some speakers, always a tendency to lip-rounding. Both [l] and [ɫ] are voiced except when the preceding consonant is voiceless.

The actual point of contact of the tongue for [ɫ] is conditioned by the place of articulation of the following consonant; thus, in *health, will they*, the [ɫ] has a dental contact (to a lesser extent, a preceding /θ,ð/ may cause a dental articulation [l̪]. e.g. in *a month late, with love*); or, in *already, ultra, all dry*, the contact for [ɫ] is likely to be post-alveolar. [ɫ] may also be strongly nasalized by a following nasal consonant, e.g. *elm, kiln.*

The velarization of [ɫ] often has the effect of retracting and lowering slightly the articulation of a preceding front vowel, e.g. *feel, fill, fell, canal*; in the case of /iː/+[ɫ], a central glide between the vowel and [ɫ] is often noticeable, and the [ɪ] element of /eɪ,aɪ,ɔɪ/ tends to be obscured, e.g. in *pail, pile, oil.* /uː/ before [ɫ] tends to be more monophthongal and nearer to C[u].

(b) *Acoustic features*[55]—The English voiced lateral is similar to nasals and /r/ in its low intensity and hence a formant structure is often only weakly apparent. There is a 'murmur' below 500 Hz (similar to nasals but of even lower intensity) which is generally considered as F1, and an F2 commonly in the range 900–1,600 Hz, a value at the low end of this range indicating a dark [ɫ]. Transitions to and from vowels are generally slower than those for nasals although faster than those for glides. A duration for [ɫ] of > 50–60 ms produces an effect of syllabicity. A spectrogram of clear [l] is shown in Fig. 43.

(3) *Variants*—The RP distribution of [l] and [ɫ] may be said to be: [l] when a vowel or /j/ follows and [ɫ] in all other positions. In word-final positions following a consonant (*fiddle, final, parcel*), syllabic dark [ɫ̩] occurs. When an affix beginning with a vowel is added or the next word begins with a vowel, (*fiddling, fiddle it, finally, parcel of books*), the lateral may remain as dark and may remain syllabic or become non-syllabic; alternatively, the lateral may become clear, in which case it is usually non-syllabic. The lateral is less likely to become clear in those cases where the following word begins with an accented syllable, where a [ʔ] may intervene, as in *real ale* [riːɫ ˋʔeɪɫ], cf. *real estate* [ˋriːl esteɪt].

Variations in the quality of the back vowel resonance associated with [ɫ] are, however, to be found among RP speakers, with a range extending from [ö], [ʊ], or [ɣ] to [ɔ̃] or [ʌ̈]; lip positions, too, vary from neutral to loose rounding. In some speech, notably that of London and the surrounding areas,[56] the tongue-tip contact for [ɫ] is omitted, this allophone of /l/ being realized as a vowel (vocoid) in the region of [ö] with weak lip-rounding or as [ɣ] with neutral or weakly spread lips, thus *sell* [seö] or [seɣ], *fall* [fɔö] or [fɔɣ], *table* [ˋtæɪbö] or [ˋtæɪbɣ]. In such speech, the lowering of /iː/ and /uː/ before [ö] is so marked that *meal, mill,* and *pool, pull,* may become homophonous or distinguished merely by the length of the central syllabic vowel element, i.e. [mɪˈö] vs [mɪö], [pʊˈö] vs [pʊö]; other confusions are likely, e.g. *rail* (RP [reɪɫ], Cockney [ræö]) and *row* (RP [rəʊ], Cockney [ræö]), *dole* (RP [dəʊɫ], Cockney [dɒö]), and *doll* (RP [dɒɫ], Cockney [dɒö]). Realizations of syllabic [ɫ̩] as a vowel are not, however, confined to Cockney; many RP speakers and especially those of London Regional RP (= Estuary English) will use [ö] for [ɫ] in words such as *beautiful, careful, people, table* etc., i.e. especially when a consonant involving a labial articulation precedes; they will, moreover, not recognize such a vocalic allophone as unusual when they hear it. The use of a vocalic allophone seems somewhat less usual in RP when other consonants precede, e.g. in *uncle, Ethel, parcel, special, spaniel,* and is

---

[55] O'Connor *et al.* (1957), Lisker (1957b), Dalston (1975)
[56] See Sivertsen (1960), Wells (1982), Trudgill (1999)

particularly avoided, as a childish pronunciation, after alveolar plosives, e.g. *little, middle*, where the consonants are regularly released laterally. On the other hand, in an artificial or somewhat precious style of speaking, [l] may be used for [ɫ].

In other dialects of English the RP distribution of [l] and [ɫ] may not obtain. In General American, in Standard Scottish English, in Australian, and in New Zealand English, as well as in large parts of the north of England (e.g. Manchester) and North Wales, dark [ɫ] may occur in all positions. In southern Irish English, in West Indian English, as well as in South Wales and on Tyneside, clear [l] may occur in all positions. Note, too, that American English has syllabic [ɫ] in words such as *fertile, futile, missile, reptile* etc., where RP retains a prominent preceding vowel [-aɪɫ]; a reduction of the vowel, similar to the present American form, occurred in seventeenth-century British English.

(4) *Chief sources*—PresE /l/ derives from OE [l,ll] (*land, climb, all, tell, apple*), from OE [hl], [xl] or [l̩] (*loaf, ladder*)—since OE front vowels tended to be diphthongized before /l/, it seems likely that /l/ in such a position was velarized in OE as it is today; from OF [l] (*lamp, close, colour, veal, able*). In many cases pre-consonantal [ɫ], especially after back or open vowels, was vocalized to [ʊ] (*walk, talk, half, folk*) in the early fifteenth century, such a pronunciation being commonly shown by the seventeenth-century grammarians; but in some cases (*halt, salt, malt*), it has been retained; in others, an /l/ has been re-introduced in spelling and pronunciation (*fault, falcon, emerald, soldier, realm*) or merely in the spelling (*calm, palm, balm*). The loss of /l/ in *could, should, would* occurred in eModE.

(5) *Acquisition of /l/ by native learners*—The lateral /l/, along with /j/ and /w/ but not /r/, is usually among the first sounds added to the nasals and plosives of children's early words. It is only rarely a problem in acquisition, and is regularly present by the age of 3;6. For a short period before its acquisition it may be replaced by /j/. Dark [ɫ] may often be replaced by vocalic [ʊ], this tendency being reinforced by the same tendency in adult English in those accents mentioned above. A voiceless [ɫ̥] may sometimes be heard in children's speech as a replacement for the initial clusters /sl-/ and /fl-/, e.g. *sleeve* [ɫiː], *fling* [ɫɪŋ].

(6) *Advice to foreign learners*—Few foreign learners will possess in their own language [l] and [ɫ] sounds with the RP distribution and many will have only clear [l], e.g. French, German, Hindi, and Spanish. It is true that, since there is no phonemic opposition between [l] and [ɫ] in English, learners will be perfectly intelligible if they use only [l]. But those whose English otherwise conforms to an RP pattern should learn to make the dark [ɫ]. In the articulation of [ɫ] there should be no 'curling back' of the tongue, as is so often advised in books on English. To overcome such a habit already acquired, the tongue-tip may be gripped between the teeth during practice. The essential feature of [ɫ] may be said to be the accompanying weakly rounded [o] or [ɔ] quality; learners should, therefore, begin by pronouncing a vowel of the [o] or [ɔ] type for the syllabic [ɫ] in words such as *bubble, people, awful*, i.e. where a labial consonant precedes [ɫ], thus—[ˈbʌbo], [ˈpiːpo], [ˈɔːfo]. A pure vowel of this kind is likely to occur in their own language. Such a pronunciation will come near to that used by many English speakers (see (3) above). The same sound sequence should then be attempted with the tongue-tip touching the upper teeth ridge, thus producing a lateral sound with the correct velarized quality. The relationship of [ɫ] and [o] can further be

established by practising the alternation of [o]–[ɫ]–[o]–[ɫ], only the tongue-tip moving and the [o] resonance continuing. The [ɫ] thus achieved should then be used in the examples of [ɫ] given in (1) above, first the syllabic cases and then the non-syllabic.

Foreign learners from some language backgrounds, in particular Slav languages, may use an over-velarized lateral in pre-vocalic positions. This should be particularly avoided, as such over-velarization is not even typical of those varieties of English which have a dark [ɫ] in all positions.

Care should also be taken to use a sufficiently devoiced [l̥] after accented (aspirated) /p,k/. Accented /p,k/ are distinguished from /b,g/ mainly by their aspiration; it is important that this aspiration cue should be made clear in the sequences /pl,kl/ by the voicelessness of the /l/. If this is not done, a word such as *plot*, pronounced with a fully voiced /l/, may be understood as *blot*. Pairs for practice, relying largely for the opposition on voiceless vs voiced [l], are: *plot, blot; plead, bleed; plight, blight; clad, glad; class, glass; clean, glean; clue, glue.*

9.7.2 Post-alveolar Approximant /r/

(1) *Examples*

> *r*—red, round, ripe, raw, rude, rope, rule
> *rr*—carry, arrive, arrogant, correct, arrest, narrative, barrister
> *wr*—write, wrote, wrinkle, wriggle, wrist, wreath, wrong
> *rh*—rhythm, rhyme, rhinoceros, rheumatism, rhetoric, rhododendron
> *word-initial*—reed, rag, raw, rude, rut, road, royal, rear
> *word-medial, intervocalic*—mirror, very, arrow, sorry, hurry, furry, arrive, diary, dowry, dairy, eery, fury
> *word-final* (/r/-link with following word beginning with a vowel (see §12.4.7))—far away, poor old man, once and for all, here at last, there are two
> *in consonantal clusters*
> (following voiceless accented plosive = fully devoiced [ɹ̥])—price, proud, tree, try, cream, crow; expression, surprise, attract, extremely, decree
> (following voiceless fricative, unaccented voiceless plosive, or accented voiceless plosive preceded by /s/ in the same syllable = somewhat devoiced [ɹ̥])—fry, afraid, throw, thrive, shrink, shrug; apron, mattress, nitrate, buckram, cockroach; sprint, sprat, street, strain, scream, scrape, history /ˈhɪstrɪ/
> (following voiced consonant in the same syllable = [ɹ]-fricative after /d/)—brief, bright, dress, dry, dream, boundary, address, tawdry, grey, grow; umbrella, address, agree, hungry; comrade, sovereign, general, miserable
> *words containing more than one* /r/—brewery, library, retrograde, rarer, treasury, gregarious, procrastinate

Compare

> /r/, /l/—raft, laughed; rush, lush; red, led; right, light; pirate, pilot; sherry, Shelley; two rocks, two locks; crash, clash; pray, play; fry, fly; grew, glue; bright, blight
> /tr/, /dr/—trip, drip; trench, drench; tram, dram; trunk, drunk; troop, droop; try, dry

/tr/, /tʃ/—trees, cheese; trip, chip; trap, chap; true, chew; train, chain
/dr/, /dʒ/—drill, gill; dressed, jest; draw, jaw; drew, Jew; dram, jam; drear, jeer; Drury, jury

(2) *Description*

(a) *Articulatory and distributional features*—The most common allophone of RP /r/ is a voiced post-alveolar approximant [ɹ]. The soft palate being raised and the nasal resonator shut off, the tip of the tongue is held in a position near to, but not touching, the rear part of the upper teeth ridge; the back rims of the tongue are touching the upper molars; the central part of the tongue is lowered, with a general contraction of the tongue, so that the effect of the tongue position is one of hollowing and slight retroflexion of the tip. The airstream is thus allowed to escape freely, without friction, over the centre part of the tongue. The lip position is determined largely by that of the following vowel, e.g. *reach* with neutral to spread lips, *root* with rounded lips. This allophone of the RP phoneme is, therefore, phonetically vowel-like, but, having a non-central situation in the syllable, it functions as a consonant.

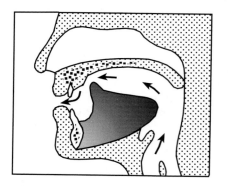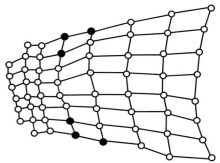

Fig. 49. *Section and palatogram of* /r/ = [ɹ].

RP /r/ occurs only before a vowel, the above description being applicable to the realizations: syllable-initially before a vowel; following a voiced consonant (except /d/), either in a syllable-initial cluster or at word or syllable boundaries; word-final /r/ linking with an initial vowel in the following word (see §12.4.7). This limited distribution applies also to other non-rhotic accents (see §7.4).

When /d/ precedes /r/, the allophone of /r/ is fricative, the /d/ closure being post-alveolar and its release slow enough to produce friction, e.g. in *drive, tawdry* and, in rapid speech, at syllable or word boundaries, e.g. *headrest, bedroom, wide road*.

A completely devoiced fricative [ɹ̥] may be heard following accented /p,t,k/, e.g. *price, try, cream, oppress, attract, across*. A partially devoiced variety of /r/ occurs: when /r/ follows an unaccented voiceless plosive initial in a syllable and, in rapid speech, at syllable boundaries, e.g. *upright, apron, paltry, nitrate, beetroot, cockroach, acrobat*; in the syllable-initial sequences /spr-,str-,skr-/, e.g.

spring, string, scream; and after other voiceless consonants in unaccented sylla-bles, e.g. *fry, thrive, shrink*. Slight devoicing may also occur, in rapid speech, following these latter voiceless fricatives, when they are unaccented and final in the preceding syllable, e.g. *belfry, saffron, necessary* /ˈnesəsrɪ/, *surf riding, birthright, horse race, cockroach, mushroom.*

(b) *Acoustic features*[57] The voiced post-alveolar approximant /r/ has a formant structure like vowels but, like the nasals and /l/, this structure is only weakly apparent. F1 is between 120 and 600 Hz, the lower the frequency the greater the perceived impression of lip-rounding; F2 is between 700 and 1,200 Hz; F3 is notable by being very close to F2. However, since the steady-state formants are likely to be very weak, /r/ is more easily identifiable on spectrograms by its steeply rising transitions (for F1, F2, F3 and F4) to a following vowel. See spectrograms in Fig. 43.

(3) *Variants*—There are more phonetic variants of the /r/ phoneme than of any other English consonant. In Refined RP, the approximant variety [ɹ] may be replaced by an alveolar tap [ɾ] in intervocalic positions, e.g. *very, sorry, marry, Mary, forever*, following /θ,ð/, e.g. *three, forthright, with respect*, and also, with some speakers, after other consonants, especially /b,g/, e.g. *bright, grow*. In the case of intervocalic [ɾ], a single tap is made by the tip of the tongue on the alveo-lar ridge, the side rims usually making a light contact with the upper molars. The articulation of [ɾ] differs from that of /d/ in that the contact for [ɾ] is of shorter duration and less complete than that of /d/, the central hollowing of the tongue typical of [ɹ] being retained; *carry* with [ɾ] and *caddie* with /d/ are, therefore, phonetically distinct. In the case of [ɾ] following /θ,ð/, a tap is made by the tongue-tip on the teeth ridge as the tongue is withdrawn from its dental position; again, the contact is of very brief duration and some tongue hollowing is retained.

In RP, too, the degree of labialization varies considerably. Although for perhaps the majority of RP speakers the lip position of /r/ is determined by that of the following vowel, some speakers labialize /r/ whatever the following vowel. In some extreme cases, lip-rounding is accompanied by no articulation of the forward part of the tongue, so that /r/ is replaced by /w/ and homophones of the type *wed, red*, are produced. Alternatively, a labiodental approximant [ʋ] may be heard as a realization of /r/ or even for both /r/ and /w/. Pronunciations of this sort were a fashionable affectation in the nineteenth and even early twentieth century. Although now generally regarded as a speech defect, they still (at least in England) seem more prevalent among those educated at major public schools.

A lingual trill (or roll) [r] may also be heard amongst RP speakers, but usually only in highly stylized speech, e.g. in declamatory verse-speaking. This trill, i.e. a rapid succession of taps by the tip of the tongue on the alveolar ridge, is often considered typical of some Scottish types of English, though a single tap or the approximant [ɹ] are more common. A tap is also the regular realization of /r/ in Liverpool and Newcastle.

A uvular articulation, either a trill [ʀ] or a fricative [ʁ], may be heard in the extreme north-east of England and also among some lowland Scottish speakers and as a defective substitution for [ɹ].

---

[57] O'Connor *et al.* (1957)

In some dialects the degree of retroflexion of the tongue for [ɹ] may be greater than in RP—[ɽ], e.g. in the speech of the south-west of England and some American English. The retroflexion of the tongue may anticipate the consonant and colour the preceding vowel articulation; such 'r-coloured' vowels may occur in this type of speech in words such as *bird, farm, lord*. A perceptual effect similar to retroflexion is often achieved by a bunching of the front and central parts of the tongue towards the roof of the mouth.[58] In this type of articulation the tip of the tongue is not retroflexed but approaches the base of the teeth.

/r/ differs in various types of English not only in its phonetic realization but also in its distribution. Many dialects of English, including General American, most types of Irish English, Standard Scottish English, and much of the rural south and south-west of England, retain the earlier post-vocalic (both pre-conso-nantal and pre-pausal) usage of /r/, distinguishing between RP homophones such as *pour, paw; court, caught*. (Some older RP speakers still retain a vocalic element representing the former /r/, keeping *pour* /pɔə/ distinct from *paw* /pɔː/.) The quality of the post-vocalic /r/ used will correspond to the types given above according to the region. A retroflexed continuant, of somewhat greater duration than the pre- or post-vocalic form, may also have syllabic function, e.g. in *water, father, ladder, paper* etc. For the use of word-final, post-vocalic /r/ as a linking form in RP, see §12.4.7.

The /ə/ in the sequence of /ər/ is frequently reduced in rapid speech by the elision of the schwa. This may leave non-syllabic /r/ pre-vocalically or it may result in a syllabic /r/. Both are possible in *conference, misery, camera, reverie, malingerer, binary, commentary, memory, victory*. The elision of both /r/ and /ə/ in *library* has similar effects. A similar elision of /ə/ can take place in the sequence /rə/ and this may result in the introduction of pre-consonantal /r/ into RP; the elision of /r/ in *parrot, barrel* may leave syllabic or non-syllabic /r/ (see further under §10.8).

(4) *Chief sources*—PresE /r/ derives from OE [r,rr] (*rise, rope, green, nearer*)—with later loss in post-vocalic positions (*horse, four*); OE [hr], [xr] or [r̥] (*ring, roof*)—[h] or the voiceless nature of [r] being lost by early ME; OE [wr] (*wrap, write, wrest, wretch*)—[w] being commonly omitted in the sixteenth century and generally by the late seventeenth, producing homophones with *rap, rite, rest, retch*; from OF [r] (*rule, remain, fruit, very*)—with later loss in post-vocalic positions (*arm, poor*). It is likely that the quality of /r/ in OE and ME was that of a linguo-alveolar trill or tap as described in (3) above. Its vibratory nature is described by writers of the sixteenth and seventeenth centuries, but /r/ had for some time exerted an influence on the preceding vowel and an [ə] resonance is identified in the sixteenth century. By the seventeenth century it is probable that the trill or tap was used only before vowels and that the approximant [ɹ] occurred, with or without friction, finally and before consonants. The change from a fricative to a non-fricative [ɹ], then to [ə], and finally to disappearance or merging with a preceding vowel in post-vocalic positions is a natural sequence. Its loss in post-vocalic positions in educated speech of the south-east of England is likely to have taken place by the end of the eighteenth century—considerably

---

[58] See Hagiwara (1995)

earlier in unaccented syllables and more generally in popular speech. As has been stated above, total loss of earlier post-vocalic /r/ is restricted socially and regionally even today.

(5) *Acquisition of /r/ by native learners*—The post-alveolar approximant, unlike the other approximants, is commonly a late acquisition, often not being contrastive until the age of 5;0. It is frequently replaced by /w/ and even when a contrast between /r/ and /w/ is present, the /r/ may have an incorrect articulation, commonly [ʋ].

(6) *Advice to foreign learners*—RP /r/ has a quality which is rarely encountered in other languages, the usual approximant variety having much in common with a vowel. Any strongly rolled *r*-sound, whether lingual or uvular, is not acceptable in RP, although it is not a question of loss of intelligibility through phonemic confusion. A weak tongue tip tap is the least objectionable substitution for RP [ɹ]; but a uvular sound, trill or fricative, as so often used by French or German learners, is generally taken as a characteristic of a marked foreign accent, despite the fact that a uvular sound is not unknown in English regional speech. It is also important that those whose own *r*-sound is of the uvular type should not make a double articulation—uvular and post-alveolar at the same time.

A foreign learner should, therefore, try to abandon his own prejudices as to what an /r/ sound should be and approach the RP [ɹ] as if it were a vowel. Any central vowel, either English /ə/ or RP /ɜː/ or a similar vowel in the learner's own language, may be used as a starting point. An approximation to the correct quality can then be achieved by maintaining the vowel sound while curling the tip of the tongue backwards. This sound can then be linked to the following vowel in a word. It is important that [ɹ] should be made unusually long in this position until the tongue articulation is established, e.g. [ɹːed].

Alternatively, practice may start from /ʒ/, in the articulation of which the tongue has a position somewhat similar to that of [ɹ], although the sound is fricative, the narrowing between tongue and roof of the mouth made too far forward, and the tongue hollowing and lateral contraction missing. From the /ʒ/ position, the tongue should be retracted, hollowed, and slightly lowered, so that the friction is lost. With both methods, it is often helpful to hold the jaws widely separated and the lips somewhat rounded. The post-alveolar affricates /tr,dr/ may also be related to /tʃ,dʒ/, applying the same principles of retraction as just described (see also §9.3.1).

Examples for practice should be chosen according to the degree of difficulty and the phonetic nature of the /r/ allophone used. Thus, the fricative variety of the second element of the affricates /tr,dr/ may be the first to be practised (to establish the post-alveolar position), but the sequence /str-/ will give greater difficulty; intervocalic [ɹ] usually presents relatively little difficulty, especially as a one-tap [r] is always permissible; the approximant in initial position may be the most troublesome articulation of all.

Learners should not be misled by the spelling into pronouncing the letter <r> in pre-consonantal and pre-pausal positions. In words such as *car, arm, horse, hurt* etc., the <r> may be taken as a sign indicating length of the preceding vowel, and in *fear, there, tour* etc, as a sign of the [ə] element of the diphthong. Nevertheless, in connected speech, the final linking /r/ form should normally be used. (See examples for practice in (1) above.)

As in the case of /l/, it should be remembered that in the sequences /pr-,br-,tr-, dr-,kr-,gr-/ the oppositions between voiceless and voiced plosives are indicated mainly by the degree of voicing in the following /r/. Thus, /pr-,tr-,kr-/ should have [ɹ̥], especially when accented, if they are not to be confused with /br-,dr-,gr-/; cf. pairs such as *pray, bray; try, dry; crow, grow.*

Many languages, including Japanese, Chinese, Tagalog, and some Bantu languages, have no distinction between /l/ and /r/. This contrast is often difficult to establish, the problem being as much perceptual as productive. Any attempt to teach the correct articulation of the sounds should therefore go hand in hand with drills to reinforce correct recognition.

9.7.3   Palatal and Labial-velar Approximants (or Semi-vowels)

(1) *Articulatory and distributional features*—A semi-vowel is a rapid vocalic glide onto a syllabic sound of greater steady duration. In English the semi-vowels /j/ and /w/ glide from positions of approximately /iː/ (with spread or neutral lips) and /uː/ (with rounded lips) respectively, e.g. in *year, west, inward, spaniel* [ˈspænjɫ]. The actual point at which the essential vocalic glide begins depends on the nature of the following sound, e.g. the glide of /j/ to /iː/ in *yeast* has a closer beginning than that of /j/ to /ɒ/ in *yacht*, and the starting-point of /w/ before /uː/ in *woo* is closer than that before /ɒ/ in *what*. When /j/ is followed by a back close vowel as in *you*, or /w/ by a front close vowel as in *we*, the starting-points need not be as close as in *yeast* and *woo*, since in the first cases the glide is essentially of a front to back (or vice versa) direction, rather than a movement of close to more open, as in the latter cases. In English, however, it is never necessary for the starting point of /j/+/iː/ or /w/+/uː/ to be so close that it falls within the frica-tive region beyond the vowel area, since English /iː/ and /uː/ are both sufficiently relaxed for a perceptible non-fricative glide to be made from a closer position within the vowel area.

Despite the fact that semi-vowels are, in phonetic terms, generally vocalic, they are treated within the consonant class, mainly because their **function** is conso-nantal rather than vowel-like, i.e. they have a marginal rather than a central situation in the syllable. /j/ and /w/ occur in the onset position of syllables either singly or as part of a consonantal cluster (see §8.2 for the treatment of the final [ɪ] and [ʊ] elements of English diphthongs as an integral part of the diphthongal glide, rather than as separable—consonantal—/j/ and /w/ occurring in the coda). Their consonantal function is emphasized by the fact that the articles have their pre-consonantal form when followed by /j/ and /w/, i.e. *the yard, a yacht, the west, a wasp*, with /ðə/ or /ə/ rather than with /ðiː/ or /ən/. Moreover, the allophones of /j/ and /w/ following a voiceless consonant are voiceless and fricative, as in *cue, quick* [kj̊uː], [kw̥ɪk], i.e. they fall within a phonetic definition of a consonant.

(2) *Acoustic features*[59]—Since /j/ and /w/ are vocalic glides (except in the case of the fricative allophones mentioned above), they may be expected to have acoustic features similar to those of vowels, i.e. a characteristic two- or

---

[59] O'Connor, *et al.* (1957)

three-formant structure similar to that of /iː/ or /uː/. In fact, as for vowels, two formants are sufficient for good recognition. Compared with /r,l/, the steady state of the semi-vowels is even shorter, e.g. of the order of 30 ms. F1 starting-point of the glide is that of /iː/ or /uː/, i.e. about 240 Hz; F2 has a starting-point within the range 2,280–3,600 Hz for /j/, depending on the following vowel, and within the range 360–840 Hz for /w/, depending on the following vowel. The transition duration of F2 is of the order of 50–100 ms for both /j/ and /w/, with that of F1 of the same or shorter duration. Spectrograms of /j,w/ are shown in Fig. 43.

9.7.4 Unrounded Palatal Approximant /j/

(1) *Examples*

> *y*—yes, yacht, young, yours, yeast, year, yak, yearn, beyond, lawyer
> *i*—spaniel /ˈspænjəl/, brilliant /ˈbrɪljənt/, senior /ˈsiːnjə/, onion, familiar /fəˈmɪljə/, behaviour, view, saviour, opinion
> *u*—(as part of [juː]) use, muse, opulent, presume, congratulate, nebulous
> *ue*—avenue, revue, revenue, argue, subdue, barbecue, pursue
> *ew,eu*—(as part of [juː]) new, mildew, nephew, spew, feud, adieu, eulogy

(*Note* 'beauty, you'.)

> *word-initial*—yield, yes, yard, yacht, yawn, union, young, yearn, yokel, year, Europe
> *following accented* /p,t,k,h/ (*only before* /uː,ʊə/)= [ç]—pew, tune, queue, cure, pure, huge; accuse, secure, peculiar, attuned
> *following* /sp,st,sk/, *voiceless fricatives, or unaccented* /p,t,k/=slightly devoiced [j̊]—spurious, stew, askew; enthusiasm, refuse; opulent, spatula, oculist; help you, kick you
> *following voiced consonant* =[j]—beauty, duty, music, new, value, view; abuse, endure, argue, manure, onion, failure, familiar, residue, senior, behaviour

(2) *Description*—The vocalic allophones of RP /j/ are articulated by the tongue assuming the position for a close-mid to close vowel front (depending on the degree of openness of the following sound) and moving away immediately to the position of the following sound; the lips are generally neutral or spread, but anticipate the lip rounding of the following vowel in cases such as *you, yawn* etc. When /j/ follows a voiceless consonant, devoicing takes place; when /j/ follows accented /p,t,k,h/, the devoicing is complete, with the result that a voiceless palatal fricative [ç] is produced. (In these cases, it is the friction rather than the glide which identifies the phoneme.)

When /j/ is the final element of accented clusters, only /uː/, /ʊə/ or sometimes /ɔː/ may follow /j/ (*pew, cure*); in unaccented clusters, /j/ may be followed by /uː,ʊ,ʊə/ or /ə/ (*argue, opulent, tenure, senior*). The sequence /h+/j/ as in *hue* /hjuː/ [hçuː] may coalesce into [ç] giving [çuː]. Such a realization entails oppositions between /i/, /h/, and [ç], raising the possibility of phonemic status for [ç]—*you, who, hue*. The number of words offering the sequence /h+/j/→ [ç] is, however, restricted (e.g. *hew, hue, human, humour*), and alternative pronunciations with

/h/+/j/ or /h/+[ç] (on the pattern of /p,t,k/+/j/) are possible. [ç] is, therefore, more conveniently treated as a realization of /h/+/j/.

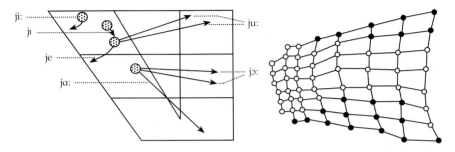

Fig. 50. *Vowel diagram and palatogram for* /j/.

(3) *Variants*—In many cases of RP /j/+/uː/, an alternative pronunciation without /j/ exists (and is extended further in American English). Earlier /juː/ or /ɪu/ sequences (see §8.9.10) have regularly been reduced to /uː/ in PresE after /tʃ,dʒ,r/, and /l/ preceded by a consonant; /juː/ is retained after plosives, nasals, /f/, /v/, and /h/ (*pew, beauty, queue, argue, tune, dune, few, view, nephew, huge*), and when /l/ is preceded by an accented vowel (*value, curlew*); but in other cases, more variation is possible, both /uː/ and /juː/ being heard, e.g. in *absolute(ly), lute, salute, revolution, enthusiasm, pursuit, assume, suit, suet, suitable, superstition, supermarket, consume, presume* etc, though /uː/ grows increasingly common in such words, being the more common after /l/ and /s/ in an accented syllable whilst /juː/ remains predominant after /θ,z/. Increasingly, pronunciations without /j/ are also heard following /n/ in accented syllables, e.g. *neutral, news*. In General American /j/ is regularly absent following /t,d/, e.g. *tune, tunic, dune, duty*, while in East Anglia /j/ may be dropped following all consonants, e.g. *beauty, music, view, argue*. The sequence /h/+/j/ is reduced to /j/ alone in some accents, e.g. in much of Wales.

Unaccented sequences of /tj,dj,sj,zj/ coalesced in an earlier state of the language into /tʃ,dʒ,ʃ,ʒ/ (see §§9.3.1, 9.4.5). In some cases, e.g. *statue, residue, issue, seizure, Christian, immediate, educate, gratitude, usual, visual, Jesuit*, both forms may now be heard, the pronunciation with /tj,dj,sj,zj/ being characteristic of careful speech; on the other hand, the occasionally heard coalesced forms in the onset of accented syllables, e.g. /ʃ,ʒ/ in *assume, presume* are regarded as non-RP. Such coalescences also occur in rapid, familiar, speech, at word boundaries, e.g. in *not yet, would you, this year, sees you* (§12.4.5).

In unaccented syllables there is often variation between /jə/ and /ɪə/, e.g. in *immediate, India, audience, tedious, idiot, hideous*. In the cases involving a preceding alveolar plosive where the /jə/ form may be regarded as the primary one, this form may occasionally be further reduced to /tʃ,dʒ/ in rapid speech, e.g. /ɪˈmiːdɪət, ɪˈmiːdjət, ɪˈmiːdʒət/. In cases such as *Romania, Bohemia, Australia, morphia*, /ɪə/ tends to be retained in careful speech, as well as in those suffixes where /ə/ has a separable morphemic value, e.g. in *easier, heavier* (see §8.12.1 for those sequences of [ɪ] plus [ə] which are better regarded as bisyllabic).

A junctural [ʲ] glide may sometimes be heard between /iː,ɪ,eɪ,aɪ,ɔɪ/ and a follow-ing vowel, e.g. *seeing* [ˈsiːʲɪŋ]; *saying* [ˈseɪʲɪŋ], *sighing* [ˈsaɪʲɪŋ], *enjoy it* [enˈdʒɔɪʲɪt], *see ants* [siːʲænts], *say all* [seɪʲɔːl], *my aunt* [maɪʲɑːnt], *toy arm* [tɔɪʲɑːm], result-ing from the relatively close quality given to /iː/ and [ɪ] and the subsequent glide to the following, more open, vowel. However, such a glide is rarely equivalent in nature to a phonemic /j/, the finishing point of the diphthong not being suffi-ciently prominent, nor the glide being long enough. The difference between phonemic /j/ and junctural [ʲ] can be seen in the opposition between *my ear* /maɪ `ɪə/ (= [maɪ ˈʲɪə]) and *my year* /maɪ `jɪə/ (= [maɪ ˈjɪə]), and *we earn* /wiː `ɜːn/, (= [wiː ˈʲɜːn]) and *we yearn* /wiː `jɜːn/ (= [wiː ˈjɜːn]). A junctural [ʲ] always has the alter-native of a glottal stop, e.g. [maɪ ˈʔɪə] and [wiː ˈʔɜːn] (see §9.2.8).

(4) *Chief sources*—PresE /j/ derives from OE [j] (itself deriving from a palatal-ized form of [g]) (*yard, year, yield, yoke, young*). PresE /j/ (+/uː/) also derives from ME [ɪu,eu] (see §8.9.10) and from loss of syllabic value of [ɪ] before another vowel in unaccented situations, e.g. in words of French origin such as *opinion, familiar, onion, William, pavilion*, where the <i> had at an earlier stage repre-sented the palatal nature of French /ɲ,ʎ/.

(5) *Acquisition of /j/ by native learners*—The palatal approximant, along with /l/ and /w/, is usually among the first consonants added to the plosives and nasals of children's first words. It is only rarely a problem in acquisition, and is regularly present by 3;6.

(6) *Advice to foreign learners*—RP /j/ presents little difficulty except where it occurs before a following close front vowel, as in *yeast, yield, Yiddish, year*, where there may be a tendency to omit the /j/ altogether. In such cases it can be helpful to make the learner say an additional [iː] instead of the [j] at the beginning of the word, e.g. [iːiːst], [iːiːld], [iːɪdɪʃ], [iːɪə] and then gradually shorten the [iː]. Spanish learners should avoid using a palatal plosive [ɟ] in accented syllables, e.g. in *yes, young* [ɟes, ɟʌŋ]. Speakers of languages like French having unaspirated /p,t,k/ should be sure to correctly devoice a following /j/, e.g. in *pew, tune, queue*.

9.7.5   Labial-velar Approximant /w/

(1) *Examples*

w—west, weather, wink, wit, wet, wagon, walk, wood, swoon, sweep
wh—which, what, where, when, whether, while, wheel, whisper, whistle, white, whisky, whist
u *(following <q,g,s>)*—quick, quiet, queen, colloquial, conquer, adequate, language, penguin, linguist, sanguine, anguish, persuade, suede, suite

(*Note* 'one, once, choir'.)

word-initial = [w]—weed, wet, wag, wasp, wood, womb, one, word, wave, woke, wire, weird, wear
following accented /t, k/= [ʍ]—twig, twelve, twin, twice, queen, quell, quick, quite, quaint, acquaint
following /sk/, *accented voiceless fricative or in unaccented syllable following* /p,t,k/= *slightly devoiced* [w̥]—square, squash, squirrel; thwart, swim, swear, swoon; upward, outward, equal; pump water, that word, take one

intervocalic, or following voiced consonant = [w]—away, aware, inward, always, language; dwindle, dwarf, guano
possible oppositions /w/, /ʍ/—witch, which; weather, whether; wine, whine; Wales, whales; wear, where

Compare

/w/, /v/—west, vest; wine, vine; worse, verse; wail, veil; weir, veer

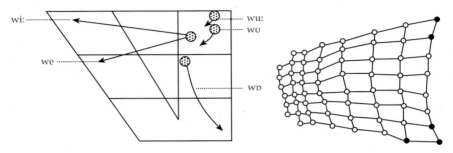

Fig. 51. *Vowel diagram and palatogram for* /w/.

(2) *Description*—The vocalic allophones of RP /w/ are articulated by the tongue assuming the position for a back close-mid to close vowel (depending upon the degree of openness of the following sound) and moving away immediately to the position of the following sound; the lips are rounded (more closely when followed by /uː,ʊ/ or /ɔː/ than when preceding a more open or front vowel—cf. *woo, wood, war*, with *what, west, we*; in those cases where /w/ precedes /uː/, the lip-rounding for /w/ is closer and more energetic than that associated with /uː/, permitting a distinction between a pair such as *ooze, woos*). This is an example of double articulation, the approximation of the articulators at the bilabial and velar places of articulation constituting two strictures of equal rank. The soft palate is raised and the vocal folds vibrate; but when /w/ follows a voiceless consonant, devoicing takes place: when /w/ follows accented /t,k/, the devoicing is complete =[ʍ], a voiceless labial-velar fricative—the friction being bilabial. In this latter case, it is the bilabial friction rather than the glide which identifies the phoneme; words such as *swoop, swoon*, are distinguished from *soup, soon*, not only by the stronger lip action associated with /w/ but also by its devoiced friction.

Consonants preceding /w/, especially initially in an accented syllable, will be lip-rounded in anticipation of /w/, e.g. in *twist, queen, swing, language, conquest*; such rounding occurs to a lesser extent at syllable or word boundaries, e.g. in *onward, bindweed, front wheel, this one*.

(3) *Variants*—The main variant, both in RP and in other types of British English, concerns the pronunciation of the spelling <wh>. Among careful RP speakers and regularly in several regional types of speech, e.g. in Scottish English, words such as *when* are pronounced with the voiceless labial-velar fricative [ʍ]. In such speech, which contains oppositions of the kind *wine, whine*, shown in (1) above, /ʍ/ has phonemic status. Among RP speakers the use of /ʍ/

as a phoneme has declined rapidly (though it is often taught as the correct form in verse-speaking). Even if /ʍ/ does occur distinctively in any idiolect, it may nevertheless be interpreted phonemically as /h/+/w/ (cf. the treatment of [ç] in §9.7.4.(2)). The fact that the stock of words in which /ʍ/ may occur (e.g. *whale, what, wheel, when, where, whet, which, whig, whin, whine, whirr, whist, whit, why*) is greater than those in which [ç] may occur, does not of itself provide sufficient argument for a monophonemic rather than a biphonemic solution.

A junctural [ʷ] glide may sometimes be heard between /uː,ʊ,əʊ,aʊ/ and a following vowel, e.g. *doing* [ˈduːʷɪŋ], *following* [ˈfɒləʊʷɪŋ], *allow it* [əˈlaʊ ʷɪt], *who asked* [huː ˈʷɑːst], *follow on* [fɒləʊ ˈʷɒn], resulting from the relatively close quality given to /uː/ or [ʊ] and the subsequent glide to the following, more open, vowel. However, such a glide is rarely equivalent in nature to a phonemic /w/, the finishing point of the vowel not being sufficiently prominent, nor the glide long enough. The difference between phonemic /w/ and junctural [ʷ] can be seen in the opposition between *two-eyed* [tuː ˈʷaɪd] and *too wide* [tuː ˈwaɪd] and between *no air* [nəʊ ˈʷeə] and *no wear* [nəʊ ˈweə]. A junctural [ʷ] always has the alternative of a glottal stop, e.g. [tuː ˈʔaɪd] and [nəʊ ˈʔeə] (see §9.2.8).

(4) *Chief sources*—PresE /w/ derives from OE [w] (*way, wolf, wash, widow, twin, dwarf*); from OF [w]—a northern French form, where Mod French has /g/ (*wage, ward, warrant, war*); from an earlier French [u] preceded by a velar plosive and followed by another vowel (*squire, squirrel, squadron*). In many cases an earlier [w] has been lost (*so, such, thong, two, sword, answer*) during the ME or eModE periods. [w] in the cluster [wr] (*write, wreck, wrist*) was finally lost in the late seventeenth century.

PresE /ʍ/ derives from OE [hw], [xw] or [ẉ] (spelt <hw> in OE) (*whale, wheel, where, when, which, whistle*). [hw] or [ʍ] finally merged with /w/ in educated southern speech in the late eighteenth century, although still deplored by normative elocutionists; /w/ occurs for [hw] much earlier—probably in ME—however, in popular speech. The reduction of [hw] to /w/ is parallel to that of [hr,hn,hl] to /r,n,l/; the relatively smaller number of French words entering the language with /w/ (compared with the numerous examples with initial /r,n,l/) may be a reason for the longer persistence of a /hw/–/w/ opposition, the imbalance between the voiceless and voiced varieties being not so marked as in the case of /hr,hn,hl/vs /r,n,l/.

In the case of *who, whom, whose*, it is the [w] element which has been lost (probably by the eModE period), due to a merging of the [w] with the following, similar, /uː/. The addition of initial /w/ in *one, once* (cf. *alone*), occurred from late ME onwards in popular speech, existed alongside [oːn,oːns] forms in eModE, and was finally adopted as regular by the end of the seventeenth century.

(5) *Acquisition of* /w/ *by native learners*—The labial-velar approximant is often the first approximant to be acquired, following fairly rapidly on the prior acquisition of nasals and plosives. It rarely presents a problem, and is usually present by at least 3;0.

(6) *Advice to foreign learners*—It is important that the vocalic allophone of /w/ should not be replaced by a consonantal sound, i.e. either a voiced bilabial fricative [β] (as in Hungarian), or a voiced labiodental fricative [v] (as in German), or a labiodental approximant [ʋ], in which there is a loose approximation (without friction) between the lower lip and the upper teeth (as in Hindi).

All such substitutions will be interpreted by the English ear as /v/. The learner should protrude and round his lips, ensuring that the teeth play no part in the articulation; if necessary, in practice, an energetically rounded full [uː] vowel should be used, e.g. *wine* being pronounced as [uːaɪn], and a clear distinction being made between this word and *vine* (see examples in (1) above). The same protruded and rounded lip action (and absence of lower teeth contact) applies to the voiceless allophone [ʍ], as in *quite, twin* etc. As in the case of the voiceless allophones of /l,r,j/, it is important that /w/ should be devoiced, especially after accented /t,k/, despite the fact that there are no exact pairs depending on the opposition [dw,gw]–[tʍ,kʍ], cf. *dwell, twelve; distinguish, relinquish; dwindle, twin; Gwen, quench.*

9.8   *Frequency of Occurrence of RP Consonants*

As a class, the alveolar phonemes emerge as those which occur most frequently in English, this being a generalization which appears to be applicable to many languages. The text frequencies of English consonants as given in Fry (1947) are shown in Table 13.

	%		%
n	7.58	b	1.97
t	6.42	f	1.79
d	5.14	p	1.78
s	4.81	h	1.46
l	3.66	ŋ	1.15
ð	3.56	g	1.05
r	3.51	ʃ	0.96
m	3.22	j	0.88
k	3.09	dʒ	0.60
w	2.81	tʃ	0.41
z	2.46	θ	0.37
v	2.00	ʒ	0.10
Total all consonants: 60.78 %			

Table 13. *Text frequencies of consonants in RP**
* (From Fry, 1947). Revised percentages (supplied by G. Perren) for /t/, /d/, and /r/ are included.

The frequencies of consonants shown in Table 13 and in other studies of text frequencies[60] show their rank order of occurrence falling into five groups:

---

[60] In addition to Fry (1947) see also Carterette and Jones (1974), Mines *et al.* (1978), Knowles (1987)

(i) /n,t,d,s,l,r/ (with /r/ much more frequent in General American because of its occurrence of pre-consonantal and pre-pausal positions);

(ii) /ð,k,m,w,z/;

(iii) /p,b/;

(iv) /f,v,h,j,g,ŋ/;

(v) /θ,ʃ,ʒ,tʃ,dʒ/.

As is to be expected from its historical origins and its restricted contextual distribution, /ʒ/ regularly occupies the lowest position. In any general text frequency count such as this, the order obtained will reflect the occurrence of 'common' words such as *the, that, which* etc., giving preponderance to /ð,w/, for example, as against /θ,j/.

There are notable discrepancies between the occurrence of voiceless and voiced members of homorganic pairs of phonemes: thus, /s,ð,k/ occur more frequently than their counterparts. Discrepancy in general frequency of occurrence is, however, less important, as far as oppositional significance is concerned, than the frequency of minimal pairs, the so-called FUNCTIONAL LOAD of contrasts. By this measure the contrasts of /θ/ vs /ð/ and /ʃ/ vs /ʒ/ carry a very low functional load, with minimal pairs being almost non-existent (*thigh* vs *thy, ether* vs *either, teeth* vs *teethe, Aleutian* vs *allusion, illusion* vs *Illuyshin, leash* vs *liege, Confucian* vs *confusion*).

PART III

Words and Connected Speech

Introduction

We have seen that speech, a manifestation of language, may most readily be investigated at the physiological and physical levels. Such investigations show, however, that it is by no means easy to analyse the data obtained for any speech event into discrete, successive units within either the articulatory or the acoustic patterns. Speech must, therefore, be considered from the phonetic point of view as an ever-changing continuum of qualities, quantities, pitch, and intensities. If, for practical purposes, e.g. in a transcription of the spoken language, we treat speech as a succession of articulatory or auditory separable units, it is largely because we impose, upon the gross material of speech, entities which we have derived (consciously or unconsciously) from a knowledge of the linguistically significant oppositions operating for any particular language system, e.g. the words, the morphemes, and (particularly important in the present context) the phonemes. In other words, a useful phonetic/phonemic account of speech describes those articulatory or acoustic features which are significant in distinguishing the phonemes (or the important allophones within a phoneme) of a language. It should not, however, be forgotten that such a linear presentation is an abstraction from the concrete material of speech rather than a statement of the gross phonetic material composing the continuum. In this respect, the sophisticated written form of English differs from the spoken manifestation of the language, for our writing explicitly represents a succession of discrete linguistic units—phonemes (nowadays imperfectly) and words.

If, however, for convenience, our analysis is based on discrete phonemic units, it is necessary to take into account the way in which such units combine in speech—both in words and in connected speech; thus, the aim of the following chapters is to show how phonemes combine in words and how varying accentual patterns apply to the syllables of words (Chapter 10), how accentual and intonational patterns occur on groups of words and sentences (Chapter 11), and how the citation forms of words change in connected speech (Chapter 12).

10

Words

10.1 *Accent*

The word, composed of one or more phonemes, has a separate linguistic identity, in that it is a commutable entity, higher than the phoneme, which may either constitute a complete utterance or may be substituted in a longer utterance for other words of its same class. It may be thought of as a shape or pattern, constituted from the qualitative and quantitative elements of its phonemes, these phonemic elements being also capable of distinctive commutation, e.g. the /t/ and /d/, in *writer* and *rider*. In addition, in polysyllabic words, the word shape has an identity determined by the relationship of its parts. Thus, *writer, rider,* may be said to have a pattern consisting of a 'strong' syllable followed by a 'weak' syllable. This pattern obtains also for *written* /ˈrɪtn/; but, in the case of *return* /rɪˈtɜːn/ or *again* /əˈgen/, the pattern is reversed. The identity of *return* and *again* depends not only on the different elements which distinguish these words from, for example, *written*, but also on the different patterns which derive from the varying prominence of the parts. The syllable or syllables of a word which stand out from the remainder are said to be accented, to receive the ACCENT.

The accentual pattern of English words is fixed, in the sense that the main accent always falls on a particular syllable of any given word,[1] but free, in the sense that the main accent is not tied to any particular point in the chain of syllables constituting a word, as it is in some languages, e.g. to the penultimate syllable in Polish, to the first in Czech, and to the last in French. Thus, in English the main accent falls regularly on the first syllable in words such as *finish, answer, afterwards*; on the second syllable in *behind, result, together, impossible*; on the third syllable in *understand, education*; or later in *articulation, palatalization* etc.

The accentual shape of a word, in terms of the degree of prominence associated with its parts, is a reality for both the speaker and the listener; but the speaker's impression of the factors which produce such a pattern of varying

---

[1] With certain exceptions, determined by the larger rhythmic pattern of the total context (see §10.4)

prominences may differ from the actual auditory cues by which the listener perceives the prominence pattern. It is, therefore, necessary to examine the factors which in English are significant both for the speaker and for the listener in producing the communicated effect of accent.

10.2   *Accent and Prominence*

Any of four factors, pitch, loudness, quality, and quantity may help to render a syllable more prominent than its neighbours. But it is principally pitch change which marks an accented syllable.

(1) *Pitch change*—The principal cue to accent is pitch prominence, which depends as much upon pitch change as pitch height. The different accentual patterns of *insult* (n.) and *insult* (v.) are easily distinguished by their pitch patterns. If a falling intonation is used, the fall occurs on the first syllable of the noun and on the second syllable of the verb.

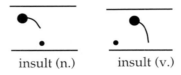

insult (n.)   insult (v.)

Similarly, if a rising intonation is used, the rise begins on the first syllable and the second syllable respectively (in these so-called interlinear diagrams syllables are indicated by dots and accented syllables by large dots):

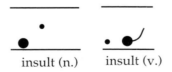

insult (n.)   insult (v.)

Pitch changes may make prominent more than one syllable in a word; thus *examination*:

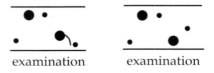

examination   examination

or, within a phrase like the following, where the first three accented syllables show a change of pitch level while the last accent involves a change of pitch direction:

The first examination was over

The final pitch accent in a word or in a group of words is usually the most prominent (and hence referred to as the PRIMARY ACCENT) while a pitch accent on an earlier syllable is usually somewhat less prominent (and referred to as SECONDARY ACCENT).

(2) *Loudness*—Accented syllables are often assumed to be louder than unaccented syllables and in many cases this may be so. Greater loudness is carried principally by voiced sounds, in which greater amplitude of vibration of the vocal folds, together with the reinforcing resonance of the supraglottal cavities, results in acoustic terms in relatively greater intensity. This strong intensity and the perceived loudness on the part of the listener results from the relatively greater breath effort and muscular energy expended on the articulation of a sound by the speaker. This effort and energy is frequently referred to as 'stress', although, because of the many different ways in which it has been used, this word is avoided here. Loudness is not by itself an efficient device for signalling the location of the accent in English. When they are said on a monotone and without undue lengthening of accented syllables, it is difficult to distinguish by loudness alone *in`sult* (v.), *im`port* (v.), *be`low*, from *`insult* (n.), *`import* (n.), *`billow*, words in which different accentual patterns are not associated with qualitative differences in the vowels.

(3) *Quantity and quality*—While accent is principally achieved by pitch change, sometimes assisted by extra loudness, among unaccented syllables some will be more prominent than others due to the quality and quantity of the vowels at their centre. (For varying prominence among sounds more generally, see §5.5.) Long vowels and diphthongs are generally more prominent than short vowels, while among the short vowels themselves /ɪ,ʊ,ə/ (when unaccented) are the least prominent and are often referred to as REDUCED vowels as opposed to other FULL vowels (as far as prominence is concerned, syllabic consonants are considered to be sequences of /ə/ plus /l,m,n,ŋ/ and hence are equivalent to reduced vowels). Indeed the reduced vowels are so lacking in prominence that they have a high frequency of occurrence in unaccented as opposed to accented syllables and /ə/ occurring only in unaccented syllables. But a long vowel in an unaccented syllable is sometimes longer than a vowel in an adjacent accented syllable, e.g. *pillow* /`pɪləʊ/, *ally* /`ælaɪ/, *frontier* /`frʌntɪə/, *phoneme* /`fəʊniːm/, *placard* /`plækɑːd/, *record* /`rekɔːd/, *expert* /`ekspɜːt/, *female* /`fiːmeɪl/. In similar cases where the unaccented syllable precedes the accent there is often alternation between a full and reduced vowel, e.g. *July* /dʒuːˈlaɪ/ /dʒəˈlaɪ/, *November* /nəʊˈvembə/ /nəˈvembə/, *proceed* /prəʊˈsiːd/ /prəˈsiːd/, *September* /sepˈtembə/ /səpˈtembə/. Some dialects, e.g. that of northern England, are more likely to retain the full vowel in these positions, particularly in monosyllabic prefixes, e.g. *obtain* /ɒbˈteɪn/ /əbˈteɪn/, *contain* /kɒnˈteɪn/ /kənˈteɪn/, *continue* /kɒnˈtɪnjuː/ /kənˈtɪnjuː/, *expect* /ekˈspekt/ /ɪkˈspekt/ or /əkˈspekt/. In some disyllables (both in RP and in other dialects) there may be alternation in the position of the primary accent with

consequent alternation in the use of a full or reduced vowel, e.g. *adult* /ˈædʌlt/ vs /əˈdʌlt/, *contact* (v.) /ˈkɒntækt/ vs /kənˈtækt/.

(4) *Conclusion*—There are therefore four degrees of prominence in English:

(a) primary accent, marked by the last major pitch change in a word (or longer utterance);

(b) secondary accent, marked by a non-final pitch change in a word (or longer utterance);

(c) a minor prominence produced by the occurrence of a full vowel but containing no pitch change;

(d) a non-prominent syllable containing no pitch change and one of the vowels /ɪ,ʊ,ə/.

10.3   *Word Accentual Patterns*[2]

Although many longer words contain primary accented syllables, secondary accented syllables, and prominent syllables based on vowel quality alone, it is the position of the primary accent which contributes most to a word's accentual pattern (and which will be the principal cue to the nuclear tone (see §11.6.1.2)). Attempts to reduce the placement of primary accent in English words to a set of rules are bedevilled by the existence of large numbers of exceptions to almost any rule. The following sections should therefore be regarded as stating tendencies rather than absolute rules. It is principally the status of the final syllable as strong or weak (together with grammatical class) which governs primary accent placement in English. Syllables are here counted as STRONG when they contain a long vowel or diphthong or a short vowel plus two consonants; otherwise they are WEAK.

English words may be divided into ROOTS and AFFIXES, including both SUFFIXES and PREFIXES. Roots include not only single free morphemes like *fool, begin*, and *understand* but also that part of a word remaining after an affix has been removed, even though such a part cannot occur on its own, e.g. *ephemer-al, tremend-ous, hospit-able*. In the next section tendencies in root stressing are, however, generally exemplified in free morphemes.

10.3.1   Roots

Somewhat different tendencies apply to verbal, adjectival, and nominal roots. Among other word classes, adverbs are generally derived from adjectival roots with no alteration to the accentual pattern, while the remaining classes rarely have more than one syllable which contains a strong syllable.

(1) *Verbs*

(a) If the final syllable is strong, it is accented, e.g. /rɪˈleɪt/, /tʃæsˈtaɪz/, /əˈraɪv/, /meɪnˈteɪn/, /əˈkɜː/, /pəˈsiːv/, /wɪðˈhəʊld/, /wɪðˈstænd/, /pəˈsweɪd/, /entəˈteɪn/,

---

[2] See particularly Chomsky and Halle (1968), Fudge (1984). For an alternative formulation involving heavy syllable as VC and extrametrical final consonants, see Giegerich (1992)

Words 225

/rɪˈfjuːz/, /əˈgriː/, /kənˈvɜːt/, /kənˈvɪkt/, /kənˈteɪn/, /ɪŋˈkluːd/, /əʊvəˈteɪk/, /rɪˈdʒekt/, /ʌndəˈstænd/, /dɪsˈlaɪk/, /əˈdɔːn/, /bɪˈliːv/, /priːsəˈpəʊz/, /ɪmˈvɒlv/, /rekəˈmend/, /rɪˈmaɪnd/, /ɪnˈtend/.

(b) Otherwise accent falls on the penultimate syllable, e.g. /səˈrendə/, /ˈwɪspə/, /ˈpɒlɪʃ/, /ˈpʌnɪʃ/, /dɪˈveləp/, /ˈwɜːʃɪp/, /ˈvɪzɪt/, /ˈgæləp/, /ˈtrævəl/, /əˈstɒnɪʃ/, /ɪkˈzæmɪn/, /ˈlɪsən/, /ɪˈmædʒɪn/, /rɪˈzembəl/.

Some exceptions:

> unaccented strong final syllables: /ˈrekəgnaɪz/, /ˈrɪəlaɪz/
> accented weak final syllables: /ɪmˈpres/, /pəˈses/, /bɪˈgɪn/, /fəˈget/, /fəˈbɪd/, /pəˈmɪt/

(2) *Adjectives*

(a) If the final syllable is strong, it is accented, e.g. /məˈtjʊə/, /sɪˈkjʊə/, /əˈfreɪd/, /əˈsliːp/, /kəmˈpliːt/, /ɪkˈstriːm/, /əˈbrʌpt/, /səˈblaɪm/, /əˈləʊn/.

(b) Otherwise accent falls on the penultimate syllable, or (with reduced vowel on the penultimate) on the antepenultimate, e.g.

> penultimate: /ɪkˈsesɪv/, /ˈnjuːtrəl/, /ˈsɒlɪd/, /ˈklevə/, /ˈfeɪməs/, /ˈrɪdʒɪd/, /ɪkˈsplɪsɪt/, /kɒnfɪˈdenʃəl/
> antepenultimate: /ˈnesəsrɪ/, /ˈdeɪndʒərəs/, /ˈdɪfɪkəlt/, /ˈdefɪnɪt/, /ˈɪntrɪstɪŋ/, /ˈpɒsɪbəl/, /ˈmaːvələs/, /ˈɪntɪmət/

Some exceptions:

> strong final syllables, unaccented: /ˈmɒrɪbʌnd/, /ˈtæntəmaʊnt/, /ɪmˈpɔːtənt/, /kəʊˈhɪərənt/, /ˈærəgənt/)

(3) *Nouns*

(a) If the final syllable is strong, it is **optionally** accented, e.g. /aɪˈdɪə/, /məˈʃiːn/, /dɪsˈpjuːt/, /kæˈʃɪə/, /aːftəˈnuːn/, /kəˈtaː/, /bəˈluːn/, /ʃæmˈpeɪn/, /kəˈʃɪə/, /pəˈliːs/, /kæŋgəˈruː/, /ˈmɪraːʒ/.

(b) Otherwise primary accent falls on the penultimate syllable, or (with reduced vowel on the penultimate) on the antepenultimate, or, rarely, on the ante-antepenultimate, e.g.

> strong final syllable, penultimate accent: /ˈprəʊfaɪl/, /təˈmaːtəʊ/, /təˈbækəʊ/, /pəˈteɪtəʊ/, /ˈwɪndəʊ/, /ˈpɪləʊ/, /ˈærəʊ/, /ˈfeləʊ/, /ˈwɪləʊ/, /ˈwɪdəʊ/, /səˈpraːnəʊ/, /kənˈfetiː/, /ˈməʊmənt/, /ˈsʌfɪks/, /ˈbærəks/, /ˈɪnɪŋz/
> strong final, antepenultimate accent: /ˈænəkdəʊt/, /ˈfærənhaɪt/, /ˈpedɪgriː/, /ˈæpətaɪt/, /ˈkætərækt/, /əˈsetɪliːn/, /ˈtelɪfəʊn/, /ˈæntɪləʊp/
> weak final, penultimate accent: /ɪŋˈkaʊntə/, /ˈlæŋgwɪdʒ/, /ˈpætən/, /kəmˈplekʃən/, /ˈpeɪpə/, /ˈfeɪvrɪt/, /ˈtʃɒklɪt/, /ˈvɜːmɪn/
> weak final, antepenultimate accent: /ˈkwɒntɪtɪ/, /ˈdɪsɪplɪn/, /ˈkæmərə/, /ˈhɪstərɪ/, /əˈnælɪsɪs/, /ˈevɪdəns/, /raɪˈnɒsərəs/, /ˈɪnəsəns/
> weak final, ante-antepenultimate accent: /ˈhelɪkɒptə/, /ˈtelɪvɪʒən/

Some exceptions:

> final accent on weak syllable: /həʊˈtel/, /pɜːsəˈnel/ (*personnel*), /sɪɡəˈret/ (*but* /ˈsɪɡəret/ in GA)

/ɪ/ sometimes functions as a reduced vowel, as in /ˈpedɪgriː/ and sometimes as a full vowel, as in /vəˈnɪlə/ and sometimes has both functions in one word, as in /ˈwɪkɪd/.

It should particularly be noted that there are two competing accent patterns for nouns with strong final syllables, one with final accent and one with an earlier accent. The final syllable in the case of (2)(b) is sometimes said to be 'extra-metrical', i.e. outside the rhythm of the word.

Cigarette illustrates the problem of deciding whether to treat a word as a single root or as a sequence of root plus affix, e.g. in the case of /sɪgəˈret/, the analysis root *cigar* plus suffix *-ette* would produce the correct accentual pattern in the same way that *disk* becomes *disˈkette*. (A similar problem arises in the treatment of compounds—see §10.3.5 below.)

10.3.2   Suffixes

Suffixes may be added to a root, e.g. *nation, national*, or they may be added to an already combined root plus suffix, e.g. *national, nationalist, nationalistic*. This part of a word to which a suffix is added are called STEMS. Some suffixes have no effect on the accentual pattern of stems and hence are called ACCENT-NEUTRAL; in the complex word the primary accent remains where it is in the stem, e.g. ˈbitter, ˈbitterness. Other suffixes regularly take the accent themselves (are ACCENT ATTRACTING), e.g. ˈdisk, disˈkette. Yet others have the effect of fixing the accent on a particular syllable of the stem (are ACCENT-FIXING): on the final syllable, e.g. ˈdefinite, defiˈnition, or on the penultimate syllable, e.g. ˈinfant, inˈfanticide (where the stem is *infanti-*), or varying between final and penultimate according to the same principle as that for roots, i.e. whether the final syllable of the stem contains, on the one hand, a short vowel in an open position or followed by only one consonant or, on the other hand, a long vowel or short vowel plus two consonants, e.g. ˈmedicine, meˈdicinal, but inˈtestine, intesˈtinal. Unfortunately, many suffixes are not entirely regular in the accentual patterns they induce, belonging in one group of words to one category, and in another group of words to another category. In many cases variation occurs which is dependent on the type of stem, i.e. whether it consists of a FREE or BOUND morpheme; thus disaˈgree, disaˈgreement but segˈment, torˈment. Where more than one suffix is applied to a stem, the last suffix determines the word's accentual pattern, e.g. ˈrational, ˈrationalize, rationaliˈzation; faˈmiliar, familiˈarity, familiariˈzation.

There are some endings derived principally from Greek which are like suffixes in that they occur attached to a number of stems, but which have other Greek elements preceding them which themselves are like prefixes, and neither element has a greater claim to be considered as a root, e.g. *phonograph, logogen, microscope*. These are not treated in this section, but dealt with under §10.3.5 as compounds, since their accentual patterning is similar to compounds.

(1) *Accent-neutral suffixes*—Included in this category are all inflexional and many common derivational suffixes. Some inflexions are non-syllabic like plural, possessive, and third person singular *-s* (but these are syllabic following

/s,ʒ,ʃ,ʒ,tʃ,dʒ/—see §10.10.2) and past tense -*t* (this is syllabic following /t,d/—see again §10.10.2); other inflexions are monosyllabic like -*er, est* (comparative, superlative) and -*ing* (progressive). Most derivational suffixes ending in -*y* (or *ie*) (e.g. -*ary*, -*ery*, -*ory*, -*cy*, -*acy*, -*ty*, diminutive -*y*, adjectival -*y*, and adverbial -*ly*) are accent-neutral, e.g. in`firm, in`firmary; `celibate, `celibacy; `difficult, `difficulty; `pot, `potty; `bag, `baggy; `usual, `usually.* Other suffixes in this category include -*ish*, -*ism*, -*ist*, -*ise*, -*ment* and agentive -*er* and female -*ess*, e.g. `fool, `foolish, `alcohol, `alcoholism; `separate, `separatist; `circular, `circularize; disa`gree, disa`greement; lead, `leader, and `lion, `lioness.* All the examples given here concern stems which are free forms; in the case of stems which are not free forms some of these suffixes fall into other categories, e.g. -*ary* as a suffix on such stems falls under (3b) below, and -*ment* will fall into (2) on verbs but into (3b) on nouns. (Note also irregular ad`vertisement.*)

(2) *Accent-attracting suffixes*—Some common derivational suffixes in this category are -*ade*, -*eer*, -*esque*, -*ette*, and -*ation* (which could be analysed into a double suffix -*ate* plus -*ion* (=/-eɪʃn/), e.g. es`cape, esca`pade; `mountain, mountain`eer; `picture, pictur`esque; `usher, ushe`rette; `private, privati`zation.* Verbal -*ate* belongs here in disyllables, e.g. mi`grate.*

(3) *Accent-fixing suffixes*

(a) On final syllable of stem—here belong -*ic*, -*ion*, and -*ity*, e.g. `chaos, cha`otic; de`vote, de`votion; `curious, curi`osity.* In the case of -*ion* most words are formed from free-form disyllabic verbal stems accented on the second syllable and -*ion* could therefore equally well be regarded as accent-neutral; however, since the final syllable of the stem is almost unexceptionally accented in bound stems as well, e.g. com`plexion, o`ccasion,* it is better regarded as accent-fixing.

(b) On penultimate syllable of stem—the number in this category is small, the most important being verbal -*ate* in words of more than two syllables, most involving bound forms, e.g. in`augurate, exco`mmunicate, `operate.*

(c) On final or penultimate of root according to the weight of the final syllable—here belongs -*ative*, which is added to a similar set of bound forms as is -*ate* in (b) above, cf. `operative, `qualitative* vs. repre`sentative, argu`mentative.* Here are also -*ency* and adjectival -*al*, e.g. `presidency* but e`mergency, `pharynx, pha`ryngeal* but `medicine, me`dicinal.*

Besides those suffixes above which have been noted as preferring one pattern when suffixed to a free form and another pattern when suffixed to a bound form, there are others which vacillate freely between two patterns. A common suffix of this sort is -*able* which is in most cases accent-neutral, e.g. a`dore, a`dorable; com`panion, com`panionable; question, `questionable; `realize, `realizable; `reconcile, `reconcilable.* However, in a number of disyllabic stems with accent on the final syllable the accent may be shifted to the first syllable of the stem: `admirable, `applicable, `comparable, `despicable, `disputable, `lamentable, `preferable, `reputable, (ir-)`reparable.* But the general pressure from the accent-neutrality of -*able* may lead to alternative pronunciations of these words with the accent on the final syllable of the stem, e.g. ad`mirable, a`pplicable, com`parable, de`spicable, di`sputable,la`mentable, pre`ferable, re`putable, re`parable* etc. To add to the confusion there are some changes in the opposite direction, e.g. `demonstrate, de`monstrable; `extricate, (in-)ex`tricable; `realize, realizable; `reconcile, *recon`cilable* (all of which have an alternative form with initial accent). In most cases the form with the shifted accent (either right to left or left to right) is still the more acceptable pronunciation in RP.

10.3.3   Prefixes

Prefixes are generally accent-neutral, e.g. *de-, dis-, in-* (and various assimilated forms like *il-, im-, in-, ir-*), *mal-, mis-, pseudo-, re-, sub-*, and *un-*, e.g. *de`foliate, disin`genuous, inco`rrect, i`lliterate, imma`ture, i`rreverent, mal`function, misre`port, pseudoscien`tific, rede`sign, sub`standard, un`necessary*. In general, such prefixes result in a doubled consonant when the prefix-final and the stem-initial consonant are identical, e.g. *un`necessary* is pronounced with a double length [nː]. (This rule does not apply to in- and its variants, so, for example, *i`llogical* is pronounced with only a single /l/.)

10.3.4   Secondary Accent[3]

When words have more than one syllable before or after the main accent, a general rhythmical pattern is often apparent, there being a tendency to alternate more prominent and less prominent syllables. Syllables made prominent in this way will retain a full vowel; additionally syllables before the primary accent will often receive a secondary accent involving pitch change (see §10.2 (1) above). If there is only one syllable before the primary accent, this is usually unaccented e.g. *a`pply, con`cern, a`round, de`ceive* etc. If there are two syllables before the primary accent, the first will often receive a secondary accent, e.g. *`rhodo`dendron, `medi`eval, `repre`sent, `maga`zine*. Indeed, as indicated by pattern (3) under §10.3.1, primary accent shows a tendency to move to the position of the secondary accent, producing, for example, `*magazine*, in General American (see also alternating accent under §10.4). Where there are more than two syllables before the primary accent, a secondary accent will fall two or three syllables back according to the presence of a full vowel, e.g. *in`feri`ority, en`thusi`astically*, but *`circumlo`cution, `characte`ristically*. As in everything concerned with word accent in English, all of this section should be taken as indicating tendencies rather than rules that are without exception.

10.3.5   Compounds

COMPOUNDS are composed of more than one root morpheme but function grammatically and/or semantically as a single word. In most cases the two roots are free morphemes themselves: the largest type of exception to this concerns the PSEUDO-COMPOUNDS under (3) below. Compounds are grammatically unitary when the combination of the grammatical classes of the two elements would not

---

[3] See Fudge (1984: 31)

normally function as the type of constituent which the compound does, e.g. *daybreak* is composed of the noun *day* plus the verb *break* but such a combination noun–verb does not normally constitute a noun phrase functioning as the subject of a sentence as in *Daybreak comes early in summer*. A compound is semantically unitary because it has a meaning representing a specialized conjunction of the meanings of its two components, e.g. *glasshouse* is indeed loosely a type of house and is made of glass but the compound cannot be used to describe any sort of glass house. Compounds may be written as one word as with *daybreak* and *glasshouse*, or with a hyphen as in *clear-cut*, or with a space between the two elements, as in *working party*; there is no systematic practice in the choice among these three ways, although there is a tendency for compounds with primary accent on the first element to be written as one word or with a hyphen, and for those with the primary accent on the final element to be written as two words.

The primary accent in compounds is most commonly on the first element, e.g. ˈdaybreak, ˈglasshouse and in some cases this type of accentuation will distinguish the compound from a more productive phrasal pattern, e.g. glass ˈhouse (but note that a contrastive accent within the phrase will produce the same pattern as the compound, e.g. *This is a ˈbrick house, not a ˈglass house*). There are, however, many compounds (judged as such on grammatical or semantic criteria) which have the same pattern as phrases, e.g. clear-ˈcut. There are also often differences between the accentuation of compounds in RP and in General American, e.g. RP ˈshop ˈsteward, ˈhorse ˈchestnut, ˈstage ˈmanager, ˈseason ticket, compared with G.A. ˈshop steward, ˈhorse chestnut, ˈstage manager, ˈseason ˈticket. Where the primary accent is on the second element, a secondary accent is usual on the first element. Where the primary accent is on the first element, a full vowel is usually retained in the final element. In the following sections the principal types of compound are exemplified together with their usual accentual patterns.

(1) *Compounds functioning as nouns*—This is by far the most frequent type of compound (and accounts for approximately 90% of compounds). Three subtypes (a), (b), and (c) can be distinguished:

(a) ˈN(oun) + N(oun) (around 75% of compound nouns)—ˈalcohol abuse, ˈadrenaline tourism, ˈbank account, ˈbar code, ˈbirthplace, ˈblood-money, ˈbomb factory, ˈbottle bank, ˈbreadcrumbs, ˈcar boot sale, ˈchild abuse, comˈmunity charge, comˈpassion fatigue, comˈputer virus, ˈcontrol freak, ˈcrime rate, ˈdeckchair, ˈdrug addict, ˈenterprise culture, ˈfun run, ˈghetto blaster, ˈguidebook, ˈkeyboard, ˈlager lout, ˈlaptop, ˈlifestyle, ˈmatchbox, ˈmountain bike, ˈmuesli belt, ˈozone layer, ˈpeace dividend, poˈlice force, ˈpressure group, ˈracehorse, ˈshopping centre, ˈstock exchange, ˈphonecard, ˈtape measure, ˈtheme park, ˈtoilet roll, ˈtorture victim, ˈwheel clamp, ˈwheelie bin. Included here are examples involving nouns in final position formed from V(erb) +er, e.g. ˈbodyscanner, ˈbricklayer, ˈcash dispenser, ˈscrewdriver, ˈscreensaver.

Some general categories of exception to the accentual pattern of ˈN+N are:

(i) man-made items, e.g. apple ˈpie, banana ˈsplit, brick ˈwall, chocolate ˈbiscuit, clay ˈpigeon, cotton ˈwool (cf. ˈlambswool), dirt ˈroad (but cf. ˈfootpath), elderberry ˈwine, feather ˈpillow, fruit ˈsalad, knickerbocker ˈglory, rice ˈpudding.

(ii) where N1 is a name: *Christmas ˈpudding* (but CF *ˈChristmas cake*, because *cake* generally produces a pattern of *ˈN+N*, e.g. (*ˈEccles cake, ˈchocolate cake, ˈcheesecake*), *Fosbury ˈflop, Highland ˈfling, London ˈRoad* (*Road* always induces this pattern whereas *Street* induces *ˈN+N*, e.g. *ˈOxford Street*). *Mexican ˈwave, Molotov ˈcocktail, Neanderthal ˈman, Norfolk ˈterrier.* (Exceptions to this exceptional category are *Aleˈxander technique, ˈBaker day.*)

(iii) where both N1 and N2 are equally referential: *acid ˈrain, aromaˈtherapy, banner ˈheadline, barrier ˈreef, boy soˈprano, cauliflower ˈcheese, fridge-ˈfreezer, garden ˈsuburb, infant ˈprodigy, junk ˈfood.*

(iv) where N1 is a value, e.g. *100% ˈeffort, dollar ˈbill, fifty p.ˈcharge, pound ˈnote, tenpence ˈpiece.*

Some other, specific, exceptions to the *ˈN+N* pattern are: *bay ˈwindow* (and all involving *window* in final position), *Channel ˈferry, combine ˈharvester, county ˈcouncil, keyhole ˈsurgery, kitchen ˈsink, morning ˈpaper, office ˈparty, star ˈturn, trade ˈunion.*

(b) *ˈA(djective)+ N, ˈN's+N, ˈN+V, ˈV+N, ˈN+Ving, ˈVing+N*—*ˈbatting average, ˈboardsailing, ˈbridging loan, ˈbuilding society, ˈbull's eye, ˈchargecapping, ˈcrow's nest, ˈear-splitting, ˈeating apple, ˈfaintheart, ˈfly tipping, ˈhack saw, ˈhand bagging, ˈjob sharing, ˈjoy riding, ˈlandfill, ˈmind boggling, ˈpay cut, ˈpickpocket, ˈpoll capping, ˈsearchparty, ˈshop lifting, ˈskateboarding, ˈstatesperson, ˈwindsurfing.* (There are many exceptions, particularly in the case of Ving +N, e.g. *alternating ˈcurrent, black ˈeconomy, compact ˈdisc, flying ˈsaucer, insider ˈdealing, living ˈmemory.*) Compounds involving these patterns are much less productive than those under (a) above.

(c) Phrasal and prepositional verbs used as nouns—*ˈburn-out, ˈbuyout, ˈcock-up, ˈlay-offs, ˈmelt-down, ˈrave-in, ˈring-around, ˈset-up, ˈshowdown.* Note also *ˈbypass.*

(2) *Compounds functioning as adjectives and verbs*—These are much more limited in number than those under (1). They divide fairly evenly between those with initial accent and those with final accent:

(a) Adjectives—(i) with initial accent: *ˈbloodthirsty, ˈgobsmacked, ˈheadstrong, ˈhen-pecked, ˈladylike, ˈmoth-eaten, ˈseasick, ˈsell-by (date), ˈuse-by (date), ˈtrustworthy, ˈwaterproof, ˈworkshy.* Those compound adjectives where N is a special application of A generally take this pattern, e.g. *ˈcarefree, ˈlovesick*, as do those involving N+ past participle, e.g. *ˈbedridden, ˈsunlit, ˈtime-honoured, ˈweatherbeaten.*

(ii) with final accent: *deep-ˈseated, ham-ˈfisted, long-ˈwinded, rent-ˈfree, skin ˈdeep, sky ˈblue, stone ˈdead, tax ˈfree, tight-ˈknit, user-ˈfriendly.* Those compound adjectives where N modifies an A generally take this pattern, e.g. *dirt ˈcheap, stone-ˈdeaf*, as do sequences of A+V+ing, and A (or ADV) +A, e.g. *easy ˈgoing, high ˈflying, long ˈsuffering, overˈripe, overˈdue, redˈhot.*

(b) Verbs—The number of compounds functioning as verbs (if we exclude phrasal and prepositional verbs) is very small. They usually involve initial accent, e.g. *ˈbabysit, ˈbackbite, ˈbadmouth, ˈbrowbeat, ˈheadhunt, ˈsidestep, ˈsidetrack, ˈwheelclamp* (but *manˈhandle*), *ringˈfence.* The sequence ADVorPREP+V generally takes final accent, e.g. *back`fire, out`number, out`wit, over`sleep, under`go.*

(3) *Pseudo-compounds*—There are some complex words (often of Greek origin) made up of two bound forms which individually are like prefixes and suffixes and it is thus difficult to analyse words such as prefix plus root or root plus suffix, e.g. *`microwave, `telegram, `thermostat, an`tithesis, `circumflex, `fungicide, ka`leidoscope, `monochrome, `prototype.* Since they have no clear root, these sequences are here referred to as pseudo-compounds. From these examples it can be seen that, as with compounds generally, the primary accent usually falls on the first element (but not invariably, e.g. it falls on the second element of *homo`phobic, hypo`chondriac* (also *`cyberchondriac*)). The accentual pattern of compounds at the same time conforms to the root pattern in 10.3.1 (3b) above, with the accent on the penultimate or antepenultimate syllable even though there is commonly a strong final syllable. The accentual patterns of pseudo-compounds are affected by suffixes as if they were simple roots, thus *`telephone, tele`phonic, te`lephonist; `photograph, pho`tographer, photo`graphic.*

Finally, it should be pointed out that the dividing line between phrase and compound is often difficult to draw. It is particularly difficult in those cases where the sequence of word classes involves regular constituents of a phrase (and where the primary accent is kept on the second item) but where the collocation has become idiomatic, as, for example, in *ethnic `cleansing, global `warming, third `world*, where A and N are regular constituents of a noun phrase but where the sequence has acquired a specialized meaning.

10.4 *Word Accentual Instability*

The accentual patterns of words are liable to change. Considerable changes of this kind have taken place within the last 300 years, in addition to the large-scale accentual shifts affecting French importations in ME. Thus, in the seventeenth century, and still in American English, a secondary accent with a strong vowel fell on the penultimate syllables of words such as *necessary, adversary, momentary*; the earlier distinction between the noun *abuse* (with primary accent on the first syllable) and the verb *abuse* (with primary accent on the second syllable) has been lost although in this pair of words a distinction is maintained by the occurrence of /s/ or /z/ finally; we no longer place the primary accent on the second syllable of *revenue, illustrate, confiscate, character* etc., or on the first syllable of *humidity, convenient, prosperity* etc.

Hesitancy and variation of accentual pattern occurring at the present time are the result of rhythmic and analogical pressures, both of which entail in addition considerable changes of sound pattern in words.[4]

---

[4] These remarks apply mainly to RP and to the patterns of isolate words rather than those variants occurring in connected speech (see §12.3); they do not take into account patterns used in other dialects, e.g. in Scottish English, *enquiry* /ˈenkwɪrɪ/, *realize* /rɪəˈlaɪz/, *advertisement* /ˈædvərˈtaɪzmənt/. For informant tests concerning the preferred variants see Wells (2000). Where there is a preferred 'correct' pattern in RP, it is marked here with * in the transcription

(1) *Rhythmic changes*—In some words containing more than two syllables there appears to be a tendency to avoid a succession of weak syllables, especially if these have /ə/ or /ɪ/. Thus, in words of three syllables, there is variation between [ˋ--] and [-ˋ-] patterns, e.g. *exquisite* /ˈekskwɪzɪt/ or */ɪksˈkwɪzɪt/, *deficit* /ˈdefɪsɪt/* or /dɪˈfɪsɪt/, *integral* /ˈɪntɪɡrəl/* or /ɪnˈteɡrəl/, *mischievous* /ˈmɪʃtʃɪvəs/* or /mɪʃˈtʃiːvəs/ (or even /mɪʃˈtʃiːvɪəs/), *inculcate* /ˈɪŋkʌlkeɪt/* or /ɪŋˈkʌlkeɪt/, *acumen* /ˈækjʊmen/* or /əˈkjuːmen/, *kilometre* /ˈkɪlɒmɪtə/ or /kɪˈlɒmɪtə/*, sonorous* /ˈsɒnərəs/* or /səˈnɔːrəs/, *precedence* /ˈpresɪdns/* or /prɪˈsiːdns/, *importune* /ɪmˈpɔːtʃuːn/ or /ɪmpəˈtjuːn/*, premature* /ˈpremətʃə/* or /premeˈtjʊə/, *inventory* /ˈɪnvəntərɪ/* or /ɪnˈventərɪ/.

Similarly, in words of four syllables, there is variation between first and second syllable accenting, e.g. *controversy* /ˈkɒntrəvɜːsɪ/ or /kənˈtrɒvəsɪ/*, hospitable* /ˈhɒspɪtəbl/* or /hɒˈspɪtəbl/, *despicable* /dɪˈspɪkəbl/* or /ˈdespɪkəbl/, *formidable* /fəˈmɪdəbl/* or /ˈfɔːmɪdəbl/, *capitalist* /ˈkæpɪtəlɪst/* or /kəˈpɪtəlɪst/, *aristocrat* /ˈærɪstəkræt/* or /əˈrɪstəkræt/; variation in second and third syllable accenting in words such as *centrifugal* /senˈtrɪfjʊɡl/ or /sentrɪˈfjuːɡl/*, metallurgy* /məˈtælədʒɪ/* or /ˈmetalɜːdʒɪ/. Television now has the pattern /ˈtelɪvɪʒn̩/* predominantly, the variant /telɪˈvɪʒn̩/ being less common.

Longer words, too, often exhibit a tendency towards the alternation of accented and unaccented syllables with various rhythmic patterns, e.g. *tuberculosis* /ˈtjuːbəkjʊˈləʊsɪs/* or /tjʊˈbɜːkjʊˈləʊsɪs/, *articulatory* /ɑːˈtɪkjʊlətrɪ/* or /ˈɑːtɪkjʊˈleɪtərɪ/, *Caribbean* /kəˈrɪbɪən/* or /kærɪˈbiːən/, *necessarily* /ˈneseserɪlɪ/ or /neseˈserɪlɪ/, *inexplicable* /ˈɪnɪkˈsplɪkəbl/* or /ɪnˈeksplɪkəbl/.

Primary accent is also unstable in some compounds, e.g. *camp-fire, lacklustre, life-size, man-handle, overcast.* However, the number of truly unstable compounds is relatively small, although many may be subject to the accentual shift described in §12.3, e.g. *afterˈnoon* but *ˈafternoonˈtea.* Many others may vary in their accentual pattern between RP and General American, e.g. *Adam's ˈapple* (RP) vs *ˈAdam's apple* (GA), *peanut ˈbutter* (RP) vs *ˈpeanut butter* (GA), *shop ˈsteward* (RP) vs *ˈshop steward* (GA), *stage ˈmanager* (RP) vs *ˈstage manager* (GA), *vocal ˈcords* (RP) vs *ˈvocal cords* (GA), *ˈseason ticket* (RP) vs *season ˈticket* (GA). As can be seen, most of these involve a shift from final accent in RP to initial accent in GA.

(2) *Analogical changes*—It sometimes happens that a word's accentual pattern is influenced not only by rhythmic pressure but also by the accentual structure of a related word of frequent occurrence. Thus, the analogy of the root forms *apply* /əˈplaɪ/, *prefer* /prɪˈfɜː/, *compare* /kəmˈpeə/, is responsible for the realization of *applicable, preferable, comparable,* as /əˈplɪkəbl*, prɪˈfɜːrəbl, kəmˈpeərəbl/ instead of /ˈæplɪkəbl, ˈpref(ə)rəbl*, ˈkɒmp(ə)rəbl*/. Again, the existence of *contribution, distribution* /kɒntrɪˈbjuːʃn, dɪstrɪˈbjuːʃn/ may account for the pronunciation /ˈkɒntrɪbjuːt, ˈdɪstrɪbjuːt/ (*contribute, distribute*) instead of the more usual /kənˈtrɪbjuːt*, dɪsˈtrɪbjuːt*/, where the first syllable is totally weakened and the last retains only a certain qualitative prominence. The case of a word such as *dispute* (n.), for which /dɪˈspjuːt/* is now more common than /ˈdɪspjuːt/, illustrates an accenting of the noun by analogy with the related verb (see the stressing of pairs of disyllabic nouns and verbs in the following section).

10.5 *Distinctive Word Accentual Patterns*

The accentual pattern of a word establishes the relationship of its parts; it may also have a distinctive function in that it opposes words of comparable sound structure (and identical spelling). Such word oppositions (for the most part disyllables of French origin) may or may not involve phonemic changes of quality.

(1) A relatively small number[5] of pairs of noun and verb may differ only in the location of the primary accent, this falling on the first syllable in the nouns and on the second in the verbs. In most cases (though not all) the differing accentual patterns for nouns and verbs can be related to the accentual tendencies of roots given under §10.3.1. Some speakers may reduce the vowel in the first syllable of the verbs to /ə/:

	Noun	*Verb*
accent	/ˈæksent/ or /ˈæksnt/	/ækˈsent/ or /əkˈsent/
digest	/ˈdaɪdʒest/	/daɪˈdʒest/ or /dɪˈdʒest/
torment	/ˈtɔːment/	/tɔːˈment/
transfer[6]	/ˈtrænsfɜː/	/ˈtrænsˈfɜː/ or /trənsˈfɜː/
transport[6]	/ˈtrænspɔːt/	/trænˈspɔːt/ or /trənˈspɔːt/

(2) In a somewhat larger number of pairs the occurrence of /ə/ or /ɪ/ in the first syllable of the verb is more regular (although the full vowel may be kept in some dialects outside RP, in particular in northern England). In a few cases there may be a reduction of the vowel in the second element of the noun:

	Noun/Adjective	*Verb*
combine	/ˈkɒmbaɪn/	/kəmˈbaɪn/
compress	/ˈkɒmpres/	/kəmˈpres/
concert	/ˈkɒnsət/	/kənˈsɜːt/
conduct	/ˈkɒndʌkt/	/kənˈdʌkt/
consort	/ˈkɒnsɔːt/	/kənˈsɔːt/
contract	/ˈkɒntrækt/	/kənˈtrækt/
contrast	/ˈkɒntrɑːst/	/kənˈtrɑːst/
convict	/ˈkɒnvɪkt/	/kənˈvɪkt/
desert	/ˈdezət/	/dɪˈzɜːt/
export	/ˈekspɔːt/	/ɪkˈspɔːt/
object	/ˈɒbdʒɪkt/	/əbˈdʒekt/
*perfect**	/ˈpɜːfɪkt/	/pəˈfekt/
*permit**	/ˈpɜːmɪt/	/pəˈmɪt/
present	/ˈpreznt/	/prɪˈzent/
proceeds	/ˈprəʊsiːdz/	/prəˈsiːdz/
produce	/ˈprɒdʒuːs/	/prəˈdʒuːs/
progress	/ˈprəʊgres/	/prəˈgres/

---

[5] The small number of disyllables involved in such accentual oppositions is shown in Guierre (1979). Out of a corpus of more than 10,000 disyllabic words, only 85 exhibited changes between verbal, nominal, or adjectival functions by means of a shift of accented syllable

[6] Also with /trɑːns-/

project	/ˈprɒdʒekt/	/prəˈdʒekt/
protest	/ˈprəʊtest/	/prəˈtest/
rebel	/ˈrebl/	/rɪˈbel/
record	/ˈrekɔːd/	/rɪˈkɔːd/
refuse	/ˈrefjuːs/	/rɪˈfjuːz/[7]
segment	/ˈsegmənt/	/segˈment/
subject	/ˈsʌbdʒɪkt/	/səbˈdʒekt/
*survey**	/ˈsɜːveɪ/	/səˈveɪ/

(* In these words, the opposition of /ɜː/ and /ə/ in the first syllable amounts to an opposition of vowel quantity; it is to be noted that the verb to *survey* may have the same accentual pattern as the noun in the particular sense of 'to carry out a survey'.)

Several disyllables do not conform to the general noun/verb accentual pattern distinction or exhibit instability, e.g. *comment* /ˈkɒment/ for both noun and verb; *contact* /ˈkɒntækt/ (n.) and /ˈkɒntækt/, /kɒnˈtækt/ or /kənˈtækt/ (v.); *detail* /ˈdiːteɪl/ (n.) and /ˈdiːteɪl/ or /diːˈteɪl/ (v.); *contrast* has a verbal form /ˈkɒntrɑːst/ in addition to the more usual form given above. In all these cases, and in that of *dispute*, already mentioned, the noun form is tending to supersede the verbal pattern.

Some words containing more than two syllables also exhibit distinctive accentual patterns (in some cases the distinction lies only in the reduced or full vowel in the last syllable):

	Noun/Adjective	*Verb*
associate	/əˈsəʊsjət, -sɪət, -ʃət/	/əˈsəʊsɪeɪt, əˈsəʊʃɪeɪt/
attribute	/ˈætrɪbjuːt/	/əˈtrɪbjuːt/
envelope	/ˈenvələʊp/	/ɪnˈveləp/
reprimand	/ˈreprɪmɑːnd/	/reprɪˈmɑːnd/
interchange	/ˈɪntətʃeɪndʒ/	/ɪntəˈtʃeɪndʒ/
compliment	/ˈkɒmplɪmənt/	/kɒmplɪˈment/ /ˈkɒmplɪment/
supplement	/ˈsʌplɪmənt/	/sʌplɪˈment/ /ˈsʌplɪment/
estimate	/ˈestɪmət/	/ˈestɪmeɪt/
prophesy	/ˈprɒfəsɪ/	/ˈprɒfɪsaɪ/

A small number of adjectives and verbs show a similar relationship in accentual pattern (again with some pairs having only a difference in the last full or reduced vowel):

	Adjective	*Verb*
abstract	/ˈæbstrækt/	/æbˈstrækt/
absent	/ˈæbsənt/	/æbˈsent/
frequent	/ˈfriːkwənt/	/friːˈkwent/
alternate	/ɔːlˈtɜːnət/	/ˈɔːltəneɪt/
intimate	/ˈɪntɪmət/	/ˈɪntɪmeɪt/
separate	/ˈsepərət/	/ˈsepəreɪt/

---

[7] The noun and verb forms of *refuse* differ also in the final consonant and the resulting variation of vowel length of /uː/

There is alternation between noun and adjective between *compact* /ˈkɒmpækt/ (n.) and compact /kəmˈpækt/ (adj.) and between *minute* (n.)/ˈmɪnɪt/ and *minute* /maɪnˈjuːt/ (adj.).

10.6   *Acquisition of Word Accent by Native Learners*

Little is known in detail about the children's acquisition of word accent. This area appears in general not to be a problem for native learners and, because of the complexities involved, it must be assumed that the accentual patterns of words are learnt individually as they are heard (unlike most foreign learners, young children hear rather than see such new words). This may even apply to morphologically complex words. Children therefore generally place the primary accent on the correct syllable of words. However, they frequently omit unaccented syllables before the primary accent, e.g. *banana* [ˈnɑːnə], *guitar* [tɑː], *elastic* [ˈlætɪ], or, alternatively, all such syllables may be reduced to a single shape, e.g. [rɪˈnɑːnə], [rɪˈtɑː], [rɪˈlætɪ].

10.7   *Advice to Foreign Learners*

Many learners come from language backgrounds where word accent is regular, on the first syllable in Finnish and German, on the penultimate syllable in Polish and Spanish, and on the final syllable in French and Turkish. But in English there is no such regular pattern and the differing accentual patterns of words are as important to their recognition as is the sequence of phonemes.

Although the accentual patterns are not as regular as in many other languages, there are nevertheless tendencies and the foreign learner can definitely be helped by learning some of these tendencies. In particular, he should pay attention to the influence of suffixes on the placement of primary accent (§10.3.2), noting whether the suffix leaves the accent on the stem unchanged (as with the inflexional suffixes, with adjectival *-y*, with adverbial *-ly* and with *-er*, and *-ish*), whether it takes the accent itself (as with *-ation*) or whether it moves the accent on the stem (as with *-ate* and *-ity*).

Learners should also pay particular attention to the role of accentual contrast in those cases where word classes are distinguished by a shift of accent (§10.5), at the same time making appropriate reduction of unaccented vowels. They should not, however, extend such variation of accentual patterns indiscriminately to all disyllables, e.g. *report, delay, select, reserve, account* etc., have the same pattern in both verb and noun/adjective functions.

10.8   *Elision and Epenthesis*

Since OE, it has always been a feature of the structure of English words that the weakly accented syllables have undergone a process of reduction, including loss of phonemes or of vowels (see also §§8.8.12, 8.8.13). The same process of reduction, with resultant contraction, may be observed in operation in PresE. It is important, however, to distinguish between cases of elision which have been established in the language for some time (although the spelling may still reflect an earlier, fuller form) and those which have become current only recently. In these latter cases, the forms exhibiting elision are typical of rapid, colloquial speech, whereas more formal speech tends to retain the fuller form under the preservative influence of the spelling. The examples of elided word forms in colloquial speech which are given below are independent of the type of reduction affecting particular words and syllables under weak accent in connected speech (see §12.4.6). They are also to be distinguished from reduced forms in various types of regional and popular speech, which are often regarded as vulgar, e.g. *recognize* as /ˈrekənaɪz/, *satisfactory* as /sæsˈfæktrɪ/, *cigarette* as /sɪˈgret/, *possible* as /ˈpɒsbl/, *Waterloo* as /wɔːˈluː/, *lovely* as /ˈlʌlɪ/ etc.

(1) *Vowel Elision*[8]

(a) *Established*—Loss of vowels under weak accent within the word has occurred at various stages of the language's development and is now, for example, established: initially in, *state, scholar, sample*; medially in, *Gloucester, marriage, evening, chimney, curtsey, forecastle* /ˈfəʊksl/, *gooseberry*; and in the final syllable in *time, name, loved, hands* (< handes), *eaten, written, cousin*.

(b) *Present colloquial*—In PresE such elision is likely to take place especially in a sequence of unaccented syllables, where /ə/ and /ɪ/ are involved. Thus, in positions after the primary accent, particularly in the sequence consonant +/ə/+/r/+ weak vowel, the /ə/ between the C and the /r/ is regularly lost, e.g. in *preferable* /prefrəbl/; similar reductions occur in *repertory, temperature, comparable, territory, lavatory, temporary* /ˈtemprərɪ/, *anniversary, vicarage, category, factory, robbery, labour-exchange* /ˈleɪbrɪkstʃeɪnʒ/, *murderer* /ˈmɜːdrə/, *customary, camera, honourable, scullery, suffering, beverage, rhinoceros, nursery, Nazareth, fisheries, treasury, natural* /ˈnætʃrəl/, *dangerous, utterance, history, ordinary*. Though labelled here as 'colloquial' these elisions may occur regularly within the speech of an individual, the fuller version not forming a part of his idiolect. A more recent development[9] concerns the sequence /r/+ weak vowel + C, in which the weak vowel may be elided, leaving a pre-consonantal (possibly syllabic) /r/ (even though /r/ does not normally occur before a consonant in RP), e.g. *barracking* /ˈbærkɪŋ/, *Dorothy* /ˈdɒrθɪ/, *pterodactyl* /terˈdæktɪl/.

In the same way, there may be an elision of a weak vowel following a consonant and preceding /l/, or the reduction of syllabic [l̩] to syllable-marginal /l/, in *grappling, doubling, fatalist, paddling, bachelor, specialist, usually, insolent, easily, carefully, buffalo, novelist, family, panelling, chancellor* etc. Note, too, frequent loss of post-primary /ə/ or /ɪ/ in *university* /juːnɪˈvɜːstɪ/, *probably* /ˈprɒbblɪ/, *difficult* /ˈdɪfklt/, *national* /ˈnæʃnl/, *fashionable* /ˈfæʃnəbl/, *reasonably* /ˈriːznəblɪ/, *parliament* /ˈpɑːlmənt/, *government* /ˈgʌvmənt/. A similar process may apply with the loss of syllabicity in the present participles of verbs such as *flavour, lighten,* and *thicken* where the /ə/ may be elided or the syllabic consonant [n̩] replaced by a non-syllabic consonant marginal to the syllable. Thus /ˈfleɪvrɪŋ/, /ˈlaɪtnɪŋ/, and

---

[8] For absorption of the second element of a diphthong before another vowel (smoothing), see §8.11

[9] Windsor Lewis (1979)

/ˈθɪknɪŋ/ in place of /ˈfleɪvərɪŋ/, /ˈlaɪtənɪŋ/, and /ˈθɪkənɪŋ/, respectively. It may be noted that some speakers make a regular distinction between the participle with three syllables and the noun of two syllables exhibiting elision, e.g. *lightning* /ˈlaɪtnɪŋ/ and *lightening* /ˈlaɪtənɪŋ/.

In pre-primary positions, /ə/ or /ɪ/ of the weak syllable preceding the primary accent is apt to be lost in very rapid speech, especially when the syllable with primary accent has initial /l/ or /r/,[10] e.g. *police, Palladium, parade, terrific, correct, collision, believe, balloon, barometer, direction, delightful, gorilla, ferocious, philology, veranda, voluptuous, saloon, solicitor, syringe, charade* etc; also, with a continuant consonant preceding and a consonant other than /l/ or /r/ following, in *phonetics, photography, thermometer, supporter, suppose, satirical, circumference* etc. Note, too, the elision of /ə/ in *perhaps* /pˈhæps/ and of /ɪ/ in *geometry* /ˈdʒɒmətrɪ/, *geography* /ˈdʒɒɡrəfɪ/.

(2) *Consonant Elision*

(a) *Established*—Apart from such consonants as have been lost through vocalization, e.g. OE *hlaford* > *lord*, OE *wealcan* > *walk* /wɔːk/, or have lost allophones in certain situations, e.g. /h/=[x,ç] in *brought, night*, the reduction of many consonant clusters has long been established, e.g. initial /wr,kn,gn,hl,hr,hn/ in, *write, know, gnaw, loaf, ring, nut*; medial /t/+/n/ or /l/ in, *fasten, listen, often, thistle, castle*; and final /mb,mn/ in *lamb, hymn* etc.

(b) *Present colloquial*—In PresE simplification of clusters continues to take place, especially involving the loss of the alveolars /t,d/ when medial in a cluster of three consonants. In the following examples, retention of the alveolar plosives is characteristic of careful speech: *exactly, facts, mostly, handsome, windmill, handbag, wristwatch, friendship, kindness, landlord, lastly, restless, landscape, Westminster, coastguard, dustman, perfectly* (and more rarely /t/ in words such as *attempts, prompts*). /θ/ is normally elided from *asthma* and *isthmus* and may sometimes be omitted from *months, twelfths, fifths, clothes*; and in rapid speech elision of /k/ in *asked* and /l/ in *only* may occur. [ɫ] is apt to be lost when preceded by /ɔː/ (which has a resonance similar to that of [ɫ]), e.g. *always* /ˈɔːwɪz/, *already* /ɔːˈredɪ/, *although* /ɔːˈðəʊ/, *all right* /ɔːˈraɪt/, *almanac* /ˈɔːmənæk/ (cf. established loss of [ɫ] in *walk, talk* etc.).

/p/ may be lost in clusters where its position is homorganic with that of an epenthetic plosive e.g. *glimpse* /ɡlɪms/. Elision is much less likely to occur in the sequence /ŋks/ in *inks*.

Whole syllables may be elided in rapid speech, especially in the vicinity of /r/ or where there is a sequence of [r] sounds, *library* /ˈlaɪbrɪ/, *February* /ˈfebrɪ/, *literary* /ˈlɪtrɪ/, *meteorological* /miːtrəˈlɒdʒɪkl/.

(3) *Epenthesis*[11]—The elision of /t/ in words like *vents* sometimes leads to the opposite tendency to insert an epenthetic /t/ in words like *dance, fence, sense, bounce* etc., so that *tents* and *tense* may sound the same as either /tens/ or /tents/.

---

[10] Such elisions in word-initial syllables are more likely when the preceding word, belonging to the same group, ends in a vowel, e.g. *the police* /ðə ˈpliːs/, *I believe* /aɪ ˈbliːv/, but *local police* /ˈləʊklpəˈliːs/, *can't believe* /ˈkɑːm bəˈliːv/

[11] See Fourakis and Port (1986) and Blankenship (1992)

Epenthetic /t/ may also occur before /θ,ʃ/ as in *anthem* /æn(t)θəm/, *pension* /pen(t)ʃən/, (but in the latter there is no coalescence to /tʃ/). Such alternation does not apply in RP following /l/, so that *else* and *melts* have distinct final clusters.

While epenthetic /t/ occurs between an /n/ and /θ,s,ʃ/, similarly, an epenthetic /p/ or /k/ may occur between an /m,ŋ/ and a following fricative, as in *triumphs* /traɪʌm(p)fs/, *warmth* /wɔːm(p)θ/, *confuse* /kəm(p)fuːz/, *Kingston* /kɪŋ(k)stən/.

Epenthesis is less common before a voiced fricative, as in *wins* being pronounced the same as *winds* /wɪn(d)z/ and in *lambs* /læm(b)z/, *rings* /rɪŋ(g)z/. If there is epenthesis in *king-size*, note that it is a /g/ that is inserted, i.e. /kɪŋ(g)saɪz/, suggesting that *king* has a different base form from *Kingston* /kɪŋ(k)stən/.

10.9   *Variability in the Phonemic Structure of Words*

In connected speech, English words exhibit variations of accentual pattern and changes of a phonemic or phonetic kind, involving assimilation and elision, especially at word boundaries (see Chapter 12). There is also often a remarkable latitude in the choice of phonemes used in words when said in isolation by RP speakers. Even with the exclusion of cases of differing phonemic inventories— e.g. the choice between using /hw/ or /w/ for *wh* words or /ɔː/ or /ɔə/ in words of the *bore* type—there remains a high degree of variability within the same variety of pronunciation. The permissible variations concern mainly vowels but cases of a choice of consonant also occur. The following are examples:

(1) *Vowels*

/iː/–/ɪ/ acetylene, economy; –/e/ economics, premature; –/eɪ/ deity, detour; –/aɪ/ Argentine, iodine

/ɪ/–/e/ alphabet, orchestra; –/aɪ/ privacy, dynasty; –/eɪ/ magistrate, holiday; –/ə/ believe, system, adequate

/e/–/eɪ/ again, maintain; –/ə/ accent, emblem

/æ/–/ɑː/ graph, translate; –/eɪ/ patriot, amoral; –/eə/ larynx, pharynx; –/ə/ agnostic, vapidity

/ʌ/–/ɒ/ constable, combat; –/ə/ bankrupt, dandruff

/ɒ/–/ɔː/ salt, wrath, Australia; –/ə/ obscure, obligatory

/ɔː/–/ʊə/ sure, poor

/ʊ/–/uː/ room, groom

/uː/–/juː/ suit, supreme, allusion

/eɪ/–/ɑː/ data, esplanade

/əʊ/–/ə/ allocate, phonetics

(2) *Consonants*

/t/–/tj/–/tʃ/ amateur

/tj/–/tʃ/ actual, Christian

/dj/–/dʒ/ educate, grandeur

/dʒ/–/ʒ/ garage

/g/–/dʒ/ pedagogic

/ntʃ/–/nʃ/ French, branch

/ndʒ/–/nʒ/ revenge, strange

/k/–/kw/ quoit
/ŋk/–/ŋ/ anxious
/ŋg/–/ŋ/ English
/sj/–/sɪ/–/ʃɪ/ associate; /sj/–/ʃ/ issue, sexual
/zj/–/ʒ/ usual, azure
/ʃ/–/ʒ/ Asia
/s/–/z/ usage, unison; /f/–/p/ diphthong, naphtha

10.10 *Phonotactics*

English does not exploit, in the word and the syllable, all the possible combinations of its phonemes. For instance, long vowels and diphthongs do not precede final /ŋ/;[12] /e,æ,ʌ,ɒ/ do not occur finally; and the types of consonant cluster permitted are subject to constraints in both initial and final positions. Initially, /ŋ/ does not occur; no combinations are possible with /tʃ,dʒ,ð,z/; /r,j,w/ can occur in clusters only as the non-initial element; initial sequences such as /fs,mh,stl,spw/ etc. are unknown. Finally, only /l/ may occur before non-syllabic /m,n/; /h,r,j,w/ do not occur in the type of phonemic analysis here used (see §8.5); and terminal sequences such as /kf,ʃp,lð,ʒbd/ etc. are unknown.

Although the general pattern of word-initial and word-final phoneme sequences is plain, there are certain problems:

(1) Some sequences are exemplified only by single words which are themselves of rare occurrence, e.g. /smj-/ *smew*, /gj-/ *gules*. Such sequences are generally included in the statements of potential clusters given under §10.10.1.

(2) Some sequences are exemplified only by their use in certain proper names, e.g. /gw-/ *Gwen* (and various other names of Welsh origin). Again, such sequences are generally included.

(3) Some sequences are exemplified only in recently imported foreign words, often themselves proper names, e.g. a number of words, including *schnapps* and *Schweppes*, involving initial clusters beginning with /ʃ/. If such words are judged to be in common use, the clusters they exemplify are included in the statements in §10.10.1.

(4) Sometimes a word or a group of words have more than one accepted pronunciation, one of which provides a unique sequence of phonemes. Thus *width, breadth, hundredth* have variants with /tθ/ or /dθ/; only the more common /tθ/ is included in §10.10.1, since /dθ/ is the less common pronunciation, and /tθ/ follows a common pattern whereby all final clusters involving plosives, fricatives and affricates are either wholly voiceless or wholly voiced. Words like *French, range* can be pronounced with /ntʃ,ndʒ/ or /ʃ,ʒ/; again, since the former is more common, the possibility of the latter is excluded. On the other hand, though many speakers do not distinguish the final clusters of *prince* and *prints* (see §10.6 above), the possibility is sufficiently widespread for both /-ns/ and /-nts/ to be considered as possible final clusters.

---

[12] It should be noted that such combinations do occur as a result of assimilation, see §12.4.5

(5) An attempt to include sequences of consonant plus syllabic nasal or lateral would unnecessarily complicate the statement of word-final clusters; such sequences are therefore taken as a variant of /ə/ plus nasal or lateral.

(6) The greater complexity of final consonant clusters is largely accounted for by the fact that final /t,d,s,z/ frequently represent a suffixed morpheme (e.g. possessive <-s>, or past tense <-ed>). However, because there are a few monomorphemic words like *axe* /æks/, *text* /tekst/, the statement of word-final clustering possibilities would not be significantly simplified by excluding such suffixes. It would, however, be simplified if /t,d,s,z,θ/ were treated as appendices or 'extrametrical' to the basic syllable structure (particularly since the sonority hierarchy is often violated—see §5.5.1–5.5.3). Such treatment of /s/ as an appendix could be extended to its occurrence in word-initial position, which would eliminate all three-member clusters in that position.

10.10.1   Word-Initial and Word-Final Phoneme Sequences

(1) *V*—The following ten vowels constitute monosyllabic words

/iː/ the letter <e>, /ə/ *a*, /ɑː/ *are*, /ɔː/ *or*, /ɜː/ *err*
/eɪ/ the name of the letter <a>
/aɪ/ the name of the letter <i>, /əʊ/ *owe*, /ɪə/ *ear*, /eə/ *air*.

In addition, /iː/ and /uː/ occur as reduced forms for *he* and *who*, and /ɔɪ/ may occur in the exclamation *Oy!*

(2) *Initial V*—All vowels occur initially. /ʊ/ and /ʊə/ occur only in foreign proper names such as *Uppsala*, /ʊpˈsɑːlə/ and *Urdu* /ˈʊːəduː/.

(3) *Initial CV*—/ŋ/ does not occur initially. /ʒ/ occurs initially before /ɪ/, /iː/, /æ/ /ɒ/, and /ɑː/ in foreign words such as *gigolo, gigue, Zhivago, jabot, genre, gite,* and *gendarme.* The other consonants generally occur before all vowels, though marked deficiencies are evident before /ʊə,ʊ,ɔɪ/.

(4) *Initial CCV*

(a) Initial CC clusters pattern as follows:

```
p  +  l,  r,  j
t  +      r,  j,  w
k  +  l,  r,  j,  w
b  +  l,  r,  j
d  +      r,  j,  w
g  +  l,  r,  j,  w
m  +          j,
n  +          j
l  +          j
f  +  l,  r,  j
v  +  l,  r,  j
θ  +      r,  j,  w
s  +  l,  r,  j,  w, p,  t,  k,  m, n,  f,  v
ʃ  +  l,  r,      w,              m, n
h  +          j
```

(b) /mj/ occurs in *muesli*, /vl-/ and /vr-/ in *Vladivostok* and *vroom*, /sr-/ and /sv-/ in *Sri Lanka* and *svelte*, and /ʃl-/, /ʃw-/, /ʃm-/, and /ʃn-/ in a number of imports from German and Yiddish, e.g. *Schlesinger, Schweppes, schmalz*, and *schnapps*. /Cj/ occurs only before /uː/ or /ʊə/ or occasionally /ʊ/. Initial /tw,dw,gw/ occur only before only a restricted set of vowels; /hw/ is excluded as an initial RP sequence, /hw/ in other dialects generally corresponding to /w/ in RP.

(5) *Initial CCCV*

(a) Initial CCC clusters pattern as follows:

```
s  +  p  +  l,  r,  j
s  +  t  +      r,  j
s  +  k  +  l,  r,  j,  w
```

(b) /s/ is the essential first element of CCC clusters; the second element is a voiceless stop; the third element must be one of /l,r,j,w/. Of the 12 potential CCC sequences /spw-, stl-, stw-/ do not occur. /CCj/ occurs only before /uː/ or /ʊə/; /skl-/ occurs only before /ə/, though the item *sclerosis* admits the variants /skle-, sklɪ-, sklɪə-/.

(c) The name of the bird *smew* provides a single example of the initial sequence /smj-/.

(6) *Final-V*—All vowels except /e,æ,ʌ,ɒ/ occur finally. /ʊ/ may occur word-finally in *to* before a word beginning with a vowel or in pre-pausal position (as well as in certain pronunciations of words like *statue*). No short vowels occur in accented open syllables.

(7) *Final VC*—/r,h,j,w/ do not occur finally in the present phonemic analysis of RP (see note to §8.2). /ʒ/ occurs finally only after /iː,ɑː,uː,eɪ/ in words of recent French origin, like *liege, camouflage, rouge*, and *beige*. /ŋ/ occurs only after /ɪ,æ,ʌ,ɒ/.

(8) *Final VCC*

(a) Final CC clusters pattern as follows:

```
p  +    t,                              θ, s
t  +                                    θ, s
k  +    t,                                 s
b  +                   d,                     z
d  +                                          z
g  +                   d,                     z
tʃ +    t
dʒ +                   d
m  +  p,               d,        f,   θ,     z
n  +    t,             d, tʃ, dʒ,     θ, s, z
ŋ  +         k,        d,                     z
l  + p, t,  k, b,  d, tʃ, dʒ, m, n, f, v, θ, s, z, ʃ
f  +    t,                              θ, s
v  +                   d,                     z
θ  +    t,                                 s
```

ð	+		d,		z
s	+	p, t, k			
z	+		d		
ʃ	+	t			
ʒ	+		d		

(b) Final CC clusters can be divided into two groups:

(i) Nasal, lateral, or /s/ plus another consonant, e.g. *jump, bend, dent, think* /θɪŋk/, *quilt, whist, cask, cusp*;

(ii) A consonant plus one of the apicals /t,d,s,z,θ/. The majority of such clusters arise from non-syllabic suffixation of past tense /t,d/; from possessive, plural, or third-person singular present tense /s,z/; or from ordinal or noun-forming /θ/ or noun-forming /t/, e.g. *laughed, behaved, dog's* or *dogs, cat's* or *cats, leads, hits, fifth, depth, product*. There are a few monomorphemic words of this sort, e.g. *act, axe, adze, lapse, corpse*.

(c) In the present analysis of RP /r,h,j,w/ do not combine with other consonants in final positions. (/r/ occurs in such positions in General American); and if the diphthongs /eɪ,aɪ,ɔɪ,əʊ,aʊ/ were analyzed as sequences /ej,aj,ɔj,əw,aw/ then /j,w/ would be said to occur in such positions (see §8.5). /g,ŋ/ do not occupy final position in a final CC cluster. /θ/ is of limited occurrence in this position: /-pθ/ occurs only after /e/, /-mθ/ only after /ɔː/ and /fθ/ only after /ɪ/. /-ln/ occurs only after /ɪ/ and /lʃ/ only after /e/. Only /dz/ occurs after all vowels; /-nz, -lz/ occur after all but two vowels. All other CC clusters show considerable restrictions in their ability to combine with preceding vowels.

(9) *Final VCCC*

(a) Final VCCC clusters pattern as follows:

(i) Final /t/ preceded by one of the following sequences:

p	+	s	
t	+	s	
k	+	s	
d	+	s	
m	+		p
n	+	s,	tʃ
ŋ	+	s,	k
l	+	s, p, k, tʃ	
s	+		p, k

(ii) Final /d/ preceded by one of the following sequences:

n	+	dʒ,	z
l	+	dʒ, m, v	

(iii) Final /s/ preceded by one of the following sequences:

p	+	t,	θ
t	+		θ
k	+	t	

```
m +  p,      f
n +     t,      θ
ŋ +        k
l  + p, t,  k, f,  θ
f  +     t,      θ
s  + p, t,  k
```

(iv) Final /z/ preceded by one of the following sequences:

```
n + d
l  + b, d, m, n, v
```

(v) Final /θ/ preceded by one of the following sequences:

```
k +              s
n + t
ŋ +        k
l  +        f
```

(b) Final CCC clusters can be divided into two groups:

(i) Those which involve a combination of the two types of CC clusters, i.e. /m,n,ŋ,l,s/ plus C plus /t,d,s,z,θ/. These nearly all involve suffixes, e.g. *jumps, cults, lists,* but there are a few monomorphemic words, e.g. *mulct, calx.*

(ii) Those which involve the double application of /t,d,s,z,θ/; the majority again involve suffixes, e.g. *fifths* /fɪfθs/, *products* /ˈprɒdʌkts/, *acts* /ækts/ (but these are all commonly reduced to /fɪfs/, /ˈprɒdʌks/, /æks/), but there are two common monomorphemic words, *text* and *next* pronounced /tekst/, /nekst/ when are not reduced, but they are also commonly reduced to /teks/ and /neks/.

(c) CCC clusters predominantly follow short vowels. Eleven of the 49 CCC final clusters occur after only one vowel (five after /ɪ/, four after /e/, one after /ʌ/, one after /ə/).

(10) *Final VCCCC*—Final CCCC clusters occur only rarely, as a result of the suffixation to CCC of a /t/ or /s/ morpheme, e.g. /-mpts/ *prompts, exempts*; /-mpst/ *glimpsed*; /-lkts/ mulcts; /-lpts/ *sculpts*; /-lfθs/ *twelfths*; /-ksts/ texts; /-ksθs/ *sixths*; /-ntθs/ *thousandths.*

(11) Final clusters involving /t,d,s,z,θ/, as well as initial clusters beginning with /s/, violate the sonority hierarchy (see §5.5.1 above) and a much simpler statement about English phonotactics (particularly that part concerning final clusters) can clearly be made if such consonants, which are all apical sonorants, are treated as appendices and excluded from the basic statement.

(12) With a vowel inventory of 20 items and the possible initial and final consonant clusters given above, it is clear that a large number of potential combinations are not utilized. Thus, unused monosyllabic words such as the following conform to an already existing pattern: /faʊd, saɪdʒ, mɒmp, bruːtʃ, pliːk, splʌk, stredʒ/. If, in addition, gaps are filled on the grounds of general patterning, it would be possible to construct words of an English phonological character with, for instance, initial /tʃʊ-, rɜː-, glɔɪ-, skɪə-, sprəʊ-/ or final /-ɔːɡ, -aɪtʃ, -uːnt, -ɑːndʒ, -ʌkst/ etc.

10.10.2   Word-medial Syllable Division

Word-medial consonant sequences are of course longer than those in initial and medial positions since they combine syllable-coda and syllable-onset positions. While word-initial naturally equates with syllable-onset and word-final with syllable-coda, any word-medial sequence has to be divided between coda and onset. (In this section syllable division is marked by a stop, e.g. /ə.ˈrəʊ.mə/.) Some of the criteria for dividing such sequences have already been discussed in §5.5.3. The three basic criteria are morphemic (syllable boundaries should correspond with morpheme boundaries); phonotactic (syllable division should accord with what we already know about syllable onsets and syllable codas from what we know of them in word-initial and word-final positions); and allophonic (syllable division should predict correct allophonic variation). These principles sometimes conflict or give no clear answer. A further principle is sometimes applied in such cases, the maximal onset principle,[13] which sets a preference for assigning consonants to onsets on the basis that onsets are more commonly complex in languages than codas. The little experimental evidence that there is[14] also suggests a general preference for onset syllabification.

The case of single medial consonants is exemplified by *motive* (with a long vowel in the accented first syllable) and by *butter* (with a short vowel in the accented first syllable). In the case of *motive*, the phonotactic principle is satisfied either way while the application of the allophonic principle is uncertain (there is no instrumental evidence about possible shortening before /t/, although it is probable that this does not apply). So, using the maximal onset principle, *motive* is generally syllabified as /ˈməʊ.tɪv/, as are other similar words with a long vowel, e.g. *autumn, suitor, survey*. In the case of *butter*, words do not end in /ʌ/ so the phonotactic principle suggests /ˈbʌt.ə/, which accords with the allophonic shortening of /ʌ/ before /t/ and the same syllabification is generally applied to similar words with a short vowel, e.g. *bitter, supper, knickers*.

Medial CC sequences are exemplified in *sequel* (with a long vowel in the accented first syllable) and *petrol* (with a short vowel in the accented first syllable). In the case of *sequel*, both /siː.kwəl/ and /siːk.wəl/ are divisions which accord with the phonotactic principle. However /ˈsiː.kwəl/ accords better with the allophonic principle whereby the /w/ following /k/ is devoiced. This syllabification applies to other cases of CC following a long vowel, e.g. *programme, perfume, protein, awkward*. In the case of *petrol* /pet.rəl/ accords with the phonotactic principle, but does not accord with the allophonic devoicing of /r/, whereas /pe.trəl/ correctly predicts the devoicing of /r/ (following /t/), but does not accord with the phonotactic principle (words do not end in /e/). Applying the maximal onset principle resolves the problem in favour of the latter solution. In *window* the phonotactic and allophonic principles would allow both /ˈwin.dəʊ/ and /ˈwɪnd.əʊ/; the maximal onset principle decides in favour of /ˈwɪn.dəʊ/. The phonotactic principle would give us /ˈplæs.tɪk/ but the allophonic principle

---

[13] See Selkirk (1982)

[14] For experimental information on syllable division word-medially, see Fallows (1981), Treiman and Davis (1988) and Treiman *et al.* (1992). Such experimentation is based principally on speakers being asked to divide up nonsense words

suggests /ˈplæ.stɪk/ because of the unaspirated /t/ and this is endorsed by the maximum onset principle as well as being in accord with the experimental evidence.[15]

The case of longer medial sequences is exemplified by *extra*. The /k/ belong in the coda of the first syllable by both phonotactic and allophonic principles and the /tr/ belongs in the onset (/r/ is devoiced). These two principles give us no solution to the assignment of /s/, which we place in the second syllable by the maximal onset principle, giving /ˈek.strə/.

All the patterns which have been dealt with so far have concerned consonantal sequences following the primary accent. Examples preceding the primary accent most frequently involve consonants containing the typical vowels of unaccented syllables /ə/ and /ɪ/ and in such examples the phonotactic principle together with the maximal onset principle generally leads to the whole sequence being syllabified with the following syllable, e.g. /ə.ˈkwaɪə/, /rɪ.ˈkwest/, /ə.ˈplɔːz/, /ə.ˈstjuːt/, /ə.ˈspærəgəs/. Similarly, in those, less frequent, cases where a full vowel precedes the primary accent the phonotactic principle and the maximum onset principle again generally apply unproblematically, e.g. /meɪn.ˈteɪn/, /sep.ˈtembə/, /taɪ.ˈkuːn/, /əʊ.ˈbiːs/, /bæp.ˈtaɪz/.

Most of the examples above have concerned disyllabic words. The general principles apply in similar fashion in longer words, with clusters before and after secondary accent behaving the same as those around a primary accent, e.g. /en.ˈsaɪ.kləʊ.ˈpiː.dɪə/, /ˈæl.juː.ˈmɪn.ɪəm/, /ˈkæŋ.gə.ˈruː/, /ˈmæk.ɪn.tɒʃ/. The morphemic principle applies regularly in compound words but note that inflexional /-ɪd/ and /ɪz/ regularly lead to resyllabification according to the patterns for monomorphemic words outlined above, e.g. /saɪt/ ~ /ˈsaɪ.tɪd/, /vaɪs/ ~ /ˈvaɪ.sɪz/.

An alternative solution to ambiguous medial sequences can be achieved with the notion of ambisyllabicity; by this means the /t/ in *butter*, the /t/ in *petrol* and the /s/ in *extra* are regarded as ambisyllabic, i.e. they straddle the syllable boundary. For plosives the compression stage could belong to the first syllable and the plosion and release to the second; for fricatives the boundary would simply be in the middle. Phonetically this seems a credible solution. Unfortunately, it would considerably complicate the overall statement of permissible clusters.

10.10.3   Inflexional Suffix Formation

Inflexional suffixes (which do not normally affect accent) follow certain rules which affect segmental aspects of pronunciation. The following regularities may usefully be listed here.

(1) *Past tense*—For regular verbs in which the past tense is signalled by the addition of an *-ed* ending, the following rules of pronunciation apply:

(a) If the stem ends in /t/ or /d/, add /-ɪd/ e.g. *exclude* /ɪksˈkluːd, ɪksˈkluːdɪd/; *guard* /gɑːd, ˈgɑːdɪd/; *rot* /rɒt, ˈrɒtɪd/; *target* /ˈtɑːgɪt, ˈtɑːgɪtɪd/. Otherwise:

---

[15] Treiman *et al.* (1992) confirmed /s/ in the onset in such sequences but found /f/ in the coda in sequences like /fl/ in *afflict*

(b) If the stem ends in any voiced sound (apart from /d/), add /-d/ e.g. *buzz* /bʌz, bʌzd/; *hammer* /ˈhæmə, ˈhæməd/; *kill* /kɪl, kɪld/; *listen* /ˈlɪsn, ˈlɪsnd/.

(c) If the stem ends in any voiceless consonant (apart from /t/) add /-t/, e.g. *arch* /ɑːtʃ, ɑːtʃt/; *immerse* /ɪˈmɜːs, ɪˈmɜːst/; *kick* /kɪk, kɪkt/; *sniff* /snɪf, snɪft/.

(2) Plural/possessive/third-person singular present tense

(a) If the stem ends in a sibilant (/s,z,ʃ,ʒ,tʃ,dʒ/), add /-ɪz/ e.g. *address* /əˈdres, əˈdresɪz/; *arch* /ɑːtʃ, ˈɑːtʃɪz/; *graze* /greɪz, ˈgreɪzɪz/; *judge* /dʒʌdʒ, ˈdʒʌdʒɪz/; *rush* /rʌʃ, ˈrʌʃɪz/. Exceptionally, the voicing of the fricative in *house* changes: /haʊs, ˈhaʊzɪz/. Otherwise:

(b) If the stem ends in any non-sibilant voiced sound, add /-z/ e.g. *blow* /bləʊ, bləʊz/; *pattern* /ˈpætn, ˈpætnd/; *regard* /rɪˈgɑːd, rɪgˈɑːdz/; *thrill* /θrɪl, θrɪlz/.

(c) If the stem ends in any non-sibilant voiceless consonant, add /s/ e.g. *laugh* /lɑːf, lɑːfs/; *pick* /pɪk, pɪks/; *resort* /rɪˈzɔːt, rɪˈzɔːts/.

(3) *Present participle*—In all cases, add /-ɪŋ/ e.g. *kill* /kɪl, ˈkɪlɪŋ/; *laugh* /lɑːf, ˈlɑːfɪŋ/; *sing* /sɪŋ, ˈsɪŋɪŋ/; *trim* /trɪm, ˈtrɪmɪŋ/. For cases where the stem ends in /ɑː,ɔː,ɜː,ɪə,eə,ʊə/, see (6) below. For stems ending in syllabic [n̩] or [l̩] the syllabic nature of the nasal or lateral is frequently retained, e.g. *handle* [ˈhændl̩, ˈhændl̩ɪŋ]; *widen* [ˈwaɪdn̩, ˈwaɪdn̩ɪŋ]. However, some speakers may insert a /ə/, retaining the same number of syllables, thus /ˈhændəlɪŋ, ˈwaɪdənɪŋ/; whilst for others the nasal or lateral may lose its syllabic function, thus [ˈhændl̩, ˈhændlɪŋ]. It should be noted that in such cases, the quality of the /l/ is altered, the dark [ɫ] of [hændɫ] being replaced by a clear [l]. (See also §10.8.)

(4) *Comparison of adjectives*—For those adjectives whose comparative and superlative degrees are formed by the suffixing of *-er* and *-est* respectively, the pronunciation of the stem remains unchanged except in the case of stems ending in /ŋ/ or /r/ (see (5) and (6) below). Thus /ə/ and /ɪst/ are regularly added, as in *easy* /ˈiːzɪə, ˈiːzɪɪst/; *great* /greɪt, ˈgreɪtə, ˈgreɪtɪst/; *big* /bɪg, ˈbɪgə, ˈbɪgɪst/.

(5) *Stems ending in /ŋ/*—When the comparative and superlative suffixes are added to stems ending in /ŋ/, a /g/ is inserted, e.g. *long* /lɒŋ, ˈlɒŋgə, ˈlɒŋgɪst/. In all other cases, the /ŋ/ is followed immediately by the suffix, e.g. participle *-ing* in *longing* /ˈlɒŋɪŋ/, adjectival modifier *-ish* in *longish* /ˈlɒŋɪʃ/, or agentive *-er* in *hanger* /ˈhæŋə/, *singer* /ˈsɪŋə/. It should be noted that monomorphemic words (not formed of a stem and affix) exhibit the sequence /-ŋg-/ intervocalically, e.g. *anger* /ˈæŋgə/, *finger* /ˈfɪŋgə/.

(6) */r/-links in suffix formation*—In the case of words which end in /ɑː,ɔː,ɜː,ə,ɪə,eə,ʊə/ (usually corresponding to an <r> in the spelling), an /r/-link is regularly inserted between the final vowel of the stem and any initial vowel of the suffix, e.g. present participles *blur* /blɜː, ˈblɜːrɪŋ/; *secure* /sɪˈkjuə, sɪˈkjuərɪŋ/; *stare* /steə, ˈsteərɪŋ/; *store* /stɔː, ˈstɔːrɪŋ/; comparative and superlative adjectives (stem +/ə,ɪst/) *clear* /klɪə, ˈklɪərə, ˈklɪərɪst/. This process applies to derivational as well as to inflexional suffixes, e.g. adjectival *-y*, e.g. *star* /stɑː, ˈstɑːrɪ/; agentive noun *-er*, e.g. *murder* /ˈmɜːdə, ˈmɜːdərə/; verb-forming *-ize*, e.g. *familiar* /fəˈmɪlɪə, fəˈmɪlɪəraɪz/. /r/-linking before inflexions where there is no orthographic <r> in the stem is unacceptable to some native speakers who have prescriptive opinions about the language, e.g. in *drawing, gnawing* /ˈdrɔːrɪŋ, ˈnɔːrɪŋ/.

10.10.4   Acquisition of Phonotactics by Native Learners

Children often have special problems with the acquisition of consonant clusters in syllable-initial positions, even after they have individually acquired the individual members of the clusters. With two-term clusters consisting of fricative + C (most commonly /s/) and C+/l,r,w,j/, there is often a reduction to the single C, e.g. *smoke* → [məʊk], *spin* → [pɪn], *please* → [piː], *queen* → [kiːn]. Clusters of /s/+/l,r,w,j/ may be reduced to either element, e.g. *slow* → [səʊ] or [ləʊ]. In the case of the fricative plus C type, a possible, somewhat later, development (which may at first glance look like a regression) involves a feature merger, whereby a single consonant replaces the two consonants of the adult cluster, the single consonant taking at least one feature from each of the two consonants, e.g. *spin* → [fɪn], *fling* → [ɬɪŋ], *sleep* → [ɬiːp], *smoke* → [m̥əʊk]. When the two elements of the cluster are used, there may still be a difficulty in timing the relationship between the two elements: for example, a short intrusive, or EPENTHETIC, vowel (typically /ə/) may be inserted, or one of the elements may be improperly lengthened, e.g. *sport* → [sᵊpɔːt] or [sːpɔːt], *slow* → [sᵊləʊ] or [sːləʊ].[16] Some sequences give particular problems: /st/ sometimes occurs with metathesis as /ts/ (no doubt because it is a homorganic sequence); clusters with /r/ are often very late acquisitions because /r/ as a single consonant is a late acquisition.

The course of development of syllable-final clusters is less well-known because the interval of time between the development of single consonants and clusters is shorter and because the development of word-final clusters is often partly a question of the learning of inflexions.

10.10.5   Advice to Foreign Learners

Foreign learners may introduce epenthetic vowels into English consonantal clusters: so a word like *sport* may be pronounced as /sə`pɔːt/ (and hence homonymous with *support*), or as /ə`spɔːt/ (and hence homonymous with *a sport*). Difficult clusters can sometimes be acquired by pronouncing a sequence of consonants across a word boundary and then dropping the earlier part of the first word: thus /st/ may be acquired by practising first with a phrase like *bus stop*, or even medially in a bimorphemic word, e.g. *mistake*, and then reducing these to *stop* and *steak*.

Many languages have only open syllables, e.g. Hindi, Italian, and Bantu languages. Speakers of such languages should be careful not to introduce a postthetic vowel, e.g. a [ə] may be added to *bit* making it sound like *bitter*.

10.11   *Consonant Harmony in the Word Structure of Native Learners*

Many of the common variations in the structure of words as they are acquired by children have been mentioned under the various sections dealing with individual

---

[16] See Gilbert and Purves (1977)

phonemes, word accent, and phonotactics. However, one type of change which occurs in child language but which is generally unknown among historical changes in the language and among foreign learners is the phenomenon which is usually called CONSONANT HARMONY (and which is really a type of assimilation, although within words as opposed to those assimilations occurring at word boundaries which are mentioned in §12.4.5). Such consonant harmony occurs during the period when children are using only one-word utterances. It involves the assimilation of one consonant to another across an intervening vowel. Most frequently the process involves de-alveolarization (i.e. an alveolar sound is changed to something else), and is regressive (i.e. a later-occurring sound influences an earlier sound) e.g. *supper* → [ˈpʌpə], *duck* → [gʌk], *dog* → [gɒg], although occasionally the process can be progressive (i.e. in a forward direction), e.g. *cushion* → [ˈkʊkən], *bottom* → [ˈbɒpəm].

11

Connected Speech

11.1 *Accent*

Connected speech, i.e. an utterance consisting of more than one word, exhibits features of accentuation that are in many ways comparable with those found in the polysyllabic word. Some parts of the connected utterance will be made to stand out from their environment, in the same way that certain syllables of a polysyllabic word are more prominent than their neighbours. Accentuation in connected speech differs, however, from the usual case of a polysyllable in that the situation of the accent in connected speech is determined largely by the meaning which the utterance is intended to convey, in the particular circumstances in which it is uttered. So, in terms of accent and reduced vowels, *She can* may be like the verb *insult* or like the noun *insult*, but not like *beacon*; and *She can go* may be like *telephone* or like *tobacco* or like *cigarette*, but not like *bachelor*.

Although accentual patterns of connected speech are freer than those of the word and are largely determined by the meaning to be conveyed, some words are predisposed by their function in the language to receive accent. These LEXICAL words are typically main verbs, adverbs, nouns, adjectives, and demonstrative pronouns. Other categories of words, such as auxiliary verbs, conjunctions, prepositions, pronouns, relative pronouns, and articles (FUNCTION words), are more likely to be unaccented, although they too may be exceptionally accented if the meaning requires it.

The examples given above illustrate the freedom of accentual patterning in utterances taken without a context. But the meaning of any utterance is largely conditioned by the situation and context in which it occurs. Thus, it must be expected that the freedom of accentual patterning of the utterance and, in particular, of the placement of the primary accent will be considerably curtailed by the constraints imposed by the contextual environment. In the case of an opening remark, or when a new topic is introduced into a conversation, there is only very limited scope for variations of meaning pointed by accentuation. Rather more accentual freedom is possible in responses; thus, in response to the statement *She*

*came last `week* an incredulous reaction might have the pattern `*Last week!*[1] (i.e.
'Wasn't it the week before?') or *Last `week?* (i.e. 'Don't you mean last month?');
or, in response to *What was the weather like?*, the reply might be *It rained every
`day* (emphasizing the continuous nature of the rain) or *It `rained every day!*
(where the fact of raining is emphasized). But, in the following dialogue, such
constraints are placed upon the accentuation, both by the context and by the
nature of the lexical words, that little variation is possible (those words likely to
be most strongly accented being printed in italic):

'Did you have a good *holiday?*'
'*Yes, very* good'
'Was the *weather* all right?'
'It was *fine* for the *first* part, but for the *rest* of the time it was pretty *mixed*.
We *enjoyed* ourselves though. We had the *car*, so we were able to do some
sightseeing, when it was too *wet* to go on the *beach*.'

Many monosyllabic function words are subject to qualitative variation (usually
including variation between full and reduced vowels) according to whether they
receive the accent or not. But use of a reduced vowel in an unaccented function
word may be inhibited by its position, e.g. *can* /kən/ or /kn̩/ in unaccented initial
and medial positions in the utterance, but /kæn/ in an unaccented final position,
e.g. *Of course she can* /kæn/. Monosyllabic lexical words usually retain their full
vowel value even in unaccented positions, e.g. *How* in *How `can she?*; or again,
in *We put the case in the hall, case* and *hall* will always keep their full vowel
wherever the primary accent is concentrated.

More than one word in an utterance may receive a primary accent. A deliberate, emphatic, or excited style of speaking often exhibits a proliferation of
primary accents; a more rapid and matter-of-fact delivery is likely to show fewer
primary accents.

In an extended dialogue in normal conversational style, the number of syllables with reduced vowels (or syllabic consonants) tends to exceed that of those
made prominent by an accent or by the presence of a full vowel.

11.2   *Prominence, Accent, and Rhythm*

In most descriptions of English pronunciation over the last 50 years the notion
of 'stress-timing' is invoked to explain English rhythm;[2] by such a theory
'stressed' syllables (including pitch accents and other syllables made prominent
by 'stress' alone) govern the rhythm of English utterances, an equal amount of
time being said to be taken between each two stressed syllables and between the
last stressed syllable and the end of the utterance, e.g.

---

[1] Note that the sign ` here shows the place of the primary accent. As the symbol `
implies, the most common primary accent involves a falling pitch; however /lɑːs wiːk/ is
in these examples at least as likely to have a rising pitch
[2] Pike (1945), Abercrombie (1967), Halliday (1967) and numerous TESOL textbooks,
e.g. Bright and McGregor (1970) and Abbott and Wingard (1981)

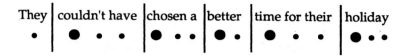

They | couldn't have | chosen a | better | time for their | holiday

However, all attempts to show such timing instrumentally have been unsuccessful,[3] and such groups are often clearly far from ISOCHRONOUS. In the above example the group containing the two-syllabled word *better* will be shorter than the three-syllabled groups *couldn't have* and *chosen a* (though probably not in the ratio 2:3), while the group *time for their* (also containing three syllables) will be longer than all three because of the full vowel on the word *their*.

Indeed, the occurrence of full vowels generally predicts the rhythm of English rather more usefully than any notion of stress (besides variation of the type exemplified above, there is often difficulty in deciding whether a syllable is stressed when no pitch accent is present—some might judge the full vowel on *their* above as showing stress). For rhythmical purposes the reduced vowels are /ə/, and /ɪ/ and /ʊ/ when they occur without a pitch accent; all other vowels are counted as full vowels. The one simple rule of English rhythm is the BORROWING RULE[4] whereby a syllable with a reduced vowel 'borrows time' from any immediately preceding syllable containing a full vowel.[5] By the predictions of the Borrowing Rule full-vowelled syllables each take approximately an equal amount of time (although in practice this will be somewhat affected by the innate length of the vowel and the consonants in the syllable). Each syllable containing a reduced vowel is much shorter, and by the Borrowing Rule a full-vowelled syllable is itself shortened if immediately followed by a syllable with a reduced vowel. The operation of the rule is shown in the following two examples (chosen to compare the predictions of full-vowelled rhythm and stress-timed rhythm) (' and ` indicate pitch accents):

(a) Those 'wallabies are `dangerous
    F F- R R R F- R R

(b) Those 'porcupines aren't `dangerous
    F F F F   F   F- R R

In these examples, syllables marked F are equally long, those marked R are equally short, and those marked F- are long syllables shortened by the following reduced-vowelled syllables. So *dangerous* is the same in the two examples, but the rhythms of *wallabies are* and *porcupines aren't* are completely different (whereas by a theory of stress-timed rhythm both sentences would be predicted to have the same rhythm). A sequence of F- followed by R is equal to a single F; but any further following R's do not take time from the F-, e.g. the single syllable of *speed* will be shortened when turned into *speedy* but will be no further shortened when turned into *speedily*.

11.3   *Weak Forms*

Lexical words (both monosyllables and polysyllables) generally have in connected speech the quantitative pattern of their isolate form and therefore retain some measure of prominence based on the occurrence of a full vowel even when no pitch prominence is associated with them.

   However, many function words have two or more qualitative and quantitative patterns according to whether they are unaccented (as is usual) or accented (in special situations or when said in isolation).[6] As compared with the accented realizations of these words (the STRONG forms), the unaccented WEAK forms of these words show reductions of the length of sounds, obscuration of vowels towards /ə,ɪ,ʊ/, and the elision of vowels and consonants. The following list of examples presents the most common of these words, first in their unaccented (normal) weak form and secondly in their less usual[7] accented strong form:

	Unaccented	*Accented*
a	/ə/	/eɪ/
am	/m̩, əm/	/æm/
an	/n̩, ən/	/æn/
and	/ənd, n̩d, ən, n̩/	/ænd/
are	/ə/ + consonant	/ɑː/
	/ər, r/ + vowel	/ɑːr/
as	/əz/	/æz/
at	/ət/	/æt/
be	/bɪ/([bi])	/biː/
been	/bɪn/	/biːn/
but	/bət/	/bʌt/
can (aux.)	/kən, kn̩/	/kæn/
could	/kəd, kd/	/kʊd/
do (aux.)	/də/ + consonant	/duː/
	vowel + /d/ + consonant	
	/dʊ/ (or [du]) + vowel	
does (aux.)	/dəz, z, s/	/dʌz/
	(e.g. *What's (= does) he like?* /wɒts iː ˈlaɪk/,	
	When's (= does) he arrive? /wenz iː əˈraɪv/)	
for	/fə/ + consonant	/fɔː/
	/fər, fr/ + vowel	/fɔːr/
from	/frəm, frm̩/	/frɒm/
had (aux.)[8]	/həd, əd, d/[9]	/hæd/

---

[6] For a full treatment of English weak forms, see Obendorfer (1998)
[7] The following 42 items occur in the first 200 most common words in connected speech: *the, you, I, to, and, a, that, we, of, have, is, are, for, at, he, but, there, do, as, be, them, will, me, was, can, him, had, your, been, from, my, or, she, by, some, her, his, us, an, am, has, shall.* It is significant that of these the following 19 have over 90% unaccented occurrences with a weak form: *at, of, the, to, as, and, or, a, his, an, but, been, for, her, we, be, shall, was, them*
[8] The distinction between auxiliary *have* and the main verb may be illustrated by examples such as *He considered what he* /həd/ *left* (weak form of auxiliary verb = what had been left by him) and *He considered what he* /hæd/ *left* (main verb, non-weakenable = what he still possessed)

has (aux.)	/həz, əz, z, s/	/hæz/
have (aux.)	/həv, əv, v/	/hæv/
he	/hɪ,iː,ɪ/[9] ([hi])	/hiː/
her	/hə,ɜː,ə,/[9]	/hɜː/
him	/ɪm/	/hɪm/
his	/ɪz/	/hɪz/
is	/s,z/	/ɪz/
me	/mɪ/([mi])	/miː/
must	/məst/[10]	/mʌst/
not	/nt,n̩/	/nɒt/
of	/əv,v,ə/	/ɒv/
Saint	/sənt, sn̩t, sən, sn̩/	/seɪnt/
shall	/ʃəl, ʃl̩/	/ʃæl/
she	/ʃɪ/([ʃi])	/ʃiː/
should	/ʃəd/ ([ʃd])	/ʃʊd/
Sir	/sə/ + consonant	/sɜː/
	/sər/ + vowel	/sɜːr/
some (adj.)[11]	/səm, sm̩/	/sʌm/
than	/ðən, ðn̩/	/ðæn/
that (conj. and rel.pron.)[12]	/ðət/	/ðæt/
the	/ðɪ/ ([ði]) + vowel[13]	/ðiː/
	/ðə/ + consonant	
them	/ðəm/ also /əm, m̩/	/ðem/
there (indef. adv.)[14]	/ðə/ + consonant	/ðeə/ (rare)
	/ðər/ + vowel	/ðeər/ (rare)
to (and *into, onto, unto*)	/tə/ + consonant	/tuː/
	/tʊ/ ([tu]) + vowel	
us	/əs, s/	/ʌs/
was	/wəz/	/wɒz/
we	/wɪ/([wi])	/wiː/
were	/wə/ + consonant	/wɜː/
	/wər/ + vowel	/wɜːr/
who	/uː,ʊ/ /hʊ/([hu])[15]	/huː/
will	/əl, l̩, l/	/wɪl/
would	/wəd, əd, d/	/wʊd/
you	/jʊ/ ([ju])	/juː/

---

[9] A weak form with /h/ is normally used when unaccented but following a pause.
[10] Often /məs/ with elision of /t/, see §12.4.6
[11] *Some* does not occur in a weak form when used as a pronoun, e.g. /sʌm maɪt `seɪ/, /aɪd `laɪk sʌm/
[12] *That* as a demonstrative adjective or pronoun always takes a full vowel, e.g. *that man* /ðæt `mæn/, *that's the one* /ðæts ðə `wʌn/
[13] There may be new tendency to use /ðə/ before vowels among younger speakers. This is first reported for American speech in Todaka (1992)
[14] As a demonstrative adverb, *there* will be accented, e.g. *there's the book* /ðeəz ðə `bʊk/.
[15] A weak form with /h/ would normally be used when unaccented but following a pause

It should be noted that verb forms such as *am, are, be, can, could, do, does, had, has, have, is, must, shall, was, were, will, would* retain a strong form when they occur finally even though they are unaccented, e.g. *Who's coming?* `I am /æm/; Who's got it?* `I have* /hæv/.

Similarly, some prepositions, e.g. *to, from, at, for*, apart from having a strong form when receiving a primary accent, also have a qualitative prominence when final and unaccented, e.g. *Where have they gone to?* (/tuː/, also /tʊ/, but not /tə/); *Where's he come from?* (/frɒm/ rather than /frəm/); *What are you laughing for, at?* (/fɔː,æt/). This applies, too, when prepositions and auxiliary verbs occur finally in a rhythmic group, including at a 'deletion site' where the following item is understood, e.g. *He looked at* /æt/ *and solved the problem*; or *people who can afford to* /tuː/ (sc. *do so*) *buy luxuries*, cf. *People who can afford to* /tə/ *buy luxuries, do so*. When a preposition occurs before an unaccented pronoun, either the strong or the weak form may be used for the preposition, e.g. *I gave it to you* (/tə/ or /tuː/); *I've heard from him* (/frəm/ or /frɒm/); *I waited for you* (/fə/ or /fɔː/); *I looked at her* (/ət/ or /æt/).

Note, too, that certain function words, not normally possessing an alternative weak form for unaccented occurrences, may show such reductions in very rapid speech, e.g. *I* (/ə/) *don't know; What's your* (/jə/) *name?; I go by* (/bə/) *bus; Do you know my* (/mə/) *brother?; for love nor* (/nə/) *money;*[16] *two or* (/ə/) *three;*[16] *ever so* (/sə/) *many;*[16] in the case of the disyllables *any, many*, a qualitative prominence may be retained on the first syllable—/enɪ, menɪ/, but fully reduced, unaccented, forms may be heard in rapid speech, e.g. *Have any more come?* /hævnɪ `mɔː kʌm/; *How many do you want?* /haʊ mnɪ dʒuː `wɒnt/. Other monosyllabic function words normally retain their strong vowels in unaccented positions, e.g. *on, when, then, one*, but again, although rather less commonly, reduced vowel forms may be heard in very rapid speech, especially when the word is adjacent to a strongly accented syllable, e.g. *What on* (/ən/ or /n̩/) *earth!; When* (/wən/) *all's said and done; Then* (/ðən/) *after a time; One* (/wən/) *always hopes.*

It may be said that the more rapid the delivery the greater the tendency to reduction and obscuration of unaccented words. Even monosyllabic lexical words may be reduced in fast speech, if they occur in a relatively unaccented positions adjacent to a primary accent, and especially if they contain a short vowel, e.g. /ɪ/, *You sit over here* /juː s(ə)t əʊvə `hɪə/; /ʊ/, *He put it there* /hiː p(ə)t ɪt `ðeə/; /ʌ/, *He'll come back* /`hiːl k(ə)m bæk/; /e/, *Don't get lost* /dəʊnt g(ə)t `lɒst/; less frequently with the more prominent short vowels /æ,ɒ/, e.g. /æ/, *They all sat down on the floor* /ðeɪ ɔːl sət daʊn ən ðə `flɔː/; /ɒ/, *We want to go* /`wiː wənt tə gəʊ/; and, finally, the diphthong /əʊ/, with its dominant central [ə] element, is readily reducible to /ə/ under weak accent, e.g. *You can't go with him* /juː kɑːnt gə `wɪð ɪm/; *He's going to do it* /`hiː z gənə duː ɪt/.

11.4   *Acquisition of Rhythm and Weak Forms by Native Learners*

Such little evidence as there is suggests that some children often start off by using the strong forms of function words. They also tend towards a constant length for

---

[16] These weak forms seem to be restricted to a limited number of phrases and, in the case of *or*, particularly occurs in linking two numbers as in the example given here

each syllable and do not apply the Borrowing Rule (see §11.2 above), or, in more traditional terms, they have a syllable-timed rhythm.

11.5   *Advice to Foreign Learners*

Rhythmical shortening of full vowels occurring before /ə,ɪ/ should be attended to; such shortenings can be practised in pairs like *short* vs *shorter, lead* vs *leading, bus* vs *buses, wet* vs *wetted, John* vs *John looked ill, one* vs *one for tea, John* vs *John'll go* etc. Those with a syllable-timed L1 like Cantonese, French, Hindi, Italian, Spanish, and Bantu languages, must give particular attention to such shortenings.

Learners who aim at a native English accent (British or American) must learn the weak forms of function words and regard them as the regular pronunciations, using the strong forms only on those limited occasions where they are used (e.g. under special emphasis or contrast, and in final positions). The reduction to /ə/ in these words will not automatically follow from the teaching of rhythm.

11.6   *Intonation*[17]

The acoustic manifestation of intonation is fundamental frequency (see §3.2.1 above) which is perceived by listeners as pitch. Pitch changes in English have three principal functions (i) they signal the division of utterances into INTONATIONAL PHRASES (besides pitch change, other phonetic cues often mark such boundaries, in particular, pause, final syllable lengthening, and changes in the speed with which unaccented syllables are produced)—boundaries between intonational phrases generally correspond syntactically with clause and major syntactic phrase boundaries; (ii) they signal syllables with primary and secondary accent, both in the citation of isolated words as already mentioned in §10.1 and 10.2, and in the longer utterances of speech; (iii) the shape of the tunes produced by pitch changes can carry various types of meaning, primarily discoursal (i.e. establishing the links between various parts of utterances) and attitudinal; particularly important is the pitch pattern beginning at the primary accent and ending at the end of the intonational phrase—often called the NUCLEAR TONE. It should be noted that, while the variation in intonation between languages (and between dialects of English) is not as great as that involved in segments, it is nonetheless sufficient to cause a strong foreign accent and in some cases lead to misunderstanding. The intonation of RP is described in the following sections. Differences between RP and GA are relatively limited; differences between RP and that of a number of northern British cities are considerable (see under §11.6.3 below).

---

[17] For a more complete treatment of English intonation, see O'Connor and Arnold (1973) and Cruttenden (1997)

11.6.1   The Forms of Intonation[18]

11.6.1.1 Intonational Phrases—The boundaries between intonational phrases may be indicated by a combination of internal and external factors. Most obvious among the external ones is pause: in the following example pauses can occur at the points where boundaries are indicated by /:

> In the past five years / the way that services are delivered to the public / from both state enterprises / and private companies / has changed almost out of recognition / If we wish to make an enquiry by telephone / we have to choose between a number of options / and then between a further series of options / and so on / Even after this series of choices / we may have to listen to canned music / for a short time / or a long time / or a very long time / So we may ring off and try the internet / and look up a company's webpage / only to be told / that if we want more information / we should ring the number we have already tried.

Often, as an alternative to pause, speakers may lengthen the final syllable before the boundary:[19] in the piece above *years* and *-prises*, and *-nies* may be lengthened (such lengthening can apply both to accented and unaccented syllables and to full and reduced vowels). A boundary can also be marked by an increase in the speed of unaccented syllables following the boundary. So the syllables of *and then be-* and *that if we* above are likely to be pronounced very rapidly and hence such syllables are also very likely to involve reduced vowels. These external cues to boundaries of intonational phrases are not unambiguous: pause and final syllable lengthening may also be used as hesitations, for example when a speaker has a word finding difficulty (see §11.7 below). The external cues to boundaries are supported by internal factors: in particular (i) if one of the pitch patterns associated with a nuclear tone is completed at a certain point this in itself may indicate a boundary (see §11.6.1.3 below), and (ii) rapid change of the pitch height of unaccented syllables will generally only occur at boundaries. Thus the syllables *so we may* above are not only likely to be said at a faster tempo but will be said at a higher level than the pitch of the preceding *very long time*. This is part of the tendency for intonational phrases to be susceptible to a DECLINATION effect, i.e. to decline in pitch from their beginning to their end, so that what are felt to be low-pitched syllables at the beginning of an intonational phrase will be higher than low-pitched syllables at the end.

11.6.1.2   Primary Accents—The pronunciation of single words and of longer intonational phrases are both described in terms of an obligatory PRIMARY

---

[18] Much recent work on the form of English intonation has been done in a newer tradition represented by Pierrehumbert (1980/87) and Pierrehumbert and Hirschberg (1990), which decomposes pitch contours into sequences of high and low tones and also detaches phrase tones and terminal tones at the end of intonational phrases. However, the treatment of intonational meaning in this newer framework has remained at a general level, and the nuclear tone approach is retained here because it remains easier to treat in this setting the local meanings produced by associations between tones and syntactic types

[19] See Beckman and Edwards (1990)

ACCENT and an optional SECONDARY ACCENT. The realization of primary accent has already been discussed in §10.2 in relation to single words. There it was stated that the final pitch accent in a word or intonational phrase is usually the most prominent (and hence is referred to as the primary accent) while a pitch accent on an earlier syllable is referred to as the secondary accent. The final pitch accent identifies the syllable which is called the NUCLEUS and begins one of a number of pitch patterns known as NUCLEAR TONES.

11.6.1.3 *Types of Nuclear Tone*

(1) *Falling nuclear tones* (`' ,`)—A falling glide may start from the highest pitch of the speaking voice and fall to the lowest pitch (in the case of the HIGH FALL) or from a mid pitch to the lowest pitch (in the case of the LOW FALL). Where there are high syllables before the primary accent, a high fall will involve a step-up and the low fall a step-down. The falling glide is most perceptible when it takes place on a syllable containing a long vowel or diphthong or a voiced continuant (e.g. /m,n,ŋ,l,z/ etc.), e.g.

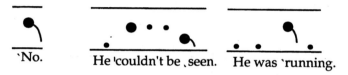

`No.    He 'couldn't be ˌseen.    He was `running.

When a fall occurs on a syllable containing a short vowel followed by a voiceless consonant (especially the stops /p,t,k/), the glide, particularly of a low fall, is so rapid that it is not easily perceptible, or may be realized merely as a low level pitch in relation to a preceding higher pitch, e.g.

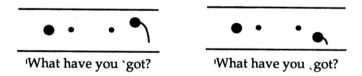

'What have you `got?   'What have you ˌgot?

Again, when syllables follow the nucleus—called the TAIL—the fall may be realised as the juxtaposition of relatively high pitch on the nuclear syllable and low pitches on the syllables of the tail, cf.

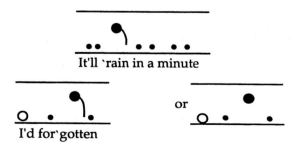

It'll `rain in a minute

I'd for`gotten   or

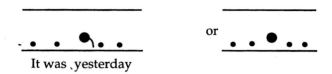

It was ‚yesterday

(2) *Rising nuclear tones* (‚ ´) —Rising glides may extend from low to mid, or from low or mid to high. When the rise ends at a high point, it is marked by ´ (a HIGH RISE); when it ends at a mid point, it is marked by ‚ (LOW RISE). Rising glides are more easily perceptible when they occur on a syllable containing a long vowel or diphthong or a voiced continuant consonant, e.g.

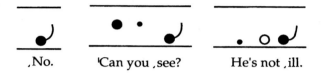

‚No.   ˈCan you ‚see?   He's not ‚ill.

When a low rise occurs on a short syllable, it must necessarily be accomplished much more rapidly, or may merely consist of a relatively high level pitch in relation to a preceding low pitch, e.g.

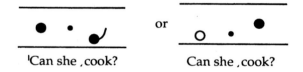

ˈCan she ‚cook?   Can she ‚cook?

With a tail, the rise is achieved by means of a lower pitch on the nuclear sylla-ble with an ascending scale on the following syllables, e.g.

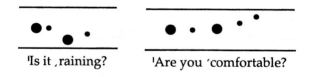

ˈIs it ‚raining?   ˈAre you ´comfortable?

When the tail is a long one, the ascending sequence of syllables of a high rise may be interrupted by a level plateau before a final upward kick, e.g.

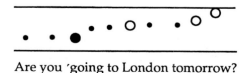

Are you ´going to London tomorrow?

(3) *Falling-rising nuclear tones* (FALL–RISE) (ˇ)—The fall and rise may be confined within one syllable, the glide beginning at about mid level and ending at the same level (or slightly above or below); in the case of a short syllable, the dip in pitch is made extremely rapidly and may be realized as an instant of creaky voice or even of cessation of voice, e.g.

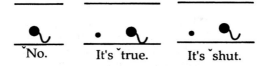

ˇNo.   It's ˇtrue.   It's ˇshut.

When an unaccented tail follows the nuclear syllable, the fall occurs on the nuclear syllable and the rise is spread over the tail (for the use of the symbol ↘ see §11.6.1.4 below), e.g.

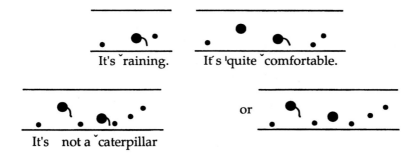

It's ˇraining.   It's ǀquite ˇcomfortable.

It's   not a ˇcaterpillar   or

When full vowels occur in tails, the fall takes place on the nuclear syllable and the rise is initiated on the last syllable carrying a full vowel, and where the fall and the rise are on separate words it accords better with tonetic reality to mark the tone with a separated ˋ and ͵, e.g.

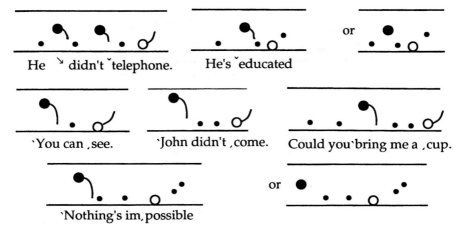

He ↘ didn't ˇtelephone.   He's ˇeducated   or

ˋYou can ͵see.   ˋJohn didn't ͵come.   Could youˋbring me a ͵cup.

ˋNothing's im͵possible   or

Sometimes a fall–rise is accompanied by a further initial rise, giving a RISE–FALL–RISE variant of the tone, e.g.

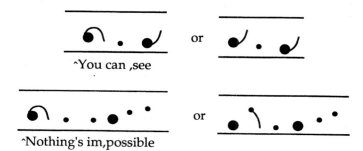

^You can ,see

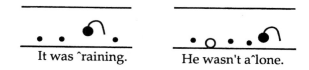

^Nothing's im,possible

(4) *Rising-falling nuclear tones* (RISE–FALL) (ˆ)—A fall may be reinforced by an introductory rise, being realized as a continuous glide on a long syllable (which may be given extra length), e.g.

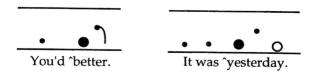

It was ˆraining.　　He wasn't aˆlone.

A rise–fall on a short syllable followed by a tail may be realized as a low accented nuclear syllable followed by a fall on the tail, e.g.

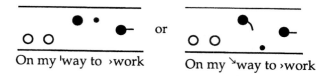

You'd ˆbetter.　　It was ˆyesterday.

(5) *Level nuclear tones* (>)—The most common level tone is a MID LEVEL, which is a very frequent tone in intonational phrases which are non-final in a sentence. If it occurs on a single syllable that syllable will be lengthened, e.g.

On my ˈway to ›work　or　On my ˇway to ›work

If a tail follows the nucleus then the unaccented syllables remain on the same level, e.g.

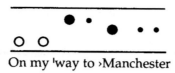

On my 'way to ›Manchester

11.6.1.4   *Secondary Accents* —A secondary accent occurs in the pre-nuclear section of an intonational phrase. It usually involves a high level pitch prominence (marked '), e.g.

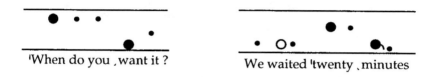

'When do you ˌwant it ?   We waited 'twenty ˌminutes

More than one secondary accent may occur in the pre-nuclear position (note that to achieve prominence each succeeding secondary accent involves a step-down), e.g.

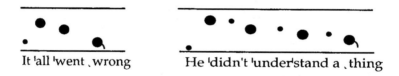

It 'all 'went ˌwrong   He 'didn't 'under'stand a ˌthing

A pitch prominence (and hence a secondary accent) may also be achieved by a step down to a low pitch (marked ˌ) following initial high unaccented syllables, e.g.

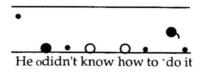

He ˌdidn't know how to `do it

Another common variant of secondary accent(s) uses one or a series of glides-down rather than levels, e.g.

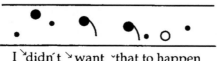

I ˋdidn't ˋwant ˋthat to happen

Glides-down of this sort are more prominent than steps.

11.6.1.5   The Pitch of Unaccented Syllables—Unaccented syllables, in addition to the fact that they are said very rapidly and usually undergo some reduction, do not normally have any pitch prominence. They may occur before the first accent (primary or secondary), between accents, or after the last (primary) accent (the nucleus).

(1) *Pre-nuclear*—Unaccented syllables occurring before a nucleus (where there is no secondary accent) are normally relatively low, whether the nucleus is a fall or a rise, e.g.

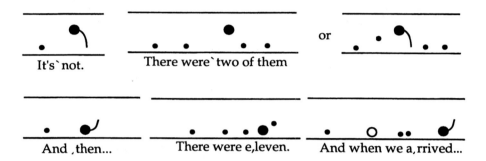

It's ˋnot.   There were ˋtwo of them   or

And ˏthen...   There were eˏleven.   And when we aˏrrived...

Unaccented syllables before a secondary accent are also usually said on a relatively low pitch, the accent having prominence in relation to them, e.g.

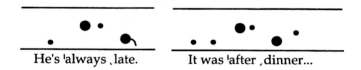

He's ˈalways ˏlate.   It was ˈafter ˏdinner...

If pre-nuclear unaccented syllables, their weak quality remaining, are said on a relatively high pitch, the effect is more emphatic and animated than if they are low in pitch, particularly if they are followed by a low nuclear tone, e.g.

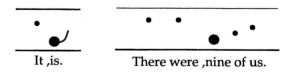

It ˏis.   There were ˏnine of us.

And, as mentioned under §11.6.1.4 above, high unaccented syllables may sometimes be used to give pitch prominence to a low accented syllable, e.g.

I ˌdon't like ˌthat

(2) *After syllables with secondary accent*—Unaccented syllables usually remain on almost the same pitch as a preceding syllable with secondary accent, e.g.

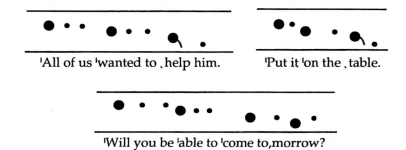

'All of us 'wanted to ˌhelp him.

'Put it 'on the ˌtable.

'Will you be 'able to 'come to,morrow?

Additional prominence is often given to secondary accents by having a descending rather than a level series of unaccented syllables following; this is particularly common before a fall–rise nuclear tone, e.g.

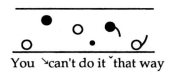

You ˅can't do it ˇthat way

(3) *Post-nuclear*—Unaccented syllables following a falling nucleus remain on a low level, e.g.

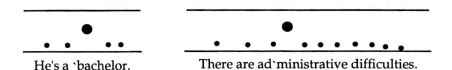

He's a ˋbachelor.

There are adˋministrative difficulties.

After a rising nucleus, unaccented syllables continue (or effect) the rise; similarly, the rise of a falling–rising nucleus may be spread over the following unaccented syllables, e.g.

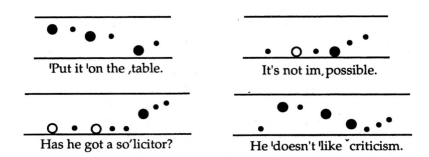

11.6.2   The Functions of Intonation

11.6.2.1   Intonational Phrasing—Most commonly, intonational phrases correspond with clauses. The clause may constitute a simple sentence or it may be
part of a compound or complex one, e.g.

/He usually comes at ten o'clock/
/He worked hard / and passed the exam/
/Because he worked hard / he passed the exam/
/It's nice / isn't it?/

But often intonational phrases correspond with smaller syntactic constituents
than the clause. The subject of a clause may receive a separate intonational
phrase of its own, e.g.

/The workers / have got a rising standard of living/
/A competitive society / is defensible/
/A lot of industry's profits / go in taxation/

Sentence adverbials and adverbials of time and place often receive separate
intonational phrases, particularly when they occur at the beginnings and ends of
clauses, e.g.

/I go to London / regularly/
/The government's got to give in / apparently / to every pressure from big
business/
/In my view / the argument should be / how to build a partnership / between
public and private sectors/
/Seriously / it seems to me / that the crucial issue/ is . . .

Only in rare cases is it obligatory for subjects and sentence adverbials to take a
separate intonational phrase; but it is an option which is often taken up, particularly when the subject is long or its status as a new topic is highlighted, or when
the speaker wishes to make an adverbial prominent.
   Other, less common, types of structure which commonly form a separate
intonational phrase are parentheticals (including vocatives and appositives) and
parallel constructions, e.g.

Lucy / will you please stop making that noise
Professor Bull / the Head of the Department / declared his support

John / this will really amaze you / actually got the highest marks
This will be achieved by hard work / by brainpower / by interactive subtlety
/ and by keeping to deadlines

Non-restrictive relative clauses, which are of course semantically similar to paren-theticals, also regularly take a separate phrase, while restrictive relatives do not, e.g.

The old man / who was clearly very upset / denied the charge
The man who appeared in the dock / looked very ill

Although there are tendencies, and some obligations, in the assignment of intonational phrases, there remains considerable flexibility. Where clauses are short, they may be combined into one group, e.g.

/I don't think he will/

While subjects are often separate phrases, objects are generally not. Nevertheless a fronted object or an object in a parallel structure may be so phrased, e.g.

This / you really ought to see
I like him / but I loathe / and detest / his wife

Besides the probabilistic correlations with grammatical units there also seems to be a length constraint; studies have suggested that in conversation and in lectures around half the intonational phrases will be three to four words in length and only in under 10% of cases will they be over eight words in length.[20] In reading aloud from prepared texts, intonational phrases are likely to be longer and are likely to be at least partly governed by punctuation.

11.6.2.2   *Primary Accents and New Information*—In previous sections intonational phrases were said to have one primary accent (= nucleus), at which point begins one of a number of nuclear tones. In very general terms, the nucleus falls on the most prominent syllable (and hence the most prominent word) in an intonational phrase. In more particular terms the nucleus marks the end of the NEW INFORMATION. Old (sometimes referred to as 'given') information is that which has either been mentioned before in the preceding intonational phrases or which is in the listener's consciousness because of its presence in the surrounding physical environment.

Sometimes intonational phrases consist wholly of new information. Very often such phrases occur out-of-the-blue or in response to 'What happened?' In cases where the intonational phrase is wholly new the nucleus falls on the relevant syllable of the last lexical item[21] (lexical item here means nouns, verbs, adjectives, adverbs, and the word 'item' rather than 'word' has been used because sometimes lexical phrases like *wind up* and *child abuse* are involved), e.g.

---

[20] Quirk *et al.* (1964: 683), Crystal (1969: 256), and Altenberg (1987: 25)
[21] Altenberg (1987: 174) found the nucleus occurring on the last lexical item in 78% of cases

Jane's had a ˈbaby
Something happened on Sunday which was quite unˈusual
I don't really want to aˈttend
He was accused of ˈdividend stripping

There are some exceptions to the rule of the last lexical item. One group of exceptions concerns intonational phrases having an intransitive verb or verb phrase whose subject is non-human or which loosely involves (dis)appearance, e.g.

That ˈbuilding's falling down
A ˈdoberman's on the prowl
The ˈdog barked. (cf. The man ˈswore)

Another group of exceptions concerns certain types of adverbial in final position. Sentence adverbials (i.e. those which modify the whole sentence) and adverbials of time usually do not take the nucleus in this position, e.g.

I go to ˈManchester usually
It wasn't a very nice ˈday unfortunately
There's been a ˈmix-up possibly
He didn't sucˈceed however

An alternative in some cases to having the adverb at the end of a sentence without an accent is to divide the sentence into two intonational phrases with the adverb getting a separate phrase on its own, e.g.

I go to ˈManchester / ˇusually
It wasn't a very nice ˈday / unˌfortunately

If a final sentence adverbial in final position takes the sole nucleus, it is contrastive, e.g.

I go there ˇusually.

Those sentence adverbials which are usually classified as conjuncts, e.g. *incidentally, therefore*, cannot take a sole nucleus in this way.

Some other types of expression, which are similar to adverbials in that they are in the nature of afterthoughts, are also common in final position with no accent; for example, vocatives and direct speech markers, e.g.

Don't you aˈgree, Peter?
Don't be a ˈfool, he said

When old information occurs at the end of the sentence, then this will be unaccented, e.g.

(Why don't you invite John to the party?)
Because I don't ˈlike John

(We had a long ˈwait)
You mean we had a ˈvery long wait

In the last example there is obviously some element of contrast present— between *long* and *very long*. Sometimes the nucleus may fall on a contrasted item even though a later item in the intonational phrase is new, e.g.

John is a quite a ˈtall man / whereas his brother is very ˈshort

In certain, very limited, cases, the whole of an intonational phrase comprises old information. One such case concerns ECHOES, i.e. where a second speaker echoes something a first speaker has just said; and the accentuation of the second speaker will follow that of the first (the tone will change to high rise), e.g.

(I couldn't ˈdo it). You couldn't ′do it?

11.6.2.3   The Meanings of Tones—Almost all primary accents in words and longer utterances have up to now been exemplified by use of the high fall nuclear tone (marked ˋ). This is the way in which individual words are usually cited in isolation. Moreover, in all styles of English speech, simple falls in pitch (whether from a high or mid starting point) account for the majority of nuclear tones (generally estimated around 50%).[22] Simple rises and fall–rises are generally estimated to account for a further 40% of tones. The preponderance of falls is usually slightly higher in conversation than in other types of speech, e.g. scripted reading. Since rises and fall–rises are often used as a cohesive device signalling more to follow, it is not surprising that they are more frequently used in reading where they will often indicate that a sentence is not yet finished.

The meanings of nuclear tones are sometimes more discoursal in nature (e.g. they indicate links or the absence of links between successive intonational phrases), sometimes more attitudinal (e.g. they indicate the speaker's doubt or certainty about what he is saying), and sometimes more semantic (e.g. they co-occur with lexical meanings which are reinforcing or limiting—this is particularly the case with adverbials). In general the meanings of tones are not directly grammatical, but grammar may indirectly be involved in two ways: (i) some attitudes are inherently more associated with questions; in particular, high rise, which often has a meaning of surprise, frequently marks an echo question (see also previous section); and (ii) the attitudinal and discoursal meanings conveyed will vary somewhat according to the syntactic sentence-type (e.g. declarative, wh-interrogative, yes/no-interrogative) with which the intonational phrase co-occurs.

Because of the variation in meaning according to sentence-type just mentioned, the description of the meanings of nuclear tones[23] which follows is divided according to the following categories: (1) major declaratives, (2) minor declaratives, (3) wh-interrogatives, (4) yes/no-interrogatives, (5) tag-interroga-tives, (6) imperatives, (7) exclamatives, (8) social formulae. In general, falling nuclear tones (whether ˏ or ˋ, and including the rise–fall) are separative, matter-of-fact, and assertive, the higher the fall the more vigorous the degree of final-ity involved; whereas both simple rises (ˏ and ′) and fall–rises (ˇ) are continuative, implicative, and non-assertive. Level tones (most common among these being the mid level) belong with the rising tones in the sorts of meanings they convey.

---

[22] Quirk *et al.* (1964: 681), Crystal (1969: 225), and Altenberg (1987: 36). But see also the higher figure reported in §12.7(1)

[23] For further information on the meanings of tones, see Halliday (1967), O'Connor and Arnold (1973), and Cruttenden (1997)

The examples are given as isolated utterances or preceded by a bracketed 'setting'. It should be remembered that the attitudinal meaning of an utterance must always be interpreted within a context, both of the situation and also of the speaker's personality. It may well happen that an intonation which is polite in one set of circumstances might, for instance, be offensive or patronizing when used by another person or in other circumstances.

(1) *Major declaratives*—Major declarative refers to those cases where the intonational phrase correlates with an independent clause, with the main clause in complex sentences, with the last clause in compound sentences, and with that part of any of these which is remaindered when a separate intonational phrase is given to an adverbial or a subject or some other part of the clause, e.g.

> *He didn't go*
> *I took an overcoat* /because it was raining
> I took the car /*and drove to London*
> The first man on the moon /*was Neil Armstrong*
> Usually /*we do it this way*
> *We do it this way* /usually

In major declaratives falling tones are the least attitudinally marked of the tones with the high fall expressing more liveliness and involvement than the low fall, cf.

> It's a very nice ˈgarden
> Of ˈcourse it is
> It's a very dull ˌbook
> The parcel arrived on ˌThursday

Fall–rise is common on major declaratives with a variety of meanings, in particular, reservation, contradiction, contrast, and warning, as in:

> I like his ˇwife / even if I don't like him
> (It's the twenty fifth today, isn't it?) Twenty ˇsixth
> John didn't succeed / but ˇPhilip did
> If you don't do it / John'll be very ˇcross

High rises are common on echoes (as already mentioned at the end of the previous section) and on declarative questions:

> (I did it in blue.) You did it in ´blue?
> So you didn't ´go?

Other tones are less common. The low rise with only other low syllables before it (i.e. with no preceding pitch accent) is complaining:

> You mustn't go aˌway

Whereas, with a high pitch before it, it is encouraging or even patronizing (this sequence is very common in speech to children):

> You'll ˈonly overˌdo things
> There's ˈno point in ˌrushing

This sequence is frequent on imperatives (see below) with a similar sort of meaning. Finally, the least common nuclear tone[24] is the rise–fall. Its meaning usually involves an element of being very impressed, or, conversely, being very unimpressed, and hence indignant or even sarcastic:

He's the head of a big firm in ˆLondon
Oh inˆdeed / How ˆnice for you

Rise–fall is often used for gossip:

Have you heard? / Jill's ˆpregnant

(2) *Minor declaratives*—Under minor declaratives are included all those parts of declarative sentences which were excluded under (1) above. Most of these occur in sentence non-final positions, e.g. subjects, adverbials, the first clause of compound sentences, and often the subordinate clause of complex sentences.

The tones used on these intonational phrases are usually from the rising group: fall–rise, low rise, and mid level. Fall–rise again carries its common meaning of 'contrast'. The difference between the other two tones in non-final position has to do with style: low rise is the most oratorical and is also typical of reading aloud, whereas the mid level carries no other meaning other than that of non-finality, which is perhaps why it alone of these three tones occurs **only** in non-final position:

What I'd ˇlike / is a drink of tea
The ˇbest person to do it / would be Bill Bailey
The ˇcrucial issue / is that . . .
We took the ˌcar / and drove to Birmingham
On my way to >work / it started to rain
Un>fortunately / it doesn't work like that
(cf. Unˇfortunately / it doesn't work like that)

Most adverbials which have a separate intonational phrase will take a rising tone but there are a number of adverbials of a particularly assertive kind which more commonly take a falling tone (e.g. *literally, certainly, honestly, by the way, of course, besides*):

Be`sides / he's had more time than he should have
By the `way / what do you think of the new chap?

As indicated by the last example, some adverbials can occur before interrogatives as well as declaratives. Adverbials also frequently occur following the main clause; in these cases the rise which occurs is almost always low rise (but the falling type again takes a fall):

I went to Canada / last ˌyear
It didn't work / unˌfortunately
He turned bright red / `literally

---

[24] For the frequency of nuclear tones, see Quirk *et al.* (1964: 681), Crystal (1969: 225), and Altenberg (1987: 37)

In the case of final subordinate clauses two sequences of tones are possible. If the previous main clause has a fall, then the subordinate clause will take a low rise. Alternatively, the main clause may take a fall–rise and the subordinate clause the fall, cf.

> I began to feel `ill / because I hadn't had enough to ,eat.
> I began to feel ˇill / because I hadn't had enough to `eat

(3) *Yes/no-interrogatives*—In RP the more usual and more polite way of asking yes/no questions is with the low rise (although a high rise is more frequent in General American); if a potentially accented syllable is available before the nucleus, then this will take a high pitch:

> (It's going to rain I'm afraid.) Do you 'really ,think so?
> (I'm really enjoying myself.) Is 'this your ,first visit to London?
> (The large size costs a pound.) Is 'that the ,new price?

A falling tone (high fall or low fall) on a yes/no-interrogative marks it as brusque and demanding:

> (Can you remember where I left my new shoes?) Are they in the `wardrobe?
> (Tom explained it all to me.) But do you under`stand it?
> (I can't find my pen anywhere.) Are you sure you brought it `with you?

A rise–fall is often used to mark a yes/no-interrogative as an exclamation:

> (He didn't even leave a message.) Now isn't that peˆculiar!
> (I'm going to Spain tomorrow.) Aren't you ˆlucky!
> (He refused to help me.) Would you beˆlieve it!

(4) *Wh-interrogatives*—The usual tone on wh-interrogatives is falling (low fall or high fall):

> (She wants you to send an apology.) What it got to do with `her?
> (You mustn't tell her.) Why `not?
> (She didn't get the job.) How do you ,know?

The alternative tone on such interrogatives is the low rise (like yes/no interrogatives, it is more likely to be a high rise in General American). The use of the rise is more tentative:

> (We're off on Thursday.) When are you ,leaving?
> (I'm afraid it didn't work.) Why did you do it ,that way?

Wh-interrogatives can be used with high rise to ask for repetition:

> (He's completely irresponsible.) 'What did you say?
> (Her name was Pettigrew before she was married.) 'What did you say she was called?

(5) *Tag-interrogatives*—Tag-interrogatives consist of a sequence of an auxiliary verb and a pronoun appended to a preceding declarative. They are most commonly negative if a preceding statement is positive, and vice versa (called 'reversed polarity' tags). Such tags have two common alternatives; a falling tone

(high fall or low fall) or a rising tone (usually low rise). Both types of tone expect agreement, the fall demanding it, the rise leaving open the possibility of disagreement:

> (It's a long way from the shops.) It's right on the outskirts /ˈisn't it?
> (I had a lovely time.) Yes / The day did go well / ˋdidn't it?
> (Lend me your copy of Shakespeare.) You will look after it /ˈwon't you?
> (Where did I put my golf clubs?) You left them in the garage /ˌdidn't you?
> (He asked me to drive him there.) But you won't be able to go /ˌwill you?
> (Who was that woman he was with?) It was his sister /ˌwasn't it?

Another type of tag has constant polarity. This type only has low rise (falling tones are impossible). The meaning conveyed is in the nature of a thoughtful echo of a statement from the preceding speaker:

> (I think he's going to emigrate.) So he won't marry her /ˌwon't he?
> (Rachel's gone out with John.) She's still seeing him /ˌis she?

(6) *Imperatives*—Abrupt imperatives have a falling tone. Polite imperatives, which are at least suggesting that the listener has a right to refuse, are said with a rising tone (most frequently low rise and sometimes fall–rise):

> (I've decided to lend him my car.) Don't be such a silly ˋfool
> (What should I do now?) Go and wash the ˋcar
> (You shouldn't have spent all that money.) Don't be ˌangry about it
> (I'm afraid I've had enough of you.) Give me another ˌchance
> (I have a very delicate job to do here.) Be ˇcareful

The use of a rising tone rather than a falling tone softens the imperative. Sometimes the rising tone is combined with a tag:

> (Can I have some more wine?) Help yourself /ˌwon't you?
> (Her nerves are terrible.) See if you can help /ˌwill you?
> (I'm doing my best.) Well / hurry up /ˌcan't you?

(7) *Exclamatives*—Exclamatives (i.e. those sentences having the syntactic form of an exclamative, i.e. an initial question word and no verb) take a falling tone (including rise–fall):

> What a beautiful ˋday! How ˋstupid he is! What a very silly thing to ˋdo!
> What a paˆlaver!

Similarly, individual words, particularly nouns and adjectives, can be given exclamatory force by the use of a falling tone, e.g.

> ˋNonsense! You ˋidiot! ˋMarvellous!

(8) *Social formulae*—It is difficult to give rules for the intonation of social formulae because it is an area where native speakers of English often have idiosyncratic habits. It is, however, generally true that falling tones generally show sincerity, whereas rising tones are used in situations where a formulaic pleasantry is appropriate. Thus *thank you* is appropriately said with a rise on being given a ticket, while a high fall is more likely if a genuine favour has been done, and a low fall if the matter in hand is boring. *Good morning* with a high fall is sincere

(and sometimes inappropriately so!), while a low fall is brusque, and with a low rise is polite (and possibly overly so!). This greeting (and many others) can also be said with the 'stylized' tone while involves a step from high level to mid level beginning on the accented syllable, thus:

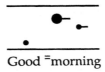

Good =morning

This tone is a special one often used on vocatives and on jocular sentences,[25] e.g.

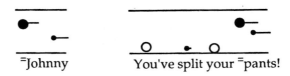

=Johnny   You've split your =pants!

(9) *Tonal sequences*—In the preceding subsections it has become apparent that some tonal sequences are very common in successive intonational phrases, particularly those within one sentence. The most common sequence involves a tone from the rising group (low rise, fall–rise or mid level) followed by a fall (high fall or low fall); and the syntactic sequences are sentence adverbial or noun-clause subject followed by a clause remainder and an initial subordinate or co-ordinate clause:

> Un>fortunately / it didn't ˇwork
> The ˇusual excuse / is that there's not enough ˇtime
> Because he gave up too ˇearly / he lost two thousand ˇpounds
> He staked everything on ˌwinning / and ended up with ˇnothing

A second sequence involves a falling tone (high fall or low fall) followed by a rising tone (almost always low rise, occasionally fall–rise): the syntactic sequences are main clause plus adverbial or main clause plus 'open' tag:

> I deny the whole ˇthing / ˌusually
> That's the best way to ˇdo it / ˌisn't it?

A third common sequence is a falling tone (low fall, high fall) plus another falling tone (low fall, high fall); this is common with sentence adverbials of the reinforcing type, with 'closed' tags, and with co-ordinate clauses which are very independent of one another:

---

[25] For full details of this tone in English, see Ladd (1979)

I go to `London / `regularly
It was a beautiful `day / `wasn't it?
(What should I do?) Take up `singing / write a `book / do an `evening class /
buy a `bicycle / `anything!

11.6.2.4   The Use of Secondary Accents—Secondary accents are produced by
pitch prominences which occur before the nucleus, i.e. they are pre-nuclear
accents. As the name implies they contribute less to meaning than primary
accents. The first secondary accent in an intonational phrase often serves to mark
the beginning of the new information, e.g. We ʹ*ran all the* ʹ*way to the* ʹ*station.*
Where there is a series of secondary accents (prominence being achieved by
'stepping' the pitch-see §11.6.1.4 above), the later accent(s), like that on *way* in
the example above, serve only to divide the new information into chunks. This
sequence of secondary accents which steps down is the most common type of
pre-nuclear accenting in RP and can occur before all nuclear tones. The other
most frequent type of sequence involves one or a series of slides (see §11.6.1.4
above); this gives more emphasis to the words taking the accents and is particularly common before the fall–rise nuclear tone, e.g. It ˇ*wasn't* ˇ*really like* ˈ*that.*

11.6.3   Regional Variation in Intonation

Within Britain the most marked variation compared with RP concerns the more
extensive use of rising tones in many northern cities; it is reported for Birmingham,
Glasgow, Liverpool, and Newcastle.[26] Rises in these cities are more frequent on
declaratives than in RP and, indeed, in some of them may typically be the most
frequent tone on declaratives. The rise may be a continuous one, as in Glasgow,
or may consist of a rise followed by a plateau (with an optional downdrift at the
end), as in Liverpool and Newcastle. Belfast (and Derry) has both types and has
the most regular use of rises of all the cities, falling tones being much less frequent
than rising ones in speakers of all educational classes (where in the other cities the
typical rising tones may be lost in more educated speakers).
    General American has less variation compared with RP than that in northern
British cities mentioned above; one notable difference is the increased use of
high rise as opposed to low rise, particularly for yes/no-interrogatives. Australia
and New Zealand are most notable for the intonational change in progress
whereby a high rise is increasingly used on declaratives;[27] it seems to be used as
a check by the speaker that the listener is paying attention and understanding,
particularly when the speaker is presenting information. This usage is now
commonly heard in England.

11.6.4   Pitch Range

In preceding sections §11.6.1.3 and §11.6.2.3 falls were divided into high falls
and low falls, and rises were divided into low rises and high rises. This sort of

---

[26] Cruttenden (1995)
[27] Guy *et al.* (1986), Britain (1992)

variation in the height of tones is referred to as accent range. However, there is another sort of variation in height which refers to the pitch of the whole intonational phrase, measured as the interval between the lowest and highest pitches. Speakers may increase the width of the normal pitch range of their intonational phrases by raising the pitch of the highest pitches. Such variation in the width of the pitch range of intonational phrases is often referred to as KEY. The most common use of key concerns the delimitation of PARATONES, a new paratone being marked by a wide key and the end of a paratone by a narrow key[28] (and often followed by an extended pause). Paratones often correspond with topics (defined in the widest sense); the most obvious use of such differences of key, paratones, and topics, is in newsreading.

There is yet another sort of variation in pitch range which involves raising or lowering both low and high pitches, so that the pitch overall is lower or higher but not wider. A low register is used for parentheticals (marked here by doubling the boundary marker), e.g.

> I ran into Jane last week // by the way / did you know she still has three children? // and she said . . .

High register is, in general, associated with greater emotional tension but nevertheless has to some extent become conventionalized. For example, the adoption of a 'little girl voice' may be used to signal helplessness.

11.6.5   Intonation and Punctuation

Punctuational usage is generally prescribed in manuals of punctuation (particularly those put out by publishing houses) according to grammar rather than intonation. Indeed, in some cases a punctuation mark has no correlate in intonation, e.g. the apostrophe marking possession or elision, and the use of spaces between words. However, in many cases punctuation is as related to intonation as to grammar.

Punctuation marks serve both to delimit, e.g. to mark the end of a sentence, or to specify, e.g. that a sentence is a question. In both areas there are clear correlations between punctuation and intonation. The use of any of the six marks, comma, semi-colon, colon, full stop, question mark, and exclamation mark, always correlates with a boundary between intonational phrases. However, there are syntactic positions where such an intonational break is very common but where the use of a punctuation mark (especially the comma) is generally proscribed. This applies particularly to the position between subject and verb. As remarked in §11.6.2.1 above, this is a very common position for an intonational break if the subject is either particularly long or contrastive. Hence, although a comma in this position is generally proscribed by manuals of punctuation, there will nevertheless be the tendency to insert a comma here because of the writer's intuition about intonational–punctuational correlations, e.g.

---

[28] See, in particular, Brazil (1975, 1978, 1985)

The best way to do this, would be to ask him first.

Specification concerns the marking of a sentence-type as a question, or an exclamation (the use of the full stop marks the sentence as a non-question and non-exclamation, but may be used for different sentence-types, e.g. statement, command, and request). Such specifiers have poor correlations with nuclear tones. The full stop usually correlates with a fall but by no means always. The question mark correlates regularly with a high rise in the case of 'declarative questions' (§11.6.2.3(1)), with a low rise very frequently in yes/no-questions and approximately half the time in tag-questions, but more frequently with a falling tone in wh-questions. Only in the case of the exclamation mark is there a regular correlation with at least an overall category of tone—it always correlates with a falling tone (usually high fall or rise–fall).

11.6.6 Acquisition of Intonation by Native Learners[29]

Many babies are excellent mimics of intonation and may produce English-sounding intonation patterns on nonsense syllables (often called 'jargon intonation') in the late stages of their pre-linguistic babbling.[30] At this same time they may also have distinction of meaning in their use of a fall versus a rise on single syllables—typically the fall is naming while the rise is requesting. Even those children who do not have this distinction during the babbling period will generally acquire it during the period of one-word utterances (which typically lasts for six to nine months during a child's second year). At the two-word stage children are capable of varying nucleus placement, although whether this is already signalling new and old information or whether it is more rigidly tied to different types of sentence is not yet clear. (It is, for example, often the case that possessives have the accent on the possessor while locatives have it on the location, cf. `Daddy car` 'Daddy's car' vs *Daddy `car* 'Daddy's in the car'). Little is known about the later acquisition of intonation, although it is likely that some uses of the fall–rise tone are learnt early. But a full mastery of the more subtle nuances of intonational meaning may not be acquired until the age of ten or even later.[31]

11.6.7 Advice to Foreign Learners

The foreign learner should pay particular attention to:

(1) Achieving a better style in reading aloud by appropriately dividing his speech into intonational phrases. Such division may be done in English in ways very similar to his native language (especially in the case of most other European languages) but nevertheless the learner should note the frequency with which sentence adverbials and the subjects of sentences are given their own intonational phrases.

---

[29] Crystal (1986)
[30] Peters (1977)
[31] Cruttenden (1974, 1985)

(2) Putting the nucleus on the focal point in the sentence. Some languages (like French, Italian, and Spanish) more regularly have the primary accent on the last word in the intonational phrase. This may sometimes mean accenting old information occurring at the end of a phrase, which is incorrect in English, e.g.

> A: Would you like to come to London with me tomorrow?
> B: No / I don't like LONdon

(3) Using appropriate nuclear tones. Learners should note that the fall–rise (especially on a single word) is rare in most languages but very frequent in English for a range of attitudinal meanings on declaratives and for subjects with their own intonational phrase. Fall–rise is also frequent on sentence adverbials in initial position, although low rise is the usual tone in final position (but those exceptional falling adverbs, like *definitely*, which take low fall or high fall in any position must also be noted).

An overuse of simple falling tones (especially high falls), together with an overuse of glides-down in pre-nuclear positions, will produce an excessively aggressive effect, while conversely an overuse of simple rising tones (including fall–rises, and glides-up in pre-nuclear position, which are uncommon in RP) will sound excessively tentative.

11.7   *Hesitations*

Pause was stated in §11.6.1.1 to be one of a number of phonetic features which are used to mark boundaries between intonational phrases. But pause can also occur in other positions: (a) before words of high lexical content or which have a low probability of occurrence in a particular context; and (b) after the first word in an intonational phrase, where it appears to be a pause for planning, i.e. the speaker has decided that he has something to say but has not yet planned it in detail.[32] Both (a) and (b) may be also used as ways of attempting to prevent interruption. Both differ from pauses at intonational phrase boundaries in frequently being filled rather than unfilled (i.e. silent) pauses. In RP filled pauses are generally filled with [ə] or [m] or a combination of the two, e.g.

> I don't agree with that / I [ɜː] think it would be better if . . .
> You see/the myth is / and I'm [ɜː] I can see from the applause . . .
> Well [əmː] I don't think I will.

This type of filled pause used in RP is not necessarily the type of filled pause used in other dialects of English or in other languages. Scottish English uses [eː], French uses [øː], and Russian uses [nː]. A quite dramatic change can be produced in the degree to which a person's speech sounds native-like by adopting the correct type of filled hesitations.

---

[32] Cruttenden (1997: 30–2)

11.8 *Voice Quality*[33]

Even more so than intonation the area of voice quality has very little scientific work associated with it, particularly on a cross-linguistic basis and this section is perforce not very systematic. Some reference has already made to the topic under §5.8 above. The term 'voice quality' refers to positions of the vocal organs which characterise speakers' voices on a long-term basis. Long-term tendencies in positioning the tongue and the soft palate are referred to as ARTICULATORY SETTINGS; those referring to positions of the vocal cords are called PHONATION TYPES. In some tone languages a phonation type may co-occur with a lexical tone (e.g. two tones may be distinguished in some varieties of Vietnamese, one simple high rise and one high rise with accompanying creak). But more generally a particular voice quality may be characteristic of an individual, of a particular language or dialect, or may be used within a language to convey a particular attitude or emotion.

The articulatory setting of a language or dialect may differ from RP. So some languages like Spanish may have a tendency to hold the tongue more forward in the mouth, whereas others like Russian may have a tendency to hold it further back in the mouth. Nasalization may be characteristic of many speakers of American English while denasal voice (which may lead to a low-grade nasal resonance in nasal consonants) is frequently said to occur in Liverpool. Tense and lax are labels which apply to the muscular tension in the whole of the vocal tract:[34] RP is generally said to be lax (making it sound 'mellow'), while French and German are said to be tense (making them sound 'metallic' or 'strident').

The most commonly described phonation types are creaky voice, breathy voice, ventricular voice (sometimes called harsh voice and involving the false vocal cords just above the vocal cords), whispery voice, falsetto (dividing the vocal cords into two halves and hence raising the pitch by an octave), and raised-larynx and lowered-larynx voices. Breathy voice is said to be used by many speakers of Danish and Dutch, creaky voice is used by many speakers of RP and particularly by speakers of Refined RP, while ventricular voice is a characteristic of many speakers of Scottish English and speakers of Cockney. Within RP (and possibly wider in English) some phonation types are associated with certain styles of speech and emotions: breathy voice is often called 'bedroom voice', whispery voice is sometimes called 'stage whisper' or 'library voice', ventricular voice is associated with anger, and lowered-larynx is called sepulchral or 'vicar's voice'.

---

[33] See Laver (1980), and Henton and Bladon (1988)
[34] The terms are also often used to distinguish between the short and long vowels of English (see §8.4.1(h) above and Chomsky and Halle (1968))

12

Words in Connected Speech

12.1 *Citation Forms and Connected Speech*

Every utterance is a continuous, changing, pattern of sound quality with associated (prosodic) features of quantity, accent, and pitch. The word (consisting of one or several morphemes) is, like the phoneme, an abstraction from this continuum and must be expected to be realized in phonetically different ways according to the context, cf. the various allophonic (phonetic) realizations of the abstract unit known as the phoneme. The word constitutes, however, a separable linguistic reality for the speaker. Whether it has a simple or a complex morphemic structure, it is an element of language which is commutable in an utterance with other members of its class, i.e. nouns for other nouns, verbs for other verbs etc. It is, moreover, often capable of constituting an utterance by itself. It must, therefore, be considered as an abstraction on a higher level than the phoneme, its separable identity having been recognized in the sophisticated written form of English by the use of spaces between words. If, however, the word is admitted as an abstracted linguistic unit, it is important to note the differences which may exist between its concrete realization when said (often artificially) in isolation and those which it has when, in connected speech, it is subject to the pressures of its sound environment or of the accentual or rhythmic group of which it forms part. The variations involved may affect the word as a whole, e.g. weak forms in an unaccented situation or word accentual patterns within the larger rhythmic pattern of the complete utterance; or may affect more particularly the sounds used at word boundaries, such changes involving a consideration of the features of morpheme and word junctures, in particular, ASSIMILATIONS, ELISIONS, and LIAISONS. In addition, it will be seen that the extent of variation depends largely upon the casual or formal nature of the utterance, the more formal and careful (and probably the slower rate of) the delivery the greater the tendency to preserve a form nearer to that of the isolate word.

12.2 *Neutralization of Weak Forms*

We have seen already (§11.3) that a number of function words may have different pronunciations according to whether they are accented (or said in isolation) or, more typically, are unaccented. Such is the reduction and obscuration of the unaccented forms that words which are phonetically and phonemically distinct when said in isolation may be neutralized under weak accent. Such neutralization causes no confusion because of the high rate of redundancy of meaningful cues in English; it is only rarely that the context will allow a variety of interpretations for any one cue supplied by an unaccented word form. The examples of neutralization which follow might occur in casual (and usually rapid) RP:[1]

/ə/ = unaccented *are, a* (and, less commonly, *her, or, of*)

> The 'plays *are* `poor
> He 'plays *a* `poor man
> She 'wants *a* `dog
> She 'wants *her* `dog (less rapidly, with reduced /ɜː/ for *her*)
> 'One *or* 'two *of* them *are* `coming (or /ɔː/ for *or*, /əv/ for *of*)
> 'Two 'books *are* `mine
> 'Two 'books *of* `mine (or, less rapidly, /əv/ for *of*)

/əv/ = unaccented *have* (aux.), *of*

> 'Some *of* ˌone piece . . .
> 'Some *have* ˌwon . . .
> The 'boys *of* 'Eton `fish
> The 'boys *have* 'eaten `fish

(The last two utterances being identical, the meaning is clear only from the larger context.)

/ər/ = unaccented *are, or*

> 'Ten *or* `under (less rapidly, /ɔː/ for *or*)
> 'Ten *are* `under

/ðə/ = unaccented *the, there*

> *There* 'seems a `chance
> *The* 'seams are `crooked

/s/ = unaccented *is, has, does*

> 'What's ('s = *does* or *is*) he `like?
> 'What's ('s = *has*) he `lost?

/z/ = unaccented *is, has, does*

> 'Where's ('s = *has*, less commonly *does*) he `put it?
> 'Where's ('s = *is*) he `going?

/əz/ = unaccented *as, has*

> 'How 'much *has* he `done?
> As 'much *as* he `can

---

[1] Byrd (1992a,b,c) found women reducing less than men

/ən/ = unaccented *and, an*

> 'On *and* `off
> 'On *an* `off-chance

/n/ = unaccented *and, not*

> 'Did*n't* he ˌdo it? /ˈdɪdn̩ːˈduː ɪt/
> He 'did *and* he `didn't /hɪ ˈdɪd n̩ iː ˈdɪdnt/

/d/ = unaccented *had, would*

> I'd ('d = *had, would*) 'put it `here

12.3   *Variation in the Accentual Patterns of Words*

When a word (simple or compound) pattern consists in isolation of a primary accent preceded by a secondary accent, the primary accent may be lost, if, in connected speech, a strong accent follows closely, e.g.

> 'thir`teen, *but* 'thirteen `pounds
> 'West`minster, *but* 'Westminster `Abbey
> 'full-`grown, *but* a 'full-grown `man
> 'after`noon, *but* 'afternoon `tea

The secondary accent in the word rather than the primary may be lost when another word with secondary accent immediately precedes, e.g.

> 'eight thir`teen; 'near West`minster; 'not full`grown; 'Friday after`noon

Such examples, and the others in this section, confirm the tendency in English to avoid adjacent accented syllables.

It is in order to avoid the placing of primary accents on adjacent syllables that 'accent shift' occurs in phrases such as 'Chinese `restaurant (but *Chi`nese*), 'outside `world (but *out`side*), 'aquama`rine `necklace (but *aquama`rine*), accents not occurring on adjacent syllables in either case. Where the accents are separated by an unaccented syllable, the accent shift is optional, e.g. *diplo`matic, diplo`matic `incident* or 'diplomatic `incident; aquama`rine, aquama`rine ti`ara, 'aquamarine ti`ara.

This tendency to the alternation of accented and unaccented syllables is so strong that the accent may be shifted in the case of certain words whose citation form contains only one, later, accent, e.g. *or`nate* but 'ornate `carvings; *u`nique* but 'unique `features; and *di`rect* but 'direct `access. The alternation tendency extends into longer utterances and may be seen in examples such as *i`dea* but *the 'idea `pleases me; recom`mend* but *I can 'recommend `several*; and in phrasal verbs such as 'come `out, 'get `in, e.g. *The 'pictures 'didn't come `out*, but *They 'came out `well* and 'What 'time will 'you get `in? but 'What 'time will you 'get in from `work?

12.4   *Phonemic and Phonetic Variations at Boundaries*

We have seen (Chapter 5) that our basic linguistic units, the phonemes, represent abstractions from actual phonetic reality. If the phoneme /t/ is given a convenient, generalized label—a voiceless alveolar plosive—it is nevertheless true that the actual phonetic realization of this consonant depends on the nature of the context, e.g. /t/ is aspirated when before a vowel (except after /s/), and dental, rather than alveolar, when adjacent to /θ/ or /ð/. Moreover, we are dealing with a sound and articulatory continuum rather than with discrete units: features of sound segment A may be found in a following segment B, and features of B in A (cf. 'transitions' of consonants, §9.2.2). If, therefore, the utterance is analysed in terms of a sequence of phonemes, account must be taken of the phonetic continuity and merging of qualities by describing the mutual influence which contiguous elements exert upon each other; in other words, tendencies towards assimilation or CO-ARTICULATION have to be noted. The tendencies outlined below are valid for colloquial English RP but may not be characteristic of other languages.

Variations of articulation may be of an allophonic kind, either within a word or at word boundaries; or, at word and morpheme boundaries, they may be of such an extent that a change of phoneme is involved, as between the pronunciation of a word in isolation and that which it may have in context. The fact that the phonemic pattern of a word is subject to variation emphasizes the potential nature of phonemic oppositions. The meaning of a word derives as much from the situation and context in which it occurs as from its precise phonemic shape, the high redundancy of English tolerating considerable variation at the phonemic level. The mutual influence of contiguous phonemes in English functions predominantly in a REGRESSIVE or ANTICIPATORY direction, i.e. features of one phoneme are anticipated in the articulation of the preceding phoneme; sometimes it is PROGRESSIVE or PERSEVERATIVE, i.e. one phoneme markedly influences the following phoneme, and sometimes it is COALESCENT, i.e. a fusion of forms takes place.

12.4.1   Allophonic Variations

Since the actual realization of any phoneme is at least slightly different in every context, it is necessary to give examples only of those variants which exhibit striking changes. The same types of allophonic variation, involving a change of place of articulation, voicing, lip position, or position of the soft palate, may be found within the word and also at word boundaries:

(1) *Place of articulation.*

(a) *within word*:

   /t/—post-alveolar in *try* (influence of [ɹ])
    —dental in *eighth* (influence of [θ])
   /k/—advanced (pre-velar) in *key* (influence of [iː])
   /n/—dental in *tenth* (influence of [θ])
   /m/—labiodental in *nymph, infant* (influence of [f])
   /ʌ/—retracted in *result* (influence of [ɫ])
   /uː/—centralized in *music* (influence of [j])

(b) *at word boundaries*:

   /t/—dental in *not that* (influence of [ð])
   /d/—dental in *hide them* (influence of [ð])

/m/—labiodental in *ten forks, come for me* (influence of [f])
/s/—retracted in *this road* (influence of [ɹ])

(2) *Voice*—devoicing of continuants following a voiceless consonant.

(a) *within word*:

/l,r,w,j/—devoiced following voiceless consonants, e.g *cry, plight, quite, queue*
/m,n,ŋ/—slightly devoiced following voiceless consonants, e.g. *smoke, snow, mutton, open* /ˈəʊpm̩/, *bacon* /ˈbeɪkn̩/

(b) *at word boundaries* (only in close-knit sequences): /l,r,w,j/—devoiced following voiceless consonants in close-knit sequences, e.g. *at last* [əˈtl̥ɑːst], *at rest* [əˈtr̥est], *at once* [əˈtw̥ʌns], *see to it* [ˈsiːtwɪt], *thank you* [ˈθæŋkju̥ː].

Note also the devoicing of word-final voiced plosive or fricative consonants before silence, and of fricatives when followed by a voiceless consonant; and of word-initial voiced fricative or plosive consonants when preceded by silence, e.g. in *What can you give?* ([v̥]); *Can you breathe?* ([ð̥]); *It's his* ([z̥]); *Near the bridge* ([d̥ʒ̥]); *They've* ([v̥]) *come; with* ([ð̥]) *some; He's* ([z̥]) *seen it; George* ([d̥ʒ̥]) *can;* ([v̥]) *very good* ([d̥]); ([ð̥]) *there;* ([z̥]) *zinc does* ([z̥]).

(3) *Lip position*—under the influence of adjacent vowels or semi-vowels.

(a) *within word*:

	Lip-spread	Lip-rounded[2]
/p/	pea, heap	pool, hoop, upward
/t/	tea, beat	two, boot, twice, outward
/k/	keep, speak	cool, spook, quite, backward
/m/	mean, seem	moon, loom, somewhat
/n/	knee, seen	noon, onward
/l/	leave, feel	bloom, fool, always
/r/[3]	read	rude
/f/	feel, leaf	fool, roof
/s/	seat, geese	soon, goose, sweep
/ʃ/	sheet, leash	shoot, douche, dishwasher
/h/	he	who etc.

(b) *at word boundaries* (only in close-knit sequences), e.g. /t,k,n,ŋ,l,s/ are somewhat labialized in cases such as *that one, thick one, thin one, wrong one, shall we, this way,* the syllables with initial /w/ carrying no accent; a rounded vowel (as opposed to semi-vowel) in an adjacent word does not seem to exert the same labializing influence, e.g. /uː/ does not labialize /s/ markedly in *Who said that?* nor /ɔː/ in *This ought to*.

(4) *Nasal resonance*[4]—resulting particularly from regressive but also from progressive lowering of the soft palate in the vicinity of a nasal consonant.

---

[2] This will apply only for those speakers who have appreciable rounding of the vowels and semi-vowels
[3] For some speakers /r/ has inherent labialization and will not be lip-spread even before a lip-spread vowel
[4] See Cohn (1990)

(a) *within word*—nasalization of vowel preceding /m/ in *ham* and /n/ in *and*, of vowel between nasal consonants in *man, men, innermost*, and of short vowels on each side of the nasal consonant in *any, sunny, summer, singer*; also /l/ in situations such as in *helmet, wrongly*; and possible slight nasalization of vowel following /m, n/, as in *meal, now*.

(b) *at word boundaries*—vowels may sometimes be nasalized somewhat by the boundary nasal consonant of an adjacent word, especially when an adjacent nasal consonant also occurs in the word containing the vowel, e.g. the first /ə/ in *bring another*, or /ɪ/ in *come in*, but sometimes also with no adjacent nasal consonant in the word containing the vowel (usually unaccented), e.g. /ə/ in *come along, wait for me*, /ɪ/ in *every night*. Approximants may also be nasalized by a nasal in an adjacent word, e.g. /l/ in *tell me*.

12.4.2   Phonemic Variations

Different pronunciations of the same word (either between two speakers or between different styles of speech in the same speaker) sometimes exhibit a different choice of internal phoneme depending on the degree of assimilatory pressure of the word environment felt by the speaker, e.g. *length* may be /leŋθ, leŋkθ/, or /lenθ/, *encounter* may have /ɪn/ or /ɪŋ/ in the first syllable, *disgrace* may have final /s/ or /z/ in the first syllable, *absolutely* may have final /b/ or /p/ in the first syllable, and *issue* may have medial /sj/ or a coalesced form /ʃ/. From a diachronic point of view, a phonemic change within a word may sometimes be attributable to the combinatory pressures exerted on a phoneme by the word environment, e.g. by labialization /wa(ː)/ → /wɒ/ or /wɔː/ (*swan, water*); /ɪr,er,ʊr/ coalesced into /ər/ (later /ɜː/) under the influence of the post-vocalic /r/ (*first, earth, curse*); and /s/ or /z/ and /j/ combined their phonetic characteristics to give /ʃ,ʒ/ (*mansion, vision*).

Many phonemic changes occur in connected speech at word boundaries (i.e. change as compared with the phonemic pattern of the isolate word form). Such phonemic variation is found in changes within the pairs of voiced/voiceless phonemes and, more particularly, in changes involving modification of the place of articulation.

12.4.3   Voiced/Voiceless Variations

Word-final voiced fricatives followed by a word-initial voiceless consonant may with some speakers be realized as the corresponding voiceless fricative, if the two words form part of a close-knit group. Thus the final /ð/ of *with* may be replaced by /θ/ in *with thanks*; the final /z/ of *was* by /s/ in *he was sent*; and the final /v/ of *of, we've*, by /f/ in *of course, we've found it*. Such a change to a voiceless fricative is an extension of the allophonic devoicing of such consonants mentioned in §12.4.1(2). The phonemic change in such examples may be complete in that a preceding long vowel or diphthong may be realized in the reduced form appropriate to a syllable closed by a voiceless consonant (See §8.4.1 (d)–(f), 9.2.1(5), 9.4(3)).

The weak form of *is* or *has* is /s/ or /z/ according to the final consonant of the preceding word, cf. *the cat's paw, the cat's gone* /kæts/ vs *the dog's paw, the dog's gone* /dɒgz/.

It is unusual in RP for word-final /b,d,g/ to be influenced in the same way by following voiceless consonants, though voiceless forms may be heard in such contexts in the speech of northern England, e.g. the /d/ of *good time* and the /g/ of *big case* may be realized as /t,k/.

It is to be noted that word- or morpheme-final voiceless consonants in English do not show tendencies to assimilate to their voiced counterparts: such pronunciations of *nice boy, black dress, half-done, they both do, wishbone, birthday*, as /'naɪz ˈbɔɪ, 'blæg ˈdres, 'hɑːv ˈdʌn, ðeɪ 'bəʊð ˈduː, ˈwɪʒbəʊn, ˈbɜːðdeɪ/ are typical of many foreign learners.

12.4.4   Nasality and Labialization

Phonemic assimilations involving nasality (i.e. anticipation or perseveration of the lowered soft palate position) would be likely to show /b/ (or /v/) → /m/, /d/ (or /z/ or /ð/) → /n/, /g/ → /ŋ/, such changes being based on roughly homorganic mouth articulations; nasalization of other sounds, e.g. /l/ or vowels, is never phonemic, there being no nasalized counterpart with approximately homorganic mouth articulation. Such phonemic nasalization as does occur concerns mainly the alveolars, especially adjacent to the negative *'nt* /n(t)/, and is characteristic of very rapid speech, often as a popular form unacceptable in RP (marked † in the examples below), e.g.

/d → n/—*He wouldn't do it* /hɪ 'wʊnn(t) ˈduː ɪt/ *good news* /'gʊn ˈnjuːz/
/d → g → ŋ/—*He wouldn't go* /hɪ 'wʊŋŋ(k) ˈgəʊ/
/d → b → m/—*Good morning* /gʊm ˈmɔːnɪŋ/
/v → m/—*You can have mine* /jʊ kŋ hæm ˈmaɪn/
/z → n/—*He doesn't know* /hɪ 'dʌnn(t) ˈnəʊ/†
/ð → n/—*He wasn't there* /hɪ 'wɒn(t) ˈneə/† *to win the race* /tə 'wɪn nə ˈreɪs/†

(In the above examples, the nasalized assimilated form may be elided altogether.)

The extension of labialization produces no changes of a phonemic kind, since lip-position is not a distinctive feature opposing any two phonemes in RP. /ɒ/ and /ɑː/ come nearest to having an opposition of lip action, but the lip-rounding for /ɒ/ is very slight and open and, in any case, there is some difference of tongue position and a considerable difference of length. Where /w/ precedes a vowel of the /ɑː/ type (and, therefore, might be expected to exert a rounding influence), either labialization has become established at an earlier stage of the development of the language (e.g. in *was, what, war, water* etc.) or two pronunciations are today permitted, e.g. *qualm* /kwɑːm/ or /kwɔːm/, *quaff* /kwɒf/ or /kwɑːf/. Labialization of /ɑː/ involving a phonemic change to /ɒ/ or /ɔː/ does not extend beyond word boundaries, e.g. in *two arms* or *the car won't go*. Some confusion may, however, occur between a strongly centralized form of /əʊ/ and /ɜː/ in a labial context, cf. *they weren't wanted* and *they won't want it*; also, with the influence of a strongly labialized form of /r/, in a pair such as *they weren't right, they won't write*.

12.4.5 Variations of Place

The most common phonemic changes at word boundaries concern changes of place of articulation, particularly involving de-alveolarization. Though such changes are normal in colloquial speech, native speakers are usually unaware that they are made. The phenomenon is essentially the same as that resulting in non-phonemic assimilation of place. Recent electropalatographic research[5] shows that phonemic assimilations of place are rarely complete, e.g. in an assimilation involving an apparent change from alveolar to labial, as in *bad boy* → /bæb bɔɪ/, some residual articulation on the teeth ridge may accompany the labial articulation. (See §9.2.6(2), §9.6.2(2).)

(1) *Regressive (or anticipatory) assimilation: instability of final alveolars*—Word-final /t,d,n,s,z/ readily assimilate to the place of the following word-initial consonant whilst retaining the original voicing. /t,d,n/ are replaced by bilabials before bilabial consonants and by velars before velar consonants; /s,z/ are replaced by palato-alveolars before consonants containing a palatal feature:[6]

/t/ → /p/ before /p,b,m/, e.g. *that pen, that boy, that man* /ðæp ˈpen, ðæp ˈbɔɪ, ðæp ˈmæn/

→ /k/ before /k,g/, e.g. *that cup, that girl* /ðæk ˈkʌp, ðæk ˈgɜːl/

/d/ → /b/ before /p,b,m/, e.g. *good pen, good boy, good man* /gʊb ˈpen, gʊb ˈbɔɪ, gʊb ˈmæn/

→ /g/ before /k,g/, e.g. *good concert, good girl* /gʊg ˈkɒnsət, gʊg ˈgɜːl/

/n/ → /m/ before /p,b,m/, e.g. *ten players, ten boys, ten men* /tem ˈpleɪəz, tem ˈbɔɪz, tem ˈmen/

/n/ → /ŋ/ before /k,g/, e.g. *ten cups, ten girls* /teŋ ˈkʌps, teŋ ˈgɜːlz/

(As a result of word-final assimilations, /ŋ/ may be preceded by vowels other than /ɪ,e,æ,ɒ,ʌ/. Thus /ŋ/ can occur after long vowels as a result of assimilation (cf. §10.9), e.g. *I've been* /biːŋ/ *gardening, She'll soon* /suːŋ/ *come, his own* /əʊŋ/ *car* etc.).

Assimilations to alveolars and between labials and velars are generally felt to be substandard in RP, although they may sometimes be heard in fast speech, e.g. *same night*, /seɪn ˈnaɪt/, *King Charles* /kɪn ˈtʃɑːlz/, *same kind* /seɪŋ ˈkaɪnd/, *blackmail* /ˈblæpmeɪl/.

/s/ → /ʃ/[7] before /ʃ,tʃ,dʒ,j/, e.g. *this shop, cross channel, this judge, this year* /ðɪʃ ˈʃɒp, krɒʃ ˈtʃænəl, ðɪʃ ˈdʒʌdʒ, ðɪʃ ˈjɪə/.

/z/ → /ʒ/ before /ʃ,tʃ,dʒ,j/, e.g. *those young men* /ðəʊʒ ˈjʌŋ ˈmen/, *cheese shop* /ˈtʃiːʒ ʃɒp/, *those churches* /ðəʊʒ ˈtʃɜːtʃɪz/, *has she?* /ˈhæʒ ʃɪ/ or /ˈhæʃ ʃɪ/

Other assimilations involving fricatives are generally felt to be substandard in RP, although /θ,ð/ may assimilate to /s,z/ in fast speech, e.g. *I loathe singing*

---

[5] See Nolan and Kerswill (1990). They also found girls less likely to assimilate than boys and /n/ more likely to assimilate than /d/

[6] See also §12.7 for stylistic variation in the frequency of assimilation

[7] Byrd (1992b) found around 78% of sequences of /s,z/ plus /ʃ/ reduced to a palato-alveolar articulation only in the TIMIT database of American English, with no effect from syntax, sex, or dialect

/aɪ ləʊz ˈsɪŋɪŋ/, *What's the time?* /wɒts zə ˈtaɪm/, *Has the post come?* /hæz zə ˌpəʊs kʌm/.

Alveolars have a high frequency of occurrence in word-final position, especially when inflexional, and so their assimilation leads to many neutralizations in connected speech, e.g. /ræŋ ˈkwɪklɪ/ (*ran* or *rang quickly*), /raɪp ˈpeəz/ (*right* or *ripe pears* or *pairs*), /laɪk ˈkriːm/ (*like* or *light cream*), /ˈhɒp mənjʊə/ (*hot* or *hop manure*), /pærɪʃ ˈʃəʊ/ (*Paris Show* or *parish show*), /wɒtʃ ʃɔː ˈweɪt/ (*what's* or *watch your weight*),[8] or, with a neutralization to a labiodental articulation, /ˈɡreɪp vaɪn/ (*great* or *grape vine*), [rʌm fə jɔː ˈmʌnɪ] (*run* or *rum for your money*).

When alveolar consonants /t,d,n/ are adjacent in clusters or sequences susceptible to assimilation, all (or none) of them will undergo the assimilation, e.g. *Don't* /dəʊmp/ *be late, He won't* /wəʊŋk/ *come, I didn't* /dɪɡŋk/ *go, He found* /faʊmb/ *both, a kind* /kaɪŋɡ/ *gift, red and black* /reb m̩ ˈblæk/.

(2) *Coalescence of* /t,d,s,z/ *with* /j/—The process which has led historically to earlier /t,d,s,z/ + /j/ giving /tʃ,dʒ,ʃ,ʒ/ medially in a word (*nature, grandeur, mission, vision*—§9.3.1) may operate in contemporary colloquial speech at word boundaries, e.g.

/t/ + /j/—*What you want* /wɒtʃuː ˈwɒnt/
/d/ + /j/—*Would you?* /ˈwʊdʒuː/
/s/ + /j/—*In case you need it* /ɪŋ keɪʃuː ˈniːd ɪt/
/z/ + /j/—*Has your letter come?* /hæʒɔː ˈletə kʌm/, *as yet* /əˈʒet/

The coalescence is more complete in the case of /t,d/ + /j/ (especially in question tags, e.g. *didn't you?, could you?* etc.); in the case of /s,z/ + /j/, the coalescence into /ʃ,ʒ/ may be marked by extra length of friction, e.g. *Don't miss your train* /dəʊmp mɪʃʃɔː ˈtreɪn/.

In very careful speech, some RP speakers may use somewhat artificial, uncoalesced, forms within words in words like *nature, question, unfortunate, soldier* /ˈneɪtjə, ˈkwestjən, ʌnˈfɔːtjʊnət, ˈsəʊldjə/. Such speakers will also avoid coalescences at word boundaries; yet other careful speakers, who use the normal coalesced forms within words, may consciously avoid them at word boundaries. (See also §12.7 below.)

(3) *Progressive (or perseverative)*—Progressive assimilation is relatively uncommon. It may occur when a plosive is followed by a syllabic nasal and the nasal undergoes assimilation to the same place of articulation as the preceding plosive, e.g. /n/ → /m/ after /p,b/, *happen, urban* /ˈhæpm, ˈɜːbm/; and /n/ → /ŋ/ after /k,ɡ/ in *second chance, organ* as /sekŋ ˈtʃɑːns, ˈɔːɡŋ, ˈbeɪkŋ/.

12.4.6   Elision

Apart from word-internal elisions (see §10.8) and those associated with weak forms, sounds may be elided in fast colloquial speech, especially at or in the vicinity of word boundaries.

---

[8] If the utterance is reduced to /ˈwɒtʃɔː ˈweɪt/, there is also the possibility of the interpretation *watch or wait*

(1) *Vowels*

(a) *Allophonic variation*—When one syllable ends with a closing diphthong (i.e. one whose second element is closer than its first, in RP /eɪ,aɪ,ɔɪ,əʊ,aʊ/) and the next syllable begins with a vowel, the second element of the diphthong may be elided. Word-internal examples of the type discussed in §7.11 (e.g. *hyaena* /haɪˋiːnə/ smoothed to [haˋiːnə]) may result in neutralization, thus *layer* /ˋleɪə/ with smoothing is the same as *lair* /leə/, *mower* /ˋməʊə/ with smoothing is the same as *myrrh* /mɜː/. Similar smoothing occurs across word boundaries, e.g. *go away* /gɜː ˋweɪ/, *I may as well* /aɪ meəz ˋwel/, *I enjoy it* /aɪ ɪn ˋdʒɔ ɪt/, *try again* [tra əˋgen] or [traː ˋgen].

(b) *Phonemic elision*—Initial /ə/ is often elided, particularly when followed by a continuant and preceded by a word-final consonant (compensation for the loss of /ə/ frequently being made by the syllabicity of the continuant), e.g. *not alone* [nɒt ˋləʊn], *get another* [get ˋn̩ʌ ðə], *run along* [rʌn ˋl̩ɒŋ], *he was annoyed* [hɪ wəz ˋn̩ɔɪd]; or again, when final /ə/ occurs with following linking /r/ (see §12.4.7) and word-initial vowel, /ə/ may be elided, e.g. *after a while* /ɑːftrəˋwaɪl/, *as a matter of fact* /əz ə mætrəv ˋfækt/, *father and son* /fɑːðrən ˋsʌn/, *over and above* /əʊvrən əˋbʌv/.

(2) *Consonants*—In addition to the loss of /h/ in pronominal weak forms and other consonantal elisions typical of weak forms (see §11.3), the alveolar plosives are apt to be elided. Such elision appears to take place most readily when /t/ or /d/ is the middle one of three consonants. Any consonant may appear in third position, though elision of the alveolar plosive is relatively rare before /h/ and /j/. Thus elision is common in the sequence voiceless continuant + /t/ or voiced continuant + /d/ (e.g. /-st, -ft, -ʃt, -nd, -ld, -zd, -ðd, -vd/) followed by a word with an initial consonant, e.g. *next day, raced back, last chance, first light, west region, just one; left turn, soft centres, left wheel, drift by, soft roes; mashed potatoes, finished now, finished late, pushed them; bend back, tinned meat, lend-lease, found five, send round, dined well; hold tight, old man, cold lunch, bold face, world religion; refused both, gazed past, caused losses, raised gently; loathed beer; moved back, loved flowers, saved runs, served sherry* etc. Similarly, word-final clusters of voiceless plosive or affricate + /t/ or voiced plosive or affricate + /d/ (e.g. /-pt, -kt, -tʃt, -bd, -gd, -dʒd/) may lose the final alveolar stop when the following word has an initial consonant, e.g. *kept quiet, helped me, stopped speaking, jumped well; liked jam, thanked me, looked like, looked fine, picked one; reached Paris, fetched me, reached Rome, parched throat; robbed both, rubbed gently, grabbed them; lagged behind, dragged down, begged one; changed colour, urged them, arranged roses, judged fairly* etc. (In the sequence /-skt/, /k/ rather than /t/ is often elided, e.g. *risked prison, asked them*.) The final clusters /-nt,-lt/, which are the only alveolar sequences which involve a change of voicing, are less prone to elision, the /t/ often remaining as [ʔ], e.g. *went down*.

Elision of final /t/ or /d/ is rarer before initial /h/, e.g. the alveolar stops are more regularly retained in *kept hold, worked hard, East Ham, reached home, gift horse, rushed home, grabbed hold, round here, bald head, jugged hare, changed horses, raised hands, moved house* etc. Final /t,d/ followed by a word beginning with /j/ are usually kept in a coalesced form, i.e. as /tʃ/ and /dʒ/, e.g. *helped you, liked you, lost you, left you, grabbed you, lend you, told you* etc.

It will be seen that in many cases, e.g. in *I walked back, they seemed glad*, elision of word-final /t/ or /d/ eliminates the phonetic cue to past tense, compensation for which is made by the general context. Such is the instability of the alveolar plosives in such a position of apparent inflexional significance that it can be assumed that the context regularly carries the burden of tense distinction. Where the juxtaposition of words brings together a cluster of consonants (particularly of stops), elision of a plosive medial in three or more is to be expected, since, because of the normal lack of release of a stop in such a situation, the only cue to its presence is likely to be the total duration of closure.

The /t/ of the negative /-nt/ is often elided, particularly in disyllables, before a following consonant, e.g. *you mustn't lose it* /ju mʌsn ˈluːz ɪt/, *doesn't she know?* /dʌzn ʃɪ ˈnəʊ/, and sometimes before a vowel, e.g. *wouldn't he come?* /wʊdn ɪ ˈkʌm/, *you mustn't over-eat* /ju mʌsn əʊvər ˈiːt/. Less common is the omission of the stops in the negative /-nt/ component of monosyllables, e.g. *he won't do it* /hɪ wəʊn ˈduː ɪt/.

Clusters of word-final /t/ and word-initial /t/ or /d/ are sometimes simplified in informal speech, e.g. *I've got to go* /aɪv gɒtə ˈgəʊ/, *what do you want?* /wɒdə ju ˈwɒnt/ or /wɒdʒu ˈwɒnt/, and less commonly /d/ before /t/ or /d/, e.g. *we could try* /wɪ kʊ ˈtraɪ/, *they should do it* /ðeɪ ʃə ˈduː ɪt/.

The elision of one of a boundary cluster of two consonants sometimes occurs in casual speech, but is usually characterized as substandard, e.g. *he went away* /hɪ wen əˈweɪ/, *I want to come* /aɪ ˈwɒnə kʌm/ (< /aɪ ˈwɒntə kʌm/, which frequently occurs), *give me a cake* /gɪ mɪ ə ˈkeɪk/, *let me come in* /lemɪ kʌm ˈɪn/, *get me some paper* /gemɪ sm ˈpeɪpə/, as well as the very reduced forms of *I'm going to* /ˈaɪm gənə, ˈaɪŋənə, ˈaɪŋnə/. Clusters in adverbs formed with -ly are also liable to reduction in rapid and/or casual speech, e.g. *stupidly* /ˈstjuːpɪlɪ/, *openly* /ˈəʊpənɪ/.

12.4.7   Liaison

(1) *Linking* /r/—As has been mentioned in §9.7(2)(a), RP introduces word-final post-vocalic /r/ as a linking form when the following word begins with a vowel. The vowel endings to which an /r/ link may, in this sense, justifiably be added are /ɑː,ɔː/ and those single or complex vowels containing final [ə] (/ə,ɜ,ɪə,eə,ʊə/), e.g. in *far off, four aces, answer it, fur inside, near it, wear out, secure everything*. Prescriptivists seek to limit the allowability of linking /r/ to those cases where there is an <r> in the spelling; nevertheless many examples of linking /r/ occur where there is no <r> in the spelling, such /r/'s being labelled as 'intrusive'. Such /r/'s are to be heard particularly in the case of /ə/ endings, e.g. *Russia and China* /rʌʃər ən ˈtʃaɪnə/, *drama and music* /drɑːmər əm ˈmjuːzɪk/, *idea of* /aɪˈdɪər əv/, *India and Pakistan* /ɪndɪər ən pɑːkɪˈstɑːn/, *area of agreement* /ˈeərɪər əv əˈgriːmənt/; and rather less frequently after final /ɑː,ɔː/ e.g. *law and order* /lɔːr ənd ˈɔːdə/, *awe-inspiring* /ˈɔːr ɪnspaɪərɪŋ/, *raw onion* /rɔːr ˈʌnjən/. Spelling consciousness remains an inhibiting factor in the use of linking /r/, but the present general tendency among RP speakers is to use /r/ links, even—unconsciously—among those who object most strongly.[9] The comparative rarity of potential contexts for

---

[9] Intrusive <r> is decried as a vice as early as Sheridan (1762)

'intrusive' /r/'s following /ɑː,ɔː/ tends to make speakers more aware of the 'correct' forms; thus *I saw it* /aɪ ˈsɔː r ɪt/, *drawing*, /ˈdrɔːrɪŋ/, are generally disapproved of, though those who avoid such pronunciations have to make a conscious effort to do so. The focusing of attention on 'intrusive' /r/'s as an undesirable speech habit has led to the use by some speakers of a pause or glottal stop in such cases of vowel hiatus, with the result that, in avoiding 'intrusive' /r/'s, they have also abandoned other linking /r/'s in favour of a vowel glide or glottal stop, e.g. in *secure it, I'm sure it does, War and Peace, winter evening*. As might be expected, in those regions where post-vocalic /r/ is pronounced and *pour, paw* are identified as separate word forms in isolation, the tendency to introduce intrusive /r/'s is less marked than in RP or in RP-influenced types of speech.

The same process is in operation whether the /r/ link inserted is historically justified (linking) or not (intrusive). The examples below demonstrate that the environment is phonetically comparable whether the /r/ link is inserted before a suffix or before a separate word and whether it is linking or 'intrusive'.

stir	*stirring*	*stir it in*		
/stɜː/	ˈstɜːrɪŋ	ˈstɜːr ɪt ˈɪn/		
dear	*dearer*	*my dear Anna*	*idea of it*	
/dɪə/	ˈdɪərə	maɪ dɪər ˈænə	aɪˈdɪər əv ɪt/	
roar	*roaring*	*roar angrily*	*raw egg*	*strawy*
/rɔː/	ˈrɔːrɪŋ	rɔːr ˈæŋgrəlɪ	rɔːr ˈeg	ˈstrɔːrɪ/
star	*starry*	*a star in the sky*	*the spa at Bath*	*schwaish*
/stɑː/	ˈstɑːrɪ	ə stɑːr ɪn ðə ˈskaɪ	ðə spɑːr ət ˈbɑːθ	ˈʃwɑːrɪʃ/

There appears, however, to be some graduation in the likelihood of occurrence as follows:

(1) The insertion of /r/ is obligatory before a suffix beginning with a vowel, where the /r/ is historically justified.

(2) The insertion of /r/ is optional, though generally present, before a following word beginning with a vowel, where the /r/ is historically justified.

(3) After [ə], even an intrusive /r/ (i.e. historically unjustified) is generally used before a following word, e.g. *vanilla essence* /vənɪlər ˈesəns/, *vodka and tonic* /vɒdkər ən ˈtɒnɪk/.

(4) After /ɑː/ and /ɔː/, an intrusive /r/ is often avoided before a following vowel, e.g. *nougat and chocolate* /nugɑːr ən ˈtʃɒklɪt/, *straw in the wind* /strɔːr ɪn ðə ˈwɪnd/.

(5) The insertion of intrusive /r/ before a suffix is often strongly stigmatized, e.g. *strawy* /ˈstrɔːrɪ/.

Phonetically (as well as historically) the resulting /r/ closes the syllable rather than being initial in the next, e.g. the /r/ of *more ice* /mɔːr ˈaɪs/ is shorter than that of *more rice* /mɔː ˈraɪs/, the latter also being associated with accent onset and possible pitch change (cf. §12.4.8).

(2) *Linking* [j,w]—In vocalic junctures where the first word ends in /iː/, /ɪ/, /eɪ/, /aɪ/, or /ɔɪ/, a slight linking [j] may be heard between the two vowels, e.g. *my arms* [maɪ ˈʲɑːmz], *may ask* [meɪ ˈʲɑːsk], *he ought* [hiː ˈʲɔːt], *annoy Arthur* [ənɔɪ ˈʲɑːθə], *beauty and* [bjuːtɪ ˈʲənd]. But this is not sufficient to be equated with phonemic

/j/; indeed, there are minimal pairs which illustrate the difference between linking [j] and phonemic /j/, *my ears* [maɪ ˈʲɪəz] vs *my years* [maɪ ˈjɪəz], and *I earn* [aɪ ˈʲɜːn] vs *I yearn* [ai ˈjɜːn]. Similarly, a linking [ʷ] may be heard between a final /uː/, /əʊ/, and /aʊ/ and a following vowel, e.g. *window* open [wɪndəʊ ˈʷəʊpən], *now and then* [naʊ ʷənd ˈðen], *you aren't* [ju: ˈʷɑːnt]; and minimal pairs illustrating linking [ʷ] and phonemic /w/ can be found, e.g. *two-eyed* [tuː ˈʷaɪd] vs *too wide* [tuː ˈwaɪd]. Alternative pronunciations, more frequent in faster speech, in the case of the sequences of diphthong plus following vowel, involve the absorption of the second element of the diphthong, i.e. of the [ɪ] in the case of /eɪ,aɪ,ɔɪ/ and of the [ʊ] in the case of /əʊ,aʊ/, giving renderings like *annoy Arthur* [ənɔ ˈɑːðə], *my ears* /ma ˈɪəz/, *window open* /ˈwɪndə əʊpən/ (see further under §8.11(8) above).

In yet another possibility, the linking [ʲ] or[ʷ] may be replaced by a glottal stop. This is most common before a vowel beginning an accented syllable, e.g. *very angry* [verɪ ˈʔæŋgrɪ] (see further §9.2.8). However, glottal stop in such cases is not so often used as in some other languages, e.g. German, and is usually associated in English with some degree of emphasis.

As regards boundaries where a consonant precedes a vowel, it is unusual for a word-final consonant to be carried over as initial in a word beginning with an accented vowel, the identity of the words being retained (see §12.4.8). Thus, *run off, give in, less often* are rarely /rʌˈnɒf, gɪˈvɪn, leˈsɒfn/ (shown because the nuclear tone, usually high fall in citation, does not begin on the consonant); and *get up, look out, stop arguing*, are not usually [geˈtʰʌp, lʊˈkʰaʊt, stɒˈpʰɑːgjʊɪŋ] (the plosives lacking the strong aspiration characteristic of an accented syllable-initial position). One or two phrases in common use do, however, show such transference, e.g. *at home, not at all*, often pronounced [əˈtʰəʊm, nɒt ə ˈtʰɔːɫ]; they may be considered as constituting, in effect, composite word forms.

12.4.8   Juncture

Despite the fact that the word may have its isolate-form identity considerably modified by its immediate phonemic and accentual context, both as regards its constituent sounds and its accentual or rhythmic pattern, phonetic features may be retained in the speech continuum which mark word or morpheme boundaries. Thus, the phonemic sequence /piːstɔːks/ may mean *pea stalks* or *peace talks* according to the situation of the word boundaries (i.e. /iː+stɔː/ or /iːs+tɔː/). In this case, if the boundary occurs between /s/ and /t/, the identity of the words *peace* and *talks* may be established by the reduced /iː/ (in a syllable closed by a voiceless consonant) and by the slight aspiration of /t/; on the other hand, if the boundary occurs between /iː/ and /s/, this may be signalled by the relatively full length of /iː/ (in an open word-final syllable) and by the unaspirated allophone of /t/ (following /s/ in the same syllable), as well as by the stronger /s/. Such phonetic differentiation depends upon the speaker's consciousness of the word as an independent entity.

The following examples illustrate various ways in which phonetic cues may mark word boundaries:

| *I scream* | /aɪ skriːm/ | : long /aɪ/, strong /s/, little devoicing of /r/ |
| *ice cream* | /aɪs kriːm/ | : reduced /aɪ/, weak /s/, devoiced /r/ |

| *why choose* | /waɪ tʃuːz/ | : long /aɪ/, short [ʃ] as element of /tʃ/ |
| *white shoes* | /waɪt ʃuːz/ | : reduced /aɪ/, long /ʃ/ |

| *a name* | /ə neɪm/ | : relatively long /n/ (beginning accent) |
| *an aim* | /ən eɪm/ | : relatively short /n/ (accent onset on /eɪ/), possibility of glottal stop before /eɪ/ |

It must be noted that the glottal stop before a vowel beginning an accented syllable in the last example is optional, and generally not used unless emphasis is required (see §9.2.8). Overuse of glottal stop in such positions is typical of some foreign learners of English.

Similarly, simple word entities may be distinguished from words composed of separable morphemes:

| *nitrate* | /naɪtreɪt/ | : devoiced /r/ |
| *night-rate* | /naɪt reɪt/ | : little devoicing of /r/ |

| *illegal* | /ɪliːgl/ | : clear [l] before vowel |
| *ill eagle* | /ɪl iːgl/ | : dark [ɫ] in word-final position possibility of glottal stop before /iː/ |

It is to be noted, however, that such junctural cues are only potentially distinctive and, in any case, merely provide cues to word identification additional to the large number provided by the context. Junctural oppositions are, in fact, frequently neutralized in connected speech or may have such slight phonetic value as to be difficult for a listener to perceive.

12.5 *Frequency of Occurrence of Monosyllabic and Polysyllabic Words*

In a running text of a conversational kind, the following approximate percentages of occurrence of words containing different numbers of syllables are to be expected: one syllable—81%; two syllables—15%; three syllables—3%. The remaining 1% of words have four syllables or more, those with five or more syllables accounting for a minute proportion of the total word list. If the 1,000 most common words used are examined,[10] it has been calculated that some 15% admit of the kind of phonemic variability mentioned in §10.9. Half of such words permitting phonemic variation are monosyllables whose phonemic structure depends upon the degree of accent placed upon them.

---

[10] Gimson (1969)

12.6   *Advice to Foreign Learners*

The foreign learner, even one aiming at a native pronunciation, need not attempt
to reproduce in his speech all the special context forms of words mentioned in
the foregoing sections. He must, however, observe the rules concerning weak
forms, should cultivate the correct variations of word rhythmic patterns according to the context, and should make a proper use of liaison forms (German
speakers, in particular, should avoid an excess of pre-vocalic glottal stops). In
addition, he should be aware of the English assimilatory tendencies governing
words in context, so as to avoid un-English assimilations such as *I like that* /aɪ
ˈlaɪɡ ˌðæt/ (incorrect voicing) or *I was there* /aɪ wəð ˈðeə/ (incorrect dental modification of the place of articulation). If his speech is to approach that of a native
speaker, he must use the special assimilated and elided word forms used in
context which have been described above. In any case, whether or not he uses
such forms himself, he must know of their existence, for otherwise he will find
it difficult to understand much of ordinary colloquial English. This knowledge is
particularly important because a second language is often learned on a basis of
isolate word forms; in the speech of the native, however, the outline of these
words will frequently be modified or obscured, as has been seen.

The foreign learner is recommended to aim at a relatively careful pronunciation of English in his own speech and, at the same time, to be aware of the
features which characterize the more colloquial pronunciation he is likely to hear
from native speakers. The following dialogue illustrates some of the differences
which may be found between a more careful and a more colloquial pronunciation:

A.   What do you think we should do this evening?
  (1)   ˈwɒt du ju ˈθɪŋk wi(ː) ʃud ˈduː ðɪs   iːvnɪŋ
  (2)   ˈwɒdʒu   ˈθɪŋk wɪ   ʃəd ˈduː ðəs   iːvnɪŋ
B.   How   many of   us   will there be?
  (1)   ˈhaʊ menɪ ˈɒv əs   wɪl   ðeə   ˈbiː
  (2)   ˈhaʊ mnɪ   əv   əs   l   ðə   ˈbiː

A.   There are   the two of   us,   and probably   the   two
  (1)   ðer   ə   ðə   ˈtuː əv ˌʌs/ ənd ˈprɒbəblɪ   ðə   ˈtuː
  (2)   ðər   ə   ðə   ˈtuː əv ˌʌs/ m   ˈprɒbblɪ   ðə   ˈtuː
        girls from next door. That'll be   four   of   us/   already
  (1)   ˈɡɜːlz frəm ˈnekst ˈdɔː/ ðætl   bɪ   ˇfɔːr əv   əs/   ɔːlˋredɪ
  (2)   ɡɜːlz   frm   neks   ˈdɔː/ ðætl   bɪ   ˇfɔːr əv   əs/   ɔːˈredɪ
        I   think they' re a   nice young couple, don't   you?
  (1)   aɪ   ˈθɪŋk ðeɪ ər ə   ˈnaɪs jʌŋ   ˌkʌpl/   ˈdəʊnt   ˌjuː
  (2)   a(ɪ)   θɪŋk   ðeər   ə   ˈnaɪʃ ʃʌŋ   ˌkʌpl/   ˈdəʊnˌtʃuː

B.   I've   only talked to   them once, but they seemed nice
  (1)   aɪv   əʊnlɪ ˈtɔːkt tə   ðəm   ˌwʌns/ bət ðeɪ   ˈsiːmd ˌnaɪs
  (2)   a(ɪ)v əʊnɪ   ˈtɔːk   tə   ðm   ˌwʌns/ bət ðe(ɪ) ˈsiːm   ˌnaɪs

	I	wonder	if	we	should	go	to	the	theatre
(1)	aɪ	ˈwʌndər	ɪf	wɪ	ʃʊd	ˈgəʊ	tə	ðə	ˈθɪˈetə
(2)	ə(ɪ)	ˈwʌndr	ɪf	wɪ	ʃg	ˈgəʊ	tə	ðə	ˈθɪˈetə

	I	can	try	and	book	some	seats	round	the	corner
(1)	aɪ	kən	ˈtraɪ	ən	ˈbʊk	səm	ˌsiːts/	ˈraʊnd	ðə	ˈkɔːnə
(2)	ə(ɪ)	kŋ	ˈtraː	m	bʊk	sm	ˌsiːts/	raʊn	ðə	ˈkɔːnə

12.7   *Stylistic Variation*

All the features of connected speech discussed in this chapter are common in the normal, fluent speech of native speakers of English and the lack of such features would be abnormal and artificial. As throughout the rest of this book, the descriptive emphasis has been on RP which is not a monolithic accent but displays considerable variation within itself. Many factors influence this variation and one which may usefully be singled out is style of discourse, e.g. whether a speaker is being either casual, or formal and hence careful.

It is important to avoid equating 'casual' and 'rapid', since slow speech is possible in a casual situation and rapid utterances can occur in more formal circumstances. It should also be borne in mind that the average rate of delivery differs from speaker to speaker regardless of discourse style.[11] Thus the degree of formality and the rate of utterance are independent variables. The generalizations which follow are based on data drawn from 20 hours of tape-recorded spontaneous conversation concentrating on the speech of six RP speakers.[12] Rate of utterance was not found to be a regular function of style, nor was style defined in terms of rate,[13] even though casualness and rapidity often co-occur. Social situations were set up that were designed to be markedly formal (e.g. an undergraduate in conversation with a professor who was a stranger to her) or markedly casual (e.g. a man in conversation with his wife). All speakers were recorded in both formal and casual situations and the speech of all of them exhibited the same trends to differing degrees.

(1) *Accent and intonation*—In all styles of speech, simple falls in pitch (whether from a high or a mid starting point) account for the majority of nuclear tones, between 60% and 70% in most conversation. The falling–rising nuclear tone accounts for roughly 20% on average. Thus it may be seen that speech exhibiting a large number of rises or rise–falls would be conspicuous in this respect. In general, intonation patterns show no marked distribution in casual speech. However, formal speech shows some concentrations of one pattern, whether repetitions of fall–rise nuclear tones or a stretch of speech with repeated rising nuclear tones, e.g. *If you pull them ˌoff / and put them in a glass of ˌwater / they grow little ˈroots / and ˌthen / you plant them in ˌsoil / and they ˌgrow / and then you 've got a ˈnother spider plant/.*

---

[11]   Byrd (1992a) found women speaking 6.2% faster than men
[12]   For details of this research, see Ramsaran (1978)
[13]   The slowest rate of utterance recorded in conversation was 189 sylls/min (3.1 sylls/sec, 7.6 segs/sec) and the fastest was 324 sylls/min (5.4 sylls/sec, 13.4 segs/sec)

Casual speech has longer intonational phrases and contains fewer accented syllables than formal speech.

(2) *Weak forms*—The use of strong and weak forms does not appear to be a matter of style except in so far as the more frequent occurrence of strong forms in more formal situations results from additional accents. The alternation of strong and weak forms is entirely regular in both formal and casual styles of speech: weak forms occur unless the grammatical word is accented. Since accents are more frequent in the intonational phrases of formal speech, strong forms occur more often.

(3) *Linking* /r/—As with weak forms, linking /r/ is frequent in all styles of speech, though an /r/ link is not necessarily used on every occasion where such an insertion would be possible (see §12.4.7). Its occurrence is of no stylistic significance. (The avoidance of intrusive /r/ results from a deliberate carefulness shown by some speakers in more formal speech.)

(4) *Assimilation*—Assimilations occur in all styles of speech. However, unassimilated forms occur more often than assimilated forms which tend to increase in frequency in the more casual style of speech, regardless of pace.

The fact that rate of utterance has no direct effect on the use of assimilation may be illustrated by examples taken from the conversation of a single speaker who has /dʒʌʃ ˈʃʌtɪŋ/ for *just shutting* (also exhibiting elision of /t/) when speaking at a medium pace in a comparatively formal situation, but /ˈhɔːs ʃəʊ/ for *horse show* when speaking very rapidly in a casual situation.

In general, although all types of anticipatory de-alveolar assimilation do occur, speakers use palato-alveolar assimilations (of the kind /ˈspeɪʃ ʃʌtl̩/ for *space shuttle*) and bilabial assimilations (of the kind /ðæp ˈpɜːsn̩/ for *that person*) far less commonly than they use velar assimilations (of the kind /ʃɔːk ˈkʌt/ for *short cut*). Such velar assimilation is also more common than coalescent assimilations (such as /d/ + /j/ → /dʒ/ as in /nəʊtɪdʒɒtsmən/ for *noted yachtsman* or /z/ + /j/ → /ʒ/ as in /bɪkəʒuː/ for *because you*). However, coalescence is frequent in common phrases such as the auxiliary verbs + pronouns of *did you, can't you* etc. /ˈdɪdʒuː, ˈkɑːntʃuː/ and may occur even in very formal conversation, e.g. *Would you like a cup of tea?* /ˈwʊdʒu ˈlaɪk ə ˈkʌp əv ˌtiː/.

(5) *Elision*—Elisions do show some correlation with rate of delivery. In all styles they become more frequent as the rate of utterance increases; but, whereas in formal speech they are almost entirely regular (e.g. alveolar plosives may be elided interconsonantally, /ə/ in pre-nuclear unaccented syllables, and /h/ in unaccented non-initial grammatical words), in casual speech they are less rule-bound. Casual speech may contain unpredictable elisions such as those of /l/ and /ð/ in *Well, that's all right* /we ˈæts ɔːˌraɪt/.

(6) *Co-occurrence of phonemic features of connected speech*—It should be noted that the occurrence of /r/ links, elisions and assimilations is optional in the sense that when the appropriate phonetic environments occur, these processes may or may not operate. The preceding sections (1)–(5) indicate some tendencies in the likelihood of occurrence. If, then, such processes do operate, they will follow the regular patterns described in §§12.4.5–12.4.7. Disregarding the occasional irregular elisions that may occur in casual and/or rapid speech, it should be added that an utterance not uncommonly contains instances of both assimilation and elision in conjunction with each other, since alveolar consonant

clusters are not infrequent in word-final position: after the elision of a final /t/ or /d/ the remaining fricative or nasal may be assimilated to the place of articulation of the initial consonant of the following word, e.g. *closed shop* /kləʊzd ˈʃɒp → kləʊz ˈʃɒp → kləʊʒ ˈʃɒp/, *hand made* /hænd ˈmeɪd → hæn ˈmeɪd → hæm ˈmeɪd/ and *just shutting* /dʒʌst ˈʃʌtɪŋ → dʒʌs ˈʃʌtɪŋ → dʒʌʃ ˈʃʌtɪŋ/. The conjunction *and* has a common weak form with /d/ elided and the /ə/ may also be elided, leaving the nasal to function syllabically, particularly after plosives. The resulting syllabic [n̩] is itself susceptible to assimilation, which accounts for pronunciations such as [wʊg ŋ̩ˈglɑːs] (*wood and glass*).

(7) *Plosive release*—One of the most stylistically significant variables concerns a non-phonemic variation in the release of plosives, particularly the voiceless series. As is explained in §9.2.4(2), a plosive usually has an inaudible release when followed by another stop consonant. However, in the most formal social situations, there is a marked increase in the number of audibly released plosives in such a context, e.g. [aɪ lʊktʰ ˈkwɪzɪkəl]. Women release their final stops more than men.[14]

(8) *Summary*—No feature is unique to one style, but some features are more common in one style than the another. In particular, pre-consonantal plosives may be audibly released when speech is formal, whereas assimilations increase in frequency as speech becomes more casual. Elision is the only feature that bears a definite relation to rate, occurring more frequently as the rate increases, however formal the situation may be. There is more fluctuation of rate in casual speech.

---

[14] Byrd (1992c)

13

Teaching the Pronunciation of English

13.1 *The Place of Pronunciation*

In the preceding chapters, the chief features of English pronunciation (especially of RP) have been set out in some detail. Clearly, a foreign learner who requires an adequate performance in the language for the practical purposes of everyday communication will not need to master all the variants described. Nevertheless, any teacher or learner must consider how much of the time given to the acquisition of another language should be devoted to pronunciation and what level of performance is necessary for efficient communication.

It can be claimed that speech, like writing, constitutes no more than the transmission phase of language, providing a signalling system for the language's more essential store of items defined in the lexicon and of syntactic rules contained in the grammar. Yet high adequacy in lexis and grammar can be negated by incompetence in the signalling phase, when the prime medium is speech. Thus, unless a learner expects to deal with English only in its written form, there is no escape from the acquisition of at least the rudimentary elements of English pronunciation. Such a conclusion implies that in any course of English a realistic amount of time should be devoted to practice in the spoken language.

However, the teaching of pronunciation presents particular difficulties. Grammatical structures can be ordered and taught in sequence; a vocabulary compiled on a basis of frequency of occurrence can be utilized for the presentation of early grammatical structures, with the addition of special sets of lexical items as situations or special purposes require. Pronunciation, on the other hand, does not permit such progressive treatment, since all phonetic/phonological features are potentially present from the very first lesson, unless vocabulary items are artificially introduced. Nevertheless, the teacher must deal systematically with the teaching of pronunciation, even though he may be forced to postpone the correction of some mistakes which occur in the early stages. In organizing his teaching he will require answers to questions such as:

(1) What form of pronunciation is to be taken as a model? (§§13.2);
(2) What level of performance is to be aimed at? (§§13.3–13.6);
(3) What general principles should underlie the teaching of pronunciation? (§§13.7).

13.2 *Models of Pronunciation*

This is a matter of special importance as far as English is concerned because of the world-wide use of the language and because of the profusion of differing spoken forms existing not only in mother-tongue areas such as Britain, North America, Australasia, and the Caribbean but also in those regions of Africa and Asia where English is used as an adopted lingua franca (see §7.3.(6)). Whatever abilities the learner may acquire in the later stages of learning English, he will be well advised at the beginning to model his productive performance on one model of spoken English and to restrict himself to a 'careful, colloquial' style (see §12.6). As he gains productive confidence he can for the purposes of widening his receptive competence gradually be exposed to other styles and important regional types. If his introduction to English is via a British spoken form, he might, when this production habit is firmly established, be encouraged to listen to General American.

13.2.1   Choice of Basic Model

Faced with the great diversity of English accents, the foreign learner might wish that there existed a neutral, all-purpose, international pronunciation of English. It is claimed by some that, as a result of the great improvement in communications, the present divergencies in English as it is spoken throughout the world will gradually be eliminated and there will emerge a universally intelligible pronunciation of English which all can use. The present evidence suggests that, if the total English-speaking population of the world is taken into account, this natural and desirable process is, as yet, making no advance. Indeed, there seems to be a growing tolerance of variation (see also §7.3(6)).

The more realistic, immediate, solution lies in the choice of one of the main native-speaker forms of English as the basic model, e.g. a representative form of British or American pronunciation, with the possibility of the selection for geographical reasons of other forms such as Australian or Caribbean. In other areas a form of modified RP taking account of local tendencies may be acceptable, e.g. 'Indian English' on the Indian subcontinent. The decisive criteria in the choice of any teaching model must be that it has wide currency, is widely and readily understood, is adequately described in textbooks, and has ample recorded material available for the learner. It is clear that, if these criteria are admitted, British RP is an important candidate as a basic model which is already taught throughout the world.

13.2.2   A Wider-based RP

The emergence of RP as a standard pronunciation has already been given some treatment, together with a preliminary assessment of the present-day situation. It is not sufficient, however, for the foreign learner to be presented with a general account of British attitudes to RP (§7.3). Not only does he require advice on whether RP is a suitable model in the first place but also guidance on acceptable tolerances and deviations from this model.

Even within Britain it is now realistic to allow considerable dilution in the original concept of the RP speaker with the new concept of Regional RPs (§7.3) in which some regional forms are admissible, e.g. /æ/ in words like *past* and *dance*, which is current throughout the north of England (as well as in General American). Nevertheless, if a model based on a British pronunciation is used for the foreign learner, General RP is still recommended as the target. But it may be permissible to allow some non-English regionalisms to intrude, including some loss of phonemic distinctions in the vowels and some phonetic variation in the realization of both the vowels and the consonants, e.g. a retroflex /t,d/ in Indian English. The extent of permitted phonemic and phonetic latitude will depend upon the type of performance at which learners, with their differing needs, are aiming.

It might be claimed that RP as a model of British English has been so diluted by the admission of the notion of Regional RPs that it should be wholly super-seded by regional standards as targets for the foreign learner. Thus, London Regional RP (= 'Estuary English'—see §7.3(6) and §7.6.3) has been claimed by some to be an emerging new standard among British speakers and hence a model towards which foreign learners should aspire, and similar claims have been made that Scottish English is not only the standard in Scotland but also positively viewed in the remainder of Britain. The position maintained in this book is that General RP remains the best British standard to aim at because it remains the most regionally neutral and, bearing in mind that any target model aimed at by foreign learners is almost certain to be diluted by their own regional character-istics, it seems appropriate that at least the initial target should be regionally largely neutral. It is also the case that the available textbooks (including this one) and the standard pronouncing dictionaries are based on General RP (even though this is in one case relabelled as 'BBC English').[1]

13.3   *Performance Targets*

Factors which will obviously determine the learner's aims are concerned with his age and his natural ability, and with his motivation and the use to which he intends to put the language. He may succeed merely in speaking English with the phonetic and phonological system of his own language, in which case he is likely to be unintelligible to listeners outside his own region or, at best, compre-hensible only to the extent that some keywords can be decoded as a result of the general context of the situation (this is the level of RESTRICTED INTELLIGIBILITY discussed at the end of this section). If an attempt is made to approximate to RP or some other native standard, his achievement may lie somewhere between two extremes. The lowest requirement can be described as one of MINIMAL GENERAL INTELLIGIBILITY, i.e. one which possesses a set of distinctive elements which correspond in some measure to the inventory of the RP phonemic system and which is capable of conveying a message efficiently from a native English listener's standpoint, given that the context of the message is known and that the

---

[1] Jones (1997), Wells (2000)

listener has had time to 'tune in' to the speaker's pronunciation. At the other extreme, the learner may be said to achieve a performance of HIGH ACCEPT-ABILITY, i.e. a form of speech which the native listener may not identify as non-native, which conveys information as readily as would a native's and which arrives at this result through precision in the phonetic realization of phonemes and by confident handling of accentual and intonational patterns.

The great majority of foreign learners will have a severely practical purpose for acquiring English and will see no great advantage in learning other than to a level of MINIMAL GENERAL INTELLIGIBILITY. Indeed, the learner may derive some advantage from retaining a clearly foreign image in his dealings with other English speakers, e.g. the waiter or the taxi driver, whose interaction in English, is unlikely to need to progress beyond a level of basic intelligibility. If the goal is of this sort, clearly, not too much attention need be paid to phonetic and phonological niceties. Such is the redundancy present in the use of any natural language that, within a defined context and with an adequate stock of words and basic syntactic patterns, considerable intelligibility can be achieved even though the pronunciation is seriously deformed. For instance, at a dinner table, someone who asks for the *potatoes*, pronounced as [bə'deːdoːz], is likely to be understood without difficulty, though it should be noted that an accentually divergent form such as ['bɒdeːdoːz] might well perplex.

There will, however, be many learners who, for academic reasons or because their work requires them to deal on equal terms with speakers in or from other regions of the world, wish to communicate easily without signalling too blatantly their regional origin; such learners will aim at HIGH ACCEPTABILITY. The foreign teacher of English constitutes a special case. He has the obligation to be as clear as possible about the model towards which he is aiming and to present to his students as near an approximation to that model as he can. Particularly if he is dealing with young pupils, his students will imitate a bad pronunciation as exactly as they will a good one; and, if he is using illustrative recorded material, his own pronunciation must not diverge markedly from the pronunciation used in it.

There remains one further and separate category of competence in pronunciation which seeks neither to imitate a natural model nor to have any international validity: it may be termed a level of RESTRICTED INTELLIGIBILITY. However undesirable such a level may be thought to be when the efficacy of English as a world language is in question, there is no doubt that for many of those who use English as a second language (even teachers of English), this is the actual situation, especially within the continents of Africa and India. Often, English is used as a lingua franca within their own country which may have a number of indigenous languages none of which is acceptable as a national language. Such types of English of RESTRICTED INTELLIGIBILITY may conform in many features of lexis and grammar to the native language of Britain or America and may thus in their written form pose no great problems of international intelligibility. But in the spoken form of transmission, interference from indigenous languages may erect a formidable barrier for listeners from other areas where English is spoken. If the interference is such that no attempt is made to do other than use the sound system and prosody of the indigenous language, however effective this may be within the country concerned, communication with native English speakers and with speakers from other countries may break down completely without recourse to written communication.

13.4   *High Priorities*

The various elements of English pronunciation will offer differing degrees of difficulty according to the linguistic background of the learner. Teaching should obviously be concentrated on those features of English which are not found in the learner's native language. There are, however, certain basic characteristics of pronunciation which seem sufficiently specific to English to constitute a priority for the great majority of learners.

13.4.1   Rhythm and Accent

The rhythm of English (be it a single word or connected speech) with the related obscuration of weak syllables is a prime distinguishing feature of the language's pronunciation. In fact, in connected speech, unaccented syllables, a majority of which include reduced vowels, considerably outnumber those carrying primary or secondary accents. For some learners, e.g. with French or Italian or Japanese or an African tone language as background, the problems of English rhythm are especially great and will require prolonged attention. The related problem of the correct accentual patterns associated with English words must be given an important and early place in any teaching programme. The correct accentual patterns of words should be learnt as they are first acquired. But this is not as large a task as might be imagined, since in ordinary connected speech monosyllables account for more than 80% of words occurring, and hence the number of words whose accentual pattern needs to be learnt is relatively small.

13.4.2   Segmental Sounds

(a) *Frequency*—It should be noted that in running English speech vowels account for some 40% and consonants 60% of the phonemes uttered (§§8.14, 9.8). The fact that RP /ə/ and /ɪ/ have a frequency of occurrence of 10.74% and 8.33%, respectively, whereas /ɔɪ/ and /ʊə/ are comparatively rare, should be taken into account in the construction of practice materials. Similarly, it is noteworthy that among the consonants the alveolar phonemes occur most frequently, whereas /ʒ/ is relatively rare. /θ/ and /ð/ regularly cause problems to foreign learners but nevertheless need to be given a high priority because /ð/ occurs in many very frequent function words, e.g. *the* and *that*, while /θ/, on the other hand, begins many common lexical words like *think* and *thank*.

(b) *Systemic oppositions*—Whatever the relative frequency of actual occurrences of the items contained in the phoneme inventory, the full system of 20 vowels and 24 consonants is complex compared with the systems of many other languages. In particular, the opposition of the close vowels /iː/–/ɪ/, /uː/–/ʊ/, the existence of a central long vowel /ɜː/ and the delicately differentiated front vowel set of /iː/–/ɪ/-/e/–/æ/–/ʌ/, together with the significant or conditioned variations of vowel length, pose problems to many foreign learners but nevertheless carry a high functional load and should assume a high priority. Similarly, in the consonant system, English has a comparatively rare complexity in its set of fricative places of articulation—labiodental, dental, alveolar, palato-alveolar, and glottal—which is in general more important than the distinctions between the voiceless and voiced pairs of fricatives (§9.4). Again, although English shares with many languages a system of plosives of the sort /p,t,k,b,d,g/, the conventions of realization will not always be the same, English preferring presence or absence of aspiration as a crucial feature, whereas many other languages, e.g. Romance or Slav, more typically make use of voicing (§9.2.1 (4)). Finally, as far as consonants are concerned, English characteristically permits a large number of consonant clusters (§10.9). Consonant clusters occur, of course, in many other languages, e.g. German and Polish, but the combinations permitted may differ from those of English. There are nevertheless other languages whose possibilities of consonant clustering are much more limited, e.g. Spanish or Italian, or whose syllables regularly have a simple CV shape, e.g. many Oriental and African languages. It is clear that in such cases much practice in English two- and three-consonant clusters will be needed to avoid the insertion of intrusive vowels—not only initially and finally in the word (where clustering as opposed to single consonants has only a 20% occurrence) but also across word and morpheme boundaries.

13.4.3   Sounds in Connected Speech

English has its own specific habits as regards both assimilation and elision (§§12.4.5, 12.4.6), but how far these are adopted by the foreign learner will depend on the performance target which he has set himself. Particularly affected are the alveolar articulations which exhibit notable instability.

13.4.4   Intonation

Although nearly all non-tone languages share certain characteristics of intonation, e.g. a tendency to use falling tunes for declarative statements and commands and rising tunes for questions and non-finality, there are some types of fall and rise (including in the latter category fall–rise) and some uses of falls and rises which are specific to English. It should also be remembered that intonation makes a most important contribution to the accentual patterning of English (pitch variation serving to accent and hence make salient those information points to which the speaker wishes to draw attention). Because of this interaction with accent, intonation may be taken to fall within the high priority category above. In addition, the cohesive and attitudinal implications of intonation become increasingly important if a high level of achievement is desired. In the early stages of learning English, although the tunes presented by the teacher should always be authentic, attention should be concentrated on the role of pitch in accentual oppositions, especially as regards the location of accented and therefore pitch-prominent (usually beginning a high fall) syllables in the utterance. Once this basic level is achieved, variations in tone shape can be introduced.

13.5   *RP High Acceptability*

High acceptability in RP is defined as a level of attainment in production which is as readily intelligible as that of a native RP speaker and which is not immediately identifiable as foreign, and as a level of receptive ability which allows the foreign listener to understand without difficulty all varieties and styles of RP. To achieve this standard the learner should be competent in all the features of current English described in chapters 7–12. His productive performance must be related to one specific type of RP. However, just as no two RP speakers of the same region (nor the same RP speaker on different occasions) speak in precisely the same way, the learner may be permitted certain tolerances in his pronunciation, provided that his speech retains an internal consistency, i.e. avoids the incongruity of a mixture of different regional characteristics. Some native speakers try to adopt particular accents in particular situations, e.g. they attempt to use an American pronunciation when dealing with teenagers and pop music. The foreign learner, however proficient he has become, is well-advised not to attempt such an effect, in the same way that he should be wary in his use of slang or non-standard grammar. The latitude which can be admitted concerns rather the phonetic realization of the segmental phonemes, i.e. the choice of allophonic variants (and in particular those of the vowels). In the following sections, the important essentials for high acceptability are listed and suggestions are made as to possible tolerances compatible with this goal.

13.5.1   Vowels

(a) *Essentials*—As mentioned in §13.4.2(b), the learner must have at his disposal the 20 vowel phonemes (12 monophthongs and eight diphthongs), together with the appropriate durational variations (§8.4), especially when these latter are significant in oppositions such as *seed–seat, heard–hurt, road–wrote* etc. Special attention must be paid to the quality/quantity complexes involved in series such as *bead, beat, bit* (§8.9.2(5)) or *food, boot, good* (§8.9.9(5)), these items illustrating the occurrence respectively of long tense /iː/, reduced tense /iː/ = [i], short lax /ɪ/ and long tense /uː/, reduced tense /uː/ = [u], and short lax /ʊ/. Although oppositions of only two phonemes are involved here, it is important in teaching to identify the three phonetic complexes so as to ensure that the vowels of, for instance, *beat* and *boot*, are not given undue length.

(b) *Tolerances*—Provided that the oppositions are retained, i.e. that the realizations of phonemes in the same context do not overlap, some latitude in performance is possible. Thus, for instance, in the series /iː,ɪ,e,æ/, the qualities produced may be somewhat more open than those indicated by the mark * in the figures of Chapter 7. Permissible **areas** (as opposed to points) of production encompassing several of the variants given in Chapter 8, are shown in Fig. 52.

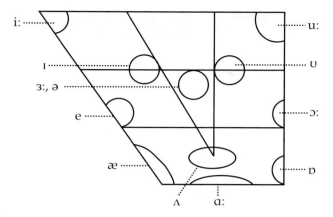

Fig. 52. *RP monophthongs: acceptable areas.*

/iː/ and /uː/, which are usually pronounced in General RP with a slight glide from a more open, centralized position to a closer, more fronted, position, may be given a pure vowel articulation with a close front or back position, respectively, similar to the qualities commonly associated with vowels of this type in other languages. Though there is a danger that such pronunciations may sound hyper-correct to the native listener, especially if the vowels used are cardinal in quality, they are to be preferred to gliding vowels whose starting point is so open that it falls within the area typical of popular regional speech—thus introducing unwit-tingly a comic incongruity if the remainder of the system conforms to the RP model.

The theoretical areas of tolerance for /ɑː/ and /ɔː/ are extensive, the limitations being imposed by the presence of /æ/ = [æː], e.g. in an opposition such as *cad–card*, and of /uː/, e.g. in *food–ford*. The variations shown in §§8.9.6, 8.9.8 may be permitted. Similarly, the variants for /ɜː/ shown in §8.9.11 may be safely used, provided that they do not overlap with the realization of /ɑː/, e.g. if an open variety of /ɜː/ is used in a word such as *burn*, this will necessitate a more retracted /ɑː/ in *barn*.

The diphthongization sometimes associated with RP /ɪ,e,æ/ mentioned in Chapter 8 seems to be growing less common and need not be adopted. However, the increasing use of a close vowel (i.e. a short /iː/) for final /ɪ/ amongst middle and young generation speakers justifies its use by foreign learners, if it is found to be easier than the traditional /ɪ/, in cases such as *happy, easy* etc. In the case of final /ə/, there is no need for a specially open variant to be used (§8.9.12(2)), an excessively open variant often being judged comic.

As stated in §8.9.2(3), there is often free variation in the use of /ə/ or /ɪ/ in some unaccented syllables. The pronunciation /ə/ appears to be increasingly preferred, e.g. for the penultimate vowel in the termination *-ity* in such a word as *quality* (/-əti/ rather than /-ɪti/), *-ily* (especially after /r/) as in *merrily* (/-əli/ rather than /ɪlɪ/) *-ate* as in *fortunate* (/-ət/ rather than /-ɪt/). Again, /ə/ or /ɪ/ are equally acceptable in the terminations *-less, -ness, -ace,* e.g. *hopeless, goodness,* *palace*, with /ə/ gaining ground; but it still seems preferable to retain /ɪ/ in *-et* as in *carpet* and essential to have /ɪ/ in *-age* as in *cabbage*, as well as in *-es, -ed* as in *horses, waited*, although pronunciations with /ə/ are gaining ground in these inflexions (besides being the norm in Australian English).

As for the eight RP diphthongs, the area of the first element is more important than the second element, which is only lightly touched on and has little prominence. Acceptable areas of onset are extensive but should not overlap (see Figs. 53, 54). The regional connotations of the quality of the starting points (as described in §§8.10–8.12) should be borne in mind: if, for instance, /eɪ/ is said with a starting-point more open than cardinal [ɛ], the impression given may be that of basilectal London speech.

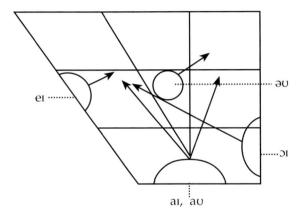

Fig. 53. *RP closing diphthongs: acceptable onset areas.*

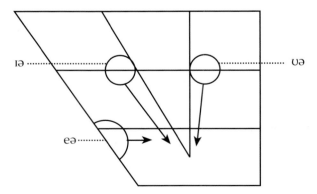

Fig. 54. *RP centring diphthongs: acceptable onset areas.*

In the case of /aɪ,aʊ/, there may be a common (open central) starting point (§§8.10.2, 8.10.5). The smoothing of /aɪə,aʊə/, though it has long been common in southern England, is not essential for the foreign learner. It should also be noted that /ʊə/ is increasingly replaced by /ɔː/ not only in words such as *poor, sure*, but also in *moor, tour* etc. (§8.12.3(3)). As for /əʊ/ (§8.10.4), the general RP form [əʊ] is most widespread and should thus be recommended, and learners are advised to avoid the diphthong having a fronted onset [ɛ̈], this variant being regarded as excessively affected.

13.5.2 Consonants

(a) *Essentials*—The full inventory of 24 consonant phonemes must be available to the speaker.

At this high level of performance, it is essential that the aspiration of voiceless /p,t,k/ in accented positions (§9.2.1(4) should be maintained as the major factor distinguishing these phonemes from voiced /b,d,g/, i.e. constituting a more potent differentiating feature than presence or absence of voicing. Learners whose mother tongue relies on voicing as the prime feature of opposition (e.g. most Romance and Slav language speakers) must take particular care. If, for instance, *pat* is realized as [pæt] rather than [pʰæt], an English listener is likely to understand *bat*, the absence of aspiration suggesting /b/ to an English ear. Similarly, /l/ and /r/ following accented /p,t,k/ (and to a lesser extent /j/ and /w/, since oppositions involving preceding voiceless/voiced plosives are rare), must be devoiced, as if thus signalling aspiration, so that *plead* and *bleed* are distinguished primarily by [l̥] in *plead* or *pray*, and *bray* primarily by [ɹ̥] in *pray*.

The articulation of /t,d/ must be clearly alveolar (§9.2.6), and when followed by the homorganic syllabics /n/ and /l/, as in *button, sudden, little, middle*, the release must be nasal or lateral respectively without an intrusive vowel (§9.2.4(4,5)). It is also characteristic of highly acceptable RP that the first plosive of stop sequences should have no audible release (§9.2.4(2)), e.g. in *actor, black tie, rugby, big dog.*

More generally, intrusive vowels should be avoided in clusters of consonants, e.g. between /s/ and /p,t,k/ as in *sport, strike, school* or in such final sequences as /lmz/ (*films*) or /lnz/ (*kilns*). Sequences of more than two consonants in simple words are comparatively rare; a greater test of articulatory skill occurs at morpheme and word boundaries, e.g. in *corkscrew, fixed price, pitched battle, sobbed bitterly.*

Alveolar /s,z/ must remain clearly distinct from dental /θ,ð/ and palato-alveolar /ʃ,ʒ/ (§9.4.4).

The /l/ phoneme should have the qualities and correct distribution of allophones mentioned in §9.7.1, i.e. [l,ɫ,l̩]. Similarly, /r/ should have a post-alveolar approximant or frictionless continuant articulation rather than any kind of trill or flap (§9.7.2). High performance RP will make use of the linking /r/, e.g. for *far away* /fɑːr əˈweɪ/ is more typical than /fɑː əˈweɪ/; and for *pour out* /pɔːrˈaʊt/ is preferred to /pɔːˈaʊt/.

(b) *Tolerances*—Certain of the variants or allophones described in Chapter 9 may be disregarded without detriment to an impression of highly acceptable performance. For instance, the devoicing of voiced consonants /b,d,g,dʒ,v,ð,z,ʒ/ in post- or pre-pausal position is not crucial: full voicing is permissible provided that [ə] off-glide is not added finally to a word such as *big* ([ˈbɪgə]) so that it is decoded as *bigger.*

Final (i.e. pre-pausal) plosives, although usually without audible release, as in *lit, lid*, may be given an explosive last stage, the resultant impression being one of careful speech. The use of [ʔ] or glottal reinforcement(§9.2.8) in connection with the voiceless plosives and affricate is never necessary; nor is the affrication or weakening of plosives mentioned in §9.2.4(6).

13.5.3   Sounds in Connected Speech

(a) *Elision*—The examples of post-nuclear vowel elision in the words quoted in §10.8, e.g. loss of /ə/ in *comparable, factory, dangerous, carefully* etc., must be regarded as optional, the retention of the weak vowel being entirely acceptable. In pre-nuclear positions, e.g. in *polite, solicitor*, the foreign learner is best advised to avoid elision of the weak vowel, a practice which is characteristic of rapid speech.

On the other hand, the alveolar consonant elisions mentioned in §10.8 can be adopted by the foreign learner, especially those involving the simplification of a three consonant cluster by the elision of a medial /t/ or /d/, e.g. in *restless, kindness*, where retention of the alveolar stop can be regarded as unusually careful.

In connected speech, considerable elision of both vowels and consonants is characteristic of a colloquial style (§12.4.6). It is not necessary, however, for the foreign learner (even with a high acceptability target) to seek to adopt all these native speaker habits. Once again, he may restrict himself to the elision of alveolar stops occurring medially in clusters of three consonants (especially when /t/ or /d/ is followed by another stop) brought together at word boundaries, e.g. in *left turn, mashed potatoes, jogged by, wind down* etc.

(b) *Assimilation*—It is assumed that the competent foreign learner will make most of the allophonic contextual assimilations mentioned in §12.4.1, many resulting from the accommodation between two articulations in the speech continuum. Certain changes which may provide cues to meaning, e.g. the devoicing of /l/ and /r/ after accented /p,t,k/ mentioned in §13.5.2(a) above are essential. In the case of assimilations involving changes of phoneme (§§12.4.2–5), especially at word boundaries, it should be remembered that these are important because they have stylistic implications. Thus, if a native speaker elides medial /t/ and /d/ in consonant clusters, it is likely that he will also assimilate word-final /t,d,n,s,z/ at word boundaries as suggested in §12.4.5. It is therefore consistent for the highly competent foreign learner to adopt similar habits. He must always be careful that in seeking to adopt an informal, colloquial style of English speech he does not introduce assimilatory habits which are characteristic of his own native language but not of English (§12.6).

However, what is more important than the development of productive skills in either elision or assimilation is the cultivation of the ability to receive and decode the highly elided and assimilated speech produced by native English speakers. Such speech must be regarded as the norm in all ordinary circumstances. The foreign student must therefore spend a considerable amount of time listening to normal colloquial English in order to acquire skill in identifying information points in an utterance (making full use of all contextual and syntactic cues and probabilities), when apparently crucial sounds are absent or when the isolate form of a word has become greatly changed in context, e.g. /ʃwɪ/ is a frequent telescoped form of /ʃəlwɪ/ (*shall we*). The native speaker is, of course, usually unaware that he makes reductions of this sort.

13.5.4   Accentuation

It has already been pointed out (§13.4.1) that the accentual features of English must form the base for the teaching of the language's pronunciation. These include the correct reduction of unaccented grammatical items (weak forms—§11.3). In connected speech, the weak forms of the most common grammatical items occur overwhelmingly more frequently than the strong forms, and, from this point of view, may be considered the usual pronunciation. However, if a native speaker is asked to pronounce common words such as *and, but, at, of* etc., he will give the rare citation (accented) forms /ænd, bʌt, æt, ɒv/ rather than the more common /ənd, bət, ət, əv/. He is genuinely unaware that he regularly reduces such words when unaccented in connected speech and will often deny that he would normally pronounce a phrase such as *And there was a knock at the door* as /ən ðə wəz ə 'nɒk ət ðə 'dɔ:/, describing such a speech style as careless. It follows that it is wiser to listen to the way in which the native speaks rather than to ask his opinion. Similarly, most dictionaries understandably record the strong pronunciation of these grammatical words, without always giving the weak alternatives. The foreign learner—at any level—must regard the strong forms as being 'marked', i.e. having a special meaning compared with the 'unmarked' sense of the usual weak forms: thus, the oppositive, emphatic meaning of *I `can* /kæn/ *come, I'm going `to* /tu:/ *London* with associated accent may be compared with the same phrases said neutrally with /kən/ and /tə/. However, the uncommon reduced forms, heard only in very rapid speech and of which some examples are given in the last part of §11.3, need not be imitated by foreign learners, even those with the highest target. The use of /jə/ or /mə/ in phrases such as *your mother, my father* has social connotations and, if employed inappropriately by a learner, could appear comically incongruous.

The proficient learner will, however, make use of those variations in the accentual patterns of words which are the result of the general rhythmic pressures of extended speech as opposed to the patterns of isolate words (§12.3). Such variation affects particularly adjectives or the adjectival element of a noun phrase, the predicative pattern (corresponding to the isolate form given in dictionaries) being regarded as normal, whereas the attributive pattern displays the variant, e.g. compare the patterns in citation or predicative situations as in *My car's `second `hand, This is `Water`loo* and the attributive variants *A `secondhand `car, `Waterloo `Station*. Such variation, 'accent-shift', is essential for high acceptability.

13.5.5   Intonation

Intonational phrasing is similar across most languages, such phrases often corresponding with syntactic clauses. However, adverbials (particularly in initial and final position) and syntactic subjects are frequently given phrases of their own, particularly in longer sentences (see §11.6.2.1). Learners will often neglect to divide long sentences into intonational phrases because the pressure to think of other aspects of the language makes them intone sentences in a wooden way. 'Chunking' a sentence into phrases will make pronunciation sound both more natural and more lively.

It is also true that there is a tendency in many languages to give the last lexical word in an intonational phrase a pitch prominence, just as is done in English in those cases where the phrase contains wholly new information. But in English in those other cases where there is old information at the end of the phrase, the major pitch prominence (the nucleus) will be moved to an earlier point in the phrase (see §11.6.2.2), i.e. old information does not receive an accent when occurring at the end of an intonational phrase. This does not apply in all languages (e.g. French, Italian, Spanish) where such de-accenting is only optional, and learners from such backgrounds must be careful to de-accent appropriately.

As regards choice of nuclear tone, once again many languages will have a distribution of falling and rising tones similar to English. But the type of fall or the type of rise may vary considerably. The high-target learner should pay special attention to the use of the fall–rise which occurs frequently in non-final positions in sentences (on dependent clauses, on adverbials, and on subjects). In RP the low rise is much more common than the high rise, particularly on interrogatives (unlike many other languages). As for falls, high fall is more common than low fall in RP (again unlike many other languages).

Learners should note that, despite what is often stated in textbooks on English language teaching, rises (usually low rise) and falls (usually high fall) both occur frequently on yes/no-interrogatives and wh-interrogatives. In both cases the low rise is the more polite tone, while the high fall is more business-like but sometimes abrupt and demanding. With tag-interrogatives, although agreement is always expected, the high fall demands such agreement while the low rise leaves open the possibility of disagreement. Learners can sound completely natural only making use of two tones, low rise and high fall, in all types of interrogatives (§11.6.2.3).

The most difficult area of intonation for foreign learners concerns its attitudinal uses. But some effort should be made to master some of the uses of fall–rise, e.g. for warnings, reservations and contradictions (§11.6.2.3).

Finally high-target learners must be aware that much of the individual tonal quality of a language is due to the types of pre-nuclear patterns which it uses. The most common pattern in RP involves a descending series of plateaux (§11.6.1.4). A series of glides-down is also common but not as common as in some other languages (e.g. North German) and if used too frequently in RP may sound aggressive. On the other hand, a series of glides-up (often heard in Norwegian and Swedish) will sound too enthusiastic. But most to be avoided is a long sequence of syllables on a low level, which will sound bored or even surly.

13.6   *Minimum General Intelligibility*

This type of performance has been described in §13.3 as one which preserves the chief elements of the RP system and is capable of conveying a message with some ease (in a given context) to a native English listener. It is regarded as essential that the accentual characteristics of English (including rhythmic features and the associated obscuration of weak syllables)[2] should be retained, as well as the ability to produce the common consonant clusters. But it is possible to reduce the segmental inventory of English very considerably and still retain a good level of intelligibility.[3] For instance, the vowel system can be reduced to a central pair /əː/ and /ə/. If this is done, the sentence /'wən də jə 'θəŋk ðə 'tʃəldrən wəl gət 'həːm frəm `skəːl?/ is not too difficult to interpret as 'When do you think the children will get home from school?', especially if the situation predisposes the listener to understand 'children' and 'school'. The disadvantage of such a reduction is that it produces a form of English unlike any natural speech, with the attendant problem that native speakers would have difficulty in teaching it.

It follows that any simplified form of pronunciation should share at least some features with most of the major natural forms of the language. In addition, the model should have three requisites:

(1) It should be at least as easy, and preferably easier, for the foreign student to learn as any natural model.

(2) It should be readily intelligible to most native speakers of English.

(3) It should provide a base for the learner who has acquired it to understand the major natural varieties of English.

Given that the accentual features common to all natural forms of English must be retained, it is in the segmental phonemes that simplification can be recommended. An amalgam of British RP and a generally accepted form of American pronunciation would seem an ideal solution, representing the great majority of native English speakers. Among the consonants the preservation of the pronunciation of post-vocalic /r/ in words like *farm, heard* is an example of closer adherence to orthography which may in fact reflect a majority pronunciation among native speakers and which might be helpful to some learners who do not wish to identify their English pronunciation with any one accent. However, apart from this potential presence of post-vocalic /r/, the major forms of native-speaker English exhibit considerable homogeneity in their consonant systems, which offer no further possibilities of simplification if they are to retain some resemblance to a natural system. Most of the simplification will therefore be in the vowel system. (This also correlates with a natural simplification made by many foreign learners, e.g. those in Africa and in Japan.)

13.6.1 Vowels

The vowel system may be simplified in both phonemic and phonetic respects, while still keeping an acceptable level of intelligibility.

(a) The centring diphthongs /ɪə,eə,ʊə/ (§8.12), for instance, are of comparatively rare occurrence (1.5% of vowels; 0.7% of all phonemes in connected speech).

---

[2] Minimally reduced forms can be employed if they are thought to be easier, e.g. /ənd/ for *and* rather than /ən/, /nd/ or /n/. See also Lecumberri and Maidment (2000)

[3] Gimson (1978)

They can always be interpreted as V + /r/ when appropriate, e.g. *peer* as /piːr/; *pair* as /peɪr/, and *poor* as /puːr/ (though in the latter case it would be more economical to replace RP /ʊə/ by ɔː/). Where there is no *r* in the spelling, e.g. in *idea, skua*, /iː/ or /ɪ/ + /ə/ and /uː/ or /ʊ/ + /ə/ would be used.

(b) Similarly, many cases of long vowels can be made to conform to the orthography by the retention of post-vocalic /r/, *farm, four, heard* might well have V + /r/, though words such as *calm* and *saw* would retain their /r/-less form. The unique case of /ɜː/ without *r* in *colonel* could conform to V + /r/ by analogy, as often in American English.

(c) Finally, it would doubtless be simpler for many foreign learners if certain phonetic adjustments in the realization of vowel phonemes were made, by using Cardinal Vowel values (§4.4.2) wherever possible. Thus, /iː,uː,ɔː/ would have cardinal values; /eɪ/ and /əʊ/ would be realized as long cardinal [e] and [o] (as they are in many forms of English); /e/ and /æ/ would be pronounced as cardinal [ɛ] and [a]; /ɑː/ would be long cardinal [a]; /ʌ/ and /ə/ would have the quality of accented and unaccented mid central [ə], with a long counterpart of similar quality for /ɜː/; /ɪ,ʊ,ɒ/ would remain as now. The resulting 16 vowel inventory would be as follows:

Six short monophthongs: /ɪ/ (*sit*); /ɛ/ (*set*); /a/ (*sat*); /ɒ/ (*sot*); /ʊ/ (*soot*); /ə/ (*another*) /əˈnəðər/
Seven long monophthongs: /iː/ (*bee, beer*); /eː/ (*pay, pair*); /aː/ (*calm, car*); /ɔː/ (*paw, pour, poor*); /oː/ (*home*); /uː/ (*do, dour*); /əː/ (*bird*)
Three diphthongs: /aɪ/ (*buy*); /aʊ/ (*cow*); /ɔɪ/ (*boy*)

(The vowel relationships are shown in the diagrams given in Figs. 55, 56, opposite.)

The following transcription demonstrates the use of such a vowel system with a full RP consonant inventory:

aɪ doːnt juːʒəlɪ kəm hiːr baɪ kaːr—ðə treːnz ə gʊd diːl mɔːr kənviːnjənt wɛn wiːr spendɪŋ ə fjuː aʊərz ɪn taʊn wɪð ðə bɔɪz. juː haf tə biː so əːrlɪ ɪf juː wɒnt tə faɪnd ə paːrkɪŋ pleːs. aɪ θɪŋk moːst garaːdʒɪz tʃaːrdʒ faːr tuː mətʃ fər puːr foːk laɪk əs. ðə reːlfeːrz tʃiːpər—so: ʃal wiː miːt ət ðə steːʃən?[4]

13.6.2   Consonants

As far as consonants are concerned, it is important that all phonemic oppositions should be maintained, though the optional /hw/ (§9.7.5(3)) may be omitted. Nevertheless, certain phonetic tolerances may be permitted:

(a) In the phonemic series /p,t,k,b,d,g/ (where presence or absence of aspiration is typically significant in initial accented positions in most native forms of English) voicing may be used as the distinguishing cue, if only the most basic type of intelligibility is the aim: thus, *pie* would be distinguished from *buy* by the

---

[4] In orthography: 'I don't usually come here by car—the train's a good deal more convenient when we're spending a few hours in town with the boys. You have to be so early if you want to find a parking place. I think most garages charge far too much for poor folk like us. The rail fare's cheaper—so shall we meet at the station?'

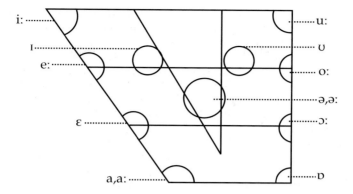

Fig. 55. *Monophthongs: simplified system.*

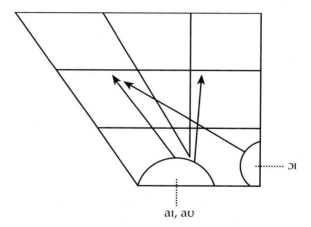

Fig. 56. *Diphthongs: simplified system.*

presence of voice in /b/ and its absence in /p/ (as is the case in the plosive systems of many languages such as those of the Romance and Slav families). Again, the loss of such an important cue implies great dependence on the context for the definition of meaning.

Less communicative harm is done if the articulation point of /t,d/ is dental rather than alveolar. Most languages use a dental contact point for this type of stop, and to do so in English entails no loss of intelligibility, though the phonetic deviation is usually immediately apparent to an English ear. It is also acceptable (from the point of view of communication) to replace, as many speakers of Indian languages tend to do, /t,d/ by retroflex [ʈ,ɖ].

(b) The sound [ŋ] may lose its phonemic status, in the sense that, besides occurring regularly before /k/ (as in *think*), it will retain a following voiced velar plosive element elsewhere, e.g. *sing, singer* [sɪŋg, ˈsɪŋgə], where RP omits [g]. [ŋ] is then a conditioned variant of /n/ before velar plosives. Thus, *hanger* and *anger* with /ŋ/ and /ŋg/ respectively in RP may both have [ŋg] if found to be easier at the rudimentary level of achievement. Such a usage corresponds to that of a part of Britain (§9.6.3). No two English words are distinguished in meaning by the opposition of /ŋ/ and /ŋg/.

(c) The complex English fricative system must be retained, but some relaxation of the articulation of the dental /ð/ is allowable in weak positions (§9.4.3), especially in the case of *the* following /s/ or /z/, e.g. in 'What's the time?' or 'Is there any left?'. In such positions, it is difficult in rapid, casual speech to articulate with any precision a truly dental sound immediately after an alveolar one. The English often replace it with a dentalized [z̪]; if a foreign learner uses a [z] sound in such positions of weak prominence, it may be hardly noticeable. It is not acceptable to replace /θ,ð/ by dental aspirated [t̪ʰ,d̪ʰ].

(d) The complex realizations of RP /l/ (§9.7.1) may be simplified; in particular, the 'clear' allophone may be used (as in some forms of Irish English) where the 'dark' [ɫ] is normal in RP, without loss of intelligibility. The devoiced [l̥] allophone following initial accented /p,k/, on the other hand, is an important carrier of meaning in an opposition such as *plot–blot*. It follows that, if voicing rather than aspiration is used as the distinguishing feature of /p,k/ vs /b,g/ as suggested in (a) above, the devoicing of /l/ after /ˈp,ˈk/ is less likely to occur; if this type of pronunciation is adopted, the listener's decoding of the message may again have to rely very heavily on the general context.

(e) There is little disturbance to comprehension if /r/ (§9.7.2) is realized as an alveolar tap or lingual roll (even in a post-vocalic position) rather than as the more typical RP post-alveolar approximant, since these variants occur in several British regional forms of speech. A uvular articulation, however, though interfering little with intelligibility once the listener has adjusted and though still occurring in the speech of some speakers in north-eastern England, is always perceived as unusual. As with /l/ in (d) above, the devoiced allophone of /r/, the main cue distinguishing *pray* from *bray*, may be dispensed with, thus forcing the context to carry a heavy burden of information. There is no loss of intelligibility if the linking /r/ is not used (§§12.4.7, 13.5.2(a)).

(f) Although the use of syllabic /n,l/ is typical of RP, intelligibility does not suffer if /ə/ is inserted even after an alveolar consonant (cf. §13.5.2(a)), as in *mutton, hidden, fasten, little, middle* etc. Following /t,d/, however, the insertion of /ə/ before /n,l/ will be perceived as strikingly unusual—and even childish.

13.6.3   Intonation

Since correct rhythm and accentuation (with the associated reduction of weak syllables) are regarded as indispensable for any level of spoken English (§13.4.1), all learners should be proficient in making use of pitch movements as important cues for signalling salient words or syllables. Those learners whose own language uses pitch variation for pragmatic rather than for lexical (tone) purposes are likely to be able to transfer much of their own intonation usage into English without serious disturbance of intelligibility. (If, however, they ignore the specifically English attitudinal uses of intonation, they will run the risk of giving an unintended impression of, for instance, abruptness or boredom.) On the other hand, those learners whose mother tongue is a tone language may find the concept of the functions of intonation as they occur in English and other European languages entirely novel. Even at the minimum level they should attempt to imitate some of the basic intonation patterns which signal a variety of discoursal and attitudinal meanings.

13.6.4   Sounds in Connected Speech

At these lower levels of performance no attempt need be made to imitate native English habits of elision or assimilation.

13.6.5   Minimum General Intelligibility: Conclusion

The result of permitting all the concessions mentioned in §13.6, involving the acceptance of an amalgam of segmental and prosodic features which occur together in no one natural form of English, is likely to be a style of speech which, though sounding markedly artificial or foreign, will be generally intelligible to most native English speakers. The native listener will need to adjust his decoding habits in much the same way that he does when listening to a native speaker using a regional accent of English which differs considerably from his own. This rudimentary form of pronunciation is not, however, to be regarded as a teaching target, but rather as a minimum level of achievement consistent with some degree of intelligibility; severe problems of communication will be caused by any greater divergence from a natural model.

13.7   *Teaching Methods*[5]

Learners' situations and requirements present so many variables that it is difficult to give advice of general applicability. Is the learner a child or an adult? Is he learning in a class with a teacher or by himself with the help of recordings or broadcast lessons? Is he to learn English pronunciation as part of a course extending perhaps over several years or is he attempting to acquire the essentials in a much more limited time? Whatever the answers to these and other questions, it must be accepted that in nearly all cases he will be seeking to learn English in an artificial fashion, i.e. very differently from the natural way in which he acquired his mother tongue, with constant exposure to the language of his family environment and with strong (instinctive) motivation to learn an efficient verbal means of communication. Nevertheless, it is some five years before he attains proficiency in the basic skills of speech production and reception.

What is clear is that, in teaching pronunciation, we are concerned especially with imparting motor and auditory skills rather than with inculcating the kind of logical agility such as may be involved in the acquisition of a new syntax. It is

---

[5] See, for example, Kenworthy (1987), Brown (1991)

true that the learner must assimilate rules for the distribution of allophones or for the assignment of intonation patterns to the appropriate discoursal or attitudinal context; he may even learn to apply rules for the derivation of word accentuation patterns from the orthography (most usefully with respect to the relation of the word accent and suffixation). But his knowledge of the rules is of little value if he is unable to apply a rule to his speech production.

Since it is generally the case that the correct pronunciation of a second language pronunciation becomes increasingly difficult to acquire after early adolescence, it is obvious that ideally it is desirable to teach pronunciation as soon as possible. With children it is often the case that the ability to mimic is retained to such a high degree that a demonstration of some feature of pronunciation, without further explanation, is sufficient (thus emphasizing how especially important it is that a teacher's own pronunciation should reach the highest level possible). When this ability is no longer present, as is the case with most adult learners, every effort must be made to overcome the interference from the sound system of the first language, through which the new, foreign (English) sounds are being filtered. Before attempting to produce English sounds, accentual or intonation patterns, it is invariably advisable to teach and establish certain basic discriminatory skills: the learner must be able (a) to distinguish with certainty between features of his own language and those of English; (b) to distinguish between the contrastive features of English.

The acquisition of such new auditory skills can be achieved by the use of extensive discrimination drills in which the learner is required to judge identities and differences in stimuli presented to him by a teacher or in a recording. Such 'ear training' is, of course, particularly important for those who aim at the higher levels of achievement in pronunciation where phonetic precision is essential. It is not generally useful to expose a learner to a tape in a language laboratory without any preliminary instruction on the features which he is expected to perceive. Moreover, even when a minimum level of discrimination has been established, learners may need specific instruction to assist correct production. The following sections give guidance for the improvement of receptive and productive skills.

Learners with different linguistic backgrounds will, of course, experience different difficulties in appreciating the distinctive elements of English. It is for this reason that a teacher should be aware of the phonetic and phonological characteristics of the mother tongue of his students (and of their particular local variety of this first language). By contrasting the features of the two languages, he will be able to predict the problems which will arise and on which he should concentrate his drills; he will also be able to make use of phonetic resemblances between the two languages which may not be readily evident to the learner.

Thus, a teacher of students whose language belongs to the Germanic or Slav families will not expect to encounter problems with the basic concept of word accentuation, which will almost certainly offer difficulty to speakers of, say, French or many Indian languages as well as to those who speak a tone language. On the other hand, as an example of the use of similarities, benefit may often be derived from relating English /ɪ/ to a vowel of the cardinal [e] type, which exists in many languages not possessing a centralized vowel such as English /ɪ/. Or again, many learners who cannot easily articulate the English 'dark' [ɫ] may in their own language have a vowel of the cardinal [o] quality, which is an excellent starting point (or even substitute) for English [ɫ] (and is indeed used by many native speakers for [ɫ]—§9.7.1).

13.7.1   Vowels

Many learners of English have difficulty with the short vowel series exemplified by *pit, pet, pat, putt, pot, put*. The series should first be presented to them, either in words having a similar consonantal frame or, preferably, in isolation. After listening, the learner should be asked to identify the items presented in a number of randomly ordered sets. (It is helpful if at this stage the learner is able to relate an English sound to a phonetic symbol or to a number, so that the success of his identification can be checked without reference to orthography, which can often be ambiguous.) In the next stage, the learner listens to examples of the same vowels (which by now he can identify correctly), but this time vowels of his own language are interspersed with the English ones; he must identify what is English and what is not.

It is of course not very helpful to give direct articulatory instruction for the production of vowels because our kinaesthetic sense of the shape of our tongue in an articulation is very limited: we are only aware of those points where the tongue contacts other articulators. Thus it is of little use to a learner to be told that, for a certain vowel articulation, the front of the tongue is raised to a close-mid position. However, there are some types of auditory and articulatory instruction which may be helpful. Use can be made of sounds which learners have in their own language and they can be told to 'try to make sound *x* more like sound *y*, or 'try to superimpose *x* on *y*', or 'try to make *x* and *y* at the same time'. Adjustments in the articulation can certainly be made by getting a learner to round the lips (either slightly or considerably); this is obviously the case for rounded vowels but can also be used to adjust the position of the tongue since rounding of the lips will generally retract the tongue. Similarly, spreading the lips (as opposed to simply unrounding to the neutral position) will bring the tongue closer to the roof of the mouth. Jaw movement can also be used to affect the tongue position: closing or opening the jaw will normally move the tongue into a more close or more open position. Sometimes a specific hint can be used for a particular vowel, e.g. /ɑː/ is the sound a doctor wants you to make when he wants to look down your throat.

13.7.2   Consonants

Similar discrimination exercises can be used in introducing possible difficult features of the English consonantal system. For instance, in the case of the importance of aspiration in distinguishing initial /p,t,k/ from /b,d,g/, it will be appropriate to present the English series for recognition (after describing the aspiration feature), and then to insert examples of strong but unaspirated [p,t,k] sounds to be identified as non-English by the student.

Direct articulatory instruction is often possible to assist in the production of consonants. For the aspiration of plosives, learners can be told to make a flame (from a match etc.) flicker or feel air on the back of the hand. For /f,v/ the upper teeth must be placed over the lower lip (and then the learner has to blow), for /θ,ð/ the tip of the tongue can be gripped between the teeth (even though in RP— but not in General American—the tip touches only the roots of the upper teeth), and for /s, z/ the tip must be put on the underside of the teeth ridge. In other cases the articulatory instructions can involve the modification of a starting point (which is not necessarily the sound the learner is using as a substitute). For /r/ a sound like [ə] or [ɜː] or [ɛ] in the learner's own language can be used as a starting point and the learner then told to curl the tip of the tongue upwards towards the roof of the mouth. For /ʃ,ʒ/ the learner can start from [s,z] and retract the tongue. For dark [ɫ] the starting point will be a back vowel (like English /ʊ/) followed by placing the tongue on the teeth ridge. In yet other cases the correct articulation of sounds can be based on other sounds with no specific articulatory instruction: /j,w/ can be taught starting from [iː,uː] and shortening, e.g. [iːɔːn] for *yawn* and [uːest] for *west*, /tʃ,dʒ/ can start from /tj,dj/ and be said rapidly, and for /h/ the learner can be told to put the tongue in the position for the following vowel and then blow. The difference between voiceless and voiced sounds is difficult to teach: it is often best to concentrate on associated factors, e.g. the shortening of vowels and approximants before voiceless consonants, the aspiration of voiceless plosives in accented positions, and the greater friction associated with voiceless fricatives and affricates.

13.7.3   Accentuation

The perceptual approach used in teaching segmental phonemes can also be employed in the case of accentual features. Learners (and especially those, such as tone language speakers, for whom the English concept of accentuation is quite new) must be taught to appreciate variation in the accentual patterns of English polysyllabic words, the varying rhythm of connected speech and the reduction of weak syllables in the utterance.

In the case of polysyllabic words, correct pattern identification (preferably by using nonsense sequences such as ['lɪlɪ,lɪ'lɪ] or ['laːlələ, lə'laːlə] etc.) should precede drills involving differing patterns in English words, e.g. be`hind vs `under; or `yesterday vs im`portant vs maga`zine vs `photograph etc. (see also §10.8). The importance of the accentual pattern of a word for its identification should be stressed, a correct accentual pattern being at least as important as the correct sequence of phonemes.

The weak forms of function words should be learnt from the beginning and their role in fluent pronunciation made clear. Exercises should be used for identifying weak forms in connected speech and particularly at the beginnings of sentences before students attempt the same sequence themselves. So too should exercises in listening and practising the borrowing rule in pairs like *bus/buses, conduct/conductor, gone/gone to, around/around the.*

13.7.4   Intonation

Learners may also by the same technique be led to appreciate the way in which pitch changes signal a shift of nucleus in a phrase where any word may carry primary accent. In a sentence such as 'This is my book', the nucleus may meaningfully be associated with any of the four words. Different versions should be presented to the learner until he is able to identify the nucleus placement with certainty. The more difficult exercises which must follow concern the recognition of the type of nuclear tone used (§11.6.1.3) and the appreciation of the pitch accents occurring before the nucleus (§11.6.1.4). As in all other drills, correct recognition must precede attempts at production.

13.8 *Pronouncing Dictionaries*

Most dictionaries of English will make use of a bilingual dictionary (i.e. one which is bilingual between English and their L1 or at least a language which they know better than English). Serious learners will make use of a monolingual dictionary designed for non-native learners like the *Oxford Advanced Learners' Dictionary* (Hornby and Wehmeier, 2000), the *Collins Cobuild* (Sinclair, 2001), or the *Longman Lexicon* (McArthur, 1981). Such dictionaries give information about pronunciation, in some cases using a transcription system similar to the one used in this book. But really serious learners, especially those aiming at High Intelligibility (§13.5), should use a pronouncing dictionary, that is, a dictionary devoted entirely to pronunciation rather than meaning. There are currently two standard dictionaries, those of Jones (1997) and Wells (2000); an older, shorter and less bulky dictionary is that of Windsor Lewis (1972).

The principal use to which a foreign learner will put such a dictionary is to look up a standard pronunciation in RP, including not only lexical words but also weak forms and names. This is generally given first for each entry, with alternative pronunciations following. The phonemic system and the transcription in Jones (1997) and Wells (2000) is virtually the same as that in this book. Additionally both use [i,u] to represent reduced forms of /iː,uː/ used in pre-vocalic positions as in [riˈækt] and [sɪtʃuˈeɪʃŋz] in the weak form of *to* pronounced [tu] and in the common pronunciation of <y> word-finally as [i], e.g. in *happy, usually, folly* and in words derived from them, e.g. *follies* as [ˈfɒliz]. They also make use of some additional symbols for sounds in foreign words. Information is also given on the primary accent and any lower accents.

It must of course be remembered that a phonemic system does not of itself tell a reader how to pronounce a word. It shows only the sequence of phonemes and the accentuation. A learner still needs to know how exactly each phoneme is realised phonetically, and sometimes differently in different positions. So he needs to know that /p,t,k/ are aspirated in syllable-initial position, less so in unaccented than in accented syllables, that /r/ is usually a post-alveolar approximant etc., etc.

Both dictionaries also give the corresponding pronunciations in General American; this can be very useful to foreign learners where the two pronunciations are not equivalent. Wells (2000) also gives information on British pronunciations which are not part of RP; this information often indicates pronunciations which the learner will meet as part of a Regional RP, e.g. /æ/ in *dance* and *example*. In varying degrees both dictionaries give notes on the pronunciation of particular words, notably the weak forms.

Marking the division into syllables is generally a useful aid to pronunciation (even though the two dictionaries differ slightly in how they do this). In looking up the pronunciation of a word for the first time, it aids the foreign learner's initial attempt at pronunciation to be able to divide the word into chunks. Since allophonic distribution often depends on syllable position, indicating syllabification aids correct pronunciation, e.g. syllabifying *appear* as /ə.pɪə/ rather than /əp.ɪə/ shows that the /p/ should be strongly aspirated.

13.9 *Assessment*

There remains the problem of the assessment of a learner's performance, from the point of view of both reception and production.

(a) A learner's achievement in comprehension can obviously be tested and quantified by measuring the amount of information which he has derived from a passage of colloquial speech, e.g. by scoring the number of information points which have been correctly received (excluding those items such as proper names etc., which may have been introduced to the listener for the first time). A score of this kind can be obtained either by questions on the text or by requiring the student to write down what he has heard. The test, when conducted with learners of high achievement, should involve passages in different pronunciation styles. The recognition of information points will, of course, be mainly concerned with the accented parts of an utterance and will be made easier by factors of redundancy and predictability. A test which involved the correct identification of intervening weak, grammatical items, and inflexions would obviously be a measure of total comprehension; although this type of detailed decoding goes beyond that which a native speaker normally employs when listening to his own language, it is nevertheless a good analytic exercise for the learner.

(b) In the case of production, an assessment of efficiency is more difficult. An atomistic approach can be used, whereby the control of phonemic oppositions is tested through the reading aloud of word lists and short sentences containing crucial minimal pairs. Similarly, lists of words exemplifying a variety of accentual patterns will test this area of the learner's proficiency. Various types of sentence (the grammatical or discoursal context being given) can also be used to assess appropriate sentence accentuation and choice of nucleus. If, however, read texts are used (even if, as lengthy passages or dialogues, they are specially contrived to exemplify the maximum number of features of segmental phonemes and connected speech), the artificiality of the procedure should be recognized and allowed for, since a certain unnaturalness of style is likely whether it is a native speaker or a foreign learner who is reading aloud.

At a higher level of achievement, phonetic quality must also be measured, the higher the level the more precise the phonetic specification in terms of the target model. Here the teacher's role is vital, since it is he who must judge (usually by ear) the extent to which the learner approaches the model. He will pay particular attention to the features of connected speech mentioned in §12.4.

The danger of an atomistic method of assessment meticulously applied is that departures from a norm will usually be found to be numerous, as much for the successful learner as for the one of lower ability. A simple aggregate of noted errors, undifferentiated in respect of their seriousness as far as communication is concerned, does not always provide a reliable indication of good or bad performance. A real assessment must be based on the intelligibility and acceptability of a learner's performance, in a situation of free discourse with a native speaker, when many of the so-called 'errors', not being perceived by the native listener, may be regarded as trivial and ignored.

Bibliography

The following books and articles are either referred to in the preceding pages or are intended as a selected list of works for further reading and consultation. The titles of certain periodicals are abbreviated as follows:

AJP	*American Journal of Psychology*
ELTJ	*English Language Teaching Journal*
ES	*English Studies*
IJAL	*International Journal of American Linguistics*
IRAL	*International Review of Applied Linguistics*
JASA	*Journal of the Acoustical Society of America*
JCL	*Journal of Child Language*
JEP	*Journal of Experimental Psychology*
JIPA	*Journal of the International Phonetic Association*
JL	*Journal of Linguistics*
JPhon	*Journal of Phonetics*
JSHR	*Journal of Speech and Hearing Research*
JVL	*Journal of Memory and Language*
Lang	*Language*
LS	*Language and Speech*
LVC	*Language Variation and Change*
MPh	*Le Maître Phonétique*
PMLA	*Publications of the Modern Language Association of America*
TPS	*Transactions of the Philological Society*
UCLA,WPP	*University of California at Los Angeles, Working Papers in Phonetics*
ZPh	*Zeitschrift für Phonetik*

Abberton, E. R. M. and Fourcin, A. J. (1984). Electrolaryngography. In C. Code and M. Ball (eds), *Clinical experimental phonetics*. London: Croom Helm.

Abbott, G. and Wingard, P. (eds) (1981). *The teaching of English as an international language*. Glasgow: Collins.

Abercrombie, D. (1948). Forgotten phoneticians. In D. Abercrombie, *Studies in phonetics and linguistics*. Oxford: Oxford University Press.

——, Fry, D. B., MacCarthy, P. A. D., Scott, N. C. and Trim, J. L. M. (eds) (1964). *In honour of Daniel Jones*. London: Longman.

—— (1967). *Elements of general phonetics*. Edinburgh: Edinburgh University Press.

Abramson, A. S. and Lisker, L. (1967). Some effects of context on voice onset time in English stops. *LS*, 10, 1–28.

Allen, W. S. (1953). *Phonetics in ancient India*. Oxford: Oxford University Press.

Altenberg, B. (1987). *Prosodic patterns in spoken English*. Lund: Lund University Press.

Amerman, J. D. and Parnell, M. M. (1992). Speech timing strategies in elderly adults. *JPhon*, 20, 65–76.

Andrésen, B. S. (1957). *-dier* and *-deer:* an experiment. *MPh*, 108, 35–7.

—— (1958). The glottal stop in the Received Pronunciation of English. Årbok: University of Bergen.

—— (1968). Preglottalisation in English standard pronunciation. Norwegian Studies in English, No 13. Oslo: Norwegian Universities Press.

Arnold, G. F. (1966). Concerning the theory of plosives. *MPh*, 125, 2–5.

Barber, C. (1997). *Early modern English*. Second edition. Oxford: Blackwell.

Bauer, L. (1983). *English word-formation*. Cambridge: Cambridge University Press.

Beckman, M. E. and Edwards, J. (1990). Lengthenings and shortenings and the nature of prosodic constituency. In J. Kingston and M. E. Beckman (eds), *Papers in laboratory phonology I: between the grammar and physics of speech*. Cambridge: Cambridge University Press.

Bell, A. M. (1867). *Visible speech*. London: Simpkin, Marshall and Co.

Bladon, R. A. W. and Nolan, F. J. (1977). A video-fluorographic investigation of tip and blade alveolars in English. *JPhon*, 1, 185–93.

Blankenship, B. (1992). What TIMIT tells us about epenthesis. *UCLA, WPP*, 81, 17–25.

Bolinger, D. L. (1958). A theory of pitch accent in English. *Word*, 14, 109–49.

—— (1981). *Two kinds of vowels, two kinds of rhythm*. Bloomington, IN: Indiana University Linguistics Club.

—— (1985). *Intonation and its parts*. London: Arnold.

—— (1989). *Intonation and its uses*. London: Arnold.

Borden, G. J. and Harris, K. S. (1984). *Speech science primer: physiology, acoustics and perception of speech*. Baltimore: Williams and Wilkins.

Brazil, D. (1975). *Discourse intonation*. Birmingham University: English Language Research.

—— (1978). *Discourse intonation II*. Birmingham University: English Language Research.

—— (1985). *The communicative value of intonation in English*. Birmingham University: English Language Research.

Bright, J. A. and McGregor, G. P. (1970). *Teaching English as a second Language*. London: Longman.

Britain, D. (1992). Linguistic change in intonation: the use of high rising terminals in New Zealand English. *LVC*, 4, 77–104.

Brown, G. (1977). *Listening to spoken English*. London: Longman.

Brown, G. (1983). Prosodic structure and the given/new distinction. In A. Cutler and D. R. Ladd (eds), *Prosody: models and measurements*. Berlin: Springer-Verlag.

Brown, A. (ed.) (1991). *Teaching English pronunciation: a book of readings.* London: Routledge.

Byrd, D. (1992a). Sex, dialects and reduction. *UCLA, WPP*, 81, 26–33.

—— (1992b). A note on the English palatalization process. *UCLA, WPP*, 81, 34–5.

—— (1992c). A note on English sentence-final stops. *UCLA, WPP*, 81, 37–8.

—— (1994). Articulatory timing in English consonant sequences. *UCLA, WPP*, 86.

Campbell, A. (1959). *Old English Grammar.* Oxford: Oxford University Press.

Carney, E. (1994). *A survey of English spelling.* London: Routledge.

Carney, E. (1997). *English spelling.* London: Routledge.

Carterette, F. C. and Jones, M. H. (1974). *Informal speech/alphabetic and phonemic texts with statistical analyses and tables.* Berkeley, CA: University of California.

Catford, J. C. (1964). Phonation types. In D. Abercrombie *et al.* (eds).

—— (1977). *Fundamental problems in phonetics.* Edinburgh: Edinburgh University Press.

—— (1988). *A practical introduction to phonetics.* Oxford: Clarendon Press.

Chafe, W. L. (1974). Language and consciousness. *Lang*, 50, 111–33.

Chafe, W. (1976). Givenness, contrastiveness, definiteness, subjects and topics. In C. N. Li (ed.), *Subject and topic.* New York: Academic Press.

Chomsky, N. and Halle, M. (1968). *The sound pattern of English.* New York: Harper & Row.

Christophersen, P. (1952). The glottal stop in English. *ES*, 33, 156–63.

Clark, J. and Yallop, C. (1995). *An introduction to phonetics and phonology.* Second edition. Oxford: Blackwell.

Classe, A. (1939). *The rhythm of English prose.* Oxford: Blackwell.

Cohn, A. (1990). Phonetic and phonological rules of nasalization. *UCLA, WPP*, 76, viii + 1–224.

Collins, B. and Mees, I. M. (1999). *The real professor Higgins: the life and career of Daniel Jones.* Berlin: Mouton de Gruyter.

Cooper, C. (1685). *Grammatica linguae anglicanae.* London: B. Tooke. Reprinted by The Scolar Press, Menston (1970). *English Linguistics 1500–1800.* No 86.

—— (1687). *The English teacher.* London: the author. Reprinted by The Scolar Press, Menston (1969). *English Linguistics 1500–1800.* No 175.

Cooper, F. S., Delattre, P.C., Liberman, A. M., Borst, J. M. and Gerstman, L. J. (1952). Some experiments on the perception of synthetic speech sounds. *JASA*, 24, 596–606. Reprinted in D. B. Fry (ed.) (1976).

Couper-Kuhlen, E. (1986). *An introduction to English prosody.* London: Arnold.

Cruttenden, A. (1974). An experiment involving comprehension of intonation in children from 7 to 10. *JCL*, 1, 221–32.

—— (1979). *Language in infancy and childhood.* Manchester: Manchester University Press.

—— (1985). Intonation comprehension in ten-year-olds. *JCL*, 12, 643–61.

—— (1995) Rises in English dialects. In J. Windsor Lewis (ed.), (1995), *Studies in honour of Professor J. D. O'Connor.* London: Routledge.

—— (1997). *Intonation.* Second edition. Cambridge: Cambridge University Press.

Crystal, D. (1969). *Prosodic systems and intonation in English.* Cambridge: Cambridge University Press.

—— (1975). *The English tone of voice*. London: Arnold.

—— (1986). Prosodic development. In P. Fletcher and M. Garman. (eds), *Language acquisition*. Cambridge: Cambridge University Press.

—— (1997). *English as a global language*. Cambridge: Cambridge University Press.

Crystal, D. and Quirk, R, (1964). *Systems of prosodic and paralinguistic features in English*. The Hague: Mouton.

Dalston, R. M. (1975). Acoustic characteristics of English /w,r,l/ spoken correctly by young children and adults. *JASA*, 57, 462–9.

Dauer, R. (1983). Stress-timing and syllable-timing re-analyzed. *JPhon*, 11, 52–62.

Davidsen-Nielsen, N. (1969). English stops after initial /s/. *ES*, 50, 321–39.

—— (1990). Old English short vowels before nasals. In S. Ramsaran (ed.).

Delattre, P. C., Liberman, A. M. and Cooper, F. S. (1955). Acoustic loci and transitional cues for consonants. *JASA*, 27, 769–73. Reprinted in D. B. Fry (ed.) (1976).

Denes, P. (1955). The effect of duration on the perception of voicing. *JASA*, 27, 761–4.

—— and Pinson, E. N. (1993). *The speech chain: the physics and biology of spoken language*. Second edition. New York: Freeman.

Deterding, D. (1990). Speaker normalization for automatic speech recognition. Unpublished Ph.D dissertation, University of Cambridge.

—— (1997). The formants of monophthong vowels in standard southern British English pronunciation. *JIPA*, 27, 47–55.

Dobson, E. J. (1957). *English Pronunciation, 1500–1700*. Oxford: Oxford University Press.

Docherty, G. J. (1992). *The timing of voicing in British English obstruents*. Berlin: Foris.

Ellis, A. J. (1869). *On early English pronunciation*. London: Early English Text Society.

Faber, D. (1986). Teaching the rhythms of English: a new theoretical base. *IRAL*, 24, 207–16. Reprinted in A., Brown (ed.) (1991).

—— (1987). The accentuation of intransitive sentences in English, *JL*, 23, 341–58.

Fallows, D. (1981). Experimental evidence for English syllabification and syllable structure. *JL*, 17, 179–92.

Fant, C. G. M. (1956). On the predictability of formant levels and spectrum envelopes from formant frequencies. In H. Lunt and H. MacLean (eds), *For Roman Jakobson*. The Hague: Mouton.

—— (1960). *Acoustic theory of speech production*. The Hague: Mouton.

Fischer-Jørgensen, E. (1954). Acoustic analysis of stop consonant. *Miscellanea Phonetica*, II, 42–59.

—— (1975). *Trends in phonological theory: a historical introduction*. Copenhagen: Akademisk Forlag.

Flege, J. E., Takagi, N. and Mann, V. (1995). Japanese adults can learn to produce English /r/ and /l/ accurately. *LS*, 38, 57–76.

Foulkes, P. and Docherty G. (1999). *Urban voices: accent studies in the British Isles*. London: Arnold.

Fourakis, M. and Port, R. (1986). Stop epenthesis in English. *JPhon*, 14, 197–221.

French, N. R., Carter, C.W. and Kœnig, W. (1930). The words and sounds of telephone conversations. *Bell System Technical Journal*, 9, 290–324.

Fromkin, V. (1971). The non-anomalous nature of anomalous utterances. *Language*, 47, 27–53.

Fry, D. B. (1947). The frequency of occurrence of speech sounds in southern English. *Archives Néerlandaises de Phonétique Expérimentale*, 20.

—— (1955). Duration and intensity as physical correlates of linguistic stress. *JASA*, 27, 765–8.

—— (1958). Experiments in the perception of stress. *LS*, 1, 126–52. Reprinted in D. B. Fry (ed.) (1976).

—— (1976) (ed.), *Acoustic phonetics: a course of basic readings*. Cambridge: Cambridge University Press.

—— (1979). *The physics of speech*. Cambridge: Cambridge University Press.

Fudge, E. C. (1969). Syllables. *JL*, 5, 253–86.

—— (1984). *English word-stress*. London: Allen & Unwin.

Garcia Lecumberri, M. L. and Maidment, J. A. (2000). *English transcription course*. London: Arnold.

Garde, P. (1968). *L'accent*. Paris: Presses Universitaires de France.

Gibbon, D. and Richter, H. (1984). *Intonation, accent and rhythm*. Berlin: de Gruyter.

Giegerich, H. J. (1992). *English phonology*. Cambridge: Cambridge University Press.

Gil, A. (1621). *Logonomia Anglica*. London. Reprinted by The Scolar Press, Menston (1969). *English Linguistics 1500–1800*. No 68.

Gilbert, J. H. V. and Purves, B. A. (1977). Temporal constraints on consonant clusters in child speech production. *JCL*, 4, 417–32.

Giles, H., Coupland, N., Henwood, K., Harriman, J. and Coupland, J. (1990). The social meaning of RP; an intergenerational perspective. In S. Ramsaran (1990) (ed.)

Gimson, A. C. (1960). The instability of English alveolar articulations. *MPh*, 113, 7–10.

—— (1964). Phonetic change and the RP vowel system. In D. Abercrombie *et al.* (eds).

—— (1969). A note on the variability of the phonemic components of English words. *Brno Studies in English*, 8.

—— (1973). Phonology and the lexicographer. *Annals of the New York Academy of Sciences*, 211, 115–21.

—— (1975). *A practical course of English pronunciation: a perceptual approach*. London: Arnold.

—— (1977). Daniel Jones and standards of English pronunciation. *ES*, 58, 151–8

—— (1978). Towards an international pronunciation of English. *In honour of A. S. Hornby*, London: Oxford University Press.

—— (1981a). The pronunciation of English: its intelligibility and acceptability in the world. *Modern Languages*, 62.

—— (1981b). Pronunciation in EFL dictionaries. *Applied Linguistics*, 2, 250–62.

—— (1984). The RP accent. In P. Trudgill (ed.), *Language in the British Isles*. Cambridge: Cambridge University Press.

—— and Ramsaran, S. M. (1982). *An English pronunciation companion to the Oxford advanced learner's dictionary of current English*. Oxford: Oxford University Press.

Grunwell. P. (1981). The development of phonology: a descriptive profile. *A First Language*, 3, 161–91.

—— (1982). *Clinical phonology*. Second edition. London: Croom Helm.

Guierre, L. (1979). *L'accentuation en anglais contemporain*. Unpublished Ph.D. thesis, University of Paris.

Gussenhoven, C. (1984). *On the grammar and semantics of sentence accents*. Dordrecht: Foris.

Guy, G., Horvath, B., Vonwiller, J., Daisley, E. and Rogers, I. (1986). An intonation change in progress in Australian English. *Language in Society*, 15, 23–52.

Haggard, M. (1978). The devoicing of voiced fricatives. *JPhon*, 6, 95–103.

Hagiwara, R. (1995). Acoustic realisations of American /r/ as produced by women and men. *UCLA, WPP*, 90.

Halle, M., Hughes, G. W. and Radley, J. P-A. (1957). Acoustic properties of stop consonants. *JASA*, 29, 107–16. Reprinted in I. Lehiste (ed.) (1967) and in D. B. Fry (ed.) (1976).

—— and Vergnaud, J. R. (1987). An essay on stress. Cambridge, MA: MIT Press.

Halliday, M. A. K. (1967). *Intonation and grammar in British English*. The Hague: Mouton.

Handbook of the International Phonetic Association: a guide to the International Phonetic Alphabet (1999). Cambridge: Cambridge University Press.

Hardcastle, W. J. (1976). *Physiology of speech production*. New York: Academic Press.

Harrington, J. (1994). The contribution of the murmur and vowel to the place of articulation distinction in nasal consonants. *JASA*, 96, 19–32.

Harris, K. S. (1958). Cues for the discrimination of American English fricatives in spoken syllables. *LS*, 1, 1–7. Reprinted in D. B. Fry (ed.) (1976).

——, Hoffman, H. S., Liberman, A. M., Delattre, P. C. and Cooper, F. S. (1958). Effect of third-formant transitions on the perception of voiced stop consonants. *JASA*, 30, 122–6.

Hart, J. (1570). *A methode*. Reprinted in B. Danielsson (ed.)(1955, 1963), *John Hart's works on orthography and pronunciation, 1551, 1569, 1570*. Two volumes. Stockholm: Almqvist and Wiksell.

Hawkins, P. (1992). *Introducing phonology*. Second edition. London: Routledge.

Hayes, B. (1982). Extrametricality and English stress. *Linguistic Inquiry*, 13, 227–76.

Henton, C. G. (1983). Changes in the vowels of received pronunciation. *JPhon*, 11, 353–71.

Henton, C. and Bladon, A. (1988). Creak as a sociophonetic marker. In L. M. Hyman and C. N. Li (eds), *Language, speech and mind: studies in honor of Victoria A. Fromkin*. London: Routledge.

Herdan, G. (1958). The relation between the functional burdening of phonemes and their frequency of occurrence. *LS*, 1, 8–13.

Higginbottom, E. M. (1965). Glottal reinforcement in English. *TPS*, 129–42.

Hockett, C. F. (1955). *A manual of phonology*. Indiana University Publications in Anthropology and Linguistics. Memoir 11 of the International Journal of American Linguistics. *IJAL*, 21, Part 1.

Hogg R. M. (1992). *A grammar of Old English*. Vol 1. Phonology. Oxford: Blackwell.

—— (1992). Phonology and morphology. In R. M. Hogg (ed.), *The Cambridge History of the English Language*. Vol. 1. Cambridge: Cambridge University Press.

—— and McCully, C. B. (1987). *Metrical phonology: a coursebook*. Cambridge: Cambridge University Press.

Hollien, H. and Shipp, T. (1972). Speaking fundamental frequency and chronologic age in males. *JSHR*, 15, 155–9.

Hornby, A. S. and Wehmeier, S. (2000). *Oxford advanced learners' dictionary*. Sixth edition. Oxford: Oxford University Press.

House, J. (1990). Intonation structures and pragmatic interpretation. In S. Ramsaran (ed.).

Hughes, A. and Trudgill, P. (1987). *English accents and dialects*. Second edition. London: Arnold.

Hughes, G. W. and Halle, M. (1956). Spectral properties of fricative consonants. *JASA*, 28, 303–10. Reprinted in D. B. Fry (ed.) (1976).

Jakobson, R., Fant, C. G. M., Halle, M. (1952). *Preliminaries to speech analysis: the distinctive features and their acoustic correlates*. Cambridge, MA: MIT Press.

—— and Halle, M. (1956). *Fundamentals of language*. The Hague: Mouton.

Jassem, W. (1965). The formants of fricative consonants. *LS*, 8, 1–16.

Johnson, S. (1755). *A dictionary of the English language*. London: Printed by W. Strachan for J. and. P. Knapton.

Jones, D. (1954). Falling and rising diphthongs in southern English. *Miscellanea Phonetica II*, 1–12.

—— (1972). *The pronunciation of English*. Fourth edition. Cambridge: Cambridge University Press.

—— (1918). *An outline of English phonetics*. Eighth edition, 1960. Cambridge: Heffer.

—— (1976). *The phoneme; its nature and use*. Cambridge: Cambridge University Press.

—— (1997). *English pronouncing dictionary*. Fifteenth edition. Edited by P. Roach and J. Hartman. Cambridge: Cambridge University Press.

Jongman, A. (1989). Duration of fricative noise required for identification of English fricatives. *JASA*, 85, 1718–25.

Kelly, J. (1981). The 1847 alphabet: an episode of phonotypy. In R. E. Asher and E. J. A. Henderson (eds), *Towards a history of phonetics*. Edinburgh: Edinburgh University Press.

Kenworthy, J. (1987). *Teaching English pronunciation*. London: Longman.

Kenworthy, J. (2000). *The pronunciation of English: a workbook*. London: Arnold.

Kenyon, J. S. and Knott, T. A. (1953). *A pronouncing dictionary of American English*. Springfield, MA: Merriam Webster.

Kingdon, R. (1958). *Groundwork of English intonation*. London: Longman.

—— (1958). *Groundwork of English stress*. London: Longman.

Knowles, G. (1978). The nature of phonological variables in Scouse. In P. Trudgill (ed.), *Sociolinguistic patterns in British English*. London: Arnold.

—— (1987). *Patterns of spoken English*. London: Longman.

Kreidler, C. W. (1989). *The pronunciation of English*. Oxford: Blackwell.

Kökeritz, H. (1953). *Shakespeare's pronunciation*. New Haven: Yale University Press.

Kurowski, K. (1987). Acoustic properties for place of articulation in nasal consonants. *JASA*, 81, 1917–27.

—— and Blumstein, S. E. (1984). Perceptual integration of the murmur and formant transitions for place of articulation in nasal consonants. *JASA*, 76, 383–90.

Labov, W. (1966). *The social stratification of English in New York City*. Washington DC: Center for Applied Linguistics.

—— (1991). Three dialects of English. In P. Eckert (ed.), *New ways of analyzing sound change*. San Diego: Academic Press.

Ladd, D. R. (1978a). *The structure of intonational meaning*. Bloomington, IN: Indiana University Press.

—— (1978b). Stylized intonation. *Language*, 54, 517–39.

—— (1979). Light and shadow: a study of the syntax and semantics of sentence accent in English. In L. R. Waugh and F. van Coetsem (eds), *Contributions to grammatical studies: syntax and semantics*. Leiden: Brill.

Ladefoged, P. (1956). The classification of vowels. *Lingua*, 2, 113–27.

—— (1962). *Elements of acoustic phonetics*. Chicago: The University of Chicago Press.

—— (1967). *Three areas of experimental phonetics*. Oxford: Oxford University Press.

—— (1971). *Preliminaries to linguistic phonetics*. Chicago: Chicago University Press.

—— (1982). *A course in phonetics*. Second edition. New York: Harcourt, Brace, Jovanovich.

——, Draper, M. H. and Whitteridge, D. (1958). Syllables and stress. *Miscellanea Phonetica III*, 1–13.

Lass, R. (1976). *English phonology and phonological theory*. Cambridge: Cambridge University Press.

Laeufer, C. (1996). The acquisition of a complex phonological contrast: voice timing patterns of English final stops by native French speakers. *Phonetica*, 53, 117–42.

Laver, J. D. M. (1974). Labels for voices. *JIPA*, 4, 62–75. Reprinted in J. D. M. Laver (1991).

—— (1980). *The phonetic description of voice quality*. Cambridge: Cambridge University Press.

—— (1991). *The gift of speech*. Edinburgh: Edinburgh University Press.

Lehiste, I. (ed.) (1967). *Readings in acoustic phonetics*. Cambridge, MA: MIT Press.

—— (1970). *Suprasegmentals*. Cambridge, MA: MIT Press.

—— (1977). Isochrony re-considered. *JPhon*, 5, 253–63.

—— and Peterson, G. E. (1961). Transitions, glides, and diphthongs. *JASA*, 33, 268–77.

Liberman, A.M., Delattre, P. C. and Gerstman, L. J. (1952). The role of selected stimulus-variables in the perception of unvoiced stop consonants. *AJP*, 65, 497–516.

——, ——, Cooper, F. S. and Gerstman, L. J. (1954). The role of consonant vowel transitions in the perception of the stop and nasal consonants. *Psychological Monographs*, No 379. Washington: DC: American Psychological Association. Reprinted in D. B. Fry (ed.) (1976).

——, ——, and Cooper, F. S. (1958). Some cues for the distinction between voiced and voiceless stops in initial positions. *LS*, 1, 153–67.

Lieberman, A. M. and Blumstein S. E. (1988). *Speech physiology, speech perception, and acoustic phonetics*. Cambridge: Cambridge University Press.

Lisker, L. (1957a). Closure duration and the intervocalic voiced–voiceless distinction in English. *Lang*, 33, 42–9.

—— (1957b). Minimal cues for separating /w,r,l,y/ in intervocalic positions. *Word*, 13, 256–67.

—— and Abramson, A. S. (1964). A cross-language study of voicing in initial stops. *Word*, 20, 384–422.

Macken, M. and Barton, D. (1980). The acquisition of the voicing contrast in English: a study of voice onset time in word-initial stop consonants. *JCL*, 7, 41–74.

MacLagan, M. A. and Gordon, E. (1996). Out of the AIR and into the EAR: another view of the New Zealand diphthong merger. *LVC*, 8, 125–47.

MacMahon, M. K. C. (1998). Phonology. In S. Romaine (ed.), *The Cambridge history of the English language*. Cambridge: C.U.P.

Maddieson, I. (1984). *Patterns of sounds*. Cambridge: Cambridge University Press.

Maidment J. (1990). Focus and tone in English intonation. In S. Ramsaran (ed.).

Malécot, A. (1956). Acoustic cues for nasal consonants. *Lang*, 32, 274–84.

—— (1968). The force of articulation of American stops and fricatives as a function of position. *Phonetica*, 18, 95–102.

Malmberg, B. (1963). *Phonetics*. New York: Dover Publications.

—— (1968) (ed.). *Manual of phonetics*. Amsterdam: North-Holland.

Matthews, W. (1938). *Cockney past and present*. Reprinted (1972) with a new preface. London: Routledge.

McArthur, T. (1981). *Longman lexicon of contemporary English*. Harlow: Longman.

McIntosh, A. (1952). *Introduction to a survey of Scottish dialects*. Edinburgh: Nelson.

Mines, A. M., Hanson, B. F. and Shoup, J. E. (1978). Frequency of occurrence of phonemes in conversational English. *L&S*, 21, 221–35.

Mugglestone, L. (1995). *'Talking proper': the rise of accent as social symbol*. Oxford: Clarendon Press.

Mol, H. and Uhlenbeck, E. M. (1955). The linguistic relevance of intensity in stress. *Lingua*, 5, 205–13.

Nolan, F. (1983). *The phonetic bases of speaker recognition*. Cambridge: Cambridge University Press.

—— and Kerswill, P.E. (1990). The description of connected speech processes. In S. Ramsaran (ed.).

Obendorfer, R. (1998). *Weak forms in present-day English*. Oslo: Novus Press.

O'Connor, J. D. (1952). RP and the reinforcing glottal stop. *ES*, 33, 214–18.

—— (1980). *Better English pronunciation*. Second edition. Cambridge: Cambridge University Press.

—— (1973). *Phonetics*. Harmondsworth: Penguin.

—— and Arnold, G. F. (1973). *Intonation of colloquial English*. Second edition. London: Longman.

——, Gerstman, L. J., Liberman, A. M., Delattre, P. C. and Cooper, F. S. (1957). Acoustic cues for the perception of initial /w,j,r,l/ in English. *Word*, 13, 24–43. Reprinted in D. B. Fry (ed.) (1976).

—— and Tooley, O. M. (1964). The perceptibility of certain word boundaries. In D. Abercrombie *et al.* (eds)

Ohde, R. N. (1984). Fundamental frequency as an acoustic correlate of stop consonant voicing. *JASA*, 75, 224–30.

—— (1994). The development of the perception of cues to the [m]–[n] distinction in CV syllables. *JASA*, 96, 675–86.

Orton, H. *et al.* (1962–71). *Survey of English dialects*. Leeds: Arnold.

——, Sanderson, S. and Widdowson, J. (eds) (1978). *The linguistic atlas of England*. London: Croom Helm.

Painter, C. (1979). *An introduction to instrumental phonetics*. Baltimore: University Park Press.

Palmer, H. E. (1924). *English intonation with systematic exercises*. Cambridge: Heffer.

Palsgrave, J. (1530). *Lesclarcissement de la langue francoyse*. Reprinted by The Scolar Press, Menston (1971). *English Linguistics 1500–1700*. No. 267.

Perkell, J. S. (1969). *Physiology of speech production: results and implications of a quantitative cineradiographic study*. Cambridge, MA: MIT Press.

Peters, A. M. (1977). Language learning strategies: does the whole equal the sum of the parts? *Lang*, 53, 560–73.

Peterson, G. E., and Lehiste, I. (1960). Duration of the syllable nuclei in English. *JASA*, 32, 693–703.

Pierrehumbert, J. (1980/87). The phonology and phonetics of English intonation. Ph.D. dissertation, Massachusetts Institute of Technology. Reproduced by Indiana University Linguistics Club Publications, Bloomington, Indiana.

—— and Hirshberg, J. (1990). The meaning of intonation contours in the interpretation of discourse. In P. R. Cohen, J. Morgan and M. E. Pollack (eds), *Intentions in communication*. Cambridge, MA: MIT Press.

Pike, K. L. (1943). *Phonetics*. Ann Arbor: University of Michigan Press.

—— (1945). *The intonation of American English*. Ann Arbor: University of Michigan Press.

—— (1947). *Phonemics*. Ann Arbor: University of Michigan Press.

Pointon, G. E. (1983). *BBC pronouncing dictionary of British names*. Second edition. Oxford: Oxford University Press.

Prator, C. H. and Robinett, B. W. (1972). *Manual of American English pronunciation*. Third edition. New York: Holt, Rinehart & Winston.

Puttenham, G. (1589). *Arte of English poesie*. London: Alex Murray and Son. Edited by G. D. Willcock and A. Walker (1936). Cambridge: Cambridge University Press.

Quirk, R. and Wrenn, C. L. (1955). *An Old English grammar*. London: Methuen.

——, Svartvik, J., Duckworth, A. P., Rusiecki, J. P. L. and Colin, A. J. T. (1964). Studies in the correspondence of prosodic to grammatical features in English. In H. G. Lunt (ed.), *Proceedings of the Ninth International Congress of Linguistics*. The Hague: Mouton. Reprinted in R. Quirk, *Essays on the English language: medieval and modern*. London: Longman.

——, Greenbaum, S., Leech, G. and Svartvik, J. (1973). *A grammar of contemporary English.* London: Longman.

——, ——, ——, and —— (1985). *A comprehensive grammar of contemporary English.* London: Longman.

Ramsaran, S. (1978). *Phonetic and phonological correlates of style in English: a preliminary investigation.* Unpublished Ph.D. thesis, University of London.

—— (1990). RP: fact and fiction. In Ramsaran (ed.).

—— (ed.) (1990). *Studies in the pronunciation of English: a commemorative volume in memory of A. C. Gimson.* London: Croom Helm.

Repp, B. H. (1986). Perception of the [m]–[n] distinction in CV syllables. *JASA,* 79, 1987–99.

Roach, P. J. (1973). Glottalization of /p/, /t/, /k/, and /tʃ/: a re-examination. *JIPA,* 3, 10–21.

—— (1979). Laryngeal-oral co-articulation in glottalized English plosives. *JIPA,* 9, 1–6.

—— (1982). On the distinction between 'stress-timed' and 'syllable-timed' languages. In D. Crystal (ed.), *Linguistic controversies: essays in linguistic theory in honour of F. R. Palmer.* London: Arnold.

—— (1991). *English phonetics and phonology: a practical course.* Second edition. Cambridge: Cambridge University Press.

Robins, R. H. (1989). *General linguistics, an introductory survey.* Fourth edition. London: Longman.

Romaine, S. (1978). Post-vocalic /r/ in Scottish English: sound change in progress? In P. Trudgill (ed.), *Sociolinguistic patterns in British English.* London: Arnold.

Russell, A., Penny, L. and Pemberton, C. (1995). Speaking fundamental frequency changes over time in women: a longitudinal study. *JSHR,* 38, 101–9.

Schubiger, M. (1958). *English intonation, its form and function.* Tübingen: Niemeyer.

Scully, C., Castelli, E., Brearley, E. and Shirt, M. (1992). Analysis and simulation of a speaker's aerodynamic and acoustic patterns for fricatives. *JPhon,* 20, 39–51.

Selkirk, E. (1982). The syllable. In H. van der Hulst and N. Smith (eds), *The structure of phonological representations.* Part II. Dordrecht: Foris.

Sharf, D. J. (1962). Duration of post-stress intervocalic stops and preceding vowels. *LS,* 5, 26–46.

Sheridan, T. (1762). *A course of lectures on elocution.* London: W. Strahan. Reprinted by the Scolar Press, Menston. (1969). *English Linguistics 1500–1800.* No 129.

—— (1780). *A general dictionary of the English language.* Reprinted by The Scolar Press, Menston (1967). *English Linguistics 1500–1800.* No 50.

Sinclair, J. (2001). *Collins Cobuild English language dictionary.* Third edition. London: Collins.

Sivertsen, E. (1960). *Cockney phonology.* Oslo: Oslo University Press.

Smith, T. (1568). *De recta et emendata linguae anglicanae.* Reprinted by The Scolar Press, Menston. (1968). *English Linguistics 1500–1800.* No 109.

Steele, J. (1775). *An essay towards establishing the melody and measure of speech, to be expressed and perpetuated by peculiar symbols.* London: Bowyer & Nicholls.

Reprinted by The Scolar Press, Menston (1969). *English Linguistics 1500–1800.* No 172.

Stetson, R. H. (1951). *Motor phonetics.* Second edition. Amsterdam: North-Holland.

Stevens, K. N. and Klatt, D. H. (1974). The role of formant transitions in the voiced-voiceless distinctions in stops. *JASA*, 55, 653–59.

—— and Blumstein, S.E. (1978). Invariant cues for place of articulation in stop consonants. *JASA*, 64, 1358–68.

——, Blumstein, S. E., Glucksman, L. Burton, M., and Kurowski, K. (1992). Acoustic and perceptual characteristics of voicing in fricatives and fricative clusters. *JASA*, 91, 2979–3000.

Stoel-Gammon, C. and Dunn, C. (1985). *Normal and disordered child phonology.* Baltimore: University Park Press.

Stone M. (1990). A three-dimensional model of tongue movement on ultrasound and x-ray microbeam data. *JASA*, 87, 2207–17.

——, Faber, A., Raphael, L. J. and Shawker, T. H. (1992). Cross-sectional tongue shape and linguopalatal contact patterns in [s], [ʃ], and [l]. *JPhon*, 20, 253–70.

Strevens, P. D. M (1960). Spectra of fricative noise in human speech. *LS*, 3, 32–49. Reprinted in D. B. Fry (ed.) (1976).

Subtelny, J., Worth, J. H. and Sakuda, M. (1966). Intraoral pressure and rate of flow during speech. *JSHR*, 9, 498–518.

Suomi, K. (1976). *English voiceles and voiced stops as produced by native and Finnish speakers.* Reports from the Department of English, University of Jyväskylä, No 2. Jyväskylä: Jyväskylän Yliopiston Monistuskeskus.

—— (1980). *Voicing in English and Finnish stops.* Publications of the Department of Finnish and General Linguistics, University of Turku, No 10. Turku: Turun Yliopisto.

Sweet, H. (1888). *History of English sounds.* Second edition. Oxford: Clarendon Press.

—— (1911). *A primer of spoken English.* Fourth edition. Oxford: Clarendon Press.

—— (1929). *The sounds of English.* Second edition. Oxford: Clarendon Press.

Thompson, H. (1990). *Stress and salience in English: theory and practice.* Palo Alto Research Centre: Xerox.

Todaka, Y. (1992). Phonetic variants of the determiner 'the'. *UCLA, WPP*, 81, 39–47.

Trager, H. L. and Smith, H. L. (1951). *An outline of English structure.* (Studies in Linguistics Occasional Papers 3). Washington: American Council of Learned Societies.

Treiman, R. and Davis, C. (1988). Syllabification of intervocalic consonants. *JML*, 27, 87–104.

Treiman, R., Gross, J. and Cwikiel-Glavin, A. (1992). The syllabification of /s/ clusters in English. *JPhon*, 20, 388–402.

Trim, J. L. M. (1959). Major and minor tone groups in English. *MPh*, 112, 26–9.

—— (1961–2). English standard pronunciation. *English Language Teaching*, 26, 1961–62.

Troubetzkoy, N. S. (1949). *Principes de phonologie* Translated by J. Cantineau. Paris: Klincksieck.

Trudgill, P. (1974). *The social differentiation of English in Norwich*. Cambridge: Cambridge University Press.

—— (ed.) (1978). *Sociolinguistic patterns in British English*. London: Arnold.

—— (ed.) (1984). *Language in the British Isles*. Cambridge: Cambridge University Press.

—— (1984). *Applied sociolinguistics*. London: Academic Press.

—— (1999). *The dialects of England*. Second edition. Oxford: Blackwell.

—— and Hughes, A. (1979). *English accents and dialects*. London: Arnold.

Vachek, J. (1964). Notes on the phonemic value of the modern English [ŋ] sound. In D. Abercrombie (ed.).

Vanvik, A. J. (1961). *On stress in present-day English*. Bergen: Norwegian Universities Press.

Volatis, L. E. and Miller, J. L. (1992). Phonetic prototypes: influence of place of articulation and speaking rate on the internal structure of voicing categories. *JASA*, 92, 723–35.

Walker, J. (1791). *Critical pronouncing dictionary and exposition of the English language*. London. Reprinted by The Scolar Press, Menston (1968). *English Linguistics 1500–1800*. No 117.

Wallis, J. (1653). *Grammatica linguae anglicanae*. London. Reprinted by The Scolar Press, Menston (1969). *English Linguistics 1500–1800*. No 142.

Ward, I. C. (1948). *The phonetics of English*. Fourth edition. Cambridge: Heffer.

Wells, J. C. (1982). *Accents of English*. Volumes 1–3. Cambridge: Cambridge University Press.

—— (2000). *Longman pronunciation dictionary*. Harlow: Longman.

—— and Colson, G. (1971). *Practical phonetics*. London: Pitman.

Wiik, K. (1965). *Finnish and English vowels: a comparison with special reference to the learning problems met by native speakers of Finnish learning English*. Annales Universitatis Turkensis, Series B, No 94. Turku: Turun Yliopisto.

Wilkins, J. (1668). *An essay towards a real character and a philosophical language*. London: J. Martyn. Reprinted by The Scolar Press, Menston (1967). *English Linguistics 1500–188*. No 119.

Windsor Lewis, J. (1969). *A guide to English pronunciation*. Oslo: Universitetsforlaget.

—— (1972). *A concise pronouncing dictionary of British and American English*. London: Oxford University Press.

—— (1979). Pre-consonantal /r/ in the General British pronunciation of English. *ELTJ*, 33, 188–90.

—— (1990). HappY land reconoitred: the unstressed word-final -y vowel in General British pronunciation. In S. Ramsaran (ed.).

Wingate, A. H. (1982). A phonetic answer to a phonological problem. *UCLA, WPP*, 54, 1–27.

Wyld, H. C. (1936). *A history of modern colloquial English*. Third edition. Oxford: Blackwell.

Index

References are to page numbers. Main references are in **bold**. Phonetic symbols are placed at the end of the appropriate letter section. Only those authors mentioned in the main text, and usually of historical interest, are included. For authors whose recent or current work has been referred to, see Bibliography.